CAREER
MANAGEMENT
for the
CREATIVE
PERSON

Also by Lee Silber

Nonfiction

Time Management for the Creative Person

Aim First!

Notes, Quotes & Advice

Successful San Diegans

The Guide to Dating in San Diego

Fiction

Tales from America's Finest City

CAREER MANAGEMENT
for the
CREATIVE PERSON

Right-Brain Techniques to
Run Your Professional Life
and Build Your Business

▼ ▼ ▼ ▼

LEE SILBER

THREE RIVERS PRESS
New York

Published by Three Rivers Press, 201 East 50th Street, New York,
New York 10022. Member of the Crown Publishing Group.

Random House, Inc. New York, Toronto, London, Sydney, Auckland
www.randomhouse.com

THREE RIVERS PRESS is a registered trademark of
Random House, Inc.

Printed in the United States of America

Design by Rhea Braunstein

Library of Congress Cataloging-in-Publication Data
Silber, Lee T.
Career management for the creative person: right-brain techniques to
run your professional life and build your business / by Lee Silber.
1. Vocational guidance.   2. Career development.   I. Title.
HF5381.S595   1999
650.14—dc21   99-12530

ISBN 0-609-80365-4

10   9   8   7   6   5   4   3   2

▼ ▼ ▼

This book is for anyone who has been asked "Why don't you get a real job?" and replied, "Never!"

▲ ▲ ▲

Contents

Acknowledgments   ix

Introduction   xi

1. What's Right About Being Right-Brained   1

2. You Have What It Takes   24

3. Ready, Set, Goals   49

4. It's Not Just a Job, It's an Adventure   72

5. Basic Training   100

6. The School of Hard Knocks   127

7. There Is No "I" in "Team"   142

8. Be Your Own Boss   167

9. Help! I Need Somebody   186

10. Expose Yourself   216

11. The Seven (Bad) Habits of Highly Ineffective
    Creative People   253

12. PMS: A Positive Mental State   310

Contact Information   335

Bibliography   336

Index   341

Acknowledgments

Mensches is a Yiddish term for bighearted people who go out of their way to help others. These caring, sharing people are like angels sent from above to help make your life a little easier. It is always good form to show your appreciation by showering them with plenty of praise (they like gifts, too), even though they ask for very little in return for all of their efforts on your behalf. I had the good fortune to have several mensches come into my life to lend a helping hand:

My agent, Toni Lopopolo, has successfully managed my career over the past few years with the kind of selflessness that only a mensch can (even if she does get 15 percent of everything I earn).

My editors, Patrick Sheehan, Alexia Brue, and Jessica Schulte, are mensches because they always do what they say they'll do, get it done on time, and then ask if there is anything else they can do. I have heard hundreds of horror stories about authors and their editors. I am so glad mine turned out to be a love story.

My writing partner, Beth Hagman, has, for the past several years (and six books), found creative ways of turning my stream-of-consciousness style of writing into concise and coherent prose (and without all the kvetching, I might add).

My mentor, Harriet Schechter, more than anyone I know, lives the life of a practicing mensch. It was Harriet who recommended me to Three Rivers Press for my previous book, *Time Management for the Creative Person*. That act alone changed my life. Yet that is not all she has done on my behalf. She also helps with promoting and publicizing my other books!

Occasionally, being a mensch requires sacrifice. My lovely wife, Andrea, likes to be a part of the process of writing my books, while sometimes what a writer really requires is the solitude that only sequestering can provide. It has become a ritual of mine to hole up in a hotel for a few weeks while finishing up a book. Even though she insists she is not a distraction, if you saw how great my wife looks, you'd know why I have to work alone.

Writing books is a natural extension for a mensch who is driven to help others any way they can. That's what drives these wonderful writers who have come before me to write some of the best books on building a career in the creative arts. They include Julia Cameron, SARK, Richard Bolles, Anne Lamott, Carol Lloyd, Laurence Bolt, Caroll Michels, Barbara Winter, Carol Eikleberry, Eric Maisel, and Linda Buzzell (for a complete listing, please refer to the bibliography).

Usually, a mensch will thank everyone and his brother, so . . . let me start my own career as a mensch by thanking my brothers, Mark and Scott, as well as the rest of my family and friends for their undying support.

Others worthy of credit include Rachel Pace (publicist to the stars), Mary-Ellen Drummond (who taught me to reach for the stars), Susan Guzzetta (a star in her own right), and everyone else who has played a supporting role in this play called my life. (There are no extras in my play; everyone has a role, is a SAG member, and gets paid above scale.)

THANKS!

Introduction

Life is to be lived. If you have to support yourself, you had bloody well better find some way that is going to be interesting.

—Katharine Hepburn

"There is no such thing as a Tooth Fairy, Santa Claus, or the Easter Bunny—and there's certainly no such thing as the perfect career." That's what many people really think, and it's sad, because there are plenty of rewarding, challenging, and fulfilling career opportunities that allow creative people to use their gifts and be rewarded handsomely for their efforts. Those who settle for less than the best simply haven't found the right job—yet. You can have it all when it comes to a creative career—if you know how.

The fact is that most people hate their jobs. They would rather be doing something else—*anything* else. It doesn't have to be that way. What if I told you that you would never have to work another day in your life? Would you be interested? When you find the right fit in a career, it no longer feels like work. You wake up every day excited about how you earn your living. This perfect harmonizing of your talents, skills, personality, and work style creates a passion and a desire as well as a feeling of contentment that is worth more than gold.

If can all be yours, if you will read this book and apply its principles.

The challenge is that the creative arts are very different from other fields. To get ahead, you sometimes have to zigzag to the top. Let me show you when to zig and when to zag to make the most of the opportunities out there.

Finding contentment in your career is a lot like looking for treasure. Using a map, you embark on a journey, an adventure in search of yourself. The thing is, there isn't a pot of gold waiting for you when you get to the spot marked "X" on the map. The buried treasure is within you. The pursuit of the gold (or the goal) is the reward. Because, when it comes to a career, there is no "there" there. It is *all* a search. Enjoying the search is what success is all about.

This is the age of opportunity for the creative person. Innovation and ideas are gold. Ridicule and red tape are being replaced with respect and rewards for the clever and creative person. The work environment and job market are changing, and they are changing for the better—for you. Are you ready for these exciting times ahead? This book will put you in a position to prosper. What parents, teachers, and bosses might see as problems (sloppiness, habitual tardiness, short attention span, nonconformism) can actually be hidden assets in the search for work in a rewarding and interesting creative career. Intuition, emotion, divergent thinking, daydreaming, thriving on chaos, big-picture thinking, cleverness, open-mindedness, and an ability to play and have fun are virtues in the right setting.

Even so, it's not exactly easy to build a career in the creative arts. You have to be able to deal with heaping helpings of rejection. It is a part of everyday life for the creative person.

There is also that funny feeling that you don't quite fit in—and you don't. Thank God. An unconventional person with unconventional ideas, you are often seen as immature, temperamental, moody, difficult, distracted, irresponsible, and irrational.

The truth is, you can be your wonderful self and still get ahead in the corporate world—or work for yourself, as many creative people do. Whichever you choose, this book will help you manage your career using a whole-brain approach that takes advantage of the way you are, without forgetting the way the world works.

Helping You Help Yourself

There is no such thing as a career—all you get are present moments.
—*Wayne W. Dyer*

It's time to move on, move up, and move out with a new mission. This book is about taking charge of your destiny so that no idiot can control your fate with a pink slip.

Most books on careers are very thorough when it comes to identifying and informing you about the problems and pitfalls of a career in the creative arts. What they lack, however, is the WHAT THE HELL AM I SUPPOSED TO DO ABOUT IT? part. I decided this was going to be a real how-to book, heavy on help and light on lengthy explanations of the challenges. You already KNOW what those are—you deal with them every day. So let's get busy and tackle them head-on. I'll try to ease up on the Zen stuff and instead offer as many practical and applicable tips and techniques as possible.

New careers are popping up all the time. The Internet needs more content. More TV channels mean more programming, which mean more programs, which mean more jobs in entertainment. There has *never* been a better time to strike out on your own and make your way as an entrepreneur (or freelance your way to success). This is your time to shine as a creative person. The future looks bright. Many of the current trends favor your preferred mode of operation—self-reliance, zigzagging to the top, rapid change, multitasking, chaos, adaptability, intuition, training and retraining.

This book will show you how to find your career niche, and then how to earn a living doing what you love. You will learn how to overcome the challenges the right-brainer faces, and how to make your nature and your creativity work for you. You'll learn how to market yourself and your art even in a crowded marketplace, survive and thrive in the battlefield that is the creative arts, be your own boss and work for others, take the "free" out of "freelance," rise to the top without stepping on too many toes, and use your natural abilities to find a perfect pitch and harmony in your work world.

The title of this book includes the words "career management," but in reality we are talking about "life management." There is a direct, undeniable correlation between your career and your life. It's less about what you do for a living than what you can live with doing. Finding fun and fulfillment at work spills over into the rest of your life. Without it, your health will suffer, your creativity will suffer, your art will suffer—and so will everybody around you. You don't need to live that way.

If you are thinking of giving up on a creative career and getting a "real" job, stop right there. When you settle for less than what's best for you, you instantly get less than you settled for. Don't sell yourself short. The regret will eat you up inside. Don't miss your chance; it may be right around the corner. Instead, get going and go for it—be bold. Use the techniques in this book to give you a leg up.

Don't let others push boulders in your path and fill your head with factoids like "most businesses fail in the first year," "it's too competitive out there," "there are NO jobs," "you don't have enough experience or talent," "you have no agent," "only the top 3 percent of the Screen Actors Guild earn enough money to live on." It's bad enough that these insecure and misinformed people are telling you why you *can't* succeed. It's worse if you believe them. Don't let anyone talk your dreams down.

This book is for creative people in all walks of life, even if I don't specifically cover your field—carpenter or composer, painter or poet, musician or magician, designer or DJ, writer or waiter/actor. It isn't meant to apply to just the glamour jobs; whatever form your creativity takes, you can apply this information.

For everyone who tells you "you can't make a living doing that," there are hundreds of examples of creative people who found a way to turn something they thought was fun and would even do for free into a fulfilling freelance career.

I will help you take your powerful creative energy and harness it, and you will beat the odds, making a living doing what you love to do. Your life will become a work of art.

Managing Your Life

There is only one success—to be able to spend your own life in your own way.

—*Christopher Morley*

Few people know what they want to be when they grow up, and even fewer creative people *want* to grow up. Maybe you won't discover your true calling until you test-drive several makes and models. Isn't it better to test-drive them in your head, using that incredible imagination of yours, than waste years on a dead-end job? One of the key things you'll work on here is defining what you want to do (not for the rest of your life, but what you want to do *now*), and eliminating the careers that aren't a fit. The choices that lead to a life of creative expression and financial security are there for the making. The catch is that creative careers are often unconventional and in some cases completely uncharted. The challenge is that there are a million different things you could do.

The key to success in any career is clarity. Becoming clear about who you are and what you want is the first part of this book. Then how to get what you want is covered in great detail. It's hard work, but this is your chance to reinvent yourself. Don't let it pass you by.

CAREER
MANAGEMENT
for the
CREATIVE
PERSON

What's Right About Being Right-Brained

I wish the real world would just stop hasslin' me.
—Matchbox 20

Success for a creative person can be tremendous. Not just in money, but in creative freedom. Look at the list of highest-paid entertainers and entrepreneurs—they're all people who don't fit any mold, but they're also people who used that fact to their benefit. (Steve Jobs of Apple Computer instantly comes to mind.) You can do it, too, in your own way, on your own time, reaching your own goals. Unmire yourself from the myths about creative people. Don't be afraid to look at your strengths *and* weaknesses. Face the fact that traditional business management, which is left-brain, logical, and linear (not to mention rigid, boring, and counterproductive), doesn't work for you. It isn't much fun, and if it isn't at least a little bit of fun, you're not going to do it. It's that simple. If it's not fast, fun, flexible, and easy, you are less likely to embrace it. Be willing to work within a system—as long as it's one you create and one that works *with* you as well as *for* you.

You Could Be Even More Wonderful

We cannot forever hide the truth about ourselves, from ourselves.
—John McCain

Creatives can have an insatiable hunger to achieve, create, accomplish. They want to be recognized and heard, receive applause and take home awards. They desire change, to create a body of work, to earn, to make deals. Many people who don't know what they want actually want too much, too fast.

The key to success is learning how to focus on what's most important. It's counterproductive to try to do *too* many things at once—nor is it good to focus on only one area of your life. One way to whittle it down (focus) and spread it around (balance) is to choose a top goal for each area of your life.

Take a good, hard look at who you are and what you want from life. Sometimes having everything be just okay, having an adequate job and a moderate life, is the biggest tragedy of all. Take the time now to find yourself, so you can live your life without getting lost and make good decisions that will lead you to the success and happiness you desire.

We are all born creative. What happens to us from kindergarten to college shapes how much of that creativity stays with us. Some, despite the best efforts of the school system and corporate America to stamp out the creative spirit, slip through the cracks, creativity intact. You are still not safe. Ninety-eight percent of the people in the world are living the left-brained life. Society tends to reward the left brain (structure, status quo) and reprimand the right brain (chaos, creativity, innovation).

You can stunt your creative spirit with disuse. You cannot lose a talent, but your skills can certainly atrophy. Yet almost any job can be done creatively. Creative careers are not exclusively in the arts. There is plenty of creativity in business, too! Entrepreneurs must be creative to survive, managing people can be done creatively, marketing certainly involves a degree of creativity, even distribution can be a right-brained affair. What makes any career interesting, exciting, and vital is the creative approach you take to it.

Researchers at the Johnson Research Foundation (an organization that tests aptitudes) found that people who ignore their creative gifts in their careers are frustrated and unhappy by midlife (or much sooner). Contentment comes from finding your greatest gifts and abilities and then developing and using them in the work you do.

The Right Brain

The only normal people are those you don't know very well.
—*Oscar Wilde*

Creativity and creative careers involve a whole-brain approach, an interaction between the left hemisphere of your brain (the detail-oriented, accountant side) and the right hemisphere (the big-picture, artistic side). The right brain comes up with the ideas and the left brain implements them. Too much right brain and nothing gets done; too much left brain and life is dull and uninspiring.

As a right-brainer, you are absolutely unique (and wonderful). There has never been anyone like you—and (until they can clone more than just sheep) there never will be again. Ponder that for a moment. Beneath all the self-doubt, guilt, fear, remorse, and distorted beliefs is a gem of a person who, more than anything, deserves to be happy, successful, and fulfilled. To have a career that is challenging and rewarding. A career that fits like a glove and is such a joy that you would do it for free—but is so valuable to others that you are paid well. And why not? You have found your place in the universe, you are making a contribution with your talent and creativity.

Once you understand yourself and what work you enjoy doing, you can work *with* your natural abilities and tendencies rather than against them. It makes life much easier. This is something that is unique to you. It is what will work best for *you*. So don't just breeze past the questions in this chapter. Make the time to really give some thought to who you are, what you want to do, and what would be the best way to go about doing it. I have always said that to find yourself you need to get lost. You need time for reflection, away from the hustle and bustle of your busy life, to open yourself to new possibilities.

Do you honestly love what you do now? Are you excited to go to work on Monday? Do you go home happy? If you answered no to any of these questions, there is a better way.

I was the perfect choice to write this book for two reasons. The first is that I am the classic creative type. I have reinvented myself more times than Edison has patents. My career path is a zigzagging winding road rather than a straight line. I am an artist, a musician, a writer, a trainer, and an entrepreneur. The second reason is that, when all was said and done, I found a way to use my natural skills and abilities in my work. As a result, I have had both happiness and success—and I am on the path, however wiggly, that best suits me. Now, let's talk about you.

Are You in Your "Right" Mind?

The following quiz should give you an indication of where your natural tendencies lie—left brain, right brain, or whole brain. Answer honestly and quickly. Don't dwell on the answers, and don't try to figure out what we're looking for. There is no "right" answer.

1. When it comes to emotions,
   a. I can articulate my feelings to others
   b. I am better at expressing my emotions through my art

2. I have always been told
   a. I'd make a great accountant
   b. I was a natural-born artist
3. Success is
   a. closely related to annual income
   b. unrelated to the money I make
4. When trying to explain how I came up with an idea,
   a. I am able to put it into terms others can understand
   b. I feel like an alien from another planet
5. When I am working on a project,
   a. I'm not happy until it's done
   b. I enjoy the process
6. It's a beautiful summer day, but I have work to do. I will
   a. get my work done first and then go to the beach
   b. go to the beach and deal with my work later
7. When it comes to a big project, my strength is in seeing
   a. The worm's-eye view (details)
   b. The bird's-eye view (the big picture)
8. When my boss puts me on the spot,
   a. I say what I mean and mean what I say
   b. I tell him what I think he wants to hear
9. Joking around the water cooler, I've been compared to
   a. Jim Bakker
   b. Jim Carrey
10. When I have several unfinished projects going at once, I feel
    a. frustrated
    b. stimulated
11. When it comes to decorating my office
    a. I find an arrangement that works and stick with it
    b. I rearrange everything at least every six months
12. Multitasking for me is
    a. doing two things at once
    b. doodling, talking on the phone, sending an E-mail, searching for a file in a teetering pile of work on my desk, listening to the radio, making faces at a co-worker, and sorting through my mail all at once.
13. When I'm asked to bring something to the office party,
    a. I bring paper plates
    b. I have a new recipe I'm dying to try out
14. I am more like

  a. Spock (logical)
  b. Kirk (intuitive)
15. After work,
  a. I go home, or maybe out with people in my work group
  b. I like to go places where people from other departments hang out
16. Before I speak,
  a. I think it through and censor it in my head
  b. I say the first thing that pops into my head
17. I'm running late for an important meeting and a dear friend calls with a relationship crisis,
  a. I explain that I am in a hurry and will call them back as soon as I can
  b. I say the hell with the meeting, my friend needs me now
18. When it comes to problem-solving,
  a. I analyze things from a logical perspective
  b. I consult my "gut" for an answer
19. My car is
  a. practical and safe
  b. stylish and fun to drive
20. I am best at remembering
  a. names
  b. faces
21. Whenever there is a crisis in my life,
  a. I retreat into myself and try to solve it on my own
  b. I prefer to talk it over with others
22. In making decisions,
  a. I tend to focus on the actualities
  b. I tend to focus on the possibilities
23. It's my birthday and my buddies in the office have thrown me a surprise party. I am
  a. embarrassed (I don't like surprises, and I don't want anybody to know how old I am)
  b. thrilled (I love surprises, and nobody believes me when I tell them my age)
24. When someone asks about my vacation,
  a. I give them names and places and brag about how much I saved on airfare (elapsed time, three minutes)
  b. I describe in intricate detail how wonderful it felt to be away, and talk about all the things I saw, the wonderful people I met, and the fun I had (elapsed time, three hours)

25. I write with my
   - a. right hand
   - b. left hand
26. I am a natural-born
   - a. learner
   - b. teacher
27. If I had two yearlong projects to choose from, I'd pick
   - a. an analysis of the company's past and future profit centers
   - b. working on the company's marketing materials
28. When I meet a prospective client or employer,
   - a. I have a written list of questions to cover
   - b. I talk off the top of my head, taking my cue from them
29. When I am learning a new software program,
   - a. read the manual and then begin
   - b. what manual? I figure out things on my own
30. I believe
   - a. you can make things happen through sheer force of will
   - b. there is a force in the universe that brings things to you
31. I just met with a prospective client/employer whom I really connected with. When I leave, I
   - a. shake their hand
   - b. give them a hug
32. If I could choose my work hours, they'd start at
   - a. 6:00 A.M.
   - b. 6:00 P.M.
33. My daily routine is most like the movie
   - a. *Groundhog Day* (very little variety)
   - b. *Ace Ventura, Pet Detective* (one adventure after another)
34. When I get the paper, I usually turn first to
   - a. the business section
   - b. the comics
35. While out to lunch with co-workers, I have an urgent call and ask them to order for me. They
   - a. know exactly what I want because I always get the same thing
   - b. don't have a clue because I am always trying something new
36. If the meeting is scheduled for 10:00 A.M.,
   - a. I arrive at 9:45; I am known for my punctuality
   - b. I try not to be the last person to show, but how was I to know traffic would be so bad?
37. If I lost my planner, I would be

a. completely lost; my whole life is in there

b. completely lost; I'm sure that's where I stuck the little purple piece of paper that has the name and number of the client who urgently needed a call-back yesterday on it (oh, well)

38. My idea of organization is

a. making a list of all the things to be done and then prioritizing the tasks

b. playing with my Post-it Notes, putting them on the wall in some sort of order

39. When I am working and the phone rings, I will

a. look at it as a nuisance and let it ring

b. look at it as a welcome break and pick it up

40. My boss likes to say

a. I keep my nose to the grindstone

b. I keep my head in the clouds

41. I learn best when you

a. tell me what to do

b. show me what to do

42. If I were on a game show and my winnings totaled $10,000 with the option to keep what I have or risk it all on one more question for double or nothing, I would more likely

a. take the money and run

b. bet it all

43. If I were going to clean out my desk, I would take the following approach:

a. do it a little at a time until I finished

b. pull everything from the drawers and do as much as I could before pushing the rest back in

44. If I were offered a promotion that involved moving to Hong Kong for two years,

a. I'd opt out because I don't speak Chinese

b. I'd be on the phone with Berlitz in two seconds flat

45. I am ready to leave for work, and

a. I know exactly where my car keys are

b. I go on a search-and-destroy mission until the keys turn up (in the fridge)

46. When I log on to the Internet, I do it with

a. a plan and a purpose; get in, get out

b. a sort of stream of consciousness, pausing to look at whatever catches my fancy

47. When researching a project,
    a. I find as many books and articles as I can and read them from front to back
    b. I ask someone for tips on the best places to look, and skim those
48. If I inadvertently offended a co-worker, I'd
    a. say nothing, hire a lawyer, and hope the whole thing blows over
    b. have a sit-down and discuss his or her feelings while apologizing profusely
49. When it comes to remembering all the things I have to do,
    a. I make a master list down to the last detail
    b. What was the question again?
50. My office/desk is organized in such a way that
    a. anybody could come in and find what they need quickly
    b. I pity anyone who has to try to figure out my system

In the above quiz, *a* answers count zero; *b* answers count 1. If your total is 15 or less, you must have bought this book for somebody else and you're just going through the quizzes for kicks, because you are one serious left-brainer. A total of 16 to 35 indicates a fairly balanced, whole-brain approach to the world, or a right-brainer who was educated in Catholic schools. You will go far if you can learn to loosen up a little. With a total over 35, you can consider yourself a right-brainer, with all the blessings and curses attached thereto. If you came up with your own answer even once, refusing to go with the choices offered, give yourself a star. You are a true right-brainer, an independent thinker, an original. To understand what all this means to your career, skip ahead to page 10.

ASK A PRO: MARILEE ZDENEK

Marilee Zdenek is an author/speaker/creativity consultant who wrote *The Right-Brain Experience* and has led seminars on the subject of creativity since 1970.

Is there a clear list of traits that creative people share?
I see creative people as unique within themselves and unpredictable. Therefore it is hard to find common denominators. I do see a difference between very successful and unsuccessful creative types. Unsuccessful creative types are not getting it together to get

their work out there. They can be extremely talented, but something is holding them back.

I consistently hear creative people talk about their fears holding them back.

Yes, it can be a fear of failure or even a fear of success. Or it may be their inability to use the left side of their brain to provide structure, commitment, or follow-through. People who tend to exhibit extreme right-brain tendencies and are highly creative can be very arrogant about it. Yet, in many cases, they could benefit from switching gears and doing more of the left-brain stuff like scheduling, financing, marketing—business-related matters. In short, they should honor the role the left hemisphere plays in their success. The first step is to work on improving their weaker side, the left brain.

Some people may never be comfortable doing left-brain things. What then?

Make a list of your strengths and weaknesses, then delegate what you don't do well or what you don't want to do. One day my CPA said to me, "Do us both a favor and stay away from the books." So I hired a bookkeeper. I put all of my receipts in a shoe box and then it's taken care of by someone who really enjoys doing it and does it well. It felt so wonderful to let this go. It was total freedom.

How do you balance your left-brain responsibilities with your right-brain tendencies?

By nature, I would do what I feel like doing at that moment. I'm kind of a free spirit that way. But, because I want to succeed, I try to counterbalance my impulsive side. I'm not a list-maker by nature, but it does seem to work, so I do it. For example, Fridays I'll turn off my computer and close my eyes and free-float through the past week and all of the things I've accomplished. Then I write expectations for the following week. First the overview, then specific details like deadlines and appointments.

Do you find that a sterile work environment is counterproductive to creativity?

The most frustrating thing is when my daughter tries to clean my desk. It drives me crazy! I need that clutter. It's important to me. It's part of the freedom I need to be creative. It's the child part of me.

The Good News

All I wanna do is have some fun. I've got a feeling I'm not the only one.
— Sheryl Crow

Many studies have shown that the creative person is more intelligent and scores higher in tests than do lawyers and doctors. While nobody uses only their right brain or left brain, most creatives tend to rely heavily on their right brains—the source of their creativity. Because of that, many of the following statements will apply to you. Even whole-brainers (those who operate equally from both hemispheres) will see some of themselves here, often tempered by the logical, stabilizing influence of the left brain.

The right-brainer is able to compare and combine two things that are not usually related. The creative mind is not limited by normal boundaries, and so can see relationships that aren't obvious to others.

The right-brainer sees abstract concepts and then is able to express them in concrete terms. You know who was great at simplifying even the most complicated things? Einstein. He described his theory of relativity as follows: "Put your hand on a hot stove for a minute, and it seems like an hour. Sit with a pretty girl for an hour, and it seems like a minute. *That's* relativity." See, I get that.

The right-brainer has a strong appreciation of art. The assumption is that creative people always "create" art. That is not the case. There are careers for people who appreciate the arts. (Not many, but it *is* an option.)

Right-brainers tend to have rich and vivid memories. Right-brainers are able to remember faces and places, but aren't so hot at names and titles. They retain images better than words. They remember themes and scenes from movies, but not the names of the actors or the director. The right brain remembers feelings—good and bad. Steven Spielberg tapped the traumas of his parents' divorce and the pain he felt as a child to conjure up the story of an extraterrestrial and a little boy.

Creative people have the pioneering spirit that it takes to do things differently, regardless of the grief they may take from (and give to) others. They are eager to go where nobody has gone before. The great unknown is more interesting and inspiring than the safe and secure. It is intoxicating to be involved with an idea on the ground level. The early stages of the creative process are magical, where anything is possible and reality is way off in the distance. (Then the left brain enters the picture and ruins all the fun.)

Right-brainers appreciate nature and have the ability to find beauty everywhere. Creative people desperately need to stop and smell the flowers, to keep in touch with life and beauty. Their super-sensitive senses trigger their creativity. For me the smell of fresh-cut grass, any painting by Gauguin, the feel of clay between my fingers, or the sound of a thumping bass line all inspire my creative juices. As a drummer, when I listen to music I can pick out the ride, hi-hat, crash, and splash cymbals. I'll ask my wife, "Did you hear what the drummer is doing there with that rim shot?" She just stares blankly at me.

Creatives respond to their surroundings. It is a blessing and a curse to be tuned in. I can collect and re-collect these sensations and recycle them in my art. Unfortunately, sensitivity to my surroundings can interrupt the creative flow, even leading to depression, anxiety, and frustration.

Being creative sometimes means being lonely in a crowd. When I start talking about intuition and inspiration with "the guys," they look at me as if I am from another planet and tell me to shut up and just watch the game.

Right-brainers welcome challenges. They are able to see the big picture and tackle problems on a global scale. They use intuition rather than facts and figures to find new and better solutions.

Although right-brainers may be in touch with trends, they're more likely to *start trends*. They are leaders, not followers. They are flexible. Passionate. Tenacious. When it comes to getting their ideas or their pet projects made they can be relentless.

Right-brainers are open-minded and less prone to prejudice. Creatives often have high ethical and moral standards. Gray-matter thinkers in a black-and-white world, they often see more than one right answer and maybe even more than one question.

The successful idea person has some way to capture ideas and refer back to them later. I have a notebook/idea catcher that is filled with winning ideas, so many there isn't enough time to try them all out.

Creatives are obsessed with their craft and improving their skills and abilities. I like to do good work. I need to do good work, even if it means fighting my way through a constrictive structure (the publishing process), going without sleep, and typing until my fingers go numb and my brain goes dead.

The Bad News Isn't So Bad

The first problem that an artist has is to survive.

—*Philip Glass*

Sometimes speaking without thinking, as in a brainstorming session, is perfectly acceptable. Sometimes right-brainers forget where brainstorming ends and real life begins, however. Saying the first thing that comes to mind makes people uncomfortable—especially when you're telling them that what they are wearing makes them look puffy. "Wait, not puffy in a *bad* way." But it's too late.

Right-brainers feel things much more deeply than most other people do. It's trying to verbally communicate those feelings to others that gets them tongue-tied. That's why they create, to express what they are feeling through art. So maybe that's not a bad thing.

Right-brainers can be impulsive. (Just say yes!) That live-for-today attitude and "being in the moment" works for the artist in them, but, to succeed, they've got to give some thought to the future. There can be long-term consequences when they play now and pay later.

Divergent thinkers often go off on tangents, and are frequently seen as scatterbrained. It's hard to concentrate when you're not inspired or interested. It takes discipline to get started and stick with the business side of creative business. Creatives can work harder than anybody if they find something they love to do. They just have a hard time learning to love math, taxes, regular business hours, and client follow-up.

Leaping ahead, seeing the big picture, creatives lose those people who want to take it step by step and see things in black and white. Sometimes this makes them angry. Right-brainers spend a lot of time dealing (or not dealing) with frustration.

For right-brainers, all play has a purpose—it's fun. This attitude makes them seem immature. Left-brainers like rules, a purpose, and a plan, even for play—and, worse, they need a *reason* to do it. I was so embarrassed when my wife came home early one day and caught me playing in the dirt with a Tonka truck. But then I realized that it was exactly this kind of playfulness that makes me creative. I was out of ideas and needed a way to break my block. It worked, too.

Right-brainers tend to be sloppy. Not disorganized, just not organized in a way an anal-retentive, uptight, left-brained person would like them to be. Many creatives feel neatness is a waste of time.

Right-brainers are particularly vulnerable to the "they are going to find me out any minute" syndrome. They may be confident about their work, but not about themselves. Insecurity often rules them. Most creative people I know believe their talent is a gift from a higher power and that it can be taken away at any time. I believe that talent is the ONE thing nobody can ever take away from you.

Alcoholism, drug addiction, depression, hubris—all are very real dangers for the right-brainer. "I thought all serious artists were self-destructive. That anybody worth their salt was going to be out there living on the edge," says Kris Kristofferson. Although right-brainers aren't necessarily self-destructive, they are prone to overindulgence, which can lead to the same thing.

Right-brainers' high ideals may make them inflexible. Many right-brainers are frustrated by the requirements of the commercial world. Once, when Jimmy Buffett was trying to land a record deal, a record executive asked him to play a song. Jimmy played "The Captain and the Kid." The executive told him, "I like the song, but why does the Captain have to die in the end? Can you change the ending?" Jimmy just walked out.

Creatives often expose a dark side to the world. Many have mood disorders and even deeper psychological problems.

Right-brainers tend to have short attention spans, which means multitasking is second nature.

Right-brainers procrastinate. Procrastination is a problem for people whose attention span is short and whose interest scope is broad. I like to have several projects going at once, and switch off whenever I reach the point of boredom and burnout.

Right-brainers don't like to be told how to do it, but they are also very clever if you just tell them what you want and leave them to their own devices. As you can see, for every so-called negative trait there is a positive side as well.

Feeling "Left" Out? The Left Brain

You will do foolish things, but do them with enthusiasm.

—Colette

Each side of the brain processes information, but the two sides process it differently. You're always using both sides of your brain; we use the terms "right-brainer" and "left-brainer" as a matter of convenience. It's a question of emphasis. The left brain is the timekeeper, the organizer, the linear thinker. Because of it, you are able to get things done—and done on time. Being resourceful and resilient and sticking with something until it is completed requires a lot of left-brained thinking.

The left brain is logical, neat and orderly, a built-in editor and critic. It's quite maddening, really. But we need this serious, buttoned-down side to take care of all the things the right brain simply doesn't deal with—and among those things is time management. The left brain can be a little compulsive, though. It will want to do the same thing the same way every time.

While the right brain can get you lost in the cosmos, the left brain can get you lost in the details. I'll spend an hour looking for just the right phrase to complete a thought while writing. When my left brain poops out on me, I hire someone to handle the details for me. It can be expensive, but maintaining a healthy right brain (which begins to starve after too much paperwork) is more important to me.

Still, your left brain is not your enemy. It will get you where you want to go, and it will get you there without wasting time or energy. It is the goal-setter, the action hero, the muscle man.

ASK A PRO: BRIAN TRACY

Brian Tracy is known internationally as a business consultant and a best-selling author and speaker.

What characteristics have you noticed when working with creative people?

I believe there are two types of creative people. There is the pseudo-creative, and then there is the truly creative. Pseudo-creatives are people who have very short attention spans—they are all over the place. They can come up with all kinds of truly wonderful ideas but rarely follow through on them. The second type is also extremely creative, but as it happens they are extremely disciplined as well. It's a most remarkable combination.

So discipline, focus, and follow-through are important?

Most of the great geniuses of history have been extremely well disciplined. They developed the capacity to concentrate single-mindedly, to be totally focused on a single problem or question for a long period of time (almost to a fault). Sidetracking is the greatest single challenge for the creative person because, when they are all over the place, they don't get anything done. As you accomplish more, you become more motivated, inspired, stimulated as you go from average to highly creative.

Would you say that the creative person is born with or without these traits?

It's very important not to give comfort and solace to people by saying that if you are a creative person you are therefore all over the place. Spontaneity is often an excuse for a simple lack of control. I'd like to dispel the myth that truly creative people are not organized. They are. They organize so they can be spontaneous.

True creativity is a disciplined, focused process. When creative people can harness the enormous power of focus and concentration, and keep the light shining on the task at hand, they can achieve a high-quality result in half the time.

Which Is Which?

To help you remember which "brain" is which, remember that the (L) left brain is the (L) logical brain and that the (R) right brain is the R-tistic side.

The Right Fit for the Right-Brainer: Creative Careers

The right road for one is the wrong road for another.

—M. Scott Peck

In the movie *The Truman Show,* the title character is living unknowingly in an artificial world created by a television producer. Everything is perfect. Truman goes about his daily routine happily. Then he begins to get restless. He hates his job and is bored with his humdrum existence. He feels he has to make a break for it and risk his life (what life?) to escape into the real world.

Living and working in a left-brained world is not easy when you operate in the right way—that is, the right-brained way. It is easy to become Trumanized by a mortgage, car payments, a 401k plan, and benefits. But going against your own nature, your instincts, and your talents turns out to be the worst possible way to live your life. You end up with ulcers, depression, deep-seated anger.

Finding the career path that matches what you enjoy doing and do well makes more sense. I say make a run for it. Find what makes you happy and fits as it should, showing off your assets.

A good fit—in a career as well as a pair of jeans—is different for different people. Some like them loose and baggy, some formfitting. It's a personal thing. All I know is, I would *never* send my mom out to buy me a pair of jeans. The same goes with your career. Styles change and sizes change, and you'll want to try them on. Only *you* know what will work for you.

For some right-brainers, *networking* is a dirty word. For others it is a never-ending source of inspiration. There are plenty of examples of famous creatives who crave seclusion. No naysayers, no distractions, no naysayers, no phones, no naysayers, no needy people. NO NAYSAYERS.

Creative people do more than their job title requires—they just can't help it. They want the education, experience, and exhilaration of doing something different, so they don't conform to strict parameters. This may cause them to clash with corporate culture, but it's an ideal attitude for working in a small company, where versatility is not only needed but prized.

The creative career is no walk in the park, even for the most talented. Audiences are fickle, deals are tough to come by, and the pay isn't always what it should be. You need to be clear about what you want, and you have to want it badly enough to work hard, but you *can* make it.

The Nearly Perfect Job

Divergers are less interested in success, more interested in self-expression. They choose unusual occupations such as inventor, or entertainer, rather than the more conventional doctor or lawyer.
                                                                —*Leona Tyler*

No job is perfect. The trick is to find a job with imperfections you can tolerate. You may be willing to work from nine to five for the opportunity to be involved in an exciting project or to have the protection of a top-notch health plan. You may put up with a mountain of bureaucratic bull so you can work with people you respect and admire. You may manage to get along with a nitpicking, anal-retentive, narrow-minded know-nothing pipsqueak of a boss in exchange for the gratification of producing work you can be proud of.

▼ ▼ ▼

ACTION ITEM

List the things you tolerate in your current job. Then, beside each item, list the trade-off (the thing that makes you willing to put up with it).

Take a look at your list. Do future or possible benefits outnumber the here-and-now benefits? Do the negatives outweigh the positives, or have you achieved a balance? At what cost?

Most of us make unconscious choices about what we can live with. Sometimes you make the wrong choices, and these are damaging to your spirit and your future. Go back to your list again and *choose*. Think about it. You will always have to tolerate things you don't like in this life, but you don't have to tolerate *everything*. Pick your battles—but don't be afraid to fight when you need to.

▲ ▲ ▲

Motivated to Be Your Best

When I work I relax—doing nothing or entertaining visitors makes me tired.

—*Pablo Picasso*

Nobody can motivate you. You must be self-motivated to make it. In *any* career, you are the boss. If you don't feel like working for weeks at a stretch, nobody will shoot you. But there is always a price.

The creative person works well in a relaxed environment. That could be a casual corporate structure, a close-knit small company, or off alone in a cubbyhole somewhere. Freedom, individuality, and being able to be yourself are serious issues for you, wherever you choose to work.

Being a nonconformist is not limited to seeing things differently. It often manifests itself in style of dress or hair, or in the hours we keep. I go to bed when many people are getting up. I love the fact that I am a night owl. I feel comfortable with those I am surrounded by at two in the morning at Denny's.

Many creatives are slightly off-kilter in basic biological ways: you get hungry at different times, your sleep patterns may be different, you get bursts of energy at times when the average person is ready for a siesta. It pays to tune in to your body. The more you can adapt your work environment and time frame to your innate physical preferences, the more comfortable you will be. It doesn't pay to work against your body.

You'll find you have boundless energy when you're on a roll. It's amazing the number of hours you can spend, the attention to detail you can muster, and the ideas you can come up with when interested. Conversely, if you aren't interested, it is almost impossible for you to focus, and you feel as if someone unplugged you from your power supply. If I were asked to sell drugs (pharmaceuticals), which is what it seems many of my neighbors are doing for a living these days (I *do* live in a nice neighborhood), I would have a real problem. I can't get enthusiastic about selling drugs to doctors and then playing golf all afternoon, I don't care how much they pay me. I want to *create* something. I may make less money, I may work longer hours, I may spend a lot of energy networking and doing paperwork and following up on contacts—but it's all worth it to have a chance at life, at contributing something positive to the world I live in.

Creatives need constant input and stimulation. That's why many creative departments, even in huge, staid corporations, have lots of tchatchkes lying around, the walls are filled with all kinds of interesting things, and there is an air of fun and play. Don't settle for a sterile office. You can't work that way.

There is a certain lifestyle that appeals to a right-brainer, one that involves experimentation, swapping, multiple positions, passion, excitement and stimulation, variety, visual input, feeling and compassion, connection and expression. For the creative person there is real value in learning and growth as well as self-expression, freedom, and flexibility in work.

Being a craftsman is difficult in this quick-and-dirty world. Speed kills creativity. Mass production kills art and uniqueness in favor of commercialism and uniformity. Yet often "success" is equated with developing an idea that can be mass-produced, that will appeal to hordes of people. This is why it's so important to understand what motivates *you,* what your concept of success is. You may be much happier making stained-glass windows for neighborhood Victorian houses than creating window patterns for a national chain of Queen Victoria's Fish & Chips. The money, the people you deal with, and the personal scope of the two are very different, although in both cases you're creating stained-glass windows.

After getting his degree in Shakespearean theory, a friend of mine was saddled with student loans and no viable means to make money without doing two things he swore he would not do—teach or enter the world of big "bidness." The reality of the situation was grim, so he reconsidered and compromised his ideals a smidgen, going to work as a consultant in a big business, Hollywood. He also teaches a class on the film industry. He is energized, is paying off his debt, and has struck a balance between selling and selling out.

Writers Who Escaped Corporate Careers

There are plenty of creative people trapped in noncreative careers just itching to get out. Some escaped to freedom and made it big:

Tom Clancy	defense analyst turned best-selling novelist
John Grisham	lawyer turned best of the best-selling authors
David Balducci	author turned storyteller (*Absolute Power*)
Joseph Wambaugh	cop turned writer of cop dramas
Michael Crichton	researcher turned writer/producer/director
Richard Paul Evans	ad executive turned author (*The Christmas Box*)
Robin Cook	physician turned author of medical thrillers (*Coma*)

Opposites Retract

If we were the same, we wouldn't be different.

—*Adam Hanft*

Research shows that the creative person likes to work with other creative people. Yet many times you are forced to work with your exact opposite. Worse still, your boss is apt to be a left-brainer. When this happens, remember this quote from Art Buchwald: "People should assume that the person in charge is an idiot—but is always treated with respect."

The truth is, we need left-brainers as much as they need us. Because if it weren't for the accountants who balance your budget and lawyers to protect your intellectual property, you'd go broke fast. Or you would have to do the number-crunching and read the fine print yourself—and that would be a waste of your most valuable asset, your creativity. Sure, there is such a thing as "creative" accounting, but the less you have to go against type and do the things you despise doing and don't do well, the more time you have for the fun stuff. You need left-brainers to fix what you break, clean up your mess, and do the deals that keep you afloat. In short, you need them as much as they need you.

Maybe these left-brainers are close-minded and uptight, but they are also bright in their own way. You can find fault with the noncreative person for not seeing the big picture, for refusing to trust your instincts, for playing it safe and avoiding risk as if it were the flu. But they see you in a different light than you see yourself. They see you as a freewheeling good-time Charley who's out of control. A high-maintenance pain in the ass. They see emotional, defensive, and overly sensitive. It's no wonder they come down on you so hard.

It may seem as though we live in different worlds, but everything actually works together quite well. We come up with the ideas and innovations, and they produce the products. We make art, and they make budgets and do cost analysis. We take an aesthetic approach, and they approach with suspicion. We want to put soul into it and create something meaningful, and they want to sell it to some guy named Sol and make meaningful money from marketing it.

If you work together, you can create magic. They can bring your ideas to life and find ways to market them to the masses. So what if they are motivated by the money and you are driven by the design? A balance between the two is not such a bad thing—usually. For you, the work is its own reward, but you are not immune to the appeal of a little outside recognition. That comes from seeing things come to fruition—which often takes the help of your frugal little friends. It can be quite motivating to be able to have a bigger budget, better equipment, and a ton of technical "toys." This takes money, though. Lots of money. Money raised by your other half.

Both sides do best when they take advantage of their strengths. The world needs unorthodox people with slightly skewed perspectives to deal with the continuing challenges that nature throws at us. So if you are misunderstood, try communicating rather than caving in.

Polarity: Opposite and Opposing Styles

Left-Brainer	Right-Brainer
Inch by inch, it's a cinch	Do it when it's down to the wire
One-track mind	Variety is the spice of life
Life is a bitch	Life is a journey
Rule maker	Rule breaker
Felix Unger	Oscar Madison
Make it profitable	Make it beautiful
Worm's-eye view	Bird's-eye view
Office like an operating room	Office like a kindergarten room
PC	Mac
Ring around the collar	Nose ring
Noose	Loose
Do it right *now!*	Do it right
One foot in front of the other	Hopscotches around
Runs	Meanders
Nose to the grindstone	Head in the clouds
Minivan	Miata
Number-cruncher	Paint by the numbers
To-*do* list	To-*be* list
Better safe than sorry	Playing it safe is sorry

The Creative Life

It's not easy being green.

—*Kermit the Frog*

Judgmental people may complain about your short attention span, calling you scatterbrained, lazy, a slob, a flake, self-centered, cynical, impatient, and so on. It takes a toll on even the most secure, and some start believing it. Don't let that be you. Fight back. Remember that you're special—one of 2 percent of the adult population. Remember that you see a bigger world than they do, and move on.

Being an unconventional person in a conventional world is a small price to pay for the joy of being a creative person. Wear it as a badge of honor. You are one of the chosen ones. Innovators throughout time have come under constant attack from critics. What it boils down to is fear and jealousy. They will never have what you have. They will never be what you can be.

I tried to go mainstream. I was an economics major! Economics! It was so *not* me. I struggled with the supply-side stuff, and I was miserable. When I finally bucked my parents' expectations and went to art school, everything clicked. I did use my economics training; it helped me put together a successful retail business—selling surfboards.

Jewel, a self-described "student of life," is more than a chart-topping musician. She has published a book of poetry, is trying her hand at acting, and is involved with her foundation. "I would never take my music for granted, but I have a lot to do, and I just get bored if I'm not sufficiently challenged. There is always a bigger risk of failure when you branch out, but I'd rather risk it. It keeps me from falling asleep."

There are a lot of risks involved with following a creative career path. Rewards don't come without risks, and it's fortunate that the right-brainer is built to be able to withstand the pressures. The option is to sit at home and watch others living their dreams on TV. It's not a hard choice, but it's one you have to make.

Van Gogh sold one painting in his lifetime, but he didn't give up. He died poor and living on his brother's generosity, but he didn't quit. Taking a risk means you could lose. There are no guarantees.

To make it in the creative arts, you must have that fire in the belly, that burning desire to succeed. You must believe that no matter what the odds, no matter what others say, you will persevere. You will do what it takes. You will learn to do the business stuff, the networking, the bookkeeping, the planning and scutwork. You will bounce back from rejection, depression, and obsession. Because disappointments, highs and lows, and critics are everywhere. Not everything will feel like a masterpiece (or even be well received). In a way, that's good. You'll keep trying to improve.

Others Agree with Me

I used to think the human brain was the most fascinating part of the body. But then I realized, well . . . look what's telling me that!

—Emo Philips

*People want to know why I do this, why I write such gross stuff. I like
to tell them that I have the heart of a small boy—and I keep it in a jar
on my desk.*

—*Stephen King*

*I saw theater people as more open and accepting and there were
fewer rules. I've never been good with a lot of rules.*

—*Matt Keeslar in* Us *magazine*

To cease to think creatively is but little different from ceasing to live.

—*Ben Franklin*

*One of the saddest experiences which can come to a human being is to
awaken, gray-haired and wrinkled, near the close of an unproductive
career, to the fact that all through the years he has been using only a
small part of himself.*

—*V. W. Burrows*

Change your thoughts and you change your world.

—*Stewart B. Johnson*

The creative mind is seldom bored.

—*Gordon A. Macleod*

When Left Is All Right

Ingenuity, plus coverage, plus work, equals miracles.

—*Bob Richards*

We live in a world where being right-handed is considered "correct." Only
10 percent of the population is left-handed, yet a high percentage of creative people are left-handed. This small difference has led to discrimina-
tion and suppression of the southpaw over the centuries. *Left* is colloquially
defined as weak, worthless, awkward, sinister, and underhanded. (I would
like to add self-reliant, witty, intelligent, intuitive, innovative, talented, and
extremely creative, but I'm not Webster.) Left-handedness was thought to
be a sign of bastardy or witchcraft during the Middle Ages.

It may be that lefties are more creative because they are wired to
the creative side of the brain. It could be that, having been pressured
to conform, they rebelled and became true originals. Among their
many traits, an ability to handle being an outcast, being "left" out and

labeled as different, has perhaps contributed to southpaws' strength of character.

Quiz: Which of the Following People Are Left-Handed?
Bill Gates
Jerry Seinfeld
Phil Collins
Peter Benchley
Leonardo da Vinci
Marilyn Monroe
Cole Porter
Kenneth "Babyface" Edmonds
Ben Franklin
Jimi Hendrix
Michelangelo
Paul McCartney
Rudy Vallee
Cary Grant
Kermit the Frog

(Answer: All but Leonard da Vinci, who was ambidextrous, and Kermit the Frog, who is left-handed, but not a person. However, Jim Henson, his creator, was a lefty.)

The list could go on for pages, but the bottom line is, if you are a lefty, you are in good company.

2

You Have What It Takes

The greatest power a person possesses is the power to choose.
—J. Martin Kohe

How many of you remember the rock group Twisted Sister? You'd probably rather forget. They were one of the first bands MTV played, in the early days of music videos. One of their songs started with an uptight father yelling at his teenage son, "What do you want to do with your life?" The son then hits a power chord on his electric guitar and blows his father out the window as he yells, "I wanna rock!"

I wish I could have done that to all those "well-meaning" people who started asking me what I wanted to be when I grew up, while I was still playing with Lego. How did I know what I wanted to be when I grew up? They would say stupid things like, "How about an engineer, since you love to build things with your little blocks?" An engineer? You have *got* to be kidding me. The funny thing is, I remember playing air guitar to *Frampton Comes Alive* in my room. I could spend hours pretending to be a rock star. Okay, so I didn't end up as a singer-songwriter. I *did* end up as a speaker-writer.

When someone says to me, "Everything happens for a reason," I want to say, "Yes, but is it *your* reason?" Life is not an accident. Through careful choices and persistent planning, you can control what happens to you. That sounds boring, doesn't it? It's not. We are talking about your future. The best way to deal with the future is to invent it!

What could be more exciting than trying to figure out what *you* want to have happen and, as they say on *Star Trek,* "Make it so"? If you live your life wandering around aimlessly, you're not likely to end up anywhere at all. If you live your life bouncing around, reacting to events and circumstances, you're giving up control over where you'll go next. This is not an ideal way to live—it's stressful and frustrating, and not creative at all.

I believe that each of us comes prepackaged with a reason for being, a *purpose*. Unfortunately, there is no operating manual or help line to make it easy to figure out what that purpose is. Once you figure it out, however, life is *soooo* much easier and better. It means that you are living *on purpose*. This translates to doing the right work, in the right environment, with the right people and using your talents and abilities in a way that benefits others as well as yourself. This purpose covers every aspect of your life, including having people to love and who care about you. (But that's another book.)

You need a compass to navigate by, a North Star to aim for (your mission or purpose) and a map so you can plot out the best (and even most scenic route, if that turns you on) way to get where you're going (your goals). You can get blown off course and explore new islands, meet interesting people in faraway lands . . . but you always have that North Star to guide you back. That's what your purpose does for you.

ASK A PRO: SCOTT KRAMER

Scott Kramer is editor and writer for a popular golf magazine and just started a golf insider's e-zine.

Did combining your passion for golf and your skill as a writer bring you bliss?

I believe people naturally assume turning a hobby into a profession is easy on the mind. Not so true. Yes, I have a passion for golf and writing, and I'm on cloud nine knowing I can earn a decent living from combining the two. But there are some drawbacks. Believe it or not, I play golf less now than before. Now, however, when I do play, it's usually at a really nice course I couldn't get access to or afford to play before.

What do you enjoy most about what you do?

Freedom is the best. I'm lucky enough to be a West Coast employee of an East Coast–based company. Therefore my hours are my own. As long as my work's in on schedule, my boss doesn't care what I do with my time.

Creativity runs a close second. I love generating something from nothing. Writing allows me to fill a blank canvas (or computer screen) with my thoughts and perceptions. That's very satisfying.

What is the most effective way for writers to land their dream jobs?

I really think freelancing is the best possible avenue to establish rooted relationships with the top editors at magazines, which eventually leads to jobs. In fact, once editors are familiar with you and your work, they'll tell you about openings long before they actually open up—allowing you to be prepared with résumé and portfolio in hand when the time arrives. Here's how I broke into the system: Any time I saw an ad in the paper for an editor, I sent in a cover letter stating that I wasn't qualified to fill the position, but "it sounds like you're short-handed with regards to writing articles." People really responded to that.

You took a pay cut to go from computer programmer to writer. Any regrets?

I've never looked back and wondered if I made a mistake. When I switched career paths, I took more than a fifty-percent pay reduction, but it was at a time in my life when I had few financial responsibilities other than rent. Besides, I was tired of writing software code all day. By contrast, writing stories was a creative escape to salvage any sanity I still had. Having money was always important to me, but I knew my editing pay would rise over five years, and I looked at the larger picture to gain perspective. In fact, I set personal goals every year to make x amount of money freelancing. Five years later, I found I was making just as much money as the programming friends I had abandoned earlier—and I'm a lot happier. Fortunately, I never considered myself a starving writer. Hopefully, I'll never have to.

What advice would you offer others who want to follow in your footsteps?

Believe in yourself and in your ability to write, and try to corner a niche so that magazines and companies eventually start calling you because you're perceived as an authority in a particular subject. From there, you can branch out.

Believe It—You *Are* in Control

"Follow your bliss."

—Joseph Campbell

When you aren't sure about what you should be doing with your life, it can feel like you're in free fall. For some, the rush of hurtling to the ground at terminal velocity is exhilarating. Some don't even seem to realize that they don't have anything (a parachute) to stop them from hitting the ground and going *splat*. In the beginning, it can be exciting to go through life without a plan or purpose. Many romantic tales have been spun about the vagabond life. Just remember that these stories are written by people who disciplined themselves not just enough to put pen to paper, but enough to sell their stories for publication.

Being in control of your life means knowing what you want and working toward it. It means waking up every morning saying, "I've got the best job in the world. I absolutely love what I do." If you can say that, everything else in your life will fall into place.

Some people know early on what they want. Comedian and best-selling author George Carlin entertained passersby on a streetcorner as a teenager with a fifteen-minute act. He would imitate the people of the neighborhood and make up wild stories about them. He says, "I used to tell everyone, 'When I grow up, I want to be an actor and comedian.'" His mother bought him a little tape recorder, and he would record sketches and skits. (That's where his "seven words you can't say on television" must have come from.)

Rosie O'Donnell was also ambitious at an early age. In the first grade, she was practicing signing her autograph in her notebook. "When I was a kid, I always fantasized my success would be to this degree. You have to dream it to live it."

They're the lucky ones. Most of us struggle for a while before we find our niche. That's okay. Enjoy the struggle. Consider it a voyage of discovery with a treasure at the end. Self-knowledge is a wonderful thing.

How to Find Yourself When You Didn't Know You Were Lost

Interests and skills together point to an occupation. More than any other factor, your skills help you translate who you are into a job.

—Carol Eikleberry

Before you can figure out your niche in the creative scheme of things, you need to understand yourself, your strengths and weaknesses, your true desires, your personal definition of success. The following questions are designed to make you think about yourself from various angles. Answer them quickly. Put down the first thing that pops into your mind (before your left brain has a chance to butt in). Don't analyze either the questions or the answers. Be honest—nobody ever has to see this but you. Now, quick and dirty:

Personal

- What is your favorite time of year?
- What is your favorite hobby?
- Where is your favorite getaway spot? When was the last time you went there?
- What social settings bring out the best in you? Worst in you?
- What is your best personality trait? Worst? How would your spouse/best friend answer that?
- What one thing would you most like to change about your personality?
- Make a list of your friends and look for common qualities they all share. Next, list the people you absolutely loathe. What qualities do they share?
- Are you a country mouse or a city mouse? Do you like more a laid-back lifestyle or one that is frantic and fast-paced?
- Are you more comfortable competing against others or against yourself?
- Which is more you—safe and secure, or reckless and risky?
- Which would you rather be—healthy and wealthy, or healthy and wise?

Professional

- Do you want more or less travel in your work?
- Where would you like to go? Would you travel by land, sea, or air?
- Would you like to do more or less public speaking in your work?
- How much money as an annual salary would make you feel successful?
- Do you prefer to work with your hands or your mind? Indoors or outdoors? With people or with things? (Can't say both. Just state a preference, even if it's marginal.)
- Which is more challenging, dealing with difficult people or difficult problems?
- What bores you?

- What would you eliminate from your job description if you could?
- Do you like to be in charge? Or do you prefer to be the power behind the throne?
- What do you like best about your work?
- If you could have anyone's job in the world, whose would it be?
- What is the most undesirable job you can think of?
- When do you prefer to work—morning, noon, or night? When would you rather *not* work? What days would you like to have off? What would be an ideal work schedule for you?
- What would you like to bring to work that you can't? Kid? Dog? Stereo?
- Do you prefer to work alone or in a group? How much of your day would you like to spend dealing with people, and how much would you like to be left alone?
- How many projects can you handle at once?
- Do you prefer stretches where you work like crazy and then take a break, or do you like to pace yourself and limit your projects?
- Which best describes the environment you would prefer to work in: at home, in a lab, in a studio, outside, in an office, on the road, on a set, in a studio, in a tall building, in front of an office, or some other situation? Big city or small town, or small city/big town?
- Do you prefer to deal in concepts or projects? Which is more satisfying, the process or the product?
- List jobs you think you would enjoy doing.
- List jobs you think you could not and/or would not do.
- What skills do you like to use the most?
- What task or talent comes easily to you?
- Name something that is always a struggle to do.
- What type of people do you enjoy working with the most?
- Do you prefer to work at a fast pace or to pace yourself?
- Do you like every day to be different, or do you prefer to slip into a consistent and comfortable routine?
- Which motivates you more, money or a mission?

Finish the Sentence

Let's play "finish the sentence." Let your intuition be your guide. Go with your gut.

- I have no trouble focusing on . . .
- My idea of the perfect day is . . .
- The most fun I can have with my clothes on is . . .

- The perfect attire to work in is . . .
- My dream is to . . .
- I have always wanted to . . .
- I am looking forward to . . .
- I wish I could do _____ more often.
- I know I have a talent for . . .
- I feel fantastic when I am . . .

Honest Answers
- This turns me on:
- This touches me deeply:
- This is the thing I value the most:
- This draws out the best in me:
- This is the person I would most like to meet:
- This is the one thing I would most like to change about my community:
- This is the best thing I can do to serve others:
- This is the kind of work I would do for free:
- This is the thing I feel most passionately about:
- This is the thing that bothers me the most:
- This is the one subject I could study forever:
- This is the one thing I get complimented on the most:
- This is the thing that makes me smile the most:
- This is the activity that gives me the most pleasure:
- This is the time in my life when I felt really good:
- This is the thing I do where time flies:
- This is the nicest thing anyone ever said to me:
- This is the thing people most ask for my help with:
- This is the one thing I could do all day, every day:

Get It Gift-Wrapped
The first luck you get in life is the genetic shuffle. You're stuck with whatever you've got. The trick is to learn the strengths in your package and strengthen them.

—*George Carlin*

People spend their whole lives working against their strengths. It's like swimming against the current. Go with the flow and use what God gave you. Your best chance for success is to select a career that allows you to use your talents and do the things you most enjoy doing. All too many people believe that if you're getting paid for it, it's work. And work is the opposite of fun. Which is why they make vacations—so you can put your life on hold for fifty weeks a year and stuff all your fun into that precious two weeks. Which is why they have sick days. Because you're sick if you think this is any way to live.

If you do what you enjoy doing and are good at it, you will be stronger and happier. Vacations will be icing on the cake.

So you're no Einstein. Ah, but you are *you,* and no good can come from comparing yourself with others. Believe in your own special gifts, talents, and abilities, and use them to earn a living as well as fulfill your life.

▼ ▼ ▼

ACTION ITEMS

- List ten adjectives to describe your top skills and abilities. What makes you great? Now, using your nonwriting hand, make another top-ten list.
- List your top ten skills. Now, of those skills, which would someone pay you for? How could you earn a living using these skills?
- What can you do to increase your marketable skills? Training, practice, gaining practical experience, or learning new equipment? What is one thing you are willing to do to improve upon your existing talent?
- Put all your talents on index cards, one skill per card. Then shuffle the cards and put them into order by the skills you like to use most. Write down the result. Now reshuffle and put them in order by which ones are most marketable. Finally, put them in order by what you do best. Compare your three lists.
- What is the thing you do that comes most naturally? Could you make a living doing just that? Has anyone else made it a cornerstone to a successful career?

▲ ▲ ▲

Test Your Inner Guide

Music is what I like to do most. It doesn't matter if I wear old clothes, or live in a hovel, or even if I starve. I just want to play music.
                                        —*George Meanwell*

You have an inner guide (if you'll pay attention to it). It's a little voice. It's seldom very loud, but there is a lot of wisdom in there. As Lieutenant Columbo put it, "Whenever I get a feeling in my stomach and ignore it, I almost always regret it."

So, as you answer the following questions, run them by your inner guide. Don't think about your answers for more than a second or two. Use your intuition. Don't give your left brain (logic brain) a chance to censor your real response. As Jiminy Cricket said, "Let your conscience be your guide."

You don't have to be precise at this point. This exercise is just to determine a general direction or an essence of what you want and where you want to go in your career. It helps to be in a relaxed state so that the messages from our inner guide can get through. The answers may come to you in words, symbols, dreams, visions, or ideas. Get them on paper (or in your computer) in some form. You need to be able to look at them later. Pay attention to your answers and don't discount them, even if they seem outlandish.

Go for it.

- Sometimes figuring out what you *don't* want in your career or life is easier (and as valuable) as trying to discover what you do want. With that thought in mind, make a list of all the things that turn you off when it comes to a career.
- Along the same lines, what path have you been trying to avoid? (Sometimes this is the one path that you should pursue.)
- What is the one thing you would *not* do for any amount of money?
- Have you ever had an epiphany about what you should do with your life, but chose to ignore it? What was it you contemplated doing?
- Create your own job description. (Don't limit yourself here. Don't think about risks. Fantasize. Enjoy).
- If you knew you would live to one hundred (without wrinkles and/or Depends), what would you do differently (we're talking career and/or education)? If you had only six months to live, what would you do differently? What would you do the same?
- What trait or talent do you think is most valuable?
- How do you like to express your creativity? What form does it take?
- What is your biggest regret?
- What rules would you want to live by?
- What is the one thing missing from your life?
- Finish this sentence: "A successful person is someone who . . ."
- Whom do you most admire? Why?
- Think back to when you were a kid, and try to recall what you most enjoyed doing. Look back at an old scrapbook or photo album, or talk to a parent for insights. (Is it a coincidence that I was my local library's Bookworm of the Year when I was a tot? I read more books than anyone else in my neighborhood. I found that out by looking through my mom's scrapbook. It was also apparent that I was a

fingerpainting Picasso, too. I looked at my old report cards, which almost all said I was a daydreamer!)
- What do you see as your role in life?
- What cause are you most committed to?
- What do you stand for?
- How can you make a difference?
- What can you do that would give you the greatest sense of importance, well-being, and self-worth?
- What person would you most like to meet/work with in your career?

Past Lives

What a wonderful life I've had. If only I'd realized it sooner.

—Colette

Okay, everything that you have done up until now is your past life. I am not saying you have to be Shirley MacLaine, but take a look at your past life as if it were a world away, in another dimension. What things worked for you, and what things did not? What did you do that helped you to succeed? What lessons did you learn from past missteps? If you retrace your steps this way, there are clues about what will work in the future. As the saying goes, "If you keep doing what you have always done, you keep getting what you have always gotten." That doesn't mean you should throw the baby out with the bathwater. Keep doing what you have always done that has worked. But take a dispassionate look at your life and career. Be honest about the areas you're unhappy with. Don't worry about blame. Just try to see where it went wrong so you can find ways to go right in *this* life.

- Write your life story from beginning (looking back) to end (as if you are very old and have already achieved all the things you want).
- What is something that makes you say to yourself (and others), "I will never do that again?" (I'm not talking about a hangover.)
- List five boneheaded things you can remember doing. Now list five things you did well in the past. Which list came faster? Which was easier to compile?
- Look at your past life and ask yourself these questions: What do I wish I had done but didn't do? What have I always wanted to do but never got around to doing?
- What are your most powerful memories from childhood, teenage years, and adulthood? Take a close look at the three memories. What do they have in common? What are the circumstances, the people involved, the tasks you were performing, the setting, the time of year?

- List your most rewarding life experiences (paid and unpaid). Are you still engaging in these activities? If not, why not? How can you bring these things back into your life?
- It is important to appreciate all the things you have and all the things you are. The more you appreciate all the things you have going for you, the more you love life. Make a list of all the things you are grateful for in your life. Start small: your health, a place to live, a car, money in the bank, people who love you . . .
- Describe yourself as a cross between two celebrities. I am a cross between Jimmy Buffett and Tony Robbins. My friend Beth is a cross between Della Street and Whoopi Goldberg.
- Write your own autobiography, or compile a collage or video of your past accomplishments.
- Draw your brain. Not the outside—though that might be fun. The inside. Mine has a very big cerebral cortex and a somewhat atrophied medulla (I really need to get out and exercise more), with bulges in the music and public-speaking areas and lots and lots of conflicting neurons in the writing area (symbolized by lightning bolts and thunderstorms).
- Draw yourself in your picture-perfect day. Put in as much detail as you can. Spend some time and thought on this one. Then pin it up where you'll see it often. This is where you want to live your future life. This is where you're going.
- Take a snapshot of your life today. Do you like what you do for a living? Are you happy? Are you using your talents? Are you able to create? Do you enjoy waking up on weekday mornings? Is it good to be home?
- Do you have enough money? Do you have a goal for the future?

This is hard work, and many people will need the services of a guidance or career counselor to help them through it. But no matter how you do this, you must do it honestly. Learn to dream aloud. It's the only way to make those dreams come true.

ASK A PRO: JOE O'BRIEN

Joe O'Brien is operations manager and talk show host of KROC-AM 1340 in Rochester, Minnesota. He's been married for eleven years and has a five-year-old daughter.

What's it like, having your own talk show?

The talk show is the fun part of my job. When I'm not in the studio, I manage a staff of eleven and am responsible for all programming, promotion, and operation of the radio station. That includes taking and responding to listener complaints and suggestions, and working with our sales department and management.

I usually get into the office before 8:00 A.M. and spend the first hour and a half doing direct preparation for the show. That includes checking E-mail and phone messages, cruising the Internet, checking four newspapers or more, talking with our news department, and preparing notes for that day's show. The morning might also include putting out one or more "fires" around the station.

I'm on air from 9:30 A.M. to 1:00 P.M. After the show, it's off to management duties—writing promos, scheduling announcers and programs, working with sales. I also represent the radio station in the community, so that means serving on boards and committees, attending meetings and events. When news breaks, I have to drop everything and deal with the crisis as it unfolds. All in all, it's a busy day. But never the same two days in a row—and never boring!

What is the best part of what you do?

It's a great creative outlet. It's satisfying because, occasionally, we'll do something or talk about something on the air that will eventually result in moving people to positive action. I had hoped to "make a difference" in whatever I did for a living. I occasionally get to do that.

What advice would you give someone who wants to break into this business? How do most on-air people get hired and get ahead?

This is an industry without a prescribed way to get to the top. It's really a what-have-you-done-for-me-lately kind of industry. My advice? Get inside a radio station whatever way possible. Start by emptying garbage if you have to. Then find a way to get in a studio. Be ready to start at terrible hours for low pay, just pushing buttons and rarely opening your mouth. This is a pay-your-dues kind of business, as there are many more people who want to do it than there are jobs to do.

Be ready to keep learning, reading, listening, watching, observing all the time. You have to have a passion for this. Raw talent alone won't do it for long. I've seen many, many people more talented than I am wash out in this business because they were lazy and didn't care about doing their best.

Finally, realize that the broadcasting world is a small one. Get to know people in the business, and keep those relationships fresh. Don't burn bridges. It's amazing how what goes around comes around in this business. You keep running into the same people over and over again.

Visualize Your Values

As a creative person you're less able to separate your work and your life than most people. You cannot ignore your values when looking at a career path. Your values, your needs as a person, should direct that path, should point you toward the right career for you. You can't be a success if you don't know what success means to you. And you can't be a success unless you incorporate your value system into every phase of your life.

Unused talent is not just a waste. It's a poison. The symptoms are boredom, low energy, stress, depression, envy. If you recognize these symptoms in yourself, it's time to do a little soul-searching. You're not doing what you should be doing, okay, got that. But what should you be doing? The following exercises might help you figure that out:

1. Make a talent map. Start by looking back to when you were young. Plot your talents on a visual time line or map at the ages of five, ten, fifteen, and twenty. Use pictures, drawings, or key words to represent each phase or age and your talents at that time.

2. Make a value tree. Draw a tree trunk and then extend branches off in all directions. In the trunk, write your biggest belief about yourself and what your life should be. In other words, your key overriding value. On the branches, write the rest of your values. Hanging from each branch, draw a fruit and put in it how these values manifest themselves. For example, in your tree trunk would be something like "freedom" as your core value. Then the branches might be labeled "ability" and "respect" or "friends" and "family." The fruit hanging down from the "respect" branch might be "fame" and "money" or "honesty" and "integrity."

Values Grid

Integrate what you believe in every single area of your life.
—Meryl Streep

Self-realization is the first step in choosing a general direction for your life, one that will bring you happiness and peace of mind—in tune with what you really want, deep down. When you figure that out, you have taken the biggest step toward getting it. In the following exercise, you'll end up with a top value for each area of your life, and a clearer understanding of who you are and what's most important to you.

You may suffer inner turmoil when your goals or actions go against your values. I've heard this described as "cognitive dissonance"—acting in a way that doesn't *feel* right. If you value a good body but eat like a pig and party, want to be a good parent but take a job that requires a lot of travel, value integrity but lie and cheat, value marriage but are too busy flirting with others or working, value creativity but never make time to create, you will feel anxiety and unease, conflict and discomfort, anger and resentment.

Cross out each value you can live without:

Children	Power	Loyalty	Health
Career	Prestige	Integrity	Fitness
Freedom	Inner peace	Spirituality	Respect
Recognition	Order	Trust	Fame
Financial security	Education	Excellence	Balance
Friendships	Family	Helping others	Travel
Adventure	True love	Kindness	Job security
Challenge	Fun	Independence	Home
Creativity	Hobbies	Profit	Awards
Integrity	Free time	Position	Tranquillity
Joy	Happiness	Wealth	Other:_____

Go through this list again and cross out as many more as you can.

Now get tough, get down to your ten top values.

Come back to this list in two days and narrow it down to your top five. Write them down.

Now check your list of values against the career you think you want, and make sure there is no conflict between the two. If there is, rethink the kind of work you should be doing.

Putting Your Talent to Work to Better the World

You can have everything in life you want if you will just help enough other people get what they want.

—Zig Ziglar

Artist and environmentalist Wyland began his career by painting life-sized murals of marine life on the sides of buildings and walls to bring attention and appreciation and public awareness to the plight of whales. The reaction was overwhelming and, over a decade later, Wyland has found immense success selling his paintings and sculptures, while continuing to make people aware of the importance of protecting marine life and ecosystems.

John Beltzer, an award-winning composer, produces personalized songs for chronically and terminally ill children. It all began when he was dumped by his girlfriend and she took their supposedly shared recording contract with her. He borrowed more than $11,000 on his credit cards and turned his parents' basement into a recording studio. He contacted an area hospital and began recording a song about a five-year-old cancer patient's favorite things. That song changed both of their lives. He told *Parade* magazine, "In the cutest little voice, she thanked me for the song. After I hung up, I sat for half an hour crying. That was the defining moment. All those years of submitting tapes to record companies and not having much happen. This is what I needed to encourage me to go on."

When Joe Montgomery saw how his four-year-old son, who had cerebral palsy, struggled with his wheelchair, he realized he could build a better one. Inspired by his son, the entrepreneur developed a new line of custom-fitted sports wheelchairs. His company, Cannondale Products, now has sales of over $163 million.

Dorothy Balsis Thompson, a TV commercial producer, sidelined her career and used her savings to found Streetlights Production Assistance Program. It trains disadvantaged individuals for entry-level jobs in the entertainment industry. Her graduates include high school dropouts, welfare recipients, and former gang members. She uses her industry influence to get them jobs.

In August of 1990, my good friend Ruth Klampert was diagnosed with cancer and told she would need six months of chemotherapy and radiation treatments. Almost immediately her hair began to fall out. During the day she wore a wig, but at night she found it impossible to sleep with the wig or a turban on. Leaving her head bare, however, she was cold. In a dream, she had the idea for Slumbercaps, a comfortable and warm cap that would allow patients to get a good night's sleep without freezing. Patients felt less exposed and vulnerable at night. Ruth placed an ad with an 800 number in *Coping* magazine. She found herself counseling cancer patients who called in their orders. In addition, she gives many of the caps away for free. Although it hasn't been a big moneymaking venture, it has been a life-enriching one.

Spirituality

Your treasure house is in yourself. It contains all you'll ever need.

—Hui Hai

I ran into an old art school buddy of mine the other day, who now makes a good living designing web sites. He had all the appearances of success—fancy car, Rolex watch, designer clothes. I still got the sense that something was missing, or wrong. Whenever I asked him who his clients were or where I could view some of his work, he changed the topic. Finally he relented, and admitted he was designing adult (i.e., pornographic) web sites. While this is completely legal and obviously lucrative, the content bothered him something awful. He was deeply religious, and his job was so diametrically opposed to his beliefs that he was losing his hair in clumps, couldn't sleep, and was ashamed to tell anyone what he was doing.

- Do you feel guilty that you don't spend enough time in this area?
- What does your value system mean to you—in three words?

You, Inc.?

It's amazing what ordinary people can do if they set out without pre-conceived notions.

—Charles Kettering

"Where your talents and the needs of the world cross, there lies your vocation," Aristotle said. The same can be said about going into business for yourself. Finding your niche and then filling it as a freelancer may seem like the best way to go for the right-brainer. There is a downside to doing it yourself, however, and what seems like a good idea at first may become a nightmare. I think it's the only way to fly, but others find it frustrating.

It takes a certain kind of breed to make it in business for yourself. First and foremost, it takes a lot of hard work. There is no quick and easy road to success. It is likely you have what it takes but, to be sure, take the test below to see if you would be better off in business for yourself or if picking up a paycheck is more your style. (I'm pulling for you to bust out on your own.)

Check off those traits that apply to you.

I am
___adaptable
___adventurous
___a collaborator
___confident
___creative
___dedicated
___disciplined
___enthusiastic
___even-keeled
___focused
___goal-oriented
___hardworking
___a multitasker
___a negotiator
___organized
___persistent
___a problem-solver
___a public speaker
___resourceful
___resilient
___a risk-taker
___a self-starter
___skilled
___strong-willed
___a salesperson
___talented

I like
___being in charge
___controlling my own destiny
___to build things from scratch
___to work alone
___networking
___learning
___writing
___talking on the phone
___working on multiple projects
___experimenting

I want

—to work at home

—to pick and choose the projects I work on

—to get away from the corporate culture

—to be in the spotlight

—to work under immense pressure

—to be responsible for my own happiness

—to travel

—to control my destiny

I can

—budget my money to survive the ups and down of freelance work

—delay gratification

—manage my time well

—be shameless when it comes to promoting myself

—work long hours for little or no pay

—take orders from and deal with difficult clients

—handle rejection well

—think big but start small

—cut back and make sacrifices if I have to

—live without having others appreciate my work

—be very self-reliant

—survive without the perks of corporate life

—fly by the seat of my pants

I have

—some money saved up

—access to more money

—the support of my family

—a skill or service that people would pay me for doing

—space for a home office

—the basic equipment needed to get started

—experience working in my field

—no fear

If you checked off the majority of these traits, you should seriously consider going into business for yourself; it'll open up whole new worlds of possibilities for you. If you checked off less than half of these traits, think very carefully before you step out on your own. You're more likely to be happy in a niche where somebody else is paying the bills (including your paycheck) and bringing in the business. While I admit my own preference for self-employment, I'm not making judgments for anybody but myself. The important thing is to be honest and to please yourself—not me or anybody else. Then take the self-knowledge you've gained and put it to work for yourself.

Take Control of Your Life (Or Someone Else Will)

What you do today, tomorrow, this week, this month, this year are all part of a bigger picture. You control your life, your time, your future—whether you use that control or not. You don't succeed by chance. You get what you focus on, good or bad, and goals give you positive things to focus on.

The following is an example of how having clearly stated wants, values, and goals can change your life:

Makeover

Cindy, twenty-six, had been married for just over two years and had worked for a large public-relations agency in the city for the same length of time. (That's how she first met her husband.) He left the firm to start his own business. After they were married, she moved into his four-bedroom home in the suburbs. She still owns a two-bedroom condo in the city that she rents to a friend.

I met Cindy at a Toastmasters meeting (she was the president of the club), where she confided that she was unfulfilled and unmotivated by her job, never seemed to have enough time to do the things she wanted to do (because she was so busy doing things that she felt she had to do), and, as a result, was extremely unhappy in both her personal and professional life.

I asked her to write down her top five values. She was very surprised to discover that her top five values had little to do with how she spent the bulk of her time.

Cindy's top five values:
1. Marriage (she and her husband rarely spent quality time together).
2. Satisfying career (her job limited her creativity and required long hours).
3. Free time (she had a difficult time saying no, and was overcommitted).
4. Financial security (her husband's new business had depleted their savings and put them in debt).
5. Fitness (she had no time to exercise).

Where the bulk of Cindy's time was spent:

1. Commuting to and from work.
2. Clubs and committee meetings (Cindy was very active in several organizations).
3. Shopping (she did all the household and personal shopping).
4. Cleaning (she was meticulous about keeping a clean home).
5. Watching television.

How she changed:

1. She switched departments within the company and became a copywriter, work that she finds much more challenging, creative, and fulfilling. Her new position also requires fewer hours and allows her to work out of her home two days a week (i.e., less commuting). She spends more time with her husband, but staying with the same company allows them to keep their health benefits and retirement plan.

2. She quit all but two of the seven committees and organizations she belonged to (one of which was the homeowners' association of the condo she rents, of which she was a board member). She also took a less active role on the two remaining committees.

3. I suggested she try shopping by catalog (I loaned her my wife's Victoria's Secret catalog to give it a try), and she now spends less time and money on shopping. Although she still enjoys going to the mall, she finds herself going less and less often these days. Her favorite store also provides a free service called a personal shopper, who looks for items in her size and tastes (and her husband's, too). For staple items like groceries, she and her husband either shop together or switch off.

4. Keeping a clean home is still very important to Cindy, but she has lowered her standards a bit. She also has a maid service come in once a month for the really tough cleaning. She realized that she likes a clean house, but doesn't really enjoy cleaning. And her husband realized that he likes a freshly mowed lawn, but would much rather lounge in a hammock than do it himself, so they also hired a neighborhood boy to mow the lawn.

5. Her husband's business is really starting to take off, but they still haven't been able to replenish their savings account. I asked Cindy why she doesn't just sell her condo rather than rent it out. She felt if she did she would be "booting" her friend out onto the street. I persuaded her to tell her friend about the situation and see what

happened. Not wanting to leave Cindy in the lurch, her friend had been afraid to tell Cindy that she wanted to move in with her boyfriend. Cindy put the condo on the market and sold it for a substantial profit. She felt much more secure having a large savings account again.

6. I made a few suggestions about Cindy's TV time to see which ones would work, and to my surprise, they all did. Cindy now circles the shows she wants to watch in *TV Guide* and tapes her soap opera to watch while she rides the exercise bike. She also reads books and started taking a karate class with her husband. They also spend time walking on the beach with their new puppy, watching the sun go down.

7. I have watched Cindy go from an extremely frazzled and unhappy (and slightly overweight, by her own admission) individual to a warm and friendly person who really seems to be enjoying life. She and her husband are planning to start a family soon, and they recently took their first vacation together since their honeymoon—to Paris.

What to Do or Not to Do

You can have it all. You just can't have it all at once.

—*Oprah Winfrey*

You can have anything in life you want; you just can't have *everything* you want. (Where would you put it all?) Many things will catch your eye, but very few will catch your heart. Those are the things we are trying to identify here.

After college, I had to choose between working in my father's company and starting my own. It was a tough choice. Too close to call, so I flipped a coin. It came up that I should work for my dad—so I flipped again. As Kenny Rogers once said, "You've got to be willing to give up good to get great."

In all seriousness, career-related decisions are the hardest to make and have the most impact on the quality of your life. As much as you may want to refute this, you *do* spend most of your life working on or at something, and you *are* to a certain extent identified with and bonded to what you do for a living. To be able to make better decisions, you must begin with yourself. What you are feeling, and what is best for YOU? No matter how selfish that sounds, the decision must be best for you, first and foremost.

Consider how this career decision utilizes (or doesn't) your likes, your talents, how much it allows you to express yourself creatively. This is a very important element to your happiness. All things being equal, go with the choice that allows you to be the most creative and gain appreciation for your talents—the ones you think are important.

Finally, go with your gut. Which direction feels right? Which one would bring you the most joy and satisfy you emotionally? Go somewhere quiet and peaceful so you can (in solitude) get in touch with your intuition.

Stephen Covey said, "Begin with the end in mind." Decisions are so much simpler when you have a mission and an overriding purpose in your life. Even so, for the divergent thinker, decision-making does not come easily. Even though you can tap your intuition for advice, you can sometimes be too hasty and impatient. A little left-brain research could help.

Shortsighted decisions can come back and bite you later. If you say, "I'll cross that bridge when I get to it," you may find out that there is no bridge. It was washed away by bad decisions. Trying things on for size (how would I look in a corporate suit?) can be fun, but taking paths that lead nowhere will limit your success. I'm assuming (and we all know how bad that is) that you want to get somewhere. If your goal is simply to gather a wide variety of experiences, consider my tongue bit and my butt out.

The goal I'm talking about, however, is to decide on the best career that is right for you right now.

Tony Robbins was the first person I heard say that all our choices are either to avoid pain or to gain pleasure. The desire to avoid pain is the greater motivator. So what you link to pain or pleasure shapes your destiny. The way most people avoid pain is to do nothing or try to do everything. Neither of those approaches will work in the long run.

If you need help setting a goal or making a decision, try these tips:

- **Ask others for their input,** especially those who have been there, done that. People you respect. Those who are removed from the situation and can rationally (i.e., unemotionally) offer advice. Get several viewpoints. Don't be afraid to ask for input.
- **Play out what-if scenarios** and consider the contingencies and consequences of each path you could take. This fast-forward thinking allows you to "begin with the end in mind" and work backward to what you should be doing now.
- **Take a left-brain approach** and research your options. Information is a wonderful thing.

- **Focus.** Instead of taking a spray-and-pray approach, set your sights and focus on the target you most want to hit.

Richard Leider, in his book *The Power of Purpose,* has a formula for making good career decisions that is both simple and powerful. The formula is $(T+P+E) \times V$. T stands for talent (where you should begin when you are considering any career choice). P stands for passion, or purpose. E stands for environment, one that meshes with your values and temperament as well as your style. V stands for vision. How does work fit in with the rest of your life? This includes where you want to live, your relationships, and so on. When all of those elements are in alignment, you can do your best work, using your talents on something you believe in, in an environment that suits you best.

ASK A PRO: FERN GORIN

Fern Gorin, M.F.C.C., is the founder and director of Life Purpose Institute in San Diego, California.

What if I don't know what I want?

The first and most important step is to undertake a thorough self-exploration. You'll want to determine who you are as a unique individual, and what you really want in your ideal career. Identify what you love to do, your gifts, talents, interests, natural abilities, and key personality traits. Reflect upon what would make a job ideal for you.

You can begin this process by listing all the key elements—the things that are important and essential to you. For example, creativity, flexible schedule, helping people, aesthetically pleasing environment, love of writing, create my own business, et cetera. Be as specific as possible. If you like to be creative, *how* would you like to be creative? There are at least sixty ways to be creative. How do you like to help people? There are at least 101 ways to make a difference.

The next step is to tailor-make a career for yourself. Most people try to fit into a particular job slot or to find a job or business they're familiar with. An alternative is to do your own self-exploration first, then tailor-make a career that fits you.

Taking into account what you want and the key elements, design a career for yourself. Look at all the options, including standard career options and creative alternatives. There are 12,007 standard job options and thousands of other creative ones. Do you prefer starting a new business, getting a new job, or staying in your present job or business and making it ideal? Keep looking and weighing the choices until you find the right match.

How can creative people make money with their talents?

For every passion, interest, talent, there are hundreds of ways to make money. I've had the pleasure of working with over ten thousand clients, and it's never ceased to amaze me how unique each person is and how many different options each person has. Creative people need to "think outside the box" and consciously explore, design, create various possibilities with their talents.

I've had clients, for example, who loved art and wanted to have their own business and make a good livelihood. Some of my clients have taken their art and made posters, greeting cards, T-shirts, mugs, and children's wallpaper. Other clients include a folk art dealer, a famous sand sculptor, an art therapist, a web page designer, a creativity center director, a commercial artist, and an illustrator.

There are hundreds of ways to combine interests. A client who loved writing, nature, animals, creative ventures, and relating to people of other cultures became an assistant editor of a world-renowned zoo magazine and started an international newsletter that goes to zoos all over the world. Brainstorm and come up with possibilities. If you get stuck, seek out the help of a professional who can assist and guide you with your ideas, as well as present new ones.

How do you know if you've found the best choice, the "perfect" career for yourself?

The best choice incorporates those things you love to do, meets your personal and financial needs, and is in alignment with your essential values. Most clients who have found their "life purpose" have a feeling of rightness, joy, inner peace, and deep fulfillment.

If someone is still questioning, still feeling unsettled, chances are they still need to address some issues. There's usually one or more of the following to be addressed:

They have not designed or created the most fulfilling career for themselves. They need to explore other possibilities.

They need to take steps to get to their ultimate goal. Perhaps while they're developing and marketing their creative talent, there may be steps to take along the way. These steps may not always be comfortable or enjoyable.

There's an inner battle, an inner conflict going on that needs to be resolved. For example, one part wants a "real job," another part wants freedom and creativity.

Addressing these issues will bring a sense of peace and resolution to your career choice.

When you're interested in so many things, do you pick one path or do you work with three or more?

You have different choices. One choice is to pick one path that incorporates your different interests and the different facets of your personality. When working with clients, I often design an umbrella, a niche that would allow them to have a focus that allows them to do many different things under that umbrella. Another choice is to have two, three, or more different things. One client, for example, had a greeting-card line called Good Cheer, a health-care line, and did shiatsu bodywork. This client made a great living doing these three things. Whether you pick one, three, or ten things to do depends on how many projects you can handle and still feel balanced, while enjoying what you're doing and producing the results you want.

▼▼3▼▼

Ready, Set, Goals

I'd rather fail at doing something I love than fail at doing something I hate.

—*George Burns*

When I ask most people what their goals are, they stammer, "Who, me?"

Yeah, you. Do you have any goals? You do? Good. Just give me one goal you have for this year. When? NOW!

"Uh, I want to make more money this year."

Okay, if I give you one dollar, you've satisfied that goal. You just made more money.

When I ask successful people to tell me one of their goals, they will say something like, "I will earn $100,000 from my writing with another book deal by the end of the year."

This goal is stated in the positive (I will), is very specific ($100,000 from my writing), and includes a deadline (by the end of the year). Bravo! HAVING A SPECIFIC GOAL, WITH A DEADLINE, IS THE KEY TO SUCCESS.

You can make excuses or discount goal setting as being too rigid and linear for the creative person, or you can get with the program and finally start making some real progress toward achieving your dreams. Quite simply, you can't get to where you are going until you know where that is.

Duh.

Having specific, meaningful goals doesn't mean having a rigid system that leaves no room to roam. It simply means that, right now, this is what you want. Don't worry about limiting yourself. You can adjust as you go. It *does* mean that you're in control of your life, have thought about what the real issues are for you, and have a perspective on new possibilities that develop.

Bottom line: Unless you know exactly what you want from your life and you can articulate it (on demand, in case we meet), you are just fooling around. You aren't serious about success and, frankly, you'll probably never achieve it.

Having goals empowers you. Having a clear picture of what you want drowns out the negatives and attracts the positive things, ideas, and people to help you reach them. Goals give you courage to go beyond what you think is possible. Setting goals creates focus and clarity, so you're not wasting your energy on dead-end jobs.

People who know Oprah Winfrey say that the key to this talk-show host/actress/entrepreneur/author's success is that she sets goals and states them out loud and clear. She then works tirelessly to accomplish them. Did you know that Oprah is the first African-American woman to own her own production company? Through that and other endeavors, she is worth roughly $500 million. She also has a mission, which is to help people better their lives while entertaining them.

Thomas Edison set goals for himself on a weekly basis. He would challenge himself on the number of inventions he would present to the patent office each week. These self-challenges worked for the great inventor. What can they do for you? Let there be light!

Rick Allen lost his arm in an automobile accident. Before the crash, he was the drummer for Def Leppard. After the horrific and traumatic loss of his limb, he was still their drummer. He said the key to his recovery was having a goal, to return to the band, and this determination helped him get back. Think about this for a second. If Rick Allen can be a professional drummer with only one arm, whatever excuse you are using is totally lame.

Don't let the seeming impossibility of your dream get in the way of setting it as a goal. What if someone said, "I love to watch movies. How can I make that my career?" What a pipe dream, you think. I have two words for you: Roger Ebert.

What Happens Without Goals

I always knew I wanted to be somebody. I just should have been more specific.

—Lily Tomlin

Many creative people have no idea who they are, what they want out of life, where they are going, or what their passion is. Afraid to limit their options, their lives become a series of compromises and unplanned events. They are spinning out of control and feel powerless to stop it. They have zigzagged their way through life, trying this and that. "Hey, I had fun," they will tell you. But deep down they feel regret. They tried to grab at it all, and came up empty-handed.

Lack of Direction.

In *Alice in Wonderland,* Alice asks the Cheshire Cat, "Would you tell me, please, which way I ought to go from here?" The Cat replies, "That depends on where you want to get to." If you don't know what you want, you can waste a lot of time and energy going in the wrong direction. In the meantime, your career and personal life can get way off course.

Forced Compromise.

A man visits a psychic, who shuffles the tarot cards and spreads them out. Confidently, she says, "You'll be poor and unhappy until you're 45 years old." "Then what?" he asks hopefully. "You'll get used to it." You wake up one day and realize your life has been a series of compromises, a series of unplanned events. As a result, you're in a job you really don't like or aren't suited for, afraid to change.

Untapped Talent.

Without goals, you can easily get caught up in the current of life, swept away by an endless stream of details. You always seem to be paddling against the current in a battle between finding time to be creative and getting things done. Once you get off course, it can be very hard to find your way back.

Boredom.

Not having a mission in life, a passion, a purpose for your talents and creativity, is the one thing most lacking in many lives. Without it, life can become dull, empty, and uninspiring. Academy Award–winning actor George Sanders (*All About Eve*) was more than just a gifted actor; he was also a talented writer, painter, musician, and linguist. He had talent, fame, wealth, and the respect of his peers. So why did he kill himself? In his suicide note, he explained that he was bored. He was bored because he didn't have anything meaningful he wanted to achieve.

Powerlessness/Cynicism.

I have heard people describe their lives as if they were passengers in a car, watching life whiz by while looking out the window. They feel powerless, and blame everyone and everything for their lack of success, time, happiness, finances, whatever. They blame the government, the economy, reviewers, traffic, foreign competition, and on and on. Until you take responsibility for your own success, happiness, and time, you will remain a victim.

Value Conflicts.

When your values and your achievements don't align, at best you end up with hollow victories. At worst, you become depressed, angry, or resentful. If you value integrity, you can't afford to lie and cheat to get what you want. If being a parent is your top priority, you shouldn't consider a job that takes you away from your children for long hours. If you say you want to start a business, but you squander your start-up capital, it might be time to look at your values again. Maybe you're just giving lip service to a value you thought you should have. Or maybe your self-destructive behavior has deeper roots.

Regret.

Do you go zigzagging through life, jumping at any opportunity that sounds interesting or fun? After years of doing this, you're likely to realize that you have nothing to show for the past decade. This will leave you unhappy, unfulfilled, unsuccessful—because you tried to live without goals.

I have witnessed this zigzag, take-each-day-as-it-comes, I-don't-need-goals lifestyle firsthand. Teddy, a close family friend and creative soul, has imagination, talent, and intelligence. Yet he dropped out of college, got married, got divorced, started a business, went bankrupt, got married, got divorced, started a business, and went bankrupt again. In between, he invented several gizmos that he never finished, working no fewer than a hundred different jobs in several completely different fields. Today he is fifty-five years old. He lives in a beat-up trailer, works at a car wash, and is flat broke. His pattern is to get extremely excited about some new idea or new job or new business, which soon turns to boredom, then failure. If what he's working on doesn't give him immediate satisfaction, he quickly loses interest and moves on to something new. He still has no idea what he wants or what makes him happy. He was always trying to hit a home run. The big score. Yet he never hit singles. This is a bright guy, with immense talent, who wasted his life.

When I recall the two unhappiest times in my life, they were both when I was goalless. First in high school, before I had set my first goal, and later, after I had achieved my earlier goals and had yet to set new ones. What I remember most about both of those times is how unmotivated I was to do anything at all.

Here's the abbreviated version of what my life was like without goals: Growing up in Southern California, my life, like that of many of my friends, revolved around the beach. I was a bona fide beach bum. My entire youth was an endless summer spent in search of the perfect wave. On a typical day, I would wake up, grab my wet suit, towel, and surfboard, and head for the beach. My friends and I would surf all morning and lounge in the sun all afternoon. (And this was on school days!) No job, no responsibilities, and, unless I got my act together, no future! Although it was a great time and I have fond memories from those days, I also remember feeling tremendous guilt. I turned my life around after setting my first goals.

Ironically, despite the success of early goal-setting, I would again be goalless. I was living on Maui (one of my earlier goals), running my own little business, and working at the Kapalua Bay Hotel. Believe me, life was good. Yet, even though I lived in paradise, I wanted more. After spending a cloudy day alone at a remote beach, I made a list of the things I wanted to do with the rest of my life. I again felt excited and energized. It was as if the sun had come out on my life. I've never been goalless since.

With Goals

If you really know what you want out of life, it's amazing how opportunities will come to enable you to carry them out.

—*John Goddard*

With goals, you get a bird's-eye view of your life. An overview. Think of being in a plane or balloon, soaring over the scenery, looking down. Everything seems so small, so clear. You get above the trivial details, above the self-doubt. This kind of perspective allows you to do the right thing, at the right time, for the right reason in the right way.

Synchronicity.

When you set goals and pick a course of action, unexpected things start to go your way. Unseen forces in the universe begin to say, "Yes!" People and resources come into your life to help. It all starts with a clearly stated goal, one that you understand and that you can communicate to others. This works even better if you have a real passion for your goals. People pick up on your passion, your commitment. They want to contribute, to be a part of your excitement, so they offer money, time, connections.

One of my favorite stories involves the actress Fran Drescher. Before she was the star of *The Nanny,* Fran was on a flight home from Paris, seated next to a studio executive from CBS. She and her husband had an idea for a TV sitcom, so she pitched it all the way across the Atlantic. When they landed, she had a deal. That is synchronicity. If she hadn't had the idea and the goal already outlined, her rise to success and the hit show might still have come to pass, because she is talented and it was a good idea, but who knows? It certainly would have taken longer.

Your mind works for you.
When you have a goal, your mind goes about searching for information and opportunities that can help. Have you ever bought a car and suddenly everyone else is driving the same car? Why haven't you noticed them before now? Your brain, to avoid overload, screens out information not essential to your survival and success. When you know what your goals are, your mind works to incorporate them into what it lets into your consciousness. This can change your life very quickly. You may get lightning-strike ideas, seemingly out of the blue. In reality, the brain is processing all kinds of input from the outside, mixing it with your goal or purpose—and eureka!

You enjoy life more (I'm not talking about living for your goals).
Your goals allow you to really live. You can enjoy the now, and still look to the future. It's like being a kid again!

People who are living their dreams and striving for meaningful goals wake up in the morning excited, full of anticipation. Don't you want to live like that? You can't wait to start the day, you're constantly stimulated, curious, eager to interact with others, passionate about what you're doing, and you're working toward real fulfillment.

Your ability to have fun and enjoy life is tied into goals. When you know what you want, what you value, what makes you happy, it's easier to make decisions which reduce stress. The directionless life is not the happiest to look back on.

Motivation.
In the movie *Field of Dreams,* Kevin Costner's character hears an ominous voice that gives him direction: "If you build it, he will come." "Ease his pain." Everyone thought he was crazy as he plowed his corn under and built a baseball field. But he didn't care what people thought—and he was rewarded in the end.

We all need something that moves us, that we enjoy doing, and that we are good at. We need to feel useful. We need to help others or belong to a cause larger than ourselves. We know we could help make this a better world, if only on a small scale.

In this world of rapid change, people have a deep need to control their own fate. Psychiatrists are well acquainted with the phenomenon. Goals are how to do it.

▼ ▼ ▼

ACTION ITEM

Make a map of your life up to this point. It could look like a treasure map, a board game, or a street map. It could be chronological, or seasonal, it can zigzag. Go from birth to where you are right now. Get creative. Draw pictures. Use your non-writing hand.

We're not talking about regrets here. Just take a look back at where you've been for clues about where to go next.

If you want to take it one step further, try drawing another map—this one of your future. Do you know where you want to go?

▲ ▲ ▲

Next Step

A meaningful life is a continuous process that includes purposeful goals as well as consummations related to them. A person's behavior becomes meaningful by virtue of the ends that matter to him, whatever they may be . . . The concepts of meaning and happiness are thus interwoven.

—Dr. Irving Singer

John Goddard has never been afraid to dream out loud. When he was fifteen, he made a list of 127 things he wanted to do in life. Not *could* do. *Wanted* to do. Included in his list were some pretty outrageous goals: climb Mount Everest, study primitive tribes in the Sudan, run a five-minute mile, and write a book. In middle age, he has become one of the most famous explorers in the world. He reached 105 of his goals and added to the list along the way, doing many exciting things.

Wish List.

You have primed the pump, now let it pour out. What do you want to be, do, have, share in the future? Don't worry about how you will get it. Just give yourself ten minutes and list everything that comes to mind. You can think in terms of what you want next year, in the next five years, or in the next ten years. It's up to you. The important thing is to let your imagination run wild—and don't be afraid to say what you want.

Wish List II.

Now do the same exercise with your non-writing hand. Disengage your logic brain and list the things you want with your other hand. It's remarkable how different your two lists can be.

Draw pictures.

If list-making isn't your game, try drawing or painting your potential goals. Don't focus on how artistic the result is, but on how many things you can imagine yourself doing, having, being. Use symbols that you'll understand when you come back to them later.

Write.

If you're most comfortable writing, write for ten minutes, nonstop, in answer to the following statement: "I am blessed and I cannot fail; this is what I would do, be, have, create, and contribute in the future."

▼ ▼ ▼

ACTION ITEM

Ask *why*. Why do I want to be famous? Get my book published? Work for myself? Land a starring role? Explore your motivations—it'll help you weed out goals that aren't your own (I want to be a doctor because my dad and grandfather and both uncles are doctors), eliminate goals that are nonfunctional (I want to be the first four-foot guard on the Celtics), and develop the courage to say out loud what you really want (I want Meg Ryan to lust after me).

▲ ▲ ▲

For Love or Money

According to a study by the Market Research Institute, here's how Americans would spend $100,000 in lottery winnings: over $87,000 would be spent on kids' education, investing in a retirement fund, and caring for aging parents. The rest would be split between a new home, a new car, and a dream vacation.

Interesting.

In another study, just 25 percent of Americans equate having lots of money with being successful. Important factors included a good marriage, being good at their jobs, and being satisfied with and in control of their lives.

I believe that when we do what we are supposed to do—meaning we enjoy it and are good at it—the money will eventually flow, as long as we believe we deserve it and we ask for it and willingly accept it. But creative, right-brained people are usually not driven by money, don't manage it very well, and have some funny beliefs about it. For instance, there are artists who believe that they *must* starve to do *real* art, that they can't have a juicy income and remain honest and true to their vision, that somehow accepting money for one's art is selling out and giving up some of one's independence.

Let's face it, money *does* buy freedom (as does a total disregard for it, too, I guess). I have had money and I have struggled. Money did not make me happy; it just created a whole new set of challenges. When I was broke, I found out that wasn't the answer, either. The solution is to have inner happiness, so that you can enjoy your riches.

There were times when I would rather go on a vacation with my friends than take a speaking engagement (I went to Key West). There was also a time when I took a training gig against my better judgment. It was for a group of stockbrokers. What do I have in common with stockbrokers? Nothing, as it turned out. It was a disaster. If I could do it over, I would not have done it for any amount of money.

I have a friend who was making millions (okay, maybe not millions, but a *lot* of money) as a financial planner. He was miserable until he decided to take a huge pay cut to pursue his passion. Are you ready for this? He wanted to mow lawns for a living. The rewards of working outdoors with his hands, and being able to see the fruits of his labor, were more important than what he made in his "other" life. He says all of his financial friends are jealous that he works in the fresh air and has the freedom to do what he pleases. He has never been happier.

I think Goethe got it right when he said, "It is not doing the thing we like to do, but liking the things we have to do that makes life blessed." Nowhere does he mention money.

Still, if you're unwilling to live on the street (or with your mother), you need to consider money somewhere in your goal-setting process. You can do that by answering the following questions:

- What specific annual income do you need to live abundantly, not just comfortably?
- What are your minimum monthly financial needs?
- How much money would it take to make you feel successful?

- What are you doing to pay off your credit card debt or your student loan?
- Where can you cut back?
- What are some other sources of income?
- What about part-time work?
- What are you unwilling to do for money?
- What negative belief holds you back when it comes to money?
- What would it take to double your monthly income? Is it worth it?
- How does it feel to be broke?
- How does it feel to be able to buy the things you want, when you want them, and still have some left over for a rainy day?
- How much money (exactly) would you need to be able to pursue your dream?

Dr. Wayne Dyer wasn't satisfied with just being a relatively unknown professor, so he wrote *Your Erroneous Zones*. After the book was published, he bought several hundred copies, loaded up his car, and hit the road with the goal to make it a best-seller. Six months later he had traveled 28,000 miles, covering forty-seven states, and had personally delivered between 15,000 and 16,000 books to bookstores. He also sought out publicity with the local media and conducted over eight hundred interviews. Because of his goal and subsequent action, *Your Erroneous Zones* became a number-one best-seller and Dr. Dyer an acclaimed author.

What Is Your Mission?

My goal was to make my living at music without compromising my own standards and my own sense of artistic integrity. And I've been able to do this for the past twenty years.

—Michael Franks

Your mission, should you choose to accept it, is the overriding principle on which to base your life and career. This gives your life clarity and focus, without stifling or restricting you.

A mission statement is written to inspire you, not to impress others. It reflects your inner desires and values, as well as the direction of your life. It is a powerful tool and should not be rushed. It may be best to start by writing everything you want to be, do, have and how you will serve others. Then cut out the repetition and keep cutting it down until it is one or two sentences long.

Then memorize it, internalize it, and live it.

Your mission statement should include an inner goal, what it will take to please you, your deepest desires and dreams. You'll also want to include an outer goal, which is how you will serve others. This "outer goal" is important because it will usually point out how you'll make money by reaching your inner goal. Your mission statement does not need to include your desire to have a Rolex, a Porsche, a beach house in Malibu, and the best tables in the best restaurants, however.

Fill in the blanks: I would like to work in_____, doing_____, and be known for_____.

This will help you focus on what's best for you. Not what's okay, good, or better, but what's BEST. This will keep you focused from day to day and year to year.

Choose a Motto

It's what I do—I'm a writer.

—*James Michener*

Having a hard time developing a mission statement? How about just a theme for the year? Make this your year to do something special. An example a colleague shared with me was this: "Streamline, focus, and hit home runs." She felt she had lost sight of the big picture and wanted to make some real progress toward her long-term goals this year.

Another colleague's theme was, "If there is no dough, just say NO." He felt he was so overextended with volunteering and other nonprofit activities that he was losing money in his business. He felt he could do more good if he maintained a profitable business.

Theme examples:

"I will focus on my writing above all else this year."

"I will show more courage in everything I do this year."

"I will get rid of all the clutter in my life this year, both physical and mental."

"I will fight for my artistic freedom this year, and make work I want to make."

"I will better manage distractions in my life and concentrate on my work."

"I will finish what I start this year."

"I will concentrate on the business side of my art."

"This is the year of growth and study."

"This is my year to make things happen."

An Alternative: The Credo

People are starved for a way of life. They are hunting for a way to be or act toward the world.

—*Sam Shepard*

What do you stand for? It's handy to have your own personal credo, similar to a mission statement but less action-oriented. A credo is a written statement of your personal values and code of behavior.

An example from San Francisco–based artist SARK: Stay loose. Learn to watch snails. Plant impossible gardens. Make little signs that say Yes and post them all over your house. Make friends with freedom and uncertainty. Look forward to dreams. Cry during movies. Refuse to be responsible.

SARK also believes in wearing pajamas to work, taking naps, and drawing on walls. She concentrates every day on what she calls her life's mission: to free creative spirits everywhere.

First and Goal

Many people have only weekends and holidays to which they can look forward, leaving the rest of the time dreading having to go to work on Monday morning. Set for yourself goals that will bring you the satisfaction that you deserve.

—*Charles Schulz*

Okay, I'm assuming you've come up with a mission statement, or at least a theme or a credo. That's your goal. Now write it down. Say it out loud. Tell it to somebody else.

Think about it. How badly do you really want this? Be careful what you wish for.

Why do you want it? If you can establish the motive, then the means and opportunity will fall into place.

Narrow it down. Be specific.

Be honest. How many plates can you spin at once before it all comes crashing down? Most creatives can and want to do many things. Perhaps you can do it all at once. More likely, you can do some now, some later. If you want to be the best at one thing, you have to focus on that one thing and let the other stuff go. What's your style? What are you willing to give up, at least for a little while?

Linda Buzzell, author of *How to Make It in Hollywood,* has the perfect analogy for your tendency to want to do ten things at once. She suggests that you think of your life as a stovetop with five burners, two in the front and three in the back, with a pot on each one. Got that picture in your head? Okay. Now, if you want to move something from the back to the front burner, you have to move a pot from the front to the back. If you want to maybe add a new pot, you have to remove an existing pot. The same is true with your goals in life. You can have five or six, but try to keep only two or maybe three on the front burner. These are your main goals, where you focus your energy and efforts.

Spell It Out

I used to be scattered, taking on any project that sounded fun, but never working toward any real, meaningful goals. I wasted a lot of time on projects that I thought were fun but not very rewarding. All that changed when I wrote a mission statement. It was the best thing I ever did. Now I make decisions based on my mission. It also reminds me to pay attention to my mental, spiritual, and relationship goals as well as my career.

—*Karen O'Connor*

There isn't really a right or wrong way to write your goals down. It's just important that you do it, and do it in a format that helps you understand and remember what those goals mean. Companies write their goals as a mission statement—a one- or two-sentence concise statement of their purpose and how they intend to achieve it.

Whether you call it goals or philosophy or mission statement, a few guidelines may be helpful as you write them down. Here are some suggestions:

State your goal in the positive.
"I will be, I will do, I will have . . ." This reinforces that you believe you will achieve that goal. For example, "I will write a book proposal."

Set a deadline.
This creates a sense of urgency and encourages you to take action. For example, "I will complete my book proposal by June of this year."

Be specific.
Your goal should be clear, detailed, and focused. Leave no doubt about what you want to accomplish. If you said, "I will complete my book proposal by June of this year," does that mean a rough draft or the final version, or that it will have been sent to an agent or publisher? Be specific. "I will complete my book proposal, have three people check it for errors

and critique it for content, correct and finalize it, and send it to my agent—and I'll do it by June."

Make it measurable.

There should be a way to recognize that you have reached your goal. If your goal is to be thin, what does that mean to you? What weight? Dress size? Waist measurement? If your goal was to write a book proposal, are you done when it's on your agent's desk or when the book is on the book-store shelves?

Make it action-oriented.

Your goal should be something that requires action and produces results. A goal to be a writer could be better stated as, "I will spend a minimum of three hours a day, six days a week at my computer, writing, another three hours a week in the library researching my book, three hours a week connecting with possible agents, editors, publishers and other business contacts (mentors, partners, financial people, etc.), working toward having my book completed and in an agent's hands by November 1." Action doesn't have to be *your* action, however. Your goal of updating your Rolodex could be stated, "I will have my secretary update my Rolodex by adding in the phone numbers of all the business cards I have collected over the last year as well as my most frequently called numbers, weeding out the numbers that have changed or become irrelevant, making sure she has it done by June."

The goal depends on only you.

Your goal should not hinge on your ability to change others. If you said, "I will get a promotion by making the boss like me," you will find it difficult to achieve. Instead, you could say, "I will earn a promotion at work by continuing to do more than my job requires, increasing my value to the company by learning new skills, and shooting for the employee-of-the-month award by the end of this year." If your goal depends only on you, though, you'd better be sure it's important enough to put the effort into. If you have no problem finding the number you need or paying for lots of information phone calls, you'll not be likely to put in the time and effort to update your Rolodex.

Time to Do Some Weeding

Don't concern yourself with how you're going to achieve your goals. Leave that to a power greater than yourself. All you need to know is where you are going and the answers will come to you.

—Dorothea Brandt

At this point, eliminate any goals that contain one of the following concerns:

1. It's not really something you want for yourself, but something you put down because it would impress or satisfy others.
2. It won't make you happier, healthier, wealthier, wiser, or more creative.
3. It doesn't involve activities you enjoy doing or do well; you wouldn't enjoy the pursuit of this goal.
4. It is illegal, unethical, immoral, would hurt others, or would damage your reputation in any way.
5. It doesn't excite or inspire you when you think of it or tell others about it.
6. It doesn't involve at least some of the resources, educational background, skills, or abilities you already possess.
7. You're not able to state it clearly.
8. You aren't willing to pay the price it will take to reach it.

If You Can See It, You Can Do It
The future is called "perhaps."

—*Tennessee Williams*

The ability to visualize your goals puts you a long way toward reaching them. (You can't hit a target you can't see.) What do they look like? Project yourself forward. See yourself living as if they were already a reality. This intensifies your desire. When you can see it, you believe it. Let's try it.

- Remember back to a day when everything in your life was perfect. Describe in detail where you were. Whom were you with? Emotions? Colors? Images/sounds/smells? What were you doing?
- Fast-forward to the future. You have everything in life you want. Spend a day in your perfect life. Where do you live? Describe the environment. What does your home look like? Walk through the house in your mind. Describe in detail. Open your checkbook. How much money do you have? What kind of business are you in? Describe what you do, where you work. What is your greatest accomplishment to date? What does your office look like?
- Now think about the present—as it should be. What is the first thing you do when you wake up? How do you spend your morning? What do you do at lunchtime? In the evening? Draw a picture of what you saw, or write a detailed description.

Visualization is a technique that works in many situations. Athletes do it, running through the game or the race over and over in their minds, well before the event itself. It gives you the opportunity to create the best result. Visualizing your future is like watching the coming attractions to a new movie, only this one stars you in the lead role in your life. Project yourself forward.

Picture yourself in your perfect career. Some of the questions in chapter 2 were designed to help you develop this image. Fill in the details, drawing it more and more clearly in your mind. These questions might help:

- What do you do all day?
- Where do you work? Indoors? Outdoors? At home?
- What time do you start work? When do you have to wake up?
- Is it a small company or a large one? Are you the boss or the employee?
- What do you wear at work?
- How many hours a day do you work?
- Whom do you work with? Do you work alone?
- Who is at the meetings you attend?
- What are the primary tasks you perform?
- What skill do you use most?
- What tools are you using?
- How are you treated by others?
- How much are you paid?
- What are some of the perks, other than salary?

Now that your perfect career is clear in your mind, answer the following questions:

- Who is doing exactly what you want to do?
- What company or career fits this profile?

Think about it. This simple exercise could point you in new directions.

Take the First Step

The first two letters of the word *goal* are *go*. So release the emergency brake and put your goal in gear by taking that all-important first step.

In *The Empire Strikes Back,* Yoda, the Jedi master, tries to teach Luke Skywalker how to engage the "force," the greatest power in the universe. In his raspy voice, Yoda instructs his pupil, "There is no *try*. There is only *do*."

To some extent, just having a clearly stated goal helps you reach it. If you put in a little effort, however, you'll reach much farther. Here are some examples of first steps. Once you get going, you build immediate momentum. It's the first step that is the hardest.

Goal	First Step
Learn to dance, cook, scuba.	Sign up for a class.
Clean and organize your home.	Set a date for a party, send invitations.
Lose ten pounds.	Use nonfat milk in your coffee.
Change jobs.	Update your résumé.
Be a better husband.	Send flowers today, do the cooking.
Be a better boss.	Compliment someone for a job well done.
Improve your attitude.	Smile at everyone you meet.
Change the world.	Buy a recycling bin and recycle plastics.
Get in better shape.	Find a gym partner and meet three times this week.

Try investing ten minutes a day in your goal. It will all add up over the long haul. Inch by inch, it's almost a cinch.

You don't have to work on just one goal at a time, either. Switch off between goals. Try to set them up so that no matter what you are doing, you are working toward one of your goals.

Excuses, Excuses

It doesn't matter how many people say it can't be done, or how many people have tried it before; it's important to realize that whatever you're doing, it's your first attempt at it.

—*Wally "Famous" Amos*

Self-limiting excuses hold back many writers from reaching their goals.

Many people, a great many, in fact, have a goal to write a book. I hear it all the time. Yet only a fraction of them ever do it. It remains "the elusive goal." I think it is more a case of wanting to "have written" rather than do the writing. Unless you have a ghostwriter, a book will not write itself. Besides, for many people, the goal is to *sell* a book. To sell a book, you first must write it (or at least a proposal). Commit it to paper, page by page. That's the part that can be, well, work. It's tough enough with a positive attitude . . .

I can't because I can't even spell my own name.	Get a spell checker or hire an editor.
I can't because there are already too many books out.	Always room for one more.
I can't because I don't have an agent.	Self-publish.
I can't because I may fail.	What's the worst that can happen?
I can't because I'll have to quit my job.	Do it part-time.
I can't because I'm too old.	Better late than never.
I can't because critics may trash it.	What doesn't kill you makes you stronger.
I can't because I don't know what to write.	Write about what you know.
I can't because I'm not an "idea person."	You don't have to reinvent the wheel.
I can't because I don't have a computer.	Typewriters still work fine.
I can't because I can't get started.	Join a writers' group.
I can't because who will watch my cat when I go on a book tour?	Deal with it! Do phone interviews.

(Hint: Remove "I can't" from your vocabulary, and replace it with "I will.")

Deadlines

Without a deadline, baby, I wouldn't do nothing.
—*Duke Ellington*

Jimmy Buffett was first introduced to flying airplanes when he was a journalism major at the University of Mississippi. Poverty and then a hugely successful career as a musician and writer got in the way of pursuing his goal of getting his pilot's license. "A few years ago, as this pirate was looking at forty, I remembered that I had vowed to get my private pilot's license by that time. Time and again I would try to pick up where I had left off with my flying lessons, but I never saw it through until the deadline I set for myself approached, and then I got serious."

When I'm working on a book and the publisher gives me a page count and sets a deadline, I find that very helpful. I know how much I have to do and when it has to be completed. If the book is to be three hundred pages and I have one hundred days until it's due, I have to write three pages per day—every day.

The deadline also serves as wake-up call. It creates a sense of urgency and forces action. I know many creative people who will not do a thing without a deadline. When their deadline looms—watch out, they work like mad.

It's the same way with any goal. Without a deadline, your goals remain just out of reach. With a deadline, you have that extra motivation that will usually help you find a way to reach them.

▼ ▼ ▼

ACTION ITEM

Find your current age on the time line. Next determine the ripe old age you believe you will live to (or when you want to retire, or some other milestone). Now subtract the years you have left. What is the one thing you want to accomplish more than anything else in the remaining years?

0   18   21   25   30   35   40   45   50   55   60   65   75

▲ ▲ ▲

Out of Focus

Years ago, I had a belief I probably acquired from watching Leave It to Beaver, *that good people (Ward Cleaver) focused effectively on their highest-priority work all day long and never got distracted, took breaks, or indulged themselves. If I goofed off, I wasn't a good person.*
—*Richard Brodie*

Many creative, inventive, imaginative people have struggled with an inability to focus at one time or another. The most successful have used this "fault" to their benefit. Jay Leno says that he has a notoriously short attention span, but he uses his agile mind and quick-wittedness to his advantage on stage and in interviews. Jim Carrey breezed through class-work and often finished before the other students. With nowhere to direct his amazing energy, he became a bit disruptive in class. Today his disruptive behavior has made him a millionaire. David Lee Roth was so hyperactive as a child that his parents sent him to a shrink. You can't deny that Van Halen benefited from Roth's energy onstage.

On the other hand, you can learn to overcome your inability to focus when it's important. Bill Gates is known to have a very low threshold for boredom, but he can focus for great lengths on things that challenge and interest him.

In the opening scene of the movie *Tucker: The Man and His Dream*, Tucker, played by Jeff Bridges, comes home with a dozen trained Dalmatians that he traded for one of his cars. His wife and kid are unfazed by this unusual behavior. Throughout the movie, which is based on a true story, Tucker appears to be every bit the spontaneous, impulsive, scattered inventor you would expect—except when it came to designing "the car of the future." There he was extremely focused, and he followed through and built the car of his dreams despite innumerable obstacles.

Focusing is not an easy thing to do. At any given moment, you have an infinite number of choices. The trick is basing your choices on your own particular strengths and weaknesses. And sometimes your weaknesses can be the deciding factor. Rick Ramage, a screenwriter, was interested in becoming a pilot when he was younger, then thought twice about it. "I tend to daydream," he admitted. "That's good for writers, bad for pilots."

To help you focus on your goal, try these simple techniques:

- **Keep it in front of your face.** Write out your goal on posterboard and hang it over your desk. Make a painting of it and hang it in the bathroom, the kitchen, above the television set—wherever you spend the most time. Make a dangle-toy out of it and hang it from your rearview mirror. Put it on a three-by-five card and carry it with you wherever you go—preferably a colored card, so you notice it every time you look inside your wallet or purse.

- **Make a "goal board"** that includes a collage of pictures representing your goals. Make it an ongoing project, growing as you do.

- **Make a game of it.** Give a point value to each of the steps you plan to take toward your goal, and come up with a grand total you need to reach the goal. Keep a running total of the points you've earned, and reward yourself when you've reached 25, 50, and 75 percent of your goal. Decide on your rewards (preferably in ascending value) beforehand and attach a picture of it to the point total you must reach to earn it.

- **Think positive.** Use daily affirmations to keep you focused on your goal. "I will do it! I will do it! Nothing can stop me from (state your goal)." Repeat your affirmation three times when you're in a quiet, relaxed state (not, for instance, while you're stalled in heavy traffic, but rather when you first wake up, before you get out of bed). Say it enough times and you'll believe it.

- **Find a goal partner,** someone who will hold you accountable for acting on and achieving your goals. Have you ever noticed that when you have a workout partner waiting for you at the gym, you're more likely to show up? You don't want to let them down—so you don't let yourself down.

- **Talk to other people about your goals.** Tell everybody. Be enthusiastic. Don't let them shoot you down.

- **Surround yourself with other people who are working toward goals,** and who are positive and excited about what they're doing.

It Was a Good Idea, But . . .

According to a gallup poll from 1993, these are the top three New Year's resolutions:

1. Improve personal finances
2. Stop smoking
3. Lose weight

And these are the top three reasons for breaking them:

1. Lack of willpower
2. Loss of interest
3. Goals set too high

Excuses for Not Having Goals, and Why They're Bogus

If you haven't already taken the steps outlined in this chapter, you may recognize yourself in one of the following excuses. As creative people, we can come up with some pretty clever rationalizations for not having written goals—and they're all bogus.

"I already have goals." Fair enough. Are they written down? Can you spell them out? True goals—the kind that work, anyway—are written down. As a result, they can be reviewed, revamped and recalled, guiding your everyday actions and decisions.

As a kid, Chuck Givens wrote down 181 goals he wanted to achieve in his life. At the top of his list was to write a hit song and open a recording studio. At twenty-two, his song "Hang On, Sloopy" hit the charts, and he used the royalties to open a recording studio. To date, Givens has achieved 160 goals from his original list.

"I set New Year's resolutions every January, and by February I'm back to my old ways. Goal-setting doesn't work." There's a big difference between goals and resolutions. One works and the other doesn't.

Resolutions are often unrealistic and impulsive. You are initially excited about them, but there is no real commitment, so you're quickly discouraged and distracted. Written goals, on the other hand, involve some real soul-searching. When you're doing what you really want to do, you're more likely to follow through.

"Setting goals is overwhelming, complicated, and too much work." This excuse really boils down to not knowing how to set goals. When you follow the steps in this chapter, you'll learn a lot about yourself—and you'll also start developing a skill that will help you do what you need to do, whether plotting a course for your life or simply losing ten pounds.

"I'm too busy living my life, man. Besides, you can't know what's going to happen in the future." Live for today, we can all die tomorrow, right? Wrong. In the United States, women live to an average age of seventy-nine and men to seventy-two. That gives you a lot of life to live—with or without goals. Having written goals gives peace of mind, clarity of thought, and hope for the future. It motivates you, guiding your daily decisions so you can make the most of that unforeseeable future.

"Written goals will make me boring and predictable, and stifle my creativity." Okay, so write them in pencil. Change or refine them as often as you like. But get them down on paper first. Otherwise you're very likely to be bored, frustrated, and stifled—the very things you want to avoid. You don't have to set your goals in concrete—but if they're in sand, the tides can come and wash them away. Setting real goals involves self-knowledge, and self-knowledge alone can help you chart a better course.

"I don't have time to set goals." Make it a priority. Do what you can now, however small it is. You'll be surprised at how little steps can add up. Being too busy can be a symptom that you're afraid to slow down and really take a look at yourself and make decisions about what to do when you grow up. Your life is frittered away on endless details and mindless errands.

"Written goals? Whew-ee, that's pretty serious stuff. I don't know if I'm ready for that big a step." Sometimes phrased as *"I'm too old/too young to set goals."* These excuses reflect closely held fears. Fear of failure, fear of success, fear of change, fear of c . . . c . . . commitment. If you let fear get in the way, you'll always play it safe, never writing that book or opening that business or taking your paintings to a gallery show. That can lead to feelings of anger, frustration, depression, and lack of motivation. The answer is to take smaller steps. Setting goals doesn't mean making sweeping changes that you're not prepared for. You don't necessarily have to quit your job; you just need to take the first steps toward achieving what you want, or you'll never get anywhere.

"What will others think if I try for more?" or *"I know I could do more, but I'm satisfied with what I have now."* Low self-esteem is a deep-down feeling that you don't deserve to be happy and successful. Why shouldn't you have all the things you desire? You deserve it as much as anyone else. Don't let others make important choices for you.

A college professor gave his class of graduating seniors a final exam in which he had three sets of questions. The first category was the hardest and worth the most points, the second and third categories were each easier and earned fewer points. Students were instructed to choose questions from only one category. When those who chose questions from the easier categories got their papers back, they were miffed by the low grades they received even though they had answered the questions correctly. They asked the professor what he was looking for. The professor smiled and said, "I wasn't testing your book knowledge, I was testing your aim."

"There are too many things I want to do, and I don't want to choose just one." You don't *have* to choose just one. You can have several goals or one overriding goal, a mission, a vision, and several goals that support it.

I can remember going to art school (and doing homework, too), running my own retail business (I maintained control over merchandising, advertising, PR, and some of the buying), working part-time as a sales representative for another company (my territory included Hawaii, so I stayed on), volunteering as a speaker for the police department's D.A.R.E. program (my way to give back), and trying to maintain a love interest all at the same time. I obviously lacked focus and, not surprisingly, goals. I was overextended, overworked, and under a great deal of pressure. As a result, I was only mediocre in some areas and downright awful in others. I eventually set very concrete goals, lightened my load, and became successful in the things I chose to focus on.

▼ ▼4▼ ▼

It's Not Just a Job, It's an Adventure

The joy of life is made up of obscure and seemingly mundane victories that give us our own small satisfaction.

—*Billy Joel*

Someone once made the observation that you spend more time planning a vacation than you do planning your career. Why is that?

Think about how you plan a vacation. You start out thinking, "Oh, I think I'd like to go someplace tropical (or historical, or educational, or exciting)." Then you start to narrow it down to specific hemisphere, then country, then type of place to stay (campground or resort), then particular place to stay, then how and when to get there. Once the reservation is made, you can look at what you're going to do when you get there—or figure to wing it.

Planning a career is a lot like that: setting a goal, then narrowing your choices down step by step until you're where you want to be. If you haven't done that yet, it's past the time to start. Don't think of it as limiting yourself—this is just one vacation, and you've got many years ahead to travel the world. But without a little planning, you're not going anywhere. Maybe you think a career will come to you. If it does, you've got a better travel agent than I do.

Life as Art

Art is about making something out of nothing and selling it.

—*Frank Zappa*

There are times in your life when everything seems chaotic. You are in full crisis mode, unsure of what to do next, unsure about everything, really. What you think you need is a vacation to escape your challenges or at least to sort things out. The truth is, you need to get a handle on your life and get control again, to make some sense out of the uncertainty. You don't need a vacation, you need a *vocation* and a plan. This will help you make it through the turbulence and come out the other side less stressed and stronger for it.

Even the rightest right-brainers need some structure in their lives. Yet creative people resist traditional planning because they think it is too structured, too limiting. It doesn't have to be. In chapter 3 you clarified your vision and set a goal. Once you have a goal, you need a plan to help you reach it. This plan is more like a map. It has footprints to show you what steps to take (and in what order), landmarks so you can tell when you are veering off course, a list of recommended provisions for this trip, and the names of some trail guides who can help you get where you're going quickly.

The starting point is here and now. The goal is to earn a living from what you enjoy doing.

Once you get there, you can do a whole lot of sightseeing, wander around, and have a good time. From your new vantage point you may decide to set out for someplace new. The steps are the same each time: choose a destination, work out how to get there, and go.

▼ ▼ ▼

FAST FACTS

According to *Working Woman* magazine, "Only eight percent of us have the career they expected to have."

▲ ▲ ▲

The Lean Years

The following stories of struggle illustrate how having a career plan—and sticking with it even when it seems like you are going nowhere and you are ready to throw in the towel—can work for you. Hang in there; you will make it, if you really want it.

When I worked for a San Diego radio station years ago, I worked closely with the owner of a club called The Spirit. This little pink place by the bay actually launched many a band's career. I remember hearing from one of the disc jockeys at the station that the band playing that night was worth going to see. When I arrived, the parking lot was nearly empty. When I went inside, there couldn't have been more than a handful of people. But the band didn't seem to care that nobody came, because they were rocking. That band was REM!

Eddie Vedder, the singer and songwriter for Pearl Jam, worked as the house roadie for a club called The Bacchanal, supplementing his income as a gas station attendant on the graveyard shift (which he claimed gave him the peace and quiet he needed to write songs). All he was interested in was music (and surfing). He told a local reporter, "I would do anything to be around music. You don't even have to pay me." But pay him they do!

In the spring of 1978, Amy Grant released her first album. That summer, after graduating from high school, she hit the road on her first promotional tour with her mother. The first stop was a record and bookstore in Southern California. The manager sent out twelve hundred engraved invitations and was expecting a large crowd. Amy was scheduled to sign autographs and sing for ninety minutes. Not one single person showed up. She performed anyway, for an audience of one, the store manager. Even her own mother left! She went on to fill venues in Southern California later in her career with as many as twenty thousand paying customers.

One singer dropped out of Texas Tech because being an architect was not his passion. Singing was what brought him joy. Everyone said it was a mistake. Six Flags wouldn't hire him to perform in the park, but they did hire him to work the rides. Still, John Denver eventually made it as a singer.

A young singer and songwriter working as a janitor at the Columbia record studio was trying to attract the attention of Johnny Cash. He slipped demo tapes of his songs to June Carter, Cash's wife. Frustrated when Cash did not respond, the aspiring singer landed a helicopter in Cash's yard one Sunday and got out with a tape in his hand, boldly saying, "You're gonna listen to my song." Appropriately called "Sunday Morning Coming Down," it became Kris Kristofferson's first big hit.

After being turned down by twenty-six record labels, this young singer-songwriter finally got a record deal. His debut album sold a paltry 324 copies and the label "lost" the tapes to his next release. He kept writing songs and performing until he was able to build up enough of a reputation to land another record deal. In 1977 his song "Margaritaville" launched a following rivaling the Grateful Dead's Deadheads (Jimmy Buffett's fans are called "Parrotheads"), and led to a twenty-five-year career.

To have one hit record is quite an accomplishment; to have several is amazing. You may not know the name, but this Grammy Award–winning artist's songs are on the tip of your tongue. "On and On," "Save It for a Rainy Day," and "It Must Be You" are from the film *Tootsie*. The interesting thing is, when Stephen Bishop attended Crawford High School in San Diego, he got a D in music. When he submitted a song for a local radio contest, it didn't make the cut. (It later became a hit.) His band finished as runner-up in a Battle of the Bands. So he moved to Los Angeles.

After seven years of hardship, he finally started to gain some attention. I included his story just so I could share one of his song titles: "I'm So Miserable Without You, It's Almost Like Having You Here." Ouch.

▼ ▼ ▼

ACTION ITEM

Think of two important transition points in your life. Write a key word for each one. What was your feeling at the time? How did it turn out? How did you plan for it?

▲ ▲ ▲

Hey, This Wasn't in the Brochure

Life is just one long process of getting fired.

—Samuel Butler

It helps to expose and explore some of the myths surrounding creative careers (and careers in general) before you go any further. Things can look pretty glamorous from a distance, but once you're within spitting distance, you realize that this isn't anything like it was advertised to be. It also doesn't help when people send you postcards about how swell everything is, when in reality the weather is stormy and the people are rude. Forewarned is forearmed—an old-fashioned way of saying "If you know what you're getting into, you're less likely to get hip-deep in it before you notice the smell."

Myth: Your career is your life.

Reality: The average person changes careers five to seven times before retirement—and creatives change careers more like five to seven times every five to seven years. It is okay to be a job-hopper in the creative arts. In fact, the future will be more like a project-to-project kind of jumping around. Even if you think you want to stick with one job, one company your whole life (are you sure you're a right brainer?), it isn't possible anymore. End of story.

Myth: Companies offer careers.

Reality: People create careers.

Myth: You climb the corporate ladder from mailroom to boardroom.

Reality: Traditional career planning is useless today. The old rules are obsolete, and paths that were once prominently marked are now grown over or washed away. Make your own path.

Myth: Glamorous fields and big titles are where it's at.

Reality: Production Assistant. Sounds prestigious, doesn't it? If you know anything about making movies, you know it's a glorified gofer position. Titles don't mean all that much anymore—managers finally figured out that a big title makes up for a small paycheck, and even janitors have become industrial maintenance engineers. I say go for the big check and let them call you whatever they want.

Myth: Work is a necessary evil.

Reality: When you find the ideal career, you'll never work another day in your life. It won't feel like work, anyway. That is total actualization.

Myth: Pick a path that involves the hot careers and you'll be sure of a job.

Reality: Don't limit yourself to what's hot or popular. Follow your passion, your curiosity. The experts don't know what's best for you, any more than your parents or friends do. You know. So stick that neck out and go for it.

Myth: Once I make it, I'm set for life.

Reality: A creative career is like a roller-coaster ride. There is a slow and steady climb (which isn't much fun) as you pay your dues, work hard, and make connections. Once you get to the top, you have just about a second to enjoy the view before you go plummeting to the bottom, ten times as fast as the climb up. Sometimes that fast drop is your choice, sometimes it isn't. The momentum of it carries you back up the next rise, however, and around the curves to the next dip and rise and the next. The point is that the creative arts don't take you on a steady uphill climb. But, unlike other professions, they offer a lot of thrills, too.

Myth: I want my first job to launch the rest of my life.

Reality: If you're waiting for a job to start your life, stop waiting. You need a life first. A sense of who you are and what you want to be. *Then* you go looking for a job. Most people make a more lasting commitment to their second career, because they've had time to figure out what they really want by then.

Myth: Changing your career will make everything okay.

Reality: The saying "Wherever you go, there you are" comes to mind. While there is no doubt the right career makes life much, much better, it won't make *you* better. A career change is external. If you're unhappy where you are now, take the time to discover why before you leap into another situation.

Myth: The most talented people get ahead.

Reality: Talent can take you only so far. Having a vision, a plan, and the willingness to treat your career as a business—that's what it takes to get ahead. In 1973 Jimmy Buffett told a disparaging guitar-playing bell-boy, "You're a fine player, and I'm not much of a player. But I'm a poet and a businessman, and one day I'll be rich and famous. And you'll always be a bellboy." That's how it turned out, too.

Myth: Some people seem to get all the lucky breaks.

Reality: You make your own luck. Behind all those "lucky breaks" is a lot of legwork, preparation, and planning. Being in the right place at the right time means putting yourself in a position to be at the right place (get out there), being prepared when opportunities arise—and having the guts to grab your chance when it comes. Many people claim they've got no chance to win the lottery. So they don't play. Are they unlucky because they will never win or unlucky because they don't take a chance? Opportunities are everywhere, but without a clear vision of what you want, you may be passing up many "lucky breaks" of your own.

Myth: Entrepreneurs are born, not made.

Reality: It's true, not everyone is cut out to make it on their own. It takes a certain type to be in business. But creative people have many of the traits necessary to be successful businesspeople. They also have some traits (like an allergic reaction to detail work) that must be overcome.

Myth: If I work harder, everything will work out.

Reality: In the military, they have soldiers digging ditches and marching around in circles. This is very hard work. What does it get them? Calluses and athlete's foot. Hard work is needed to make it in the creative arts, but working smart and taking time out to let ideas percolate is needed even more.

Myth: You have to have a college degree to make it in the arts.

Reality: Although a college degree can't hurt (Einstein believed it did), you become an artist by *doing*. Building your skills, portfolio, and relationships while actually creating something is the best way to learn. If you do go to school, consider an art or music school, geared to the practical realities of the life you want to live. Liberal arts colleges and higher degrees are a waste of your time (unless you want to teach).

Myth: There are simply not enough jobs in the creative arts to go around.

Reality: You only need one. Don't have a defeatist attitude, or you're already defeated. Somebody is going to get a book deal or record contract, or sell their software idea. Why *couldn't* it be you?

Myth: The entertainment industry is glamorous, so get any job you can.

Reality: The above-the-line people (writers, producers, directors, actors) definitely have some perks, but for the most part it is hard work, long hours, a lot of sitting around, weeks and months away from your (real) family when on location, and total insecurity between jobs. As for the below-the-line people (film crews), it is just a job like any other. Not everyone gets to go to Cannes or fondle Oscar.

Myth: The only real artists are starving artists. At least they have some integrity.

Reality: Some art forms simply do not pay well, no matter how many dues you pay. But making money at your art does not mean you're a sell-out. It means you're smart enough to find a market for what you love to do.

Myth: Do what you love and the money will follow.

Reality: If it were that simple, don't you think *everyone* would be making it big-time? The real message behind this myth is that it is much more pleasurable to do what you love for a living. Because you love it, you do your best work and work hard. As a result of those factors, the money finds you. Hopefully, before you're dead.

Myth: You have to be famous to make a fortune.

Reality: Anyone who has had any degree of fame will tell you it doesn't pay the bills! Being respected by your peers and adored by your audience is awesome, but there are plenty of people you've never heard of who are quietly making millions. Fame is not the goal; it is a sometime by-product of doing good work.

Myth: If you don't like having a boss, you should work for yourself.

Reality: That's true—as long as you don't have any clients, partners, publishers, agents, fans, etc. Freelance clients will work you harder and try to pay you less than any "real" boss. They don't care about your other clients, other commitments, cash-flow problems, or the fact that their deadline comes smack in the middle of the first vacation you'd planned in years.

Myth: When you work for others you are just an employee, a peon.

Reality: I heard this statement from a second-grader recently— "You're not the boss of me!" *You* are the boss of you, and nobody else. An entrepreneurial mind-set will help you get ahead, no matter where you work or who you work for.

Myth: You can't start at the top.

Reality: Well, actually, you can. Start your own business, and you'll be owner, boss, CEO. You'll also be gofer, publicist, bottle washer. Entry-level jobs are necessary. Use them. Take advantage of opportunities to learn.

Myth: The more you make, the happier you'll be.

Reality: The more you make, the more you make. Money creates its own problems, and happiness is something else altogether.

Myth: There is no such thing as job security anymore.

Reality: Your job security is your talent and skills. Build on each experience, developing new skills and making key contacts along the way. Be willing to change, adapt, learn, and reinvent yourself. Be a problem-solver and self-starter, innovative and productive. You will not only survive—you'll thrive.

Myth: It's too late to start over.

Reality: It is never too late to look for and pursue your passion. "Over the hill" just means that there is another hill waiting for you to climb.

Myth: Start looking for a new job when you are ready for a change.

Reality: Always be on the lookout for opportunities. Keep that résumé updated and handy.

Myth: Jobs are like marriage.

Reality: Jobs are more like dating.

Myth: I have to settle for whatever comes along.

Reality: What you want, wants you. You only have to settle if you're unwilling to go out there and meet your life halfway.

Myth: Once I have a college degree, my training is complete.

Reality: Ongoing training and education are critical. They are your best guarantee for any kind of job security. Keep current.

Myth: Day jobs must be waiter, cabbie, or phone sex.

Reality: Although those are actually good day jobs for the creative person for a number of reasons, it might be even better to find temp work or entry-level work in your field. That way you learn from the inside out, make contacts, and learn about opportunities firsthand.

Myth: Everyone is out to steal your ideas.

Reality: Very few people have the intent, ability, follow-through, or malice to steal your ideas. Don't let this fear hold you back. Do what you can to protect yourself and your ideas, and then go out and spread the word. Make something happen.

Myth: You need an agent, a book deal, a record deal to make it.

Reality: There are ways around the gallery/publisher/studio when it comes to getting your work out there. Be a do-it-yourselfer.

Myth: Temping is temporary.

Reality: Temping has proven to lead to full-time positions more times than people think. If you don't treat it like a temp job, they won't treat you like a temp, and eventually you may land your dream job.

Myth: When you figure out what your dream is, everyone will support you.

Reality: The sad thing is that more people try to sabotage you than support you. Their insecurities and envy are their problem, not yours.

Myth: If you're all over the place, you've got a better chance of catching a big break.

Reality: Lack of focus is one of the biggest problems creatives have. In fact, I would say that focus is the difference between flourishing and floundering.

Myth: Only anal-retentive left-brainers try to plan out their lives and careers.

Reality: Even creatives need a plan—a loose plan with a tight vision.

Choosing Your Destination

Unusual people have unusual jobs.

—*Saturn automobile commercial*

Not too long ago, I was surfing at a spot known for big south swells. It was HUGE this day. I was with my brother and some friends and, against my better judgment, I paddled out. After a thirty-minute pounding, I finally made it outside the impact zone. There were only a few other people out, and the conditions were ominous—wailing offshore winds, cold water, and fifteen-to-eighteen-foot death sets that seemed to come out of nowhere. I just wanted to get one wave and go in. Since it would be my only wave, I decided to go ahead and take off on the biggest wave of the day.

I dropped in (or more like took the elevator to the bottom of the wave) and turned as hard as I could (I wasn't about to look back). As I was about to get tubed on a wave big enough to hold a bus (a double-decker bus!), I saw my brother paddling frantically to get out of the way of the monster I was riding on. I turned up into the wave to avoid hitting him, but went too high, and the lip of the wave and I became one. The force of it flipped me around and drove me down into the churning water. The impact knocked the wind out of me. I swam as hard as I could to get to the surface.

Just as I figured I was about to break through the surface, I hit the bottom. *I was swimming the wrong way!* I wanted to cry. I had used all of my energy, my lungs were burning because I was completely out of air, and I felt a wave of hopelessness come over me. I really thought that was it.

I managed to turn myself around and push off the bottom with my legs. As I headed for the surface, everything went black. I barely made it. I was exhausted. Fortunately, I was able to hold on to my friend's board as I spent the next few minutes puking and getting my wind.

The point of this story is that if you expend all of your energy in the wrong direction, you can drown.

I know a guy who has lived a most interesting life. When each career move became more bizarre than the last, I cheered him on. After he got married, however, he decided he wanted to live a more conventional life. He used his travels, experiences, and unusual skills to start a company the puts out guidebooks for hikers.

I am all for zigzagging one's way through life and having multiple careers. It is the way your mind wants to work, and it keeps you interested. At the same time, if you could focus on one career at a time, you would be much more successful. How can you combine all of your interests and experiences into one career?

▼ ▼ ▼

ACTION ITEM

List your skills and talents, highlighting the ones you think are most important, that you most enjoy using. Think of three jobs or careers that use all of your highlighted ones. Choose the one that sounds best to you, and find out more about it.

▲ ▲ ▲

Use an Umbrella

The nature of the work is to prepare for a good accident.
—Sidney Lumet

Realistically, at most you should pursue only three paths at once. If they all come under the umbrella of one career, all the better. This means everything you do feeds one or more aspects of your career. That is exactly how my career is laid out. When I am doing workshops, I am selling books. When I am writing books, I am building up credibility for my workshops. When I do my radio talk show, I am building interest in my books and workshops.

An umbrella title like *designer, inventor,* or *performer* can get you started on a career path while you're still exploring possibilities. Don't get me wrong, though. The more focused you are on what you want, the easier it will be to plan your career and the more opportunities will arise. If you can say you're an artist and define the medium you want to work in, you have an edge, a niche.

This will not hem you in. It is simply where you are today and where you want to go *at this time.* You can always adjust your course. Make a choice now, however, and you have an edge over all those wandering generalities out there. You can remain flexible and take advantage of opportunities within your niche. You can go as slowly as you like, but knowing where you're going also lets you go faster if you like.

Make sure you match up who you are to what you want. Take another look at your responses to the questions in the preceding two chapters. Don't deny these needs and preferences just because an interesting opportunity arises.

Harold Hannaker quits his job to try to find meaning in his life. He meditates for six months. Nothing. He hears of a Tibetan monk who has lived atop a mountain for thirty years and knows what the meaning of life is. So Harold hops on a plane and flies to Tibet. He treks to the top of the mountain to talk with this holy man. When he gets to the top (no small feat), he says, "I risked everything to come here and see you because you know the meaning of life. Please tell me, what is it?" The lama looks at him and says, "Life is a stream." The guy stares at the lama with a puzzled expression and asks, "What do you mean, 'life is a stream'?" The lama raises his eyebrows and shrugs his shoulders and says, "Okay, life is not a stream."

Only you know what the meaning of life is. It's an inside thing.

Kick It

I was a complete flop at getting a regular job.

—*Frank Capra*

If you think it is impossible to make it and that you may have set your sights too high, consider this. Doug Blevin's chances of being an NFL kicking coach were pretty slim, considering that there are only thirty teams. Add to that the fact that he was never an NFL kicker himself— heck, he'd never kicked a football in his life. Doug Blevins was born with cerebral palsy. Yet, despite all those people who told him it was unrealistic and even impossible to dream of coaching in pro football, he didn't listen. Today, Blevins, who uses a motorized cart to get around, is the Miami Dolphins kicking coach.

NOTHING is impossible if you want it badly enough.

Pay Attention to Your Dreams

No one travels so high as he who knows not where he is going.

—*Oliver Cromwell*

How do you know if you have chosen the best path for you? Do what I call the "sphincter check." If your bunghole gets tight and you feel something in the pit of your stomach when you think about it (fear is a good sign), then you're likely on the right track.

Remember this, "dream job" means it is *your* dream. Not anyone else's.

When I was a kid, I wanted to be a drummer. My parents wanted me to play accordion. I kid you not. There were two problems: How the hell was I going to get in a rock band playing accordion, and what girl in her right mind would date an accordion player? (I was twelve, and these were key issues in my life at the time.)

So we compromised, and I began taking bass lessons, an instrument for which it turned out I had a natural affinity. I liked the bass, and I did meet girls and play in rock bands. But, as anyone who ever played in a band with me will tell you, I spent half of all practice sessions on the drums. I even played the bass like the drums, with a lot of slapping and popping. I just couldn't get it out of my system. There was something magical about beating a drum that I didn't get from stroking a string. To make a long story longer, I picked up a set of used drums and began to teach myself how to play. That was almost fifteen years ago, and I still play today.

Companies that Coddle Creative People

Chiat/Day, an award-winning ad agency, coddles its creatives. There are no assigned desks or offices or fancy titles. You check out a computer, which you can take home to do your work if you like. There are no time cards. The creative people who work there are empowered to decide what needs to be done and how long it will take.

Other big companies that are friendly to creatives include Microsoft, Motorola, 3M, Rubbermaid, and Hewlett-Packard.

Unusual Careers for Creatives

There are a lot of careers on the fringes of other creative careers, where the competition is less aggressive and the rewards can be more money:

makeup artist
CD package designer
stage designer
fashion illustrator
art therapist
police sketch artist
display merchandiser
lighting designer
exhibit designer
animator

medical illustrator
web designer
ghostwriter
critic
floral designer
jingle musician
clip-art artist
CD-ROM director/producer
game designer
restaurant publicist
cookbook author
greeting card writer/designer
speaker/trainer
magician
comedy writer
tour manager/publicist
miniature set constructor
special-effects artist
bonsai culturist
banknote designer
cartoonist
crossword puzzle maker
graphic artist
mime (please, no more mimes!)

What's Out There? Look Before You Leap

Life is trying things to see if they work.

—Ray Bradbury

Early in the planning process, you need to find out everything you can about the field you think you want to go into. What exactly do you do day-to-day in this career? What are the trends? How did others get their start? How do you get ahead? What are the negatives, the benefits?

I'm saying this and I can see you nodding (you are either nodding off or agreeing with me), but very few creative people actually do this kind of legwork. I'm not kidding about this. It is not optional. Find out everything. You don't have to take notes, but read, talk to people, check out web sites, do some recon. Do some interior investigating, too.

- Talk to people who are doing what you think you want to do. Maybe follow them for a day. I never realized how much traveling I would have to do as a speaker/trainer/author. Everyone thinks it is so cool to be on the road, meeting new people and seeing the country. Let me tell you, it sucks. Airplanes, airports, hotel food, airplane food, long drives, setting up, testing and breaking down equipment, jet lag, colds and flu galore—these are just some of the joys of life on the road.

- Read biographies of successful people to see what it took. Are you willing to move back home with your parents during the start-up phase of your career? Work a second job? Work in the garage? Move to another city?

- Go to trade shows, make lunch dates with people in the field you're interested in, do informational interviews (on the phone if you can't meet them), search the Yellow Pages, check out chat rooms and web sites online, ask your librarian where to look for information, request literature from interesting companies, call associations, read trade journals. Get the dirt.

- Research gives you more confidence. The more you know, the less you stress. Absorb all the information you can, and then go with your gut. Let your instincts be your guide. Make informed decisions about how much you want to earn, whom you will work with, what tools and talents you need to master, the hours, the environment, the stress level. Then you can move forward with a sound decision about what you want to do. You can avoid quite a few pitfalls this way.

▼ ▼ ▼

FACTOID

Ten thousand new jobs a day are created in the United States, mostly in the "knowledge work" sector.

▲ ▲ ▲

Really Odd Jobs

You can blaze your own trail. You don't have to follow in anyone else's footsteps. Here are some trailblazing examples:

Bill Nye was an engineer and part-time comedian in Seattle when he created the character "The Science Guy," a kind of Mr. Wizard who makes science exciting, entertaining, and explainable on public television. Part of what makes his unusual career cool is that he gets to do show-and-tell every day! I have tuned in (okay, so it's not just for kids) and seen him parachute (to demonstrate wind velocity), jam with the band Soundgarden (something to do with sound), and strip to his shorts in a meat locker to illustrate that cold doesn't give you a cold. It all started when he appeared on a Seattle comedy show wearing a lab coat and safety goggles, and dunked an onion in liquid nitrogen. The onion shattered, the audience went wild, and he won a local Emmy Award for the bit. Nye now has a contract with Disney.

Quentin Proulx has played the Peanut Man for Planters Peanuts, Waldo for Mattel, The Cat in the Hat for Loews Resorts, and the Striding Man for Johnny Walker Scotch. He gets paid big bucks to make executives laugh, performing at trade shows and conventions. He's created a nice niche on the fringe of the entertainment industry, and the multitalented Proulx loves what he does.

Frank Bender combines artistry and intuition with forensic training to help solve crimes as a facial reconstructionist. (I never knew such a career existed, either.) Before getting into this unusual field, he was a photographer just getting by (he hated his job), who yearned to paint and sculpt. He took night classes to learn the craft. His life changed when a friend at the medical examiner's office invited him to the morgue for a visit. While looking around, they came to a corpse that was part of an unsolved case. The friend explained that without knowing what the badly decomposed woman looked like (yes, this is gross, sorry), there was no way to solve the crime. Bender said, "I know what she looked like." He created a sculpture of her face based on bone structure, and within six months she was identified, based on Bender's work.

Shelley Freeman and Walt Wilkey restore mannequins for a living. They also make lifelike replicas of dummies that are used in place of the actors in films where the celebrity is blown up or beaten or worse. Their mannequins have appeared on TV on *Seinfeld* and *NYPD Blue,* in commercials for Nike, and in films like *Mulholland Falls.* Have you ever seen "Mannequin Sculptor" on anyone's résumé before?

Trendy Travel

The factory of the future will have only two employees—a man and a dog. The man will be there to feed the dog. The dog will be there to keep the man from touching the equipment.

— *Warren Bennis*

Become a trend watcher. See what the future holds for you and your talents. Ask yourself, "How does that affect me and what I am doing? How can I benefit from it? Where do I fit in with these new developments?" Personalize it and then capitalize on it. It's a waste of momentum to ignore the trends altogether and say, "The heck with it, I'm gonna do what I'm gonna do no matter what." Even Picasso followed trends sometimes. He always expressed himself in his own way, however, and often he created his own trends.

I have been a graphic artist for so long that I can remember setting lead type. Just kidding. I do remember when everything was pasted up by hand. I remember copy being set on a machine that punched a tape that was run through a computer the size of a refrigerator, which printed out justified type. I also remember doing a lot more hand rendering. There isn't much call these days for paste-up artists, but graphic artists with computer skills are in demand everywhere. Many people in the printing industry have seen their jobs change radically in the last three decades. Most have retrained, upgraded their skills, and kept their jobs. The first ones to embrace computer technology were there to meet the new demand, getting better jobs and far better pay than they had before.

Want to know what the fastest-declining profession is, according to the U.S. Census Bureau? Letterpress operator.

You don't need to dial 411 to learn that the latest trends favor the right-brained, creative person. The entertainment industry is booming, which is an area loaded with creative people. Web sites need content, which means writers, photographers, and artists. Web sites need designers, too.

One of the best trends in the last decade is flex time. Are you kidding me? This is exactly the way you like to work. Creativity does not follow a time clock, so why should you have to quit at 5:00 P.M. when you are on a roll? If you stay late working on a project, why should you have to show up at 9:00 A.M. the next morning? Dress codes are relaxing, and that also favors us.

With outsourcing and project work becoming more and more common, there is a need for people like you to come in, solve problems, and move on to new and more interesting things.

Bottom line: heavy lifting is out, and all things creative are in. It's your time to shine, baby!

Show Me the Money

If you really want something, you can figure out how to make it happen.

—*Cher*

Sometimes you have to go where the money is. The states with the most Forbes 400 members are California, New York, Texas, and Florida. Areas with the highest per capita income are San Francisco, South Florida, and New York City. (Check the living expenses for San Francisco and New York, though. There's always a trade-off.)

Career Trends

I will be an artist or nothing!

—Eugene O'Neill

Drumroll, please. As I write this, the number-one area of opportunity for the creative person is . . . animator. Over and over again, this is listed as *the* best field for fun, financial gain, and fit for the creative person.

Ten years ago there were only two computer graphics staffers at Industrial Light & Magic (George Lucas's animation and special effects company). Now there are three hundred. In addition, most Hollywood studios have established in-house animation departments. The demand for animators is expected to rise by 23 percent in the next decade. The entertainment field in general is expected to boom. The demand for film and TV employees is expected to increase five times faster than the country's overall growth rate.

Another area of opportunity is in software development (no kidding). In fact, information technology is the nation's largest growth industry overall. The rapid rise of the Internet has spawned jobs galore for geeks—er, the technically inclined, that is—as well as creative types interested in marketing and design. Think about it: as the Internet becomes more commercial (bummer), there will be a need for more advertising. As it also becomes more visual, more entertainment-oriented, there will also be a demand for creative arts we probably haven't even thought of yet.

Specific jobs for the creative person with rosy outlooks in the coming years include actors, architects, artists (commercial and otherwise), consultants, dancers and choreographers, designers, desktop publishers, inventors, landscape architects, marketers, musicians, photographers, public-relations people, writers, any jobs related to marketing to the Hispanic community, anything in the entertainment industry, and anything involving the Internet. There has also never been a better time to break out and start your own business.

Travel Agents and Traveling Companions

Accepting good advice increases one's own ability.

—Goethe

Who are the most successful people in your field? Would it be possible to write, call, E-mail, or meet with them and ask for their advice? Could you learn more about their path by reading articles about them? How did they get where they are? Any patterns you could follow? What are they doing that you are not?

The best thing I ever did for my career was write a book about famous and successful people, asking them questions about how they made it. I learned more from talking to them than I ever did from any schoolbook. I picked up on their love for what they did, their enthusiasm and their energy. Success is contagious, and the advice you can glean is great. Brainstorm with others for ideas on how to get where you want to go.

Are you worried that the path others have taken no longer exists, or that they somehow had it easier? I bet there is someone who made it to where you want to go with fewer resources than you have, and greater obstacles. Read their stories. Talk to them and get ideas. More than that, get fired up!

Q & AAAA
One way to make your career plan (once you have a goal in mind) is to do a simple Q&A:

> **Question:** What would it take to reach my goal?
> **Answer:** Specific things you will need to be, do, have, and share.
> **Action:** Action steps you will take.
> **Acknowledge:** Monitor your progress with benchmarks and deadlines.
> **Adjust:** If your plan is not working, ask a better question.

The Zoom Lens
Right-brainers are big-picture people, but when it comes to detail (the devil is in the details) they get distracted. The possibilities are limitless, which makes the concept of planning a career overwhelming. The answer is to break it down, then simplify it and streamline it further.

- Who is doing what I want to do?
- What steps did they take to get there?
- What could I do to follow in their path?
- Whom could I ask how they did it?
- What obstacles might I face along the way?
- How will I deal with those obstacles?
- What are some possible solutions?
- What are the decision makers along the way looking for?
- What do I have to do to meet those needs?
- What will I need to acquire along the way?
- Where is the action happening?

- Where will I need to go to give myself a better shot?
- Where am I now?
- What can I do to close the gap between what I want and where I am now?
- How can I build a bridge from where I am to where I want to be?
- Who can help me reach my goal?
- Where do I need to be to have the best chance to make this happen?
- What skills do I need to acquire?
- What am I selling?
- Can I make a living at this?
- Who is my audience?
- How can I best reach them? Get it to them?
- What's in it for them?
- How much do I want?
- How can I simplify the process?
- What do I need to do to support this?
- What steps do I need to take? In what order?
- What action can I take right now, today?

Work Backward

- Visualize exactly what it will look like, feel like, be like when you reach your goal. For instance, you want to have a novel published by a large publisher and sold and promoted nationwide. Picture yourself signing your finished book for anxious readers.

- Whom must you persuade to publish your book? An editor.
- How can you get an editor to buy your book? You need a literary agent.
- How do you get a literary agent? You need to write a proposal.
- How do you write a proposal? You need to get a book or hire an expert on the subject.
- Whom do you know who has a book published and may know an agent?

What to Pack?

The desk is a dangerous place from which to watch the world.
                                                        —*John le Carré*

There is something to be said for having a "beginner's mind" and going off without a suitcase, to make it without a clue about what you're going to need. Sometimes that approach works because if you really knew all the things that are "required" to make it, you might just say, "Forget it, there is no way."

If I had known the odds against making a book deal with a large publisher, I am sure I would still have gone for it, but not with the same optimism people are always talking about when they speak about me. "Lee, you are so upbeat, I guess you must know something the rest of us struggling writers don't." Actually, I don't know squat. I just go for it and figure out what I need as I go along. That has served me well, because it helps me believe that anything is possible. When someone starts to feed me the "nine out of every ten businesses fail in the first three years" garbage or "the odds of getting a book deal are fifty thousand to one," I put my fingers in my ears and start to sing "La la la la la la. I don't want to hear it!"

You must hone your craft, but not to the point where all you do is practice and never get any real-world experience. Learn when good enough *is* good enough, and go out there and show them what you can do. Look for opportunities to prove yourself. Take the leap.

When starting over—and you will start over, at least once in your life—look for transferable skills you have picked up along the way.

Learn how to use a computer. Don't quibble, and don't act scared. The computer is your friend.

Take classes, any kind of classes that will feed into your ultimate goal. Community colleges offer many skills-oriented classes very inexpensively.

Be humble. Learn the nuts and bolts. Designers don't just know how to design. They know how the production process works. It makes all the difference in developing cost-effective, intelligent work.

Starting Out

As a younger man, I wrote for eight years without ever earning a nickel, which is a long apprenticeship, but in that time I learned a lot about my trade.

—James Michener

It's not where you start that matters, it's where you finish. That's why I love Quentin Tarantino's story. He got his start in the entertainment industry working as a clerk in a video store. Talk about beginning at the bottom! After the success of his film *Pulp Fiction,* the director/screenwriter/actor became a household name.

It may be that in the early years of a career (or a career change) you have to get the coffee, make the copies, and do the grunt work. Do it with a smile and some savoir-faire. Give people more than they ask for. Keep your eyes and ears open. Enjoy this time, because there will be a whole new set of challenges when you take the next step along your path.

I still meet people who are unwilling (and unrealistic) about the price they have to pay to make it. They are unwilling to wait their turn. Though I admire that ambition, I notice they are easily frustrated when things don't go their way fast enough, and they give up prematurely. Sometimes they have built a life that requires a lot of maintenance and money. They must earn x amount to meet their bills, so they are not just unwilling, they are unable to relocate, work long hours, and make sacrifices.

One guy I met at one of my seminars introduced himself as a lawyer. He hated it. He wasn't suited for law. He was bored, uninterested, and going crazy. (Even though he made a heap of money, drove a brand-new Porsche, and he and his wife traveled all the time, he was miserable.) So I asked him, "What is your passion?" His reply was that he loved to paint. Again I asked the obvious question: "Why not go for it?"

He later told me that he went home to tell his wife the good news. He was no longer going to practice law, he was going to be a painter. The look on her face compelled him to ask, "If I do become a full-time painter, it will mean a huge cut in salary, we may have to sell the house, and we probably won't be able to travel anymore. But it is my dream to do it. If I give up the law to paint, will you still love me?" She looked at him and smiled. "Of course I'll still love you. I'll miss you, but I'll love you."

Many of my generation came out of the box with high expectations, and when they were unable to speedily reach the lofty heights they set for themselves, they moved on, abandoning their true calling. They were swinging for the fences and striking out. I was trying to hit the ball to all fields, taking what the pitcher gave me and working the count in my favor. A series of singles led to the success I have achieved. Just try to put the bat on the ball.

Many creative people must follow a long, tough road. As actress and entrepreneur Sheryl Lee Ralph says, "No matter which entertainment career you consider, you've *got* to love it. You've got to want it more than anything because it's so hard to make it and there's so much competition and so much rejection . . . You should be doing this because you love it, and you should be willing to sacrifice and even starve for a while."

The following are a few examples of famous people who worked their way up:

Clothing magnate Geoffrey Beene's first job was as a window designer for I. Magnin in Los Angeles. The head of the store was so impressed with Beene's work that he encouraged him to try his hand at fashion design. Ralph Lauren also started at the bottom in fashion industry. His first job was as a salesperson at Alexander's and then as assistant buyer in the men's department at Allied Stores in New York.

Ann Brashares works for a book producer that specializes in books for teens. Her job is to dream up book series ideas, match up the ideas with authors, and sell the whole package to a publisher. She got her start at the company by doing clerical work. An ambitious woman, she would read manuscripts and offer suggestions. She took work home on weekends and soon became an associate editor.

Lori Campbell is the creative director and owner of her own ad agency. She started out as a secretary, with the dream of becoming a copywriter. After hours, she worked on two of the agency's accounts and built up her portfolio. Eventually, she was hired away to write copy for another firm.

Leo Buscaglia, the bearded best-selling author (known as Dr. Hug) who wrote books on loving, began his career by speaking in every state, meeting and hugging the people who would later buy his books. "I spoke to anyone who wanted to hear me, including one thousand nuns who could pay me only in homemade bread."

Rick Ralston founded Crazy Shirts in 1962 (you could buy one of his custom designs for four dollars). The store was housed in a grass shack that had formerly stored gardener's tools in Waikiki. If you have ever traveled to Hawaii, California, or Florida, then you know how Crazy Shirts has grown. You probably have one of his shirts in your drawer right now.

Julie Greenwald worked her way up from personal assistant to senior vice-president of marketing at Def Jam Records. Greenwald plans music video commercials, comes up with CD covers, and plans press coverage for the label's artists.

Before true-crime writer Ann Rule became a best-selling author, she was a struggling single mother writing articles for *True Detective* magazine. "There were times when I thought to myself, 'We're really poor, and we'll never pull out of it. I will never get to eat in a restaurant again.'" She can buy one now.

Whoopi Goldberg was a single mom and welfare recipient who worked as a dishwasher at the Big Kitchen restaurant in San Diego before making it as a stand-up comic and then as an actress.

Mimi Leder was the first female cinematography student to graduate from the American Film Institute's graduate program in 1975. Afterward, she worked in television as a script supervisor to pay the rent. Her dream was to be a director, so she made a short film to show what she could do. It led to directing an episode of *L.A. Law*—right after she had given birth. "Here I am, leaking milk, with ice packs on my breasts and my arms folded over them—and trying to direct." Her work caught Steven Spielberg's eye, and she was tapped to direct George Clooney and Nicole Kidman in SKG's *The Peacemaker.* She is known for pioneering the fast, you-are-there style of television's *ER*.

Tonight Show host and noted auto enthusiast Jay Leno's first job was as an auto prepper, washing and polishing new cars at Wilmington Ford in Andover, Massachusetts. One day he bumped into the general manager (literally) and dropped an armful of hubcaps. He was fired on the spot. Distraught, he wrote a letter to Henry Ford II and told him what had happened; he got his job back. Later, during college, he wanted to work at a Rolls-Royce dealership, but the owner said there were no openings. So he started washing the cars anyway. When the owner noticed him working, he hired him.

When Tony Bennett was sixteen, he got a job as a singing waiter at a restaurant called Ricardo's. He earned tips by taking requests and singing "these silly little songs. And I loved it. I thought to myself, 'I want to sing for the rest of my life, I don't care if I'm successful or not.'"

Author Toni Morrison, single mother, moved in with her parents and took a job as an editor with a textbook subsidiary of Random House. During her "spare" time, she managed to write her first novel, *The Bluest Eye,* by working late after her children were asleep. The book was a critical success and her next book, *Sula,* earned a National Book Award nomination. Today the Nobel laureate and Pulitzer Prize–winning author has six novels to her credit, three of which were best-sellers.

Quotable

Do you realize what would happen if Moses were alive today? He'd go up to Mount Sinai, come back with the Ten Commandments, and spend the next eight years trying to get published.

—*Robert Orben*

When life throws you down, try to land on your back, because if you can look up, you can get up.

—*Les Brown*

The man at the top of the mountain didn't just fall there.

—*Unknown*

If you want the rainbow, you gotta put up with the rain.

—*Dolly Parton*

It might take months or years for a wish to come true, but it's far more likely to happen when you care so much about it that you'll do all you can to make it happen.

—*Fred Rogers*

The harder I work, the luckier I get.

—*Thomas Jefferson*

To take the difficulties, setbacks and sorrows of life as a challenge which makes us stronger, rather than unjust punishment which should not happen to us, requires faith and courage.

—*Erich Fromm*

There are no menial jobs, only menial attitudes.

—*William Bennett*

Quiz: Match the celebrity to his/her odd job.

This just goes to show you that there is no such thing as an "overnight" success.

1. Annette Bening	a. once performed as a box of lemon-chiffon pie mix in a commercial
2. Kathy Najimy	
3. Keenan Ivory Wayans	b. worked at an ice cream parlor
4. Ted Danson	c. peanut vendor at Shea Stadium
5. Brad Pitt	d. worked as a cook aboard a scuba boat
6. Dennis Quaid	e. encyclopedia salesman, greeting card designer
7. Chris Rock	f. typed entries for the Yellow Pages
8. Michael Douglas	g. bagger, then checker at Vons grocery store
9. Kenneth Cole	h. bellboy at Oakland Airport Hilton
10. Cameron Diaz	i. mental hospital orderly
11. Robert Duvall	j. go-go dancer
12. Sandra Bullock	k. wore a chicken suit to promote El Pollo Loco
13. Michelle Pfeiffer	l. sold vacuums, worked as a legal secretary and an oyster shucker
14. Ellen DeGeneres	
15. Drew Carey	m. manager of a McDonald's
16. Barry Manilow	n. worked at TCBY Yogurt
17. David Hyde Pierce	o. waiter at Denny's
18. Dustin Hoffman	p. janitor
19. Clint Eastwood	q. worked the night shift sorting mail at the post office
20. George Clooney	r. drew caricatures at the mall and sold women's shoes
21. Goldie Hawn	

22. Frank Zappa   s. clown at Astro World
23. Jim Carrey   t. worked in the CBS mailroom
24. Harrison Ford   u. replaced filters in swimming pools
25. Tom Hanks   v. carpenter/yacht broker/department store buyer
26. Courteney Cox   w. gas station attendant (Mobil Man of the Month)
                             x. sold ties at Bloomingdale's
                             y. clerk in a swimming pool supply store
                             z. delivered singing telegrams dressed as a rabbit

Answers: 1(d); 2(z); 3(m); 4(a); 5(k); 6(s); 7(i); 8(w); 9(c); 10(n); 11(q); 12(b); 13(g);
14(l); 15(o); 16(t); 17(x); 18(f); 19(u); 20(r); 21(j); 22(e); 23(p); 24(v); 25(h); 26(y).

Survival Tips

*Never leave a position of your own volition unless there's somewhere
else to go, preferably upward.*

—Marilyn Grabowski

Money both helps and hurts when planning a career. Too much, and you
get soft and are unwilling to take any risks. Too little, and you can't function. Even so, that is the biggest obstacle people throw out when it gets
down to the nitty-gritty of planning a career: How do I survive while I
make my move?

How much do you need, bare minimum, to get by? What is your
bottom-line per month? Is there anything you can cut out to lower that
number while you get going? What is more important to you, time to work
on your craft or a nice car, recreation, toys? Most people use material
comforts to make up for lack of substance in their life, relationships, and
career. Is that what you're doing?

Could you be a monk for a while? Quit smoking, get a roommate, live
on cereal? If the answer to this is NO WAY, I have to ask, how badly do
you want a career? Seriously, if you aren't willing to suffer just a little to
get what you want, maybe it isn't right for you. This is what I mean when
I say *passion*. If you have real passion for a goal, a career, an expression
of your creativity, no obstacle will loom too large. If you don't have it,
every obstacle will seem insurmountable.

Check your pulse. Maybe this isn't what you really want to do. Go
back to chapter 3 and think again.

There are always ways to get more money. Can you borrow from your
brother? Ask your parents for a "loan"? Use your savings? Be a stripper?
Move in with your parents? Sleep on the floor of your studio? Ride a
bicycle instead of driving a car? I'm not saying these are necessarily the

best way to go, but they are options for those who are willing to bet it all and do whatever it takes to make it. Use your creativity to solve your money problems.

The up-and-down cycles common to the creative career can cause financial trouble if you don't plan for them. As someone who goes from project to project, I have had good times when the money has rolled in and lean times when I wanted to roll up my pantlegs and wade into the wishing well and collect the coins. Creative people have to be disciplined enough to plan for the droughts by saving some during the boom time so they don't go bust when it gets tight. But don't be so afraid of the downtime that you take every job that comes your way, whether it ties in to your plan or not.

If you aren't willing to let go of what you have and go for what you really want, you aren't committed enough. And the fact is, the more you are willing to risk, the more likely you are to make it. It also seems that the less you care about and need money, the more it comes to you.

When you get too involved in protecting what you have, it stifles your growth. Hoarding what you have gives an illusion of safety, but, as the saying goes, "A ship in the harbor is safe, but that's not what ships are for."

Waiting for Your Ship to Come In

Sometimes I feel like a figment of my own imagination.

—*Lily Tomlin*

Do you think you are above having to work a "real job" to tide you over while you work your plan? Consider this: Einstein worked for years in the patent office, even after he achieved some of his fame.

Try to find a job within your industry (for an actor, it could be a behind-the-scenes job, for a dancer it might be assisting the choreographer or teaching kids to dance, for an author it could be writing ad copy or reporting for the local newspaper). That way you can hone your skills and make contacts while getting paid.

Meanwhile, you don't have to put your creativity on hold. You can make any job more creative, interesting, lively, or varied. Deliver the mail backwards. Sing and dance while you sweep the floors. Read during the slow times at the newsstand cash register. As long as you make sure the results are excellent, you can do it your way.

Teach what you know. Who would pay you for what you know? When you're starting out, think of community groups, small businesses, local publications—they are all on tight budgets, and most are willing to let you learn while you earn.

Don't quit your day job when you are first starting a freelance business. Take a leave of absence or go to part-time or switch your hours around, but hang on to those benefits and that regular paycheck as long as you can.

Do temp work. It won't necessarily stay temporary.

Don't use all your creative energy on your day job so that you are so drained when you get home that you can't create. If you slave away all day, have something for your "real" creative career.

Who Is in Control of Your Future?

How do I work? I grope.

—*Albert Einstein*

Choose either *a* or *b* for the following questions:

1. Success in a creative career is the result of
   a. dumb luck
   b. hard work and preparation, as well as being in the right place at the right time
2. Which better describes how you feel about the job market for creatives?
   a. It's extremely competitive and there aren't enough good jobs to go around.
   b. Somebody is going to get hired, and it should be me.
3. Do you feel powerful or powerless?
   a. My life is controlled by others.
   b. My life is determined by my own actions.
4. Can you control what happens to you in the future?
   a. Yes, by taking the advice of Viveca at the Psychic Network.
   b. Yes, by setting a goal and making a plan to reach it.
5. How do you see your life two years from now?
   a. Why plan for the future when I could be dead tomorrow?
   b. I will be able to support myself with freelance work in two years.
6. The future of my chosen profession is
   a. Just a minute. I'm calling Viveca now.
   b. I've checked it out, and my field is growing by leaps and bounds. I'll probably need to learn some new software this year to keep up, though.

(Obviously the *b* answers are better.)

Planning Against the Odds

When you feel as though it is pointless to plan because of the overwhelming odds against you, author Linda Buzzell suggests picturing a stadium filled with people. These are all the people in the world who want to do what you do. This is your competition. Don't panic because it's packed. Let's start helping some of them to the exits.

Those who have no talent or training, please leave the park. (Hey, where do you think you're going? That doesn't mean you. Stay in your seat.)

Remove all the people who aren't willing to sacrifice and pay their dues.

Take away the people who don't have the fortitude to make it.

Eliminate the people who don't believe in themselves enough.

Remove people who sabotage their success.

Gone are the people who have no plan, who are wandering around aimlessly.

Now look around. (It looks like the crowd at a Marlins game.)

There are still people there, but there is room at the top, plenty of room in the middle, and loads of space at the bottom. You are unique, and with a vision and a plan, you *can* make a start and work your way to where you want to be.

For the Record

A *vocation* is what you want to do with the rest of your life. It is your "calling."

A *career* is the line of work you are in and the work you do. You change careers, but rarely change vocation.

A *job* is what you are doing at this moment.

Basic Training

The preparation for tomorrow is to do your best today.

—*Lou Gossett Jr.*

In the creative industries, you can get away with creative approaches. These are skills that aren't taught in most colleges, but they can make or break your career aspirations. That's why this is an in-depth look at how to get what you want. It isn't always the most qualified or talented person who gets the job. Haven't you ever sat and watched a movie or read a book and said, "I can do better than that"? But you *aren't* doing it, and they are.

So here is how to get hired, get ahead, go out on your own, and get what you want. Some of these skills are pretty straightforward, others make use of your creativity, and still others will force you out of your comfort zone, but all of them are keys to your career success.

Boot Camp

Don't confuse talking with kicking ass.

—*Richard Marcinko*

Do you think you have what it takes to make it in a creative career? Do you, mister!?

How about a woman who wanted so badly to work at Reebok in the basketball division (they didn't have an opening at the time) that she recruited (on her own) fourteen players to wear Reebok shoes? Hoorah!

How badly do you want that position? When a newspaper told a young writer that she was too inexperienced to work for them and that she would crumble under the workload, she sent the editor five story ideas every day for a month. She got the job.

How are you using your creativity to get what you want? Are you interested in the basic training and advanced techniques that can help you? I can't hear you!

When the founder of Dress for Success New York, an organization that provides free business suits for disadvantaged women to wear to job interviews, was looking for advisers, she bid at a fund-raising auction for an evening with Gloria Steinem and won. She used the time to discuss her ideas, and Steinem became not only an adviser but a contributor.

These are examples of people who used creative approaches to get what they wanted. They broke the rules of engagement and launched an all-out assault. They met with resistance and won the war. Even if the odds are stacked against you (there is *soooooo* much competition, yadda, yadda, yadda), that doesn't mean you can't get the job you want. Don't fight fair. This is war! Charge!

▼ ▼ ▼

FAST FACTS

What workers believe is most true about sending a résumé in response to a help-wanted ad:

1. Needs an attention-grabbing tactic to be read.	25%
2. Goes into a big pile with the other résumés.	23%
3. Sender has no control over their fate.	20%
4. Company will call immediately.	12%
5. Must send again to be noticed.	8%

▲ ▲ ▲

Name, Rank, and Serial Number

Show me a person who can't distill a life into two pages and I'll show you a scatterbrain or an egomaniac.

—James Kennedy

Résumés for the creative person are different (in more ways than one) from the traditional résumé. For example, a young man just out of college applied for a job at a top-notch ad agency. As you might expect, he lacked experience. (He was so green he didn't know that many employers *do* check the facts on your résumé.) His résumé was a total work of fiction—very creative, in fact. A few days later he got a call from the vice-president of the agency, who said, "Your résumé is full of distortions, half-truths, and bald-faced lies. Welcome aboard."

A résumé will not get you a job, but you still have to have one. The résumé will get you in the front door, and without one you will probably be led out the rear exit.

Many books are available on how to write résumés and cover letters. If you want the basics (put your name and phone number on it, keep it to two pages maximum, and so on), read one of them. The following advice is for right-brain types willing to invest some of their creativity in job-hunting.

What to Include

The difference between the right word and the almost right word is the difference between lightning and the lightning bug.
—*Mark Twain*

It isn't what's *not* in your résumé that matters, it's what you *include* that keeps you from getting hired. Employers are looking for reasons to exclude you. Here's what you *should* list:

- Include a unique hobby. It makes for an interesting conversation-starter during an interview. "I see here you're a lion trainer in your spare time." You also don't want to seem one-dimensional. "So, what do you do in your spare time?" "I write code on weekends. Programming is my life." I have actually heard of underqualified candidates getting hired *because* of their diverse backgrounds and hobbies.
- List software programs you are proficient in, and any technical skills you possess.
- Include your web site address, if you have one. You can show off your work and include a few peeks at the real you. Don't go over-board with the personal touch, however. There are things a prospec-tive boss doesn't want to know.
- Focus on your experience related to the position you are going for, not your greatest accomplishment.
- Your greatest strength as a creative person can be a combination of strengths. Don't be afraid to include a diverse background. It is also acceptable in the creative arts to be a job-hopper. Don't be embar-rassed by a lot of short-term stints.
- The artist's résumé should include exhibitions and performances, (most recent) commissions, awards and honors, grants and fellow-ships, radio and TV appearances, a bibliography (credits), educa-tion, training (voice, dance, etc.), teachers, teaching experience, or career-related experience.

- Include appropriate trade associations, such as the Screen Actors Guild.
- Stress *results,* not just facts. If you worked on a project that won an award, made money, or produced some impressive numbers, put it down. "My team developed an innovative ad for XTC toilet paper; their business doubled in the six months of the campaign."
- Keep it simple, silly. If something doesn't sell you or help you land *that* job—cut it.

Subtleties

Résumés are the junk mail of the nineties.

—*Unknown*

Big companies have employment departments that sort through résumés and eliminate most using a written job description. You don't even get a chance to appeal to the person who needs you until you've passed inspection by a bureaucrat. What does this mean? Quite simply, your form had better be correct, your spelling flawless, and your résumé complete with addresses and telephone numbers of past jobs and references.

Even among the bureaucrats, however, you need to stand out. Just remember, you're probably facing a conservative, anal-retentive detail pusher, so don't go overboard. Spend money on the paper—get the best quality you can. Paper sends a subtle message of professionalism, money, power.

Make sure the copy is readable. Keep margins wide and spacing open for a clean, uncluttered look. You might use an interesting font, but be careful. Avoid using colored type. Keep it simple and direct, paring it down to as few words as possible while still conveying your experience, education, and goals. Make sure the reader can find the information they need at a glance.

Many creatives like to use oddly shaped or oddly folded résumés for visual impact. While this technique will make your résumé stand out in a pile, it still has to fit in a regular file folder. Remember who you're dealing with, here.

The most effective résumé makes a connection between you and the reader. Use a photo to make eye contact. If you become a person to them, they're less likely to stick you in the dumper. Don't be shy. Even a passport-type photo will do, but I have seen outstanding résumés with a full-body (I don't mean naked) shot filling the right margin. Use your creativity. Photos, particularly faces, draw the eye and afford your résumé more attention that it would otherwise get.

Don't be dumb, cute, or overly gimmicky. The shoe (get my foot in the door) or the fork (I'm hungry for this job) doesn't cut it. Show them you're clever, yes, but show them you're serious about getting this job, too.

The ultimate compliment you can pay a prospective employer is to customize your résumé to match the position (all you need is a computer with a laser printer, along with some information about the company and the job you want). If you can't do that, use the cover letter to make very clear what your goals are and what position you are seeking.

Not sure what approach to take? Most résumé companies put your information into a standard format. They're really only useful if you can't type and you don't have a clue. Instead, borrow the résumé of someone who got a job like the one you want—or even just someone who got a job. Ask to see their résumé and—without copying it verbatim—use it as a guideline.

A colleague of mine occasionally does résumés for people, but they're expensive (about triple the going rate). She did only two last year—and both people got the jobs they were going after. Ask around, see if there's a résumé specialist in your town.

Money always makes an impression. This does not mean including a twenty in the envelope, it means special delivery—and "special" is getting more special all the time. That FedEx or Express Mail packet used to scream, "Open me first! I'm important!" Now it just says, "Stick me on top of the junkpile." Try a courier. Depending on how conservative your prospective employer is, try having a singing telegram service (not strip-a-gram) deliver your résumé personally.

Match your résumé to the medium. Have an electronic résumé and a paper version. Be prepared with a slimmed-down E-mail and fax version. A fax version can't include a photo, fancy type, small type, or screens, and should be limited to a single page. Send a fax version only if it is requested and time is of the essence.

Keep your résumé up-to-date, adding to it as you get credits or meet important people who are willing to serve as references. This is one place where name-dropping is valuable. If you didn't get the job the first time, try sending your résumé in again whenever you have a major addition.

Don't wait for the perfect credentials, references, and/or experience, though. Hand out your résumé, fax it, post it on the Internet, mail it—just get it out there. The sooner you do that, the sooner you will land your dream job.

Résumé Killers

Poor grammar and spelling will lose you that job. Would *you* hire someone who said, "Worked *party*-time at my last job," "Worked in the *pubic* school system," "typing speed of 40–50 *rpm*"? Have at least two people proof your résumé before you send it anywhere, and pay attention to their comments.

Nouveau Résumé

Creativity can solve almost any problem. The creative act, the defeat of habit by originality, overcomes everything.

—*George Lois*

When applying for a position in the arts, you have the advantage of being able to use your creativity to stand out. That said, *there is a paper-thin line between class and crass and fun and foolish.* Here are some clever gimmicks that helped some of my friends stand out. It should be noted that some of these were too clever for their own good.

Baseball card. I did this with my speaking résumé. (I didn't include that stick of cardboard gum.) It worked well.

Baseball bat. A friend had his résumé burned into a bat. He was hired by a professional baseball team.

Bottle of wine. Applying for a position in a winery, an applicant made her résumé into a bottle label. She was hired.

Panties. At my wife's company, an applicant going for a position doing window displays sent a pair of her panties with the note, "My mother told me to never leave home without clean underwear." We are still trying to figure this one out. She did *not* get hired.

T-shirt. A graphic artist put his résumé and picture on T-shirts and sent them out to prospective employers. He got more job offers than he could handle, and went into business for himself instead.

Booklet. I made my brochure into a CD booklet, with pictures of myself (including one at about nine months old) and my books, information written in story style, and clear contact information. It's been well received.

Brick. A woman had her résumé engraved and attached to a brick. She was interviewed—and hired.

Denim. Looking for a creative position with a jeans company, one applicant printed her résumé on a piece of denim. She was hired on the spot.

Web site. My friend Troy, an illustrator and web designer, puts samples of his work and links to web sites he's designed on his own web page.

Press release. Looking for work in a PR firm, one woman made her résumé read like a press release. She was hired.

Doll. One hopeful sent a Beanie Baby with her résumé. Bribes don't work—not even retired Beanie Babies.

Standee. A very attractive woman sent a large cutout of herself from the waist up in a sexy outfit. It was tied with a ribbon that read, "If you want to see the rest of me, call for an interview." It worked.

Audio résumé. A guy I know sends audio résumés that people can listen to in their cars. It has worked several times. (If only he could keep the jobs he gets.)

Mock-up of product package. One person went ahead and did a mock-up of a new package, using his résumé as the contents. It didn't work.

Pizza box. I read about a guy who sent a pizza to companies he wanted to work for. His résumé was printed underneath the pizza. It worked.

Other possible gimmicks include making a movie poster, a comic strip, a video, a playbill, a menu, or a magnet. Optimize your gimmick by making sure it connects to the type of work you're looking for. Be sure the copy—in whatever form—is clear, concise, and easy to read. You don't want to waste a great idea because the pizza grease obscured your name and number.

Cover Letters

Without a cover letter, you may as well not bother sending a résumé. The cover letter adds depth to your package and allows some of your personality to come through. Also, you get to explain in more detail why you should be considered for this job. When writing your cover letter, use the following guidelines:

- The first sentence must be a grabber. That's the only part that gets read in most cover letters.
- Take the attitude that you are looking for an opportunity to work with this wonderful company or on its exciting project. State some common interests. Read up on the company and its personnel—and let it show. Refer to any personal relationships you have with anyone in the company.
- Keep it short—one page, double-spaced, with wide margins. At that, busy people will only skim it.
- This is really a marketing letter. That means sell the sizzle and not the steak. Count how many "I's" you have in your letter. Try to turn each "I" into a "you" or a "we" or a "your company" by asking

yourself, "How does what I have to offer benefit them?" "My experience, bold style, and media connections can help your company increase visibility at major industry trade shows."

- DON'T be boring. Drop the formal rhetoric and let your personality shine through with a more conversational tone. Show some enthusiasm for the job.
- Put it on your own letterhead, along with a logo. If you don't have a letterhead, create one, or have the best artist you know create one.

Portfolios

A portfolio is a sight-seller, a visual documentation of, and testimonial to, your talents, skills, and accomplishments, as well as evidence of your experience. Interior designers, photographers, craftsmen, illustrators, production artists, fine artists, performance artists, animators, television or film techs all use portfolios.

What goes in it? Your art, whatever it is, put into concrete form—photos of original art, printed pieces (including books), storyboards, projects you have worked on, and prototypes. You may have to create some mockups or pieces to fill in the gaps and show off your creativity. (Many times, working with clients, you do your best work only to have a committee cut it down to nothing.)

At the back, you might include press clippings, letters of recommendation, awards, articles you have had published, photos, seminar certificates, or exhibition history. Lead with your best and dump the rest. An inferior piece drags the whole body of work down.

Portfolios are usually used during an interview, which gives you the opportunity to point out the best parts, explain how and when different pieces were done, and answer questions. It pays to have a mini-version of your portfolio printed up to leave behind. An artist I know has a page with six of her best pieces printed in color, with her name, address, and telephone number at the bottom. It was expensive to produce, but it allows her to build on the personal impression she makes at an interview. Clients don't forget her, and sometimes call many months after a presentation.

Donna Blaurock wrote a book titled *Cheatnotes on Life*. She sends it or leaves it behind when job-hunting. It makes a lasting impression.

- Keep your portfolio visual. This is not a résumé. Minimize type, using it only to date and place each piece. You can even use a video, particularly if you are involved in the performing, television, or animation arts in any way.

- Consider whether you want to focus your portfolio on an area in which you are a specialist, or show off your versatility. If you want to do mostly slick, expensive work, weed out the nonprofit, small-time, budget-conscious stuff. If you're pitching to a client who has a commitment to community, include your pro bono work and be sure to point it out.

- To have a complete portfolio, you will have to document everything and save samples of your work. Start your own performance file. Ask existing clients for several copies of each printed piece (you might not get one otherwise).

- Make it flexible and easily updated. Think ahead. If to update your portfolio you have to move every single piece one slot up, it's too much trouble. Use a three-ring binder or portfolio with removable pages.

- Make it portable. Reduce to fit, limit the number of pieces you include (be selective), or make a brochure illustrating your best work.

- Keep a backup of original pieces in case they are ever lost or damaged. Laminate pieces that might get damaged. Artwork should be clean, neat, and well organized. Dog-eared, damaged, or dirty materials show off your carelessness and lack of attention to detail.

- Portfolios can be on disk, online, in a scrapbook, in a display book, on slides, organized as a press kit, on audiotape or videotape, in a brochure, or in PowerPoint. Try to suit the medium to medium, if you get my drift. Cartoonists or graphic artists might put samples of their work on a Zip disk; a speaker or musician would send tapes.

- Video is becoming a popular way to introduce yourself. You can include interviews, mood music, credits, and graphics for a very effective presentation. Keep it short and front-load it. Make a nice jacket cover—never send a black box. Use this medium to showcase your talents. Customize it as you would a résumé. Make it match the position you are going for. Use a professional studio to get the lighting and sound quality you need. If you can't get in to see "Mr. Big," getting a tape, video, CD, portfolio, or script in his hands is the next best thing.

- Professional photos are a prerequisite for actors. Make sure the picture is high-quality, is reproduced well, looks like you (not a glamour shot), and includes contact information on the back. In fact, you can put your whole résumé on the back. If you print your résumé on clear or white full-page labeling material, you can customize the résumé each time you send your photo out, smoothly pasting it onto the back of the photo.

- Have postcards of your work made, and send them to prospective clients.

ASK A PRO: DOUG HALL

Doug Hall is a professional musician (French horn) and entrepreneur.

What are some of the biggest mistakes people make when auditioning?

Not knowing the music that is requested, i.e., the style, tempo, or emotion of a piece, Mozart versus Brahms or Beethoven or Mahler or Strauss. Also knowing the style of playing of the ensemble you are auditioning for—Chicago Symphony versus Los Angeles Philharmonic. Try to know the acoustic that you are going to play in. One time I auditioned for the Minnesota Symphony, and the reverb in their hall was so long that at times I thought I was playing a duet with myself, a very unnerving event. Basically, you need to do your homework.

What are some of the techniques you use when auditioning?

For a symphony audition, you must pretend that you are performing with an orchestra when you are really by yourself. The best visualization for me is to have a few bars playing in my head before the excerpt requested, so I feel as though I'm playing with the orchestra, and very focused on placing my part with the whole orchestra, thus fooling myself outside of the audition. Before going on, I usually do some yoga to stretch, and breathe . . . and to relax the mind to focus on the performance to come.

What should you bring with you to an audition?

A good book. You might need to hang out a long time, and you don't want to overpractice on the audition day. Water and snacks—you might not have time to get food. Your own music, instrument, and repair kit, résumé, calendar, business cards, an extra shirt if you sweat when you're nervous. Maybe a CD or tape deck to listen to your study music.

How do you get auditions in the first place?

National auditions for orchestras are advertised in the musicians' union paper and now on the Internet. You send your résumé, then they will send you the audition list. If requested, you send a tape and hopefully you are then invited. With your own money, you find a way to travel to that orchestra audition and get home.

Interviews and Auditions

Every encounter with another person is an opportunity to make them like you and help you further your aims in life.

—Barry Farber

If you went to interview with Thomas Edison, he might give you a light-bulb and ask, "How much water will it hold?" There are two ways to figure this out. The first, using mathematics, takes about twenty minutes. The second is to remove the base, fill the bulb with water, and then pour the water into a measuring cup. Elapsed time, one minute. If you chose the latter approach, you'd hear Edison say, "You're hired!"

It isn't always about the perfect answer to the overused question. Often it's your passion and personality that gets you business. Rhino Records says they look for "passionate people who are passionate about music and life." If you don't feel passionate about the job you are interviewing for, maybe you shouldn't be there.

Steve Jobs of Apple Computers says he looks for creative and talented people. He wants idea generators. "I used to think a good person was worth two mediocre workers. Now I think a good person is worth fifty mediocre workers."

Interviewing is an art. It is one you can master. It is about a positive, confident attitude, a pleasing personality, genuine enthusiasm, a track record, and goals for the future. You don't have to have the best credentials if you interview well.

There are lot of similarities between a job interview and a first date. On both, you are probably very nervous beforehand. To calm your nerves, you may ask a friend for some background on your date. What does this person like or dislike? You'll want to make a good first impression, so you make sure you look and smell your best. (Don't be late.) Maybe you bring a little gift. You begin by feeling each other out (figuratively, please), asking questions and getting to know one another. (You'll want to have good breath.) You are on your best behavior, showing off your good manners. Your date may ask about your past; try your best to not bad-mouth your exes. You share a good laugh, look for commonalities, and decide whether you want to spend more time with each other. They tell you they will call you.

That's where the similarity ends. As Jerry Seinfeld once pointed out, you don't have the potential to get naked at the end of a job interview.

Make It YOUR Interview

I knew so much about the company I was able to ask as many informed questions as my interviewer. As the session wore on, our roles reversed. I became the interrogator.

—Victor Kiam

An interview should be a collaboration. Ask the interviewer a couple of questions. Get them talking about themselves. Flatter them a little. Be a good listener. Pretend you are going on a talk show. Prep yourself with an anecdote or two, do your research, know your subject matter, prepare for the tough questions. Have a thirty-second commercial about yourself all ready to go. Sell yourself. Don't be wimpy.

Interviewers know within the first few minutes whether or not they want to hire you. Psych yourself up or calm yourself down before you enter, whichever one is more *you*. Are you the warrior or the peacemaker? Pep talk or yoga?

Make a good first impression. Body language speaks volumes about you. Walk in confidently, shake the interviewer's hand like you are serious, sit up, and keep your chin up.

Rehearse the basic interview questions like "Tell me a bit about yourself," so that you have a ready response instead of a stream-of-consciousness-type answer. The other one that can trip you up is, "Where do you see yourself in five years?" Five years!

Be ready to explain any gaps in your résumé. They may also ask you what your greatest shortcoming is.

Turn the focus around from how you desperately need this job or your car will be repossessed, and emphasize your prospective employer's needs. Talk in terms of benefits to *them*.

How *can* you meet their needs? They may not make the connection from your qualifications, so draw them a map. "My skills and experience as a web-site designer with Amazon.com can help put your company on the web and sell lots of widgets."

Still insecure about that interview? Try these ideas:

Put yourself in their shoes. What would you want to hear if you were they?

Use metaphors (this helps them to understand quickly what you are trying to say), stories (people remember stories), quotes (they say it all so succinctly), statistics (this shows you know your stuff), and examples (proof you've done it before).

Bring your portfolio and make it a show-and-tell experience.

Bring a notepad with you. At the least, you can pretend to write things down to ease your nerves. More likely, the whole interview will be an out-of-body experience and you'll want to write down what they ask you to send, and any other notes to help you write your thank-you letter.

Be yourself and be sincere. Cristin Cricco, an assistant to the editor-in-chief at *Cosmopolitan* magazine, said, "I had no previous magazine experience, but Bonnie hired me over several more qualified applicants because she felt I was the most down-to-earth and enthusiastic."

Be positive at all times. Give concrete answers with examples. How you are a team player or made money for the last company is always good.

Here's one thing that will set you apart from 99.9 percent of the other applicants: having clear goals and a focus for your future and being able to articulate them.

Give away an idea or two. This shows them you've got ideas, anyway. Don't restructure their company on the first interview, though.

Bring extra copies of your résumé, a mini-portfolio, a list of references, a business card, or a brochure—something you can leave with the interviewer when you go. (Nice and neat. Don't pull a folded one out of your pocket.)

Try to end the interview with a win. Have one ready for the inevitable, "Do you have any questions?"

Make a strong or graceful exit. Sum up what you have discussed, and ask what the next move is. Close with what you can do for them. People remember only the first and last things they hear.

Send a thank-you letter, whether you got the job or not. It's your last chance to make a good impression.

Think positive. Have your social security card and driver's license with you.

Don't Do It

You only have one chance to make a good first impression.
Make it count.

> —Markita Andrews (record holder for most Girl Scout
> cookies sold)

There are few things that will guarantee you don't get the job, so don't go for the interview unless you want to be hired. No matter how good you are at sabotaging yourself, an experienced interviewer is liable to see right through to how wonderful you are.

Assuming you want this job, keep that little saboteur under control.

Don't be late (arriving all stressed, sweaty).

Don't interrupt, or you are liable to jump to false conclusions and talk yourself right out of a job. Focus, listen, and *then* respond.

Don't have hickeys, and don't show your tattoos.

Don't complain or put down previous employers. Most companies are looking for problem-solvers, not problem people.

Don't smoke before an interview. If you absolutely must, bring mints—strong mints.

Don't have facial piercings in. In fact, downplay your appearance. You want them to focus on your work, not on your nose ring.

Don't get too comfortable. A savvy interviewer will try to create a friendly, relaxed atmosphere to get you to lower your guard and give you the chance to give them a reason not to hire you. The interviewer is not your friend, so don't start telling them about the time you . . .

Don't resort to tired old clichés like "I'm good with people" or "I'm a real fast learner." Don't make me wanna puke. Yes, make the same point, just find a new way to say it.

Don't act rushed. Relax, take your time to answer questions.

Know when it's time to leave. Don't overstay your welcome.

Don't give away the store. Some things they can't legally ask you come out when they ask you the "tell me a little about yourself" question. "Well, I'm a thirty-year-old lesbian Jew—oh, and I was fired from my last job for stealing company secrets and selling them to China." They can't ask you about that, so remember, "Don't ask, don't tell."

Don't worry too much about your grades, or let the fact that you didn't finish college make you insecure. Focus on your creativity, your work ethic, your street smarts, and your hustle. Keep in mind that Bill Gates dropped out of college, and it hasn't hurt him all that much.

Don't try to be so cool that you look uninterested. You know what I'm talking about. You don't want to act like you care too much, so you play it cool. It's okay to have a been-there-done-that attitude, but at least look like you want to do it again, for them.

Don't be rude to the secretary or receptionist. She or he can make or break you.

Auditions

There are so many reasons you're not picked that you can't even worry about it.

—*Robert De Niro*

Auditions are more difficult than interviews because they aren't interactive. You don't get a chance to work on the interviewer, and often you'll lose out for purely superficial reasons—things you can't do much about. You might hear "You're too short" one day, and "You're too tall" the next. That kind of rejection is frustrating and can destroy your self-confidence.

Auditions can be time-consuming, stressful, demeaning, and fruitless. Still, it's a part of the creative life for actors, musicians, models, and dancers.

The real trick to mastering auditions (beyond your virtuosity) is overcoming nervousness and self-doubt. It's mostly mental, because chances are you've got the chops. Relax, think positive—be positive, project positive.

"The distinction really isn't between those who audition well and those who don't, but rather between those who intend to be paid and those who aren't convinced their skills are worth the money," says Ed Hooks, who wrote the book on auditioning for actors.

Use the waiting time wisely to study, rehearse, relax.

It's about talent, skill, and proficiency in your craft as much as it is about passion. Put in the work beforehand. Know what you're doing. Ask for the script or music before the audition, and work with it.

Visualize success. *See* yourself getting the part. Go into the audition convinced you will get it.

Attitude is everything. Hint: positive, but not Up With People positive. Be enthusiastic, but don't overdo it.

Get a good night's sleep before an audition.

Don't drink or use any controlled substance before an interview or audition. Whether you believe this or not, people *can* tell when you're lit, and it won't help your chances. (One Angels reliever admits to drinking ten cups of coffee and going through two cans of chew before pitching. He says the nervous energy gives him an edge. For an audition, however, shaky hands, a full bladder, and being too hyped up are usually counterproductive.)

Do NOT be late. Yeah, we've said that before. It bears repeating.

Get them to come to your live performance. If you can get key people to see you perform rather than going to an audition, this has gotta be better than the other way around.

Life's a Pitch

If you can't convince them, confuse them.

—*Harry S. Truman*

In Hollywood, it's all about the pitch (remember Robert Altman's *The Player*?). Many creative careers are dependent on being a good pitch person. It's part salesmanship, part stage performance, and part public speaking skills, mixed in with a bit of chutzpah. In some fields, being able to pitch is a matter of career life and death.

It's much easier when you know they need what you've got and how you can help them get what they want. Start out by asking, "Who needs what I have? How badly do they want it?" The more you know the answers to those two questions, the less pressure will be on you, and the easier it becomes to pitch yourself.

Quiz: Traits of Successful Sellers

competitive	persistent
extroverted	confident
agreeable	enthusiastic
self-reliant	intuitive

Circle the traits that you have.

How to Sell Without Selling Your Soul

To get others to do what you want them to do, you must see things through their eyes.

—David Schwartz

Selling your talent is tough. It may even be distasteful, especially if you don't believe in yourself. Many creatives defend their inability to sell as an unwillingness to sell out. Get off your high horse. I am not the devil because I believe you have to get the word out.

As a creative, you are always pitching your stuff, wherever you are, whomever you're talking to. You pitch your mother so she'll get off your back and stop talking about that management program at Bloomingdale's. You pitch people you want to work for, and those you want to work for you. Your style is a pitch of its own, a demonstration of your uniqueness.

To get paid, to make a living, you have to sell. You don't have to lie, cheat, deceive, or wear polyester suits and gaudy ties. To sell effectively, you must help people, heal them, entertain them, fill their needs. These are good things.

Don't treat selling as if it were beneath you. If you don't think you can do it, then you can't. The sooner you accept that you have to do it, the better. Everyone sells something: ideas, information, talent, skills, products, dreams, energy, art. If you have something to offer, and you want to earn money for it, you sell.

That doesn't mean you can't have fun with it. One salesman went around in a limo. His chauffeur would roll out a red carpet and announce him. Good icebreaker.

While waiting for his flight out after being turned down for a job, one savvy salesman bought a life-insurance policy naming the prospect as beneficiary and sent it to him with a note that said, "I'm thinking about you." He got an appointment.

Saturday Night Live was very competitive. To get airtime, you had to be able to sell your ideas. Yet if you got a spot on the SNL team, your name was made. Your career was in your own hands. That's not an isolated situation. You must be prepared when opportunity knocks.

Try to get some intelligence on your client. People like to do business with those who know what the hell they are talking about. They will test you. You need them to say yes to your plan, tape, project, promotion. You must motivate them. Find out what it will take to get them to say yes. Work backward. Contact industry spooks, or do your own investigation. Build up a good case. Talk with others who know the client and may have some tips. Visit their web site to gain insights.

Be clean and neat. Even if you don't think personal hygiene is important, you can be assured those around you do.

Don't get hung up on the first no. New York mayor Ed Koch was recuperating from a heart attack when Mother Teresa came to visit him. He offered her a chocolate chip cookie. She refused, saying that in India when someone offers you food you never take it, because they may starve if you eat their food. "But, Mother, these are the greatest cookies in the world," persuaded Mayor Koch. Mother Teresa replied, "Wrap them up."

People want what they can't have. Sold out. Standing room only. For a limited time. I'm booked solid through July, but I think I could squeeze you in the first week of August.

Shut up and listen. Ask questions and let them do the talking. Don't ever ask a question to which they can answer no.

Trust your gut. Use your intuition to judge the situation and react.

People buy from friends. So make more friends, treat people like your friends. Borrow other people's friends. Keep in touch with old friends (neighbors, classmates, cellmates, whatever). Get referrals, testimonials, leads—and work them.

Be passionate. Being pumped will influence people more than what you actually say.

Don't be dull! Don't be desperate. Interject some humor, an anecdote, a personal story, an example. Make it real. Entertain, personalize it with your wit. Relax and have some fun.

Be ready to pitch on a moment's notice. Have your verbal brochure ready to go. It should be so well rehearsed that it doesn't sound rehearsed.

Lead with your best stuff, and keep it short. Be clear and concise about what you're selling. One to two minutes is a good pitch.

Sincerity sells. Don't be a phony. Be yourself. (Not everyone will warm to you, but at least you aren't selling out.) Always be sincere, *whether you mean it or not.*

Persistence pays off. Walt Disney was turned down by 403 banks before he found financing to make a mouse-themed park.

Set realistic sales goals. Make three calls today.

Act *as if.* Don't lie about your background, but I have read enough biographies to know that when someone is asked if they can play bass guitar and they are a guitarist, they still say yes. (Hey, it's only two fewer strings and a different clef.)

Know the difference between a quote and an estimate. One you can fudge on, but the other is final.

Always have something to give. A demo tape, brochure, video, photo, one-sheet. Carry them with you at all times.

No matter what you are selling, stress the benefits. People are influenced by WIIFM (what's in it for me). Tap into that. What is their dream, their desire? Sell them on it.

Be reliable so they will want to hire you again. Never miss a deadline.

If they say no, ask for a referral to someone else who might like what you have to offer.

Don't take no personally. If you don't get it, who did? Why? What did they do? (Sleep with the boss?) What do they have that I don't? (Big breasts?) How can I improve? (Get implants?) I'm kidding. Jeez.

Don't handicap yourself by saying, "I am not a salesperson." You can be whatever you want to be. "Think of sales as a matter of common sense with good manners added on," says Barbara Winter.

What is your bottom line? Ask them what theirs is. "What will it take to close this deal?" Find ways other than money to negotiate. Let them make the offer first.

Recognize a poor fit when you see one and back down gracefully. "You need to be comfortable with your accompanist. It's a very personal choice, and I will understand completely if you don't feel I'm the right person for the job." Give them an easy exit, and they may recommend you to someone else.

The Customer Isn't Always Right

Prospects are perishable, handle with care.

—*Zig Ziglar*

The customer will cheat on you, lie to you, nag and complain, throw a tantrum, give you the cold shoulder, and then try to rob you blind. Learn to live with it.

The Proposal (The Paper Pitch)

Publishing is an act of commerce.

—*Richard Snyder*

A proposal is just that—you propose a book, story, idea, or position. You do it on paper, in a letter or more formally (read the books on proposals in the library), then sign and date it at the bottom. A proposal clearly outlines the job, giving a time frame and sometimes a cost estimate. Many graphic artists use proposals as the contract for work simply by adding the line, "Tender of a check for (dollar amount) constitutes acceptance of this proposal in full."

You will need to write detailed proposals for many kinds of government or nonprofit work, grants, and long-term or extensive consulting work. Read the books, and hold yourself in. The government and most nonprofits have no sense of humor and no sense of style, and are usually about twenty years behind the times. Play the game their way until you get in the door.

Many writers use a query letter instead of a proposal. It's simpler, basically outlining a story idea, telling why it's a good idea (particularly for the publication being pitched), offering details on art or photographic support, and a time frame. Don't forget to include as many ways to reach you as possible (telephone, fax, E-mail).

An editor is not your enemy, although he or she may not have time to discuss your project right now. Respect the editor's time, and you're likely to get more of it. When you send in your proposal, you should follow it up with a phone call. One. Don't keep calling if you don't get an answer right away. It may seem like months to you, but it's probably minutes to the overworked person on the other end of that phone.

If you're sending a full-fledged proposal, read a book on proposal format or ask the publication or agent for their preferred proposal format—and follow it. Then spend some time creating a great cover letter. Answer the five *w*'s in the cover letter (who, what, when, where, why). Sum it up in one sentence.

Be aware of the bottom line. Show your project has potential. Back it up with statistics, details, references.

Address it correctly. Send it to the proper person, and spell his or her name right.

Sloppy says lazy. Triple-check for typos. Have someone else read it. Read it backward. Print it out. Let it sit. Read it aloud.

Show that it has commercial value.

Flesh out the problems in your proposal early. Show how you'll handle potential obstacles. Think it through.

Know who the audience is. Do your homework!

Focus, focus, focus. Establish your premise clearly and then support it in a logical fashion.

Explain how you can promote it.

Thirty Seconds to Yes

There is no such thing as soft sell and hard sell. There is only smart sell and stupid sell.

—*Charles Brower*

Simplify your message so that it is crystal clear. In general, you'll have about 30 seconds of someone's attention before they lose interest.

Energy and enthusiasm are catching. You'll be more likely to make someone else excited if you're excited first (this works in many areas of life, not just your career).

Practice and be ready for objections and negatives. Treat it like a game.

Volley with your prospect as in tennis, then go for the kill.

Talk in terms they understand.

End with a call to action.

Put yourself in their shoes. What would it take to get me to buy if I were they?

Take the risk away. Do it on spec. Consignment. Barter. Guarantee.

If selling yourself is a problem, get an agent. An agent serves as a buffer. They cover their fees by getting you more money than you could get on your own. Some will work for you on a contingency basis.

Use Your Experience

Tired of pounding the pavement looking for a job, Humphrey O'Sullivan sat down one day and invented the rubber heel.

Where the Jobs Are

This is how the people I talked to found their positions in the creative arts:

1. Networking
2. Targeting companies directly
3. Classified ads (in the trades)
4. Employment agencies and headhunters
5. Job fairs

Most jobs are available only on the black market, a sort of secret underground network of insider information and connections. Staying in the loop is definitely your best way to find out about positions opening up, but it isn't the only way.

The first step is to get on the phone, call your contacts, and tell them what you are looking for. Put out feelers. Call in markers if you have to. You need leads. Ask them to place a "Godfather" call on your behalf to get you an interview. If they don't know of anything specifically, ask them for the name of someone who might. You are building a bridge to an interview at this point.

Who needs what you have to offer and will pay for it? Who can say yes to hiring you to fill that need? How can you get to this person? Whom do you know who knows him or her? Start making your hit list.

To add to your list, do some research. Read industry magazines, *Who's Who* directories, check out the web sites for companies you have targeted, go to the library, and check databases. Knowledge is power.

Once you have a reasonable list put together (no fewer than five names), go where those players are. Attend trade shows, conferences, openings, festivals, expos. When you do contact them, ask yourself this question: "How can I help them? What can I do for them?" Ask them to lunch to share some of your ideas. That's why it's called give-and-take, with the "give" coming first.

What's the difference between being persistent and being a stalker? I'm not sure, but I would bet sifting through someone's trash or sniffing their shoes would probably be going too far when it comes to pursuing a position (and the person who can give you that position). Remember in the movie *Something About Mary*, when Matt Dillon's character was listening to Cameron Diaz's character with high-tech listening devices and using that information to get her to want to date him? That is stalking! But finding out as much as you can about someone and then selling them on you is perfectly ethical. More than that, it's necessary.

Use a variety of techniques in your job search, especially when you are targeting the same company. Mix it up. An E-mail here, a fax there, along with some phone calls, should do the trick. One risky technique is to take out a want ad in the trade papers to announce that you are looking for a position. It would be better to take out an ad to announce that you graduated, won an award, a grant, have a new exhibit, a concert, an accomplishment of some kind. At the least, it builds name recognition in a positive way.

Send your prospective employer a congratulatory card if they did something worthy, one of your newsletters, an invitation to one of your shows (and give them the VIP treatment), a postcard announcing your latest book, play, etc. Keep reminding them you're out there.

Cold calls are the worst. What you need is for someone to warm up the prospect with a quick call on your behalf. It shows that someone is willing to vouch for you. It's called a "Godfather" call because the person calling on your behalf is saying in effect, "It's okay, he's a friend of ours." You want I should whack da guy?

The next best thing is to get permission to name-drop. Impressive references (and the right references) can mean the difference between getting hired and being shown the door. This kind of third-party endorsement from a respected individual is priceless (even though it's free). Keep your references updated on your latest accomplishments.

Look, I never said it would be easy. You have to have a thick skin and realize it's a numbers game. You will hear several (hundred) noes before you hear a yes. *No* is only a two-letter word. It can't hurt you.

Make friends with the gatekeepers. Charm them and make them your allies. Find out their names and use them. Send gifts! Thank them for their help, drop them a card. An insider in the company can carry the torch for you, get your tape in the hands of the president, line up a meeting with the human resources department.

Have business cards and letterhead made up (a logo would be good), have a professional outgoing message on your voice mail, get a beeper, fax, access to E-mail—make getting a job (or that particular client or project) your full-time job, and treat it like a business. You are the VP of Marketing for YOU, Inc.

▼▼▼

FAST FACTS

Nine out of ten Americans agree that an attractive smile is an important asset.

▲ ▲ ▲

Dress

*Everything should be a confluence. The way you dress reflects the
way you live, reflects the kind of work you do, reflects the kind of
person you are.*

—Jamie Lee Curtis

What you wear says a lot about you. Be an original; don't worry so much
about what others say or think. It shows a lot of confidence to dress in
your own style. The only caveat is "keep it clean." Nails, hair, teeth,
clothing, body, mouth. Clean counts for a lot.

Dining

If you can't say anything good about someone, sit right here by me.

—Alice Roosevelt Longworth

The job was his. A $100,000-a-year public-relations position with a large
firm. All that was left to do was go to lunch and close the deal. When the
applicant didn't remove his napkin from the table throughout the meal,
the firm decided to pass on him. Why? They figured if he didn't
know basic table etiquette, he wasn't going to be able to handle the company's PR.

A lot of deals are won and lost over a meal. The business lunch is a
skill you might want to master. At the very least, it'll save you some
embarrassment.

A lot of business is done over dinner (and lunch and breakfast), and
there is an art to dining well. Remember the scene in *Get Shorty* when
Danny DeVito's character is dining with Travolta and Rene Russo? You
know, you start out all kissy-kissy, then he orders something not even on
the menu.

My wife says I have no lips and a small mouth. I do, too, have lips, but
it does seem as though I struggle with certain foods. For that reason, I
will order the easiest thing to eat when I am going to a business lunch.
Even if you have a big mouth and poochy lips, you'll want to eat light.
You aren't there for the food, anyway, and it's hard to talk business
through a heavy meal.

Make reservations beforehand if you are the one asking. It also means
YOU pick up the check. Tell the server (not the cashier with the golden
arches on her sleeve) or the maître d' beforehand to bring the check to
you. If you are hosting, pick a place you already know, but check first to
see if the others have any preference. Don't go to Al's Steak 'n' Ribs if

you're going to be dining with a vegetarian. Make sure your guests know how to get there. Call to confirm with them a day before the meeting.

The guest sets the pace. If they order tequila, then I follow their lead. In most cases, however, you should avoid alcohol at a business meal. This is no time to get stupid. You need a clear head.

Promises, Promises

If you tell the truth, you don't have to remember anything.

—*Mark Twain*

There are two rules to keep in mind in your business career. First, when you give your word, always keep it. Second, don't give your word.

Okay, don't give your word lightly. Don't say, "Yeah, I'll take care of it," when it's one of a million things you already have to do and they are all starting to slip through the cracks. It's far better to underpromise and overdeliver.

If you stick with that simple rule, you'll come out ahead, and still have time for a life. Other rules you'll be tested on are

Protect your reputation with your life. Don't put your name on ANYTHING you don't believe in. I have declared a moratorium on multilevel marketing plans. Not all of them are bad, but I don't feel comfortable having my name attached to anything that may not be above-board or that has a good chance of failing.

Don't pass the buck. Never say, "That's not my job," or "That's not my fault." Handle it. "How can I correct this for you?" "How can I help?" "I don't know, but I'll find out and get right back to you."

Don't be a whiner. Shut up and do what needs to be done. Be a problem-solver, not a problem child.

Suck it up. If you screwed up, admit it, apologize, take steps to prevent it from happening again, and do whatever it takes to makes things right. Don't be defensive (or you'll be seen as offensive). Learn from your mistakes.

Be a doer, not just a sayer. I believe we are judged by what we say, but, more important, by what we say we will do. Be known as someone whose word is gold, who gets things done. Be the person they'd want to go into battle with.

Do [It] Unto Others

Honesty is something you can't wear out.

—*Waylon Jennings*

Do you believe in karma? I do. I found a wallet at the beach. I turned it in with all the cash still in it. Not less than a week later, I was involved in a boating accident and I got a call from a guy who found several items from my boat on the beach, including my wallet. When I went to pick them up and offered him a reward, he refused. That's karma in action.

When you're working with people—and you're going to work with people, like it or not—it pays to follow some simple rules. First and foremost, treat support people with respect, and that is exactly what you get back. This is so simple, but so few people ever do it. Even little niceties like saying thank you are too much for some people. Don't be one of them.

Take the high ground when there are disputes. Don't get involved in other people's arguments, but don't be afraid to stand up for yourself, either. Don't lose your cool. Don't burn bridges.

People will lie to you, cheat you, steal your ideas, stab you in the back. Don't get mad. You have the power here. Don't deal with them and they can't mess you up. Cut them out of your client list, your life, your world. Forgive, but don't forget.

Reach out and touch someone. Give away ideas, leads, and praise. Helping the other person is, in a roundabout way, helping yourself. You get back what you give.

The key to office etiquette is "Fix what you break and replace what's out."

Be honest. Be on time. "Tardiness is inexcusable in my mind. If I can get to work on time, so can my employees," said Eileen Ford, president of Ford Models, Inc.

Sending twelve-page faxes will tie up somebody's machine and may tick them off far out of proportion to the crime. Call first before you send a big fax or a huge E-mail attachment, and make sure it's okay.

Do This, Too

Copulation was, I'm sure, Marilyn's uncomplicated way of saying thank you.

—*Nunnally Johnson on Marilyn Monroe*

Thank-you notes that are sweet, funny, anecdotal, personal (handwritten), and entertaining show that you care and that you are thinking about others, which in turn leads them to think about you. This shows off your class, thoughtfulness, discipline, and organizational skills, and sets you apart from 90 percent of the people out there.

I send thank-you cards for even the smallest thing. *Don't* take people for granted. Make them feel appreciated and important. It takes so little time, but it is *the* most important thing you can do for your career!

Don't Do It

Have a character, but don't be a character.

—*Richard Marchinko*

Working in an office has become increasingly political. It may be difficult for you, but to get ahead you're going to have to be politically correct at least part of the time. This means:

Don't interrupt people when they are talking. Bite your tongue, let someone else be the star. (Nobody likes a know-it-all.)

Don't brag about your new car, new boat, new home. It makes you look insecure.

Don't gossip or talk behind people's back.

Don't fight on the phone with your significant other where everyone can hear.

Keep your money problems to yourself. It's nobody's business but your own.

Don't talk about your sexual escapades. Keep your personal life personal. As much as it is inappropriate, you will be judged by what you do in your personal life. If you are in a position of power and your codependent relationship is known to everyone, it may undermine your authority. You don't want to become a joke.

Keep religion and politics to yourself in your working relationships. While business friendships often flower and become more personal, you should continue to avoid possible sources of conflict. That's what your spouse is for.

Nobody can keep a secret. If you have a tattoo on your butt and you don't want everyone to know about it, keep your shorts on.

Don't leave papers lying out that you don't want people to read.

Watch your mouth. You never know who is listening. There have been lawsuits against men who told smutty jokes in the hearing of others who were offended, even though the jokes were not told to them.

Big brother is watching. Don't put anything in an E-mail you wouldn't tell someone to their face.

Leaving on a High Note

If you can't be kind, at least be vague.

—*Judith Martin*

Take this job and shove it! Ooohhh, how good that would be to say to your ex-boss. "I'd really like to say it's been a pleasure to work for you, but I can't. I really can't."

Sorry, but I am going to have to advise you to bite your tongue—again. Exiting with dignity and class (although not as satisfying as tying the boss up and dragging him behind your car) is the way to go. You want a positive parting (and a we're-going-to-miss-you party). I know it can get ugly. Norm Macdonald and NBC had a bitter parting when NBC executive Don Ohlmeyer (allegedly) said that Norm wasn't funny on *Saturday Night Live*'s "Weekend Update" and should be let go. Macdonald eventually quit, but not before slinging some mud of his own. The result? NBC canceled ads that promoted Macdonald's new movie.

It is a small world in many of the creative arts, and word gets around pretty quick, good or bad. To get even, an ex can spread ugly (and untrue) rumors that will take months of spin control to overcome.

So, when you break up, mean it when you say, "But we can still be friends." Who knows? The production manager for a failing magazine left on good terms, taking a job that offered more security. Five years later, after she was laid off from her new job, she ran into her old editor. She asked him to let her know if he heard of any openings. He hired her on the spot for the new magazine he and a partner had just started up.

Your old colleagues and clients (even your former employer) are potentially your best sources for future freelance work. You may even be able to do freelance work for a company you're leaving while they find a replacement.

Don't forget to take your Rolodex and contacts files before you quit. Otherwise you may find your things boxed up, sans your most valuable assets. Save copies of any work you did for your portfolio. It's much harder to go back and get them later.

Ask for referrals and letters of recommendation before leaving. Tell the people you work with what your plans are. They may be able to help by sending you clients or getting you an interview. Get everyone's address, E-mail, and phone numbers and stay in touch.

Don't go down with the ship. If things are sinking faster than the *Titanic,* abandon ship. If you get a better offer, there's no reason to stay. If you are about to hear "You're fired," it's time to go. If the company does things that are unethical, get out before you're tarred with the same brush.

The School of Hard Knocks

You can get by on charm for about 15 minutes. After that, you'd better know something.

—H. Jackson Brown Jr.

The more work you can do, the more work you'll have. Continued learning is a way of life now. You must embrace it. You must always be trying to improve and update your skills. This is different for different professions in the arts, but if I were an actor, I would continue to take acting lessons, maybe some voice lessons, stay fit, and continue to work on my craft. In addition, I would look into directing, screenwriting, and other transferable skills. The more hats you can wear in today's job market, the more in-demand you become.

What are hot skills? Skills that help you earn more. Skills that are in demand in *your* field. What's marketable today? Just about everything.

I have to admit that I learn the things I am interested in. I learn deeper when I know I can apply these things to what I do. It's also easier to learn when you are interested. I am going to go against conventional wisdom and recommend that you improve upon your strengths first before you focus on upgrading your deficiencies. Many creative people dabble in many trades and master none—and they are struggling. Be the best at something and pretty darn good at ancillary skills within that same genre.

I'm a drummer. I can also play the bass a little, play some percussion instruments, and in a pinch I'll sing backup. They are all related, but first and foremost I'm a drummer. Master your instrument. Master your craft. Then start training yourself to get in shape for the changes you see ahead in your field. Just as in school, read ahead rather than cram at the last minute.

It also pays to learn basic business skills. It helps you understand the company you work for, it helps you run your own company and personal finances. It helps when you have to hire people, because you actually know what you're hiring them for. And it keeps you from failing through ignorance.

To be successful, you must learn, know, become more than you are. If you do not evolve, you perish.

▼ ▼ ▼

FACTOID

Seventy-five percent of workers will need more training to keep up with the changing requirements of their jobs.

▲ ▲ ▲

Quiz: Your Skills

Check off the skills you feel you are proficient in. Circle the ones you think you need to work on. You don't need and won't want to do everything on this list.

critical thinking
writing
public speaking
problem solving
researching
phone skills
sales
desktop publishing
managing people
managing projects
drawing
negotiating
proposal writing
follow-up
personal hygiene
positive thinking
planning
goal-setting
time management
public relations
Internet/Web browsing

letter writing
web designing
bookkeeping
mail handling
team building
networking
self-starting

A Few Words on Skills

Study. Learn from the wise. Look to those who are doing what you would like to do, and figure out what it is that they are doing that makes them successful.

—*Wesley Snipes*

I'm not young enough to know everything.

—*J. M. Barrie*

It is books that are a key to the wide world; if you can't do anything else, read all that you can.

—*Jane Hamilton*

The key to success in the arts is to build a strong infrastructure that includes business basics, writing, speaking, selling and being the master of your domain—learn your craft inside and out.

—*Lee Silber*

Don't just learn something from every experience, learn something positive.

—*Allen Neuharth*

I think the most important thing in the world for career and social success is for a person to be well read.

—*Liz Smith*

If I had been technically trained, I would have quit.

—*King Gillette*

In the beginner's mind there are many possibilities, but in the expert's mind there are few.

—*Shunryu Suzuki*

A mind, like a home, is furnished by its owner, so if one's life is cold and bare he can blame none but himself.

—Louis L'Amour

Never leave a position of your own volition unless there's somewhere else to go, preferably upward. If you are unhappy or dissatisfied with your job, discreetly look around.

—Marilyn Grabowki

Self-Educated and Self-Made

I may have been the only person in my high school class who didn't go to college—but I am also the only one who's sold 8 million records.

—Carnie Wilson

Steve Jobs, co-founder of Apple Computers, abandoned his studies at Reed College to build his business.

Dan Aykroyd, the actor, had no professional music training when he and John Belushi formed the Blues Brothers. But he taught himself to sing and play the harmonica, and their first album, *Briefcase Full of Blues,* sold 2.8 million copies (to say nothing of *The Blues Brothers* movie). He is also a screenwriter (*Ghostbusters*), an entrepreneur (The House of Blues nightclubs and restaurants), and a successful actor.

Richard Branson, the founder of the Virgin Group, was a high school dropout who became a millionaire by the age of twenty-three.

Michael Dell started Dell Computers in his college dormitory room during his freshman year. As the business boomed, he dropped out of school, never to return.

Bill Gates dropped out of Harvard before he finished his studies, and look at HIM!

Self-Taught

The only thing that interferes with my learning is my education.

—Albert Einstein

Award-winning designer Todd Oldham says the fashion industry is about intuition and style, and that he hires people with "personal style and lovely manners, people who are secure and grounded." He got his start doing alterations at the Ralph Lauren store in Dallas, but never went to fashion school. "There are a lot of jobs for people with no paper credentials. I learned all the necessary technical skills by practice, by playing around."

We place too much emphasis on formal education, and not enough credit is given to the people who get out there and do something. Many creatives are impatient with traditional forms of schooling and are consumed by a need to be working in their art. So they make something happen.

Lisa Kudrow, Anjelica Huston, and Aerosmith wear Sage Machado's pearl and gemstone jewelry. Her wares are carried at Neiman Marcus, yet she's never had any formal training. "There is nothing you can't learn through experience," says the successful designer/entrepreneur.

Your education and technical know-how become obsolete faster than potato salad on a hot summer day. The answer is continuous training, ongoing learning. You will need to brush up on your skills and use "mental floss" to stay current. That means YOU take responsibility for updating your skills through conventional or unconventional means.

Put yourself in the line of fire when it comes to opportunities to learn new skills. Soak it all in.

Take on projects that cause you to stretch and grow. Don't dodge a job because you don't have the skills; just allow yourself twice as much time to do it, and learn as you go. If you need to learn a new software program, start a project that requires it. People tend to learn what they need to know *now*, and nothing convinces you that you need to know something like struggling with tools that you don't understand or looking for functions you can't find.

Learn in your car by listening to tapes. This doesn't work for everybody, but it's great for auditory learners.

Be a sponge. Pay attention, listen, and learn from those around you. That's what little kids do. Be a little kid again—look at the world through wondering eyes, treat all those big people as giants and geniuses.

Read biographies and pay attention to interviews. Try to apply the lessons they learned to your own situation. (It's the next best thing to being there.)

Be in the know. Read your industry trade magazine (a must!).

Pass it on. I have found that the best way to learn something is to teach it to others. It's also a great way to keep your art fresh. I speak at a local high school every year, in a program where authors come to read to the kids. It keeps my love of my art alive while providing a service.

Take your skills and abilities into other fields. I always wanted to be a performer, but I always thought it would be as a musician. I ended up as a trainer, yet I am still performing in front of crowds, staging shows and getting the applause.

Develop skills in several media. Fine art, graphic art, computer art. The graphic artist who can draw is worth about 20 percent more in the job market. The graphic artist who can't use the major layout programs on a computer is worth about 80 percent less.

Experiment. Sometimes the best way to learn something is by playing around. A songwriter I know says she ended up writing her own songs because she was so bad at learning anybody else's.

Get out of your comfort zone. If you are bored at work, transfer to a different department or serve on a team outside your normal area of expertise. If you run your own business, get involved in community work—it's good PR, a different set of people and ideas, and it ultimately benefits your business if your community improves.

Learn the language of your industry. Don't talk about the "thingie" or the "doo-wah." Clarity of ideas depends on clarity of language. That's why each discipline has developed specific words to denote very specific things. For instance, type, typeface, font, and typestyle all have different meanings.

Learn a foreign language that's important to your industry (Japanese, Spanish, and German are the biggies right now, with Chinese on the charts with a bullet). Turn your car into a mobile university, and practice language skills while you drive. You can learn to swear at the other drivers in a whole new language. Or take a total-immersion course. How does learning Spanish in Costa Rica sound?

Be prepared. Many companies do not provide enough training for new recruits. They want plug-in people who can produce right away. That's why it's up to you to get up to speed beforehand. The San Diego Chargers drafted quarterback Ryan Leaf in the first round of the NFL draft in 1998. Even before training camp began, he watched films of the team, studied the playbook, and worked with coaches. During training camp, he spent off-days learning his position. He basically put himself through a crash course on being an NFL quarterback. The incumbent, whose job as the first-stringer was being challenged, did the absolute bare minimum. As I am writing this, Leaf won the starting job before the first preseason game. The other quarterback . . . they don't think he will even make the team.

Take advantage of any and all training the company offers. Sign up for everything. This is not just for your edification—you'll make contacts and connections with more people, and you'll impress the heck out of your boss.

Personal training matters, too. Employers these days are looking for such skills as critical thinking, networking, creativity, resourcefulness, initiative, decision making, and team skills.

Do some cross-training. Try other jobs, skills, teams, departments, projects, become more versatile, multitalented—and, as a result, indispensable.

Stay physically fit. Your mind works better, you have more stamina, and you present a better appearance.

Become a bookworm. Go to the library and introduce yourself to a librarian. It is one of the best things you can do to expand your knowledge. They are experts at helping you find information fast—and they love to do it. I use the public library all the time. I do trademark searches (for free) and research books (like this one), and until I started surfing the Internet, read magazines that I was interested in but didn't want to subscribe to (or be hassled for reading at the convenience store).

Read everything, because you never know where a connection will come from. I am convinced that I'll be able to use something from *Playboy* in a book one day. Well, whatta ya know, I did!

Practice, practice, practice. Have you ever met someone who is "book smart" but has no practical sense? Use what you learn. Test it out. There is no replacement for hands-on learning.

Use all your senses. The more senses you can attach to a bit of information, the better you'll remember it. See it, feel it, trace it on the table with your finger, say it aloud, sing it, dance it, taste it in your imagination.

Attend shows, exhibits, concerts, movies. Listen to speakers (that's not self-serving, is it?). Be an active participant. Ask questions. Whenever I go to a concert, I focus my binoculars on the drummer and watch his or her technique. I always walk away with a trick or two.

Get more experience. Take a day job or an internship, volunteer, do temp work.

"Gee, Lee, that all sounds great, but I don't have the time." *Make* the time. Set aside one evening a week to learn and grow.

▼ ▼ ▼

FAST FACTS
A survey by the Society for Human Resource Management identified a lack of creativity and innovation as the top skill weakness.

▲ ▲ ▲

Thrill Skills
Do what you do so well that people want to see you do it again—and when they do, they will go out and tell others.

—*Walt Disney*

Communication Breakdown

A study in the Washington Post *says that women have better verbal skills than men. I just want to say to the authors of that study: Duh.*
　　　　　　　　　　　　　　　　　　　　　—Conan O'Brien

Americans are more afraid of speaking in public than they are of snakes or of heights. Those other things can *kill* you. Jerry Seinfeld noted that people are more afraid of speaking in public than they are of dying. Which means they'd rather be in the casket at a funeral than the one giving the eulogy.

Communication skills are a major consideration when hiring an employee. People make judgments about your competence, credibility, and intelligence based on your communication skills. Your ability to express yourself clearly can propel you forward or hold you back. Remember *Pygmalion* (*My Fair Lady* to all you philistines out there)?

The ability (and willingness) to listen is *the* best communication skill. After that, learn to be a better rapper. Don't ramble. Get to the point and shut up.

Know when to drop the slang and clean it up. "Gnarly, dude," and "F——king A!" aren't likely to make a hit with your grandmother, and some of your bosses, clients, and co-workers will be more sensitive than even she is. Freedom of speech is bulls——t. Suit your language to the situation. "Well, sorrrrrrrry, I, like, can't help it."

It's been said that inside every successful artist is a potentially successful writer, probably because both express themselves from the inside out. Work on your writing skills. Start a journal, write letters, send clever E-mails, make that memo sing. In the movie *The Secret of My Success,* Brantley Foster (played by Michael J. Fox) says, "Davis, that wasn't a memo, it was a work of art."

Become a wordsmith and expand your vocabulary. Unless you're a lawyer, however, this means learning the correct word (syntax), not the biggest one (puffery).

Write It Right

I think when I was younger, I wanted to tell everybody everything because I thought I was so damn interesting. Then I heard the snoring.
　　　　　　　　　　　　　　　　　　　　　—David Duchovny

Business correspondence tends to be formal, rule-bound, and formatted. Whole books are devoted to the subject, so we'll just touch on the basics a creative businessperson will need to communicate in letter form:

Keep business correspondence to one page. Use an inverted-pyramid format, writing the key points in the beginning and working down to your least important point at the bottom.

Ask for action. Tell the recipient what to do, how to do it, when to do it.

Create and save form letters on your computer, so you don't have to reinvent the wheel every time you need to write a similar letter. Adjusting to fit is much easier than starting from scratch.

Don't be a know-it-all, don't be a bore. Think before you write. What is your point? What do you want the recipient to do? Use your left brain to clarify, organize, and define your thoughts before writing. Don't be a rambler—this will not help you win friends or influence people.

Don't trust spell-check alone. Let someone else proofread it, go through it backward. Double-check names, titles, numbers. Poor spelling and grammar will give the reader a poor impression of you, your product, and the point you're trying to make.

Make your mail stand out with an interesting stamp and a handwritten address. First class is better than bulk, Priority really gets attention, FedEx is better, courier gets read first.

Use wide margins and a clear typeface, double-spaced. Make the address legible and correct. Make it as easy as possible for them to respond—include a self-addressed, stamped envelope, your phone number and E-mail address.

Stamp the envelope "Urgent" or "Confidential" if appropriate.

Keep postcards handy for quick notes. Handwritten notes make more impact today.

Send a reply on the original letter. An editor I know scribbles notes on submissions and sends them back.

When you write a complaint letter, get to the point, give details, ask for something, if that's the goal. I want my money back, a free month's supply, an apology. Otherwise, complaint letters are a waste of your time.

P.S. Use the postscript! People read and remember them.

Calculation

Computers aren't intelligent, they only think they are.

—Unknown

If a train was traveling at sixty miles per hour and . . . The right brain and math go together better than you would think. Music, traditionally thought to be a function of the right brain, is actually closely associated with mathematics, in the left brain. I used to beat myself up over my lack of interest and proficiency in math. I rationalized, "But I can write and draw and play music, so who needs math anyway?"

I do, you do, we all need to know at least the basics. For me, that just means business math. You need to keep your checkbook balanced, pay the bills, give the IRS a nod at regular intervals, and squirrel some cash away for the future. A calculator helps. There are some good, simple computer programs that help you keep your finances (should you have any) in order. If you just can't get with the program, find someone who can. There's always your spouse, or a part-time bookkeeper. Nothing will hurt your chances for success like a bankruptcy.

In terms of higher math, 90 percent of the jobs in this country don't require it. Physics is something else again. Many artists, particularly animators and special-effects artists, work with the fundamentals of physics every day. The underwire bra was created by a costume designer working with a busty star—now, there's a physics problem for you! Architects must deal with mathematical, physical and functional problems on every project. Don't reject a discipline because it's supposed to be hard for creatives. The really creative mind will find a way to deal with the world around it, even if that world includes algebra.

Get High on Life

To acquire knowledge, one must study; to acquire wisdom,
one must observe.

—*Marilyn vos Savant*

"Stop fooling around. You're wasting your life. When are you going to grow up?"

Ever hear those phrases? I did. After college, I moved to Maui. Not only did I not know what I wanted to be when I grew up, I didn't want to grow up. I spent a year there. Some (like my parents) might say that it was a wasted year. I'd say it was wonderful. There were opportunities galore. It was easy to be almost anything you liked. There weren't enough people to fill all the jobs. I did freelance graphic arts, started my own art supply business, sold sunglasses, worked in the aquatics center at a resort, crewed on a sailboat, hung around George Benson's recording studio volunteering to do just about anything, and was a suntan consultant (that was my favorite job).

It was a time for reflection. It was the time of my life! So many of the people who came to Maui on vacation (to escape from their dull existences and jobs they despised) said the same thing to me: "Gosh, I wish I had done what you are doing before I settled down. You are *so* lucky." What I heard in their voices was regret—something I don't have any of.

I decided that I didn't want to have a life that I had to take a vacation from. So far, so good.

Go find yourself. Take off. Travel. Experience life. There is plenty of time to get a regular job. Self-knowledge gives you direction and improves your self-esteem—two keys to a better career.

Get some culture and round out your experiences. You create from the inside out, and it is difficult to create meaningful work when you have no life experiences.

Learn how to do things you've always dreamed of doing. Traveling to other countries allows you opportunities to try out careers that are closed off to beginners in the States. My friend Tito became a big-time disc jockey in Prague. Another friend broke into acting in Australia.

When you return, be able to describe to your employers how you benefited from this time. Did you learn leadership skills (I led a group of volunteers at a youth camp), written skills (I wrote and created a newsletter for the hotel I worked at), speaking (I led tours through the Amazon rain forest), teaching (I taught kids how to snowboard at the ski resort), language (I learned to speak Australian for beer when I was "down under"), or teamwork (I worked with the natives to implement a satellite link in the South Pacific)? Your list may include learning and using computer skills, creativity, resourcefulness, typing, planning, managing, publicity, fund-raising, and so on.

Explore your personal interests and see if any of them lead to your next career, or at least an exciting life. Test-drive various career options, have some fun, and don't have any regrets when you do settle down into a career.

ASK A PRO: DONNA PINTO

Donna Pinto (author of *Cheatnotes on Life*) and her fiancé decided to take a yearlong honeymoon around the world. It meant quitting their jobs, selling their cars, giving up their apartment, and saving every penny they made for a year, while also planning their wedding. Six months before leaving for London, they sent résumés to a number of British holiday companies, applying for jobs as "chalet representatives," the only position that allowed couples to work together. They landed jobs managing a British ski chalet in Norway, giving them the chance to work together and live in a European ski resort town, save money, and have a memorable honeymoon. To finish off their year abroad, they also decided to write a book on work and travel opportunities around the world.

What was the best part of taking time off to see the world?

There is nothing better than the freedom an extended travel experience can bring—not having to live with time constraints, work or school pressures, deadlines, a *TV Guide,* a boss, or an alarm clock. Lots of time to read, write, reflect, and think about the future. Learning and experiencing something new and different every day; meeting really cool people from all over the world and having stimulating conversations; trying all kinds of food and being exposed to diverse cultures and customs. Gaining a new appreciation for home, family, friends, and a comfy bed!

Would you recommend that recent graduates and others who aren't sure what they want to do with their life take off for a while and see the world?

What could be better than taking time out from peer, parental, and societal influences and exposing yourself to new cultures, people, and experiences? I think there is way too much pressure on young people to establish careers before they really know themselves. Travel not only teaches you about the world and other cultures, it's a great way to get to know yourself, build self-esteem, and buy more time.

Two months in Europe after college fueled my desire to further pursue "time out" from a more conventional career path. After only one year of the so-called "real world," I left a somewhat glamorous job in magazine advertising sales to work for Club Med in Mexico. A lot of friends and family thought I was crazy, but it turned out to be the best career/life move I could have made.

What lessons have you learned?

Traveling all over the world took me out of my comfort zone at times, and made me more aware and appreciative of all that we have in the United States. The lessons I learned while abroad will undoubtedly have a far greater impact on me as a person than anything I learned in all my years at school.

What advice could you offer someone thinking of following in your footsteps?

Don't worry about what skeptics may think or say. There will always be people who think what you want to do is crazy. Do what's in your heart. Make a plan and go after your dreams. There's plenty of opportunity for those who are seeking a similar path. As the saying goes, "When the student is ready, the teacher appears."

Experience: Internships, Apprenticeships, Day Jobs

Be willing to serve time as an intern in the office of the profession you've chosen. Get all the experience you can. Then make yourself invaluable to your company. Then ask for a raise.

—*June Cunniff*

The American Council on Education reports that nine out of ten colleges now offer structured work experience connected to career interests. Many high schools now also offer "career day," internship, and "partnership with business" programs, allowing young people a chance to get a taste of what it's like to work in fields they think they might be interested in. Some companies, particularly those in creative arts, start new employees out as interns. At Industrial Light and Magic, animators start out as interns, graduating to journeyman-type (paid) positions only after they prove themselves.

Some internships pay a stipend, but most don't. One high school student who spent the summer working for a pre-print service bureau—he intended to study graphic arts in college and wanted to expand his computer expertise—made himself so useful they started paying him. Don't count on it happening to you. If you go into an internship, figure you're being paid in experience, contacts, a reference for your résumé, and the chance to test-drive a career before you make any real commitment to it.

Surprisingly, there is a lot of competition for these nonpaying positions—and some disappointment when you find out that, while you may be rubbing shoulders with great ones, you'll be doing it from behind the mail cart, receptionist's desk, or filing cabinet. If you can't find an appropriate internship, try volunteering. When women began to enter the job market the numbers of volunteers dropped dramatically, and workers are desperately needed in almost every nonprofit organization.

Joyce Szymansk, the director of public relations for the Harlem Globetrotters, has this advice for the up-and-comer: "Do an internship for little or no pay. I worked an unpaid, one-year internship with a sports team immediately after college. I learned my way around a pro sports PR office and made a lot of contacts. One of those contacts led me to a full-time position with another organization."

I have a somewhat different story about interning. While I was in art school, I interned with an ad agency that specialized in the entertainment industry. That led to an internship with Paramount Pictures. With an insider's view into the film industry, I quickly realized it was not for me. It sounds glamorous and wonderful, but when I tried it on for size, I found that it was not a good fit.

An internship can get your foot in the door. Nordstrom, for example, makes everyone start at the bottom (even the Nordstrom family members work in the stockroom at first). In companies like this, you are expected to rise through the ranks, so they're set up to make that possible. Hollywood talent agencies are the same way, excepting that instead of the stockroom you begin in the mailroom. You work your way into being an assistant to an agent and then a full-fledged agent.

Can you make it big this way? Let me throw out one name: David Geffen. Once inside William Morris, he realized from observation that he could easily do the work the top agents were doing. He saw that all they did was talk on the phone, and thought, *I can do that, too!*

Maria Bartiromo interned at CNN after college and was eventually hired as a production assistant, a job she did for five years. She then made an on-air demo tape of herself in front of the camera, sent it to CNBC, and was hired as a field reporter.

The secret is, don't think like an intern or they're liable to treat you like one. Make the most of each opportunity, work hard, and connect with people (not the Monica Lewinsky kind of connection).

Temporary Insanity

It seems today there are three kinds of jobs: temporary, part-time, and overtime.

—*William Bridges*

According to the National Association of Temporary and Staffing Services, 38 percent of all temporary jobs turn into permanent positions.

Ninety percent of today's businesses use temps. Manpower, Inc. (a temporary service provider), is the largest employer in the United States. By 2007, 37 million people will be temping. There are business reasons for this; it allows companies to keep their permanent payrolls down, and give themselves staffing flexibility. They don't have to give you notice when they decide they don't need you anymore. If they don't like you, they can just cancel with no reason required. You've got no say where they put you, and no grievance process if they don't treat you well. They pay more for the service (*you* don't get paid more, the temp company gets theirs off the top), but they don't have to do the taxes and insurance paperwork on you—that's handled by the temp company.

How does temping benefit you? It is a good way to learn skills and practice them under fire, sample different careers or positions within those careers, get an insider's perspective of different companies, scout out a field while making no commitments, get your foot in the door, and perhaps land a permanent position. It also gives you a lot of flexibility in terms of amount of work you do. If you're writing a novel, you can set up to temp two days a week to pay the rent, while leaving yourself five days a week to write.

Saturday Night Live regular Molly Shannon wasn't sure how to make it in show business, so she started to learn by temping for showbiz agents and "read everything on their desks when they weren't around." She looked at client lists, trying to figure out how *she* could get on that list. She decided to put on a one-woman show and "started calling the five hundred people whose names I collected from working all over town." The place was packed, and a career was born.

Look for niches in the company you're temping for, and make it obvious that you can fill them. Find creative ways to solve problems that arise, and then offer to do it freelance, as a permanent employee, or part-time. If you are lucky enough to work on a successful project, you can take some credit, which will pop off your résumé.

A few temp agencies will help train you (to make you more valuable to them). Ask them about sending you to seminars, workshops, trade shows. Maybe you can use their equipment during off hours. A friend of mine made her demo tape at the recording studio she was a receptionist for. She did it during the wee hours of the morning when nobody was there.

7

There Is No "I" in "Team"

Working with people is difficult, but not impossible.
—*Peter Drucker*

The creative person is a jazz musician (improvising and experimenting) living in a pop music world (formula thinking, tried and true). When the two worlds collide, there can be a fusion and some pretty impressive music (the Dave Mathews Band comes to mind) or an explosion.

Why are some people so difficult to deal with? There are several reasons, among them the fear of change. Some people are trying to hang on by their fingertips to old and crusty ways of doing things. I call it complacency. They call it "We've done it that way since 1820!"

Frightening, really. These are not confident people.

It could be the enormous amount of pressure people are under. Think about films and the mixture of big budgets, tight deadlines, collaboration, and egomania, and you get a fairly combustible mix. It's safer to do it the way it was successful before. Which is why all the films you're seeing are remakes of films that were first made fifty or even five years ago.

It could be the bottom-line people (stockholders, CEOs, middle-management types) who want to squeeze one more penny out of every project. Which means you won't get enough time, money, staff, or support to do the job right.

Creative people want to make something impressive, something to be proud of, damn the costs. The innovator (that's you again) is often more concerned with the work than the bureaucracy and doesn't deal well with paperwork, punctuality, policy, and other left-brain rules and regulations. Through compromise, things can work out, but they can also turn ugly quicker than you can say "You're fired!"

This is reality. If you want to see your work produced, you have to learn to deal with management types, committees, and idiots. At the same time, it's important to take steps to minimize their (negative) effect on you. Two steps, in fact: First, minimize interaction with them; communicate through memos or E-mail. Second, use behavior-modification techniques; if they start saying something negative, *leave.* A friend had a grandmother who drove her whole family crazy. She didn't like anything or anybody, and she constantly carped. She'd complain about my friend's sister to his mother and vice versa, and told her few friends how badly her daughter and granddaughter treated her. They couldn't understand why she never complained to my friend. The answer was simple: as soon as she started to complain about anybody, he'd get up and say, "Well, Grandma, it's time to leave." And he left. Since she liked him to visit her, she found nice things to say when he was around. Oddly enough, she never complained about him, either.

▼ ▼ ▼

ACTION ITEM

Who are these people? This quiz will help you find and weed out the worst offenders. On a piece of paper, write your name and circle it. Around you, write in your friends/clients/co-workers. Circle each one and draw lines to connect them to you. Try to include all the people you spend time with. Think about your recent interactions with these people. Inside the circle, under each name, fill in a happy face (they are positive people), a sad face (negative people, but ones you still want in your life), or a crazy face (they drive you crazy); this last category comprises the ones to get out of your life if at all possible. You might want to think again about those sad faces, too. Every negative person in your life slows you down, holds you back, and affects your own happiness and success.

▲ ▲ ▲

Types of Difficult People

They steal your ideas, destroy your deadlines, talk about you behind your back, take advantage of your generosity, criticize you and your ideas, and sabotage your success. They manifest as, and morph into, several different forms, but they're all difficult people. Understanding them may help you learn to deal with them. I like to give them funny names so I don't take them so seriously and get so mad at them. I'll start by naming a few of my (least) favorites. I am sure they have mutated again and you will find new strains.

Bean Counters. So concerned with bottom-line thinking that they can't create, or let you create. The only results that matter to them come in dollar form. They can't see the forest because they cut down all the trees.

Beanie Babies. They are so sensitive that you walk on eggshells around them, afraid you may hurt their feelings. You can't argue with them even when they're wrong—*especially* when they're wrong.

Mommie Dearests. Control freaks who have to have their hands in everything. They like to look over your shoulder while you work, criticizing your thought before you get a chance to complete it.

Frosted Flakes. They don't do what they are supposed to when they are supposed to, so what you were supposed to do gets all screwed up. Somehow you're the one whose failure gets noticed.

Jeopardy Junkies. They know it all. Anything you can do, they can do better, faster, or cheaper. The worst kind will also be condescending.

Moody Blues. They get really excited about a project or idea, but just as easily lose interest. They can be swayed easily. They'll approve your design, then call you back later, saying their next-door neighbor looked at it and thought it would be better in lime green.

Chicken Littles. They always see the glass as half-empty and too big. Afraid to take risks, they tend to be overly critical. They will want twenty proofs instead of two, thirty takes instead of three, and still not be quite happy.

Tootsie Pops. Hard to get to know and sometimes nasty, they are protecting the soft stuff inside. It takes a lot of licks to get inside a Tootsie Pop.

Humpty Dumpties. They can't make a decision. They sit on the fence and waffle back and forth until you push them. Then they fall and you have a mess to clean up.

Knife Throwers. Can't trust them as far as you can throw them. They will take credit for your ideas and tell everyone you slept with the boss.

Momma's Boys. They can't do anything for themselves. They get by on their charm and good looks, but are as shallow as a baby's bath. You end up doing their work for them, or they will throw a tantrum.

Poopie Heads. Just real jerks. Bullies. Nasty, mean.

Wizards of Oz. Little tyrants who are insecure, intimidated, and irritable. They often put up a big front, but these are never the real decision-makers.

Belittlers. Either they run you down to your face or they do things like mask a criticism in a compliment.

Understand that you're a difficult person, too, and pity them for having to deal with you.

Are You a Difficult Person?

Just like there are good witches and bad witches, there are good bitches and bad bitches. Be a good bitch. A good bitch knows when to use her powers—and uses them in the fight for good, not evil.

—Karen Salmansohn

Have you read Dale Carnegie's *How to Win Friends and Influence People* in the past two years? If your answer is no, read it now. This book changed my life. I was a "difficult person." No doubt about it. Once I read that book and used what I learned, I started to notice that being understanding and unassuming actually gave me more power. I started to notice how much nicer people were, because *I* was more agreeable. I learned that instead of freaking out and going "Springer" (think TV show, not dog) on people, I was able to get what I wanted and help others get what they wanted. I was more sincere. Had a more pleasing personality. Became a better listener. Saw things from the other person's perspective. Let others save face.

Are you a difficult person? Yes, you are. That is not up for debate. The question is, how difficult are you, and can you change? Here's a checklist:

- Do you find yourself arguing all the time with those around you?
- When was the last time you sent someone a thank-you note?
- Are your calls returned promptly by others?
- Would you rather be feared or respected?
- Have people told you that you are difficult to work with?

I have a friend who says, "Everyone I work with is an idiot." That is a bad sign.

I Love My Job, but I Hate My Boss

Have I buried the hatchet with Al Davis? Yeah, right between the shoulder blades.

—Former Oakland Raiders quarterback Ken Stabler on his ex-boss, Al Davis

When it comes to lousy bosses, what goes around comes around. It's too bad it couldn't come around a lot sooner. I heard a boss say to a worker once, "I didn't say it was your fault. I said I was going to blame it on you." The guy gets points for honesty, but I still wouldn't want to work for him.

Just remember that you are your own boss. You are the CEO of your own firm. Your boss is your number-one client. Serve that client well, and you have a happy customer. You control your own destiny.

Tom Peters takes this thought one step further and states that we are all artists—great ones. So make whatever you do a creative work. Be a Picasso of production, a Rembrandt of the receiving department, a Michelangelo of management, or a Gauguin of gofering. Life is art, and even the bad times are part of the experience that will contribute to your creativity in the future. And you can call me Pollyanna.

If you have a hard time working with someone, it might be that they are left-brained (anal-retentive, compartmentalized, and detail-oriented) while you are right-brained (innovative, creative, big-picture-oriented). Think about it. These people are control freaks. They have a hard time letting go and letting you do your work. They don't *get* you. They don't understand that the creative process takes time. It may look as if you aren't doing anything when you are conceptualizing. (That's your "get out of jail" card, by the way. Use it.) You do not usually toe the company line, you don't wear the right clothes, clean your desk off at the end of the day, fit their image of a good employee. They feel there is only one way to do things. You're engaged in finding new ways to do everything. You're concerned with aesthetics while they are interested in profits.

The two can go together. In fact, the two *must* go together to create a successful business. It takes some giving in on both sides. For your part, instead of ticking them off, find ways to give them what they want while you get what you want.

Remember, your boss is not your mother. If your boss has to remind you to pick up after yourself, finish what you start, and get to work on time, it's no wonder they are treating you like a child. You must earn their trust and respect.

Apple executive Guy Kawasaki recommends that you just wait a difficult boss out. Eventually, he or she will implode. He also suggests making yourself so attractive that you get hired away or transferred out.

Be an untouchable. The doer, the expert, the superstar, the son-in-law.

Kawasaki's Bosses

In Guy Kawasaki's book, *How to Drive Your Competition Crazy,* he describes the different types of bosses:

Schmexpert. Half schmuck and half expert. They can't solve any problems and they know just enough to be dangerous.

Egomaniac. No one else in the company can do as good a job (in their own opinion), so they try to do everything themselves. They also take all the credit.

Wanna-be. Wants to be something he's not, like a visionary or an innovator.

The Peter. He's petered out and can't handle his present position, much less future challenges. He never wanted to be the boss anyway.

Boy Wonder. Arrogant, with the self-confidence of someone who hasn't been tested yet.

The Company Man. Not better or brighter than his peers, he's just outlasted everyone. (Not big on change.)

Techno Dweeb. Relates better to a computer or a mechanical device than he does to people.

How to Deal with Difficult People

Having a penis makes some men feel like they have a license to be a dick.

—Karen Salmansohn

My favorite way to deal with difficult people is not to get involved with them in the first place. If you know from their past behavior they aren't easy to get along with, put some distance between you. If you don't have any background on them, trust what your intuition says about them.

Unfortunately, you don't always have a choice. They might be part of the package in what is otherwise your dream job. Don't let difficult people ruin your career. Deal with them.

Don't give them any ammo to load their gun with. Don't bash and bad-mouth others, or put yourself in compromising positions that could be held over your head later. Not everyone can be trusted or should be trusted with sensitive material, and you can't always spot the untrustworthy ones. (Linda Tripp is a perfect example.)

Don't be so gullible when it comes to taking what people say for granted. Most people tell white lies. Some tell deep, dirty, dark ones. A healthy dose of skepticism is a good thing.

Don't burn your bridges until you get to them. In the heat of frustration, I once wrote a nasty note to the head of the travel department. I ticked off the one person who controlled my scheduling. For months afterward, I was on the worst flights and stuck in the dingiest hotels.

The jerk store called. Remember when George Costanza on *Seinfeld* had the perfect reply to an insult, but didn't think of it until he was in his car? He went to incredible lengths to set the situation up so he could use his great line. Don't anticipate problems. Don't prepare for them. Don't bring difficulties onto yourself.

Being angry saps your mental energy and thus your creativity. Don't let things fester. Let it go or let it out, but don't let it eat you up.

Step outside. Don't blow up in front of clients, peers, or others who will label you a hothead. Have a cooling-off period. Count to ten—or ten thousand. Deal with problem people in private whenever possible.

Don't put all your efforts into one basket. If you have only one client, and you have a falling-out, where does that leave you?

You can't please everyone. Stop caring so much what others think. If you are an idea person, some people will attack you and your ideas. These people give you a chance to defend your ideas—it's a great creative boost, even if you lose the argument. Thank them.

Attack the problem and not the person. Take the emotion away and deal with facts. Use logic and reason.

Let them save face. Give them an easy way out. Don't rub anybody's nose in anything.

Give people a reputation to live up to. The DMV in Virginia uses "Grateful Grams" that say "thank you" in several languages. They also use "Bravo Cards" to say thanks, with boxes to check for things like "Thanks for the quick response," or "You made my day." Put up a "brag board" where you can post praise for others and where everyone can see it.

Pick your fights carefully. Weigh the consequences before you step in and start whaling away.

Rechannel your anger into something positive. Harness it and use it, preferably on something physical (not beating your dog). Clean your office. Go for a run.

The customer isn't always right. You don't have to put up with abusive clients. Stand up to them. Bullies will back down when you stand up for yourself.

Put it in writing. Write out exactly why you are mad. Go into graphic detail about what you would like to do to the person who makes you angry. Then tear it up, take a deep breath, and move on.

Love your enemies. In Karen Salmansohn's book *How to Make Your Man Behave in 21 Days or Less, Using the Secrets of Professional Dog Trainers,* she explains the power of compassion in getting people to behave the way you want them to. "The dog/man/child will want to behave better when a warm, loving bond is firmly established. Ditto for clients and fellow employees." People respond better to positive reinforcement than to abuse. Throw them a Scooby snack, don't hit them over the head with it.

Don't play the blame game. It *is* your fault.

Consult people before making a major decision that affects them.

Take a walk in their shoes to try to figure out why they are doing the things they are. Usually they are oblivious to their bad behavior. Figure out what they want. Seek to understand and be understood.

It all boils down to this: You can't change people, so you have to set limits about how much crap you are willing to put up with. You *can* change the way you deal with them, and limit the amount of crap you dish out. That's not just a business lesson, it's a life lesson.

Opposites Attract

It's the things in common that make relationships enjoyable, but it's the little differences that make them interesting.

—*Todd Ruthman*

There's a category of "difficult people" that you not only shouldn't avoid, but should embrace. They add a dimension to your life that you need—even though it's not always comfortable. Your opposites—they're usually your best friends, your favorite clients, your toughest teachers. They balance you. The attraction is instinctive.

Nature tends to even things out. When two messy, disorganized people get together, one of them usually takes on the role of the neat, organized, responsible one. When the zany, spontaneous, let's-have-some-fun-and-clean-up-later person meets the neat, organized, and highly structured person, it's a highly combustible mix, but dangerous only if you light the fuse. Pack rats almost always marry neatniks—it's nature's way of keeping us from being buried by our stuff. Don't fight it. Be grateful.

Keep an open mind and a positive outlook, and almost any relationship can work—and work well.

Our opposites sometimes seem unemotional, uptight, logical, regimented, responsible, detail-oriented, insensitive, and always in control. Which translates (in a positive world) to: stable, responsible, mature.

Our opposites can see us as careless, carefree, unpredictable, undependable, impulsive, emotional, scattered, messy, irrational, illogical, and impatient. Which translates (in a positive world) to daring, interesting, and fun.

When you combine those lists, you get a nice blend of character traits. When you team up with an opposite style, you get a broader perspective, a better balance, and, often, far more accomplished.

Working with Your Opposite

The best time I ever had with Joan Crawford was when I pushed her down the stairs in Whatever Happened to Baby Jane.

—*Bette Davis*

Working with your opposite style can be either beneficial or extremely stressful and frustrating. Some styles just clash too much, and some people just can't be flexible enough to make such relationships work. The boss who micro-manages you (because she doesn't know what you do or understand how you do it) is a good example. A manager who gives you unrealistic deadlines (with no time to conceptualize) or bogs you down with unnecessary tasks and assignments you are ill-suited for can decrease your productivity and hinder your creativity.

"My time-management skills are fine. My managers are bad and I have to pay the price. Everything is last-minute or an emergency. No planning. Or I have to wait for them to do their part until I can do mine. I'll have nothing to do, then everything comes due at the same time." This is a common complaint. Creatives are often toward the end of the list of project completion. If the people responsible for getting materials or information to you are late, you're put into a time crunch. Ditto when the boss comes in and changes everything around in your carefully constructed layout. In small businesses, this often means you work through the night. Corporations, however, extend the timeline (corporations being so very structured) or add personnel and charge extra. Don't be afraid to take the corporate approach.

If you have to fight for time to do your job right, fight for it or suffer the physical and mental debilitation of stress. If you can't fight or you lose the battle, look for a different client, a different job, or a different department/boss within your company.

The following suggestions may help you get your business relationships working for you:

Be clear about what you do best, and how much time you need to do it. Ask for more time, more autonomy.

Ask for input, clear instructions. Write them down and get them okayed.

Write out your job description. Have your boss write out your job description. Then exchange lists, discuss the differences, and write a realistic job description together.

Respect your manager's opinions and point of view. Don't try to change things until you understand why they're done the way they are.

Don't volunteer for work that doesn't excite you. Do volunteer to help your boss out whenever you can, on projects that fit your talents or complement a project you're already working on.

Be flexible. Deadlines and needs change. You're unlikely to be able to work on one thing at a time until it's done. Learn to juggle—you'll enjoy it.

Communicate. Talk to your boss or the people up the line from you, so you know at least the outlines of the project before it hits your desk. That way, you can do your conceptualizing ahead of time. It's liable to be the only time you get.

ASK A PRO: SHERRY LANSING

Sherry Lansing, a chair with Paramount Pictures, is responsible for bringing you such films as *Forrest Gump, Clear and Present Danger, Braveheart.* In an industry dominated by men, she uses her quiet strength to take control.

"You can be strong without being tough. What I have found in life is that most people want you to tell them the truth. They can take a no if you say it to their face. What's painful is when you don't give people the truth."

Teamwork Wins Games

In the production of a good play with a good cast and a knowing director, there is formed a fraternity whose members share a mutual sense of destiny.

—*Arthur Miller*

TEAM stands for Together Everyone Achieves More.

When all its members are doing what they are supposed to, and pulling together for a common goal, a team can far outperform an individual. Pool your resources with those around you to combine and conquer.

Tony Gwynn, a seven-time batting champion, knows what his role on the team is. "I try to stay within myself and what I'm capable of doing, and not what other people think I should be doing. My forte is to put the bat on the ball and get it into play. That's my role on the team. To me, that's what this game is all about. When everyone in the lineup does their job—the team benefits."

I formed my team of reliable vendors, specialists, and timesaving services over a period of time. Like any team, you can trade, cut, and sign team members based on their contribution (or lack thereof). Start by making a list of your team members. Next to their names, write what their strengths are.

The ideal size for a team is five to ten people, with a maximum of twelve. A balanced team consists of a leader, an innovator or creative type, a warrior and motivator (someone you want to go to battle beside), a workhorse (someone who unselfishly does what needs doing), a superstar (you need talent and skill), and a specialist or role player (someone you can bring in to fill a specific need).

Teams that play together stay together. Don't be all business. We all work harder for people we like, respect, and enjoy being with.

Why Delegate? Because You Can

None of us is as smart as all of us.

—Ken Blanchard

Mic Mead, the founder and president of Adventure 16, a company that specializes in hiking and camping gear, said, "If there is any one key to success, I think it's delegation. Hire the very best people you can, pay them accordingly, and then trust them."

He explained to me that he has served and can serve any function in the company, but was always able to find someone who could do it better than he could. "The one function I really do serve, as CEO, is to keep everyone focused on a vision."

Time Is Money

A close friend of mine who lives on the island of Maui was coming to town for a visit. (I often wondered where you go on vacation when you live in paradise.) His plane was to arrive in the middle of the night. When I go to Maui, he always picks me up at the Kahalui airport. Much as I would have liked to reciprocate, I don't live on island time. Instead, I chose to pay for a shuttle to pick him up. The way I figured it, the twenty bucks it cost to hire the shuttle actually saved me money. I did the math. Going to the airport would have taken at least two hours of my time. Is my time worth more than ten dollars an hour? I think so.

Test someone with a tiny task before you give them a big job. Do the research, get referrals, check with the Better Business Bureau, interview them, do background checks, and, finally, trust your gut instincts.

Consider this an investment of time and energy that will save you a lot of time—and potentially a lot of grief—in the long run.

To Delegate or Not to Delegate—That's Not a Question

A man's gotta know his limitations.

—*Dirty Harry*

You delegate all the time, and you don't even know it. You go out to eat and the chef cooks for you. You take a taxi and someone else drives for you. Hop on a plane and someone pilots the plane for you. (While you are doing all this running around, someone watches your kids for you.) See, it's not that hard to give up some control to get control of your life.

Successful people learn how to delegate and collaborate. Eventually, you have to. Michael Dell, founder and CEO of Dell Computer Corporation, had to make the transition from the head of a small start-up company to the CEO of a large corporation. The former "whiz kid" is still in charge of the company he founded while in college in 1984, but he was smart enough to focus on his strengths (spotting trends and developing new technology) and hire a team of computer industry executives to cover his weaknesses (details and day-to-day operations).

Jimmy Buffett and his backup band, The Coral Reefers, tour the country each summer, playing before hundreds of thousands of fans. Jimmy once toured the country in a station wagon—solo. He had to handle all the books, schedule the gigs, negotiate the contracts, and, of course, perform. He said in an interview, "The first thing I learned was you find dependable people and let them do the job for you, and not try to run everything yourself."

Creatives are not born team players, but they somehow learn how to play in a band, be a cast member in a play, participate in a creative team. Almost all creative endeavors require a team effort. (The artist, the agent, the studio.) The more the creative person understands and embraces the team concept, the better off—and more successful—he or she becomes.

Others want to help, to contribute, to be challenged. But you have that Lone Ranger mentality, and you're proud of it. "I'm a do-it-myself kind of person. When the copier broke, my assistant wanted to call a repairman, but I insisted on calling him myself."

If you have trouble giving up control, you can take on the extra work of being team leader. "Ability is the art of getting credit for all the home runs that somebody else hits," said baseball manager Casey Stengel. Just remember, it's extra work—and not necessarily work you're suited for.

Myths About Delegating

The world is full of willing people; some willing to work, the rest willing to let them.

—*Robert Frost*

Delegate means "to trust to others." *Efficiency* loosely translates into "getting someone to do a job you hate." Neither of these are easy to implement, partly because you have your own definitions of what *delegate* means. Sometimes you don't know how to find or manage a delegatee.

Let's explore and explode some of the biggest myths about delegating.

Myth: It would have been easier to do it myself.

Reality: Not if you gave it to the right person and explained it properly. Besides, if you try to do everything yourself, you stunt your creative growth, and the growth of others, too.

Myth: It won't get done right (i.e., done to your high standards).

Reality: There is right and then there is different. You would be surprised what some people can do, if you give them a chance. Maybe they will have a fresh approach or an innovative breakthrough you never would have considered. Your way is not the only way. Let it go.

Myth: Nobody can do it but me.

Reality: That's what you think. Nobody is indispensable, and if you think doing everything makes you so, you're wrong. It makes you tired, it makes you cranky, it eventually makes you sloppy. It makes people *want* to find a replacement for *you*.

Myth: People will hate me if I dump things on them.

Reality: First of all, don't dump. Teach, guide, encourage. People want to contribute, to be a part of something, to feel needed, to learn. You learn and grow by helping someone else develop, by giving them work and a chance to learn from you. You also gain a disciple who will help you get through the everyday stuff.

Myth: I must do it all, or people will think I am lazy or incompetent.

Reality: They will think that anyway. Just kidding. It is not a sign of weakness to be unable to do it all yourself. It is a sign of intelligence. When you value your time, others will, too.

Myth: My employees will respect me if they see I work harder than anyone. Longer hours, getting my hands dirty with the nitty-gritty tasks.

Reality: You may be demonstrating insecurity about your position. You want to be liked, but in the process you lose respect. You could end up sacrificing more important things like developing new markets or creating new products. If you're the manager, be the manager, not a glorified worker.

Myth: If I enjoy doing it, I should keep it for myself.

Reality: You may be ignoring high-payoff tasks by continuing to do little fun tasks of no real consequence. The fact is, we all enjoy the sense of accomplishment a mindless, familiar, easy-to-complete task can provide. In the long run, however, you're spending time you can't afford.

I have to admit that delegating is one of my weaker areas. I took a good, hard look at why I am reluctant to give away control. I realized that my upbringing taught me that "if it is to be, it's up to me." "If you want things done right, do them yourself." "The buck stops here."

▼ ▼ ▼

ACTION ITEM

Make a list of all the things you do in a typical day. Then objectively look at your list and determine:

- How many of the things I did today should have been delegated to someone else?
- Why do I choose to do it all myself? What can I do to overcome this cycle?

ANOTHER ACTION ITEM

1. Whether you work for yourself or for someone else, write a job description for yourself.
2. Know what you do best. List your strengths.
3. Know what your weaknesses are. Don't be afraid to admit them.
4. List the strengths of your staff, people around you (freelancers you can hire, your team).
5. Make a list of all the things you do in a day. What could (should) you delegate? To whom?
6. List the things you absolutely hate to do, and those that are least satisfying.
7. If you were able to work only half a day, which are the things you would have to do, want to do, delegate?
8. What things do you keep putting off, things you won't or can't do yourself?
9. A friend of mine keeps a file in his drawer called his GAG file (Go Away or Get Help). In it are tasks that he would rather not do, or that he gives to his staff. Some things just sit in there that never really needed to be done in the first place.

▲ ▲ ▲

Now, Whom to Delegate To

Don't do anything someone else can do for you.
—*Bill Marriott Sr.*

Why keep a dog and bark yourself? You need to find some way to delegate when:

- You are exhausted and can't finish everything.
- You are great at coming up with ideas, tons of them, but you never get around to the follow-through. You are a starter, so you need a closer.
- It takes you eight hours to do a job that someone else could manage in only four.

Whom can you delegate to? Not everyone has an assistant, and the secretarial pool (if there is one) isn't always available or cooperative. Here's another chance to use your creativity.

When you are ready to throw up your hands and yell "I quit!" maybe it's time to get some professional help. (Not that kind.) Consider hiring a temp or a freelancer or a consultant, or even taking on an intern. Those options are usually cheaper and less complex than adding an employee.

When you do hire help, check them out thoroughly. Call those references. Then make sure you clearly state what you want and that you are both in agreement about deadlines, wages, and outcome expected. Get it in writing, even if you're bartering services.

When you first get an assignment or start a project, start asking yourself about who can help. Know what others around you are capable of and do best. Use these people for all they are worth. Everyone has their strengths.

Henry Ford had an unusual philosophy when he wanted to delegate an unpleasant task. He would assign it to the laziest man he could find. His reasoning was that within a day or two, the lazy worker would come up with a quick and easy way to do it.

When choosing whom to delegate to, keep the following tips in mind:

Match the task to the person's strengths.

Take advantage of offers of assistance, even when they were made long ago.

Look for someone who can do it better, faster, with more attention to detail, or at least for someone with the time to pay attention to detail.

Ask for a volunteer. These people are usually more motivated, at least in the short term.

Let family members help out around the house. If you're on a deadline and working all hours, it's nice to come home to a tidy house and dinner on the table.

Ask for help. People may not know that you need it. Really.

How to Get Others to Do It for You, Not to You

Never make your appeal to a man's better nature; he may not have one. Always make your appeal to his self-interest.

—*Lazarus Long*

"Idiots!" That's what an editor—not *my* editor, naturally—said to me about her writers. "Why do they feel like they have to check back with me on every little detail? At this rate, I might as well write the whole damn thing myself!" she exclaimed.

Being careful to tread lightly, I suggested, "Maybe the problem isn't with them, maybe it's you." Before I could explain what I meant, she pointed her bony finger at the door and screamed, "Get out!"

I hope she will read this chapter, which explains how to delegate effectively and avoid the pitfalls and problems she seems to be facing. The goal is to get others to do things for you without a whole lot of effort on your part.

Try to create win-win situations. Make helping you a rewarding, appealing experience. Be generous with your support and your praise—but not your time.

Everyone is the center of their own universe, the star of their own movie. They have their own agendas, no matter how altruistic you may believe them to be. You must figure out a way this assignment benefits them.

Give them a reason to want to do it. What's the value to them? Sell them on the benefits, the rewards. These can be long-term or short-term, monetary or social or personal. If one motivator doesn't work, find one that will.

The right person for the right task. Know their strengths and weaknesses and match the task to their strength. Good managers put people in situations where they know they can succeed.

Let the person have input in the beginning so they will take ownership of the job. Use the Dale Carnegie approach. You may even go so far as let them believe the idea was theirs.

Listen carefully. Be sure they understand the assignment. Have them repeat it back to you. Encourage them to ask questions up front.

Word things carefully and clearly. Avoid fuzzy words like *soon, good, safe, do the best you can, expensive.*

Give complete instructions. Be crystal clear about what you need and when you need it. Put it in writing for easy reference, so they don't have to keep coming to you with questions. Give them examples of what you are looking for.

Grant enough authority for them to be able to complete the task. Give them the tools and resources they need.

Don't micro-manage. Hands off. Let them solve their own problems; that's how they will learn. Be available if they need you. Try to avoid taking things away from them. Allow for a few mistakes along the way.

Be willing to pitch in, in a pinch. Remember, though, you are the coach, not a player. You should be able to enjoy seeing them succeed; you shouldn't have to suit up and take the field.

Keep an open mind. Let them do it their way. You might even learn something in the process.

Stress the final outcome you seek, not how to go about it. JFK said, "We're going to the moon. You're in charge." He never told them *how* to do it.

Give constructive criticism. If you are hypercritical, however, they will get gun-shy, won't take any risks, and will feel they have to check with you about every little nitpicking detail. Be supportive, be clear, offer specifics of how they went wrong and how to fix it.

Track their progress. Mark key due dates on your calendar and check them off.

Better sooner than later. Ask them to report problems early, before it's too late.

Reward and thank and compliment them for their efforts on your behalf. Be generous. It's *your* time they're saving.

Pitch the fun aspects of whatever task or project you are delegating. John Madden, the former Raiders head coach and current play-by-play announcer, says that as soon as a person hears the word *business,* they know you're not talking about fun. Use that creative mind of yours to find some fun in any task you delegate. Just don't decide that it's too much fun to give away.

▼ ▼ ▼

ACTION ITEM

Who was the best supervisor/manager you ever worked for? What made them so great? List four things they did.

▲ ▲ ▲

True Story

Whatever we have accomplished has been because other people have helped us.

—*Walt Disney*

The best supervisor/manager I ever worked for was Coach Jones, manager of a baseball team I played for years ago. He got the most from his players, and it was by far my best year. We were a winning team, even though we didn't necessarily have the best players. How did he do it?

- He set a good example for us to follow. He was always the first one at the ballpark and the last to leave. (He was also a great player himself.)
- He put people in situations he knew they would succeed in—and succeed we did. As our confidence grew, we got even better.
- He was compassionate and caring about us as players, but also as people.
- He created a fun, family-type atmosphere on the team.
- He believed in us and trusted us, no matter what.
- He was always upbeat and positive and gave his players a reputation to live up to. If I walked by while he was talking to another coach, he would say things like "That's my best pitcher over there," loud enough so I could hear.
- He punished his players in private, never in front of the others.
- He was fair and treated his players equally, regardless of whether one was a star or a role player.
- He never, ever, gave up on you, even if you wanted to quit on yourself.
- He would monitor your progress and help you make adjustments.
- He asked for feedback and listened to it.
- He was patient and understanding when you made a mistake.
- He gave you the tools and resources you needed to win.

What Motivates People

To get others to do what you want them to do, you must see things through their eyes.

—*David Schwartz*

To get people to do things, pitch in. You have to figure out what their motivation is, and appeal to it. Here are some things that motivate people:

- Money
- Recognition

- Career advancement
- Winning
- Being part of a team
- Usefulness
- Time off
- Food (don't underestimate this one)
- Job security
- Challenge
- Responsibility
- Growth
- Knowledge
- Comfort
- Respect
- Open bar (just kidding)

Name four more.

Meetings, Meetings, and More Meetings

A committee is a group that keeps minutes and loses hours.

—*Milton Berle*

When all is said and done, was more said than done? That's how most meetings end up. Do you need to be there? I can't tell you how many hours I have wasted at meaningless meetings. Now I am very selective about the meetings I attend, and try to do things over the phone or through E-mail. Teleconferencing can save an expensive and time-consuming flight. One company realized this and built a chat room into their web site for brainstorming sessions. The benefit was that people wasted less time on trivial matters, spent less time commuting to a central meeting place, and everyone could print out a transcript of the meeting.

Many creative people feel that an agenda is constricting and hinders spontaneity. I disagree, as long as the agenda doesn't account for every second and has some built-in space for brainstorming. An agenda keeps even a diverse group on track and moving along. Less time is wasted discussing inconsequentials or getting to the point.

Creatives may be more satisfied with a meeting if good information was shared, while a noncreative type is only concerned with results. A balance between these approaches is the goal.

Why Call a Meeting?

The best size for a committee is one.

—*Anonymous*

Good reasons: To brainstorm ideas, get information, disseminate information, make a decision, get input on a decision, answer questions.

Bad reasons: To get out of the office or to look busy.

Using Name Tag Games to Liven Up a Meeting

As usual, the serious me is working hard, but the real me is having fun.
—*John Reed*

Based in part on a great book called *Name Tags Plus* by Deborah Shouse, the following are great ways to break the ice in large meetings where people don't know each other:

1. Write three things about yourself on the name tag. Make one of them false, and let others try to guess which is which.
2. Write three clues to what your first job was; let others guess.
3. Write your favorite vacation spot or a place you'd like to visit.
4. If you won a million dollars, what would you do? Write it on your name tag.
5. Write your favorite year (or age), and discuss why.
6. Write three things you have on your nightstand.
7. Stranded on a deserted island, what food/album/item would you take?
8. You're ten years old, home alone. What do you eat?
9. What do you do to relax?
10. Name three people you admire most; be ready to discuss why with others.
11. If they made a movie about your life, what would the title be? Whom would you cast to play you?
12. Name the best book you read or the best movie you saw recently.
13. Write out the best piece of advice anyone ever gave you.

How to Get the Most from Group Meetings

The great dividing line between success and failure can be expressed in five words: "I did not have time."
—*Robert Hastings*

- Be prepared. Get a copy of the agenda in advance so that you can form your own agenda.
- Watch for what was *not* said; read body language.
- Watch yourself for rambling. Don't wander.
- Get involved, ask questions.

- Don't monopolize discussions. You can't learn much from listening to yourself talk.
- Take notes, but be brief. Don't be so busy writing that you don't hear what's said.
- Listen intently to others, and don't interrupt.
- Get to the meeting early and choose choice seating.

One-on-One Meetings

Creativity can solve almost any problem. The creative act, the defeat of habit by originality, overcomes everything.

—*George Lois*

As a creative in business, you might have frequent one-on-one meetings with a client. There are several ways to make these both more productive and less time-consuming:

Make the client come to you whenever possible, saving you the commuting time. That way, you won't forget something important for the meeting—you'll just have to dig it out.

Time it right. If you are not a morning person, make your meetings in the afternoons. If you are a morning person, meetings during your peak hours can be a waste of your valuable creative time.

Bring your appointment calendar to avoid conflicts and to write down due dates of tasks.

Call the day before to confirm the meeting.

Bring a calculator, writing supplies, etc.

Be prepared. Before you leave for a meeting, make sure you have everything you need with you. Not having all relevant stuff can mean a trip back to the office, having to reschedule, or an unproductive meeting.

If you commit to doing something, do it.

Write the person's phone number in your calendar when you set up a meeting, in case you have to cancel or confirm.

Show up on time or early. If the person you are meeting is frequently late, bring something to read, your cellular phone, or some minor paperwork to do while you wait. *Turn your phone off during the meeting.*

Give yourself a cushion between meetings in case the first one runs over. Otherwise you'll be running late all day.

Walk and talk, meet at a park, at the gym, on the beach. It can be a healthy alternative to meeting over a meal, and the surroundings can be inspirational in more ways than you'd expect.

Beat the lunch crowd and hold your luncheon meetings early. You'll get faster service, with no wait for your food or the check.

Use a pending meeting as a deadline and make sure you're ready.

Meeting Etiquette
- Be on time.
- Listen before you speak.
- Humor can defuse a potential conflict.
- Disagree, but don't fight and don't yell.
- Don't dismiss others' ideas. Try to build on them.
- Avoid side conversations.
- Avoid trivial matters.
- Start and end on time.

Presentations
Eye contact is a humanizing element in an often impersonal world.
—*Michael Gelb*

Nothing, I repeat, nothing, can advance your career as much as good presentation skills. (I didn't say public speaking, because that freaks too many people out.) As a creative person, you have to be able to sell your ideas, promote yourself (or your product, book, film, CD). The ability to make effective presentations and be heard can mean the difference between success and failure. You may have the best ad campaign for the client, yet someone who was able to "sell" theirs better may beat you out.

I remember the first time I was asked to give a talk. I thought I was going to die (partly because it was in front of a group of teenagers for the police department's DARE program). After a while I discovered two things: first, I really enjoyed speaking in front of groups and, second, I wasn't very good at it.

One of the best things I ever did to further my career and develop self-esteem was to join Toastmasters. (Toastmasters is not an organization that fixes toasters or drinks a lot. They are an international organization to help people develop their communication skills. Join! I urge you strongly!) The club I belonged to (I was a member for eight years and reached Accomplished Toastmaster status) was loaded with creative people, which was a networking bonanza.

Since then, I have become a frequent guest on talk shows, a nationally known seminar leader, and a part-time radio talk show host.

When You Are Asked to Speak, Don't Freak
All the great speakers were bad speakers at first.
—*Ralph Waldo Emerson*

Not everybody has to know how to speak in public. However, it's a useful skill to have. It can work in your favor when you must do interviews, make presentations (that's how you get gigs, you know), manage meetings, or deal with your public when you hit the big time. The ability to give a talk about your art can help set you up as an authority, which increases your value in the marketplace as well as your visibility.

Why wouldn't you want to speak out? I'm sure you don't lack for subject (or opinions) to speak about. Maybe it's low self-esteem. Having an audience gaze up at you raptly as you talk is a great ego-booster. Maybe you're afraid because of your tendency to wait until the last minute. Preparation equals confidence.

Other options to help you become a better speaker include the following:

Set a clock in plain view (to you, not the audience; I use a travel alarm) to keep track of time. Don't look at your watch (rude) or go over the allotted time (extremely rude).

People remember the first and last things they hear, so start with a bang, state your main points as a preview, and then end with a solid close (poem, quote, joke, story) and a review of what you covered. The classic format is, tell 'em what you're gonna tell 'em, tell 'em, and tell 'em what you told 'em.

Practice, practice, practice!!! Sure, you risk sounding a little rehearsed, but the flip side is far worse. If you are not prepared, you are more nervous, you have no idea how long your talk will be, you may leave important things out, or you may ramble off and lose sight of the main point.

Keep it simple. Ask yourself, "What is the one thing (the main point) I want them to take away from this talk?" Then stick to that, with appropriate embellishments.

Use personal examples. Give them a piece of *you*. They'll appreciate it and you'll seem more real. If you're going to poke fun at anyone, start with yourself.

Be sincere. As motivational speaker Zig Ziglar says, "People don't care how much you know until they know how much you care about them." Be sincere.

Less is more. Lincoln's Gettysburg Address was short, as was Martin Luther King's "I Have a Dream" speech. Leslie Hore-Belisha, the British statesman, said, "To make a speech immortal, you don't have to make it everlasting."

Involve the audience at least once every ten minutes or so. It helps keep them awake.

Be prepared for the question-and-answer segment. Have answers ready for the most frequently asked questions.

Make eye contact. I like to find a friend right away and then work the room. Don't make people uncomfortable and stare, but hold eye contact for a second or two.

Drink lots of water before and during your talk. Lukewarm water with lemon is best. (Ice water causes your throat muscles to constrict.) Stay away from caffeine and alcohol before a talk.

Move around, but don't pace. Use hand gestures and movement to keep the audience from getting bored, and to emphasize key points.

Don't make off-color jokes or use bad language. Be careful not to offend anyone.

Practice in front of a live audience before the real talk. This is very helpful. Ask for feedback. I've practiced in front of my wife, who is a great audience; if she doesn't laugh at a joke, I know I'm in trouble. Use a tape player to record your practice talks, or tape your actual talk and listen later. You can always find ways to improve.

Know your audience beforehand. The best speakers spend time asking meeting planners questions, and customizing their talks to match the audience. Doing your homework beforehand can save you a lot of embarrassment later. On the TV series *The Jeffersons,* George Jefferson was excited when he found out he'd been elected "Small Businessman of the Year" and was asked to say a few words at the awards banquet. When he arrived, he was surprised to learn that "Small Businessman" didn't mean he ran a small business—it meant *he* was a small person in business.

Prepare your own brief and accurate introduction and ask that it be read, rather than have your introducer improvise. That way, you won't spend the first few minutes of your talk correcting your name and explaining that you're not a billionaire, just a millionaire. Type your introduction of yourself so it can be read easily by the introducer. Phonetically spell out names or strange words. Use a large type size.

Be enthusiastic. Any nervousness or lack of information can be overcome by being excited about your topic.

Work on your vocal quality and projection. Speak from your diaphragm, and breathe. Practice improving your voice by changing your voice-mail message or answering machine message, or by leaving messages to yourself and listening back every day.

Slow down. The most common mistake is to talk too fast. Prepare less material than you think you need, and force yourself to slow down.

Have funny replies ready in case you get hecklers.

Eliminate distractions. Disconnect any house phones in the room.

Use word pictures, metaphors, graphics, and stories. The more senses you can involve in your talk, the better your audience will listen and retain. Remember, "facts tell, but stories sell."

Don't script your speech. Use an outline and key words or phrases as reminders in your notes. If you are not going to be behind a lectern (which is better), use index cards for notes rather than pieces of paper. You can use different-colored cards for different sections of your talk. (Green for intro, yellow for main points, red for your close.) If you use overhead projections, write notes on the flip-frame protectors. Make sure your notes are big enough to read at a quick glance. Use key words.

Nervousness and fear are perfectly natural. Breathe deeply, say "Relax" to yourself, ask to be the first one to talk if there are several speakers (get it over with), use notes if they make you feel more secure, tell yourself "I'm excited" instead of "I'm freakin' scared out of my mind." (See the difference each can have on your mental state.)

Use visual aids, but don't make them the focus of your talk. *You* are the message. Visual aids are good for highlighting key points. My rule of thumb is no more than five points per page. Use pleasing colors. *Check spelling!*

Make sure you have directions to the place you're giving your talk, and leave time to get lost anyway. Arrive at least thirty minutes early.

Call a few days before your talk to find out how many will be attending (if you have a handout, you need to know how many to bring), and make sure the event hasn't been canceled.

Check out the room and the equipment beforehand. You can never be prepared for everything that can go wrong, and believe me, I have seen almost everything happen (heart attacks, a rat in the room, fire alarms, earthquakes). The more things you are prepared for, the better. (During the fire alarm, I remembered from school to tell people to leave the room single-file, no pushing and shoving, walk, don't run.)

Remember, the audience WANTS you to succeed. Nothing is more painful than watching someone bomb onstage. So they are on your side from the beginning. If you are still frightened out of your wits, try visualizing the audience naked—I hear it's an effective technique.

8

Be Your Own Boss

Your most important sale in life is to sell yourself to yourself.
—*Maxwell Maltz*

I can just hear you saying, "Ptui! I don't need no stinking résumé. I don't need to deal with a lousy boss. I'll just start my own business!"

If you think you're going to get around dealing with authority figures by starting your own business, think again. To be successful in any business, you have to have clients. Clients are the same as bosses—only, if you're lucky, you'll have even more of them. They have power over you (pay or no pay, referral or none). They often come in committee form (God help you!), and you don't have any of the protections a corporate structure provides.

You've also got Uncle Sam looking over your shoulder, making sure you do your bookkeeping.

And if you think your own business will give you lots of free time, you must consider that if it's *your* business, you're *always* working.

When you start out, you won't even be a small business. Small business is categorized as ten to fifty employees. Most creatives start—and many stay—as one-man bands. One person (usually with some subcontractors, like a bookkeeper or a sound studio). That's a microbusiness, and it isn't even mentioned, covered, or protected in any city or state legislation. They will charge you for a business license, however, and check the zoning if you work out of your home. They will expect you to know, understand, and abide by sales tax, payroll tax, business improvement district tax, self-employment tax, and independent contractor laws. You will get no support from your local chamber of commerce, and the Small Business Administration is likely to consider you beneath their notice.

You're on your own, baby. So keep that résumé up-to-date.

If that little diatribe didn't scare you off, you might just make it on your own. Read on.

▼ ▼ ▼

FAST FACTS

According to Opinion Research, 57 percent of adults ages eighteen to twenty-four would like to own their own businesses. Ages twenty-five to forty-four, 96 percent would like to work for themselves.

▲ ▲ ▲

Now the Good Stuff

Is your desk a prison where you're grueling or a garden where you're blooming?

—Anonymous

I have noticed that what corporate America sees as faults and flaws in the right-brained person are assets when it comes to working for yourself. Things like intuition, imagination, and innovation are exactly the things needed. Don't fault yourself for not fitting into the nine-to-five world. Be glad that you have what it takes to work "outside the box."

Most creatives in business for themselves work over sixty hours a week. Why would anyone want to work long hours, often for very little pay? Maybe because they live in the Third World, making clothes and trinkets for Americans, or maybe because they don't want to do anything else. Your work is like your child; you want to take care of it, nurture it, grow it, and despite all the diapers you have to change (and what's in them), you love it.

Maybe you shouldn't marry your work, but it becomes a very tempting mistress. You have the freedom to make your own hours and pick and choose which projects you will work on (and which clients you will work with). You don't have some dork telling you what to do all the time. You can make as much or as little as you want. The only glass ceiling is the amount of work you are willing to do.

There's more. You control your own destiny. The rewards that come from all that hard work belong to you. You own your ideas. There is an unlimited income potential. It is both challenging and constantly changing; it's hard work, but you feel as if you are hardly working because it is a labor of love. You set the priorities—you can work less and have more free time, or work more and make more money. You set the hours—I like to work from midnight to 3:00 A.M. My partner does her creative work from 8:00 A.M. to noon.

So why did I start the chapter with all that negative stuff? Working for yourself isn't easy, but it *is* doable! I am sick of hearing about how half of all businesses fail after the first year. Half of all marriages fail, too. Does that stop people from getting married? Think of it this way: Half of all businesses MAKE it!

Right-Brainers in Business

Not using aptitudes you are blessed with tends to cause a lot of frustrations, and can inhibit career success.

—Stephen Greene

There are several misconceptions about creative people that may keep you from going into business for yourself. Although there may be very good reasons you should not attempt self-employment, these are NOT among them.

Artists are like children. Wrong. You may have a childlike quality, but you're not childish. "People seem to think artists are like helpless children that need constant guidance; I don't feel I have to be deemed an imbecile and a child because I am an artist," says singer Natalie Merchant, formerly of the group 10,000 Maniacs.

You'd be happy playing all day long. So the creative person likes a good time more than the next guy, is that such a crime? To the creative, work very often *is* play, and I personally think that's the best way to live.

You're defensive about your way of doing something. This one may not be so far off the mark. You've probably had to defend yourself for most of your life. "My mother would describe me as somewhat of a problem child. I was very imaginative. I was only interested in doing things that interested me, as I still am. I've never had the discipline to do things other people's way," says John Cusack. It might help to be able to prove that you know what you're doing.

You can come up with ideas quickly. According to Dave Barry, "The creative process is a slow, frequently tedious one." The constant pressure to come up with inspiration on demand can be wearing. You need time to conceptualize, to let ideas percolate, to do your best work. Time management can help give you that time, even when nobody else will.

You don't care about business. Guitarist Steve Laury told me this one day: "Just having a great idea is not enough. It takes so much mental energy to keep yourself alive in the music business. It's not enough to just be a great player or composer, unfortunately. Many great musicians and composers died poor." Just because you're creative doesn't mean you don't yearn for success, for recognition, for financial security. And you actually have a natural gift in this direction, if you learn to recognize and use it.

There's only one way to be organized, and you can't handle that kind of regimented, structured, right-angle style of time management. This is half right. You probably can't and definitely shouldn't try to regiment your lifestyle, killing your creativity in the process. But there are many ways to be organized, and you're creative enough to find one that will work for you.

Organized means sterile, cold, dull, rigid, or inflexible. Wrong. Organized means being able to find what you need when you need it. "Once you can concentrate on organizing, ideas fall into place with an almost audible click," says Jane Harrington.

You work better under pressure. What does that have to do with anything except eventual heart failure, ulcers, or stroke? It is okay to turn up the heat from time to time, if you do it on your terms, keep it under your control.

You were born disorganized, born with some sort of cleaning disability. That's baloney. You can organize yourself; it's just that nobody else can organize you. As long as you can function and those around you don't want to kill you, what's the problem?

You're antisocial. You do need your space at times. When I was finishing up this book, I spent a week in a hotel—away from phones, visitors, and even my wife. But once the book is finished, look out!

You're a little crazy (all your dogs aren't barking). Crazy? No. Off-center, maybe. Don't keep trying to judge yourself by irrelevant standards. It's a colossal waste of time.

You're stubborn (single-minded). Hah! You're more likely to have ten or twenty things going on in that incredible brain of yours. And there's nothing wrong with sticking to your guns when you know you're right. (Unless you're disagreeing with me, of course.)

You're absentminded and forgetful. If you have ten things going in your mind at once, it's understandable that you lose one every now and then. If you're totally involved in a project, it's not surprising that everything else falls by the wayside. I call it focus, not flaky.

Homework

A logical, rational methodology handcuffs any possibilities for a thrilling creative solution that can make miracles.

—George Lois

Millions work at home, facing some unique challenges, and the rewards can be great. One problem with working at home is that your personal life and work life tend to blend into one. Keep them separate by doing office work in your home office only, even if it's just a corner of the bedroom. Keep regular office hours.

One of the problems of a home-based business is that the work is always near and, for some, always beckoning. They tend to overwork, with no separation between work and play. Let the demands of work determine your schedule. If you want a break, take on less work.

Work at the times you work best. That's the beauty of working at home—you can work at odd times, or whenever the muse hits you. Your "regular office hours" could be 8:00 A.M. to noon and 9:00 P.M. to 1:00 A.M. Your only limitations are the need to be available to your clients, and the need to be available to friends and family.

Ask family and friends to respect your hours and your need for uninterrupted time when you're working at home. Balance that by giving them your uninterrupted attention when office hours are over.

Some people thrive in a home-based business environment; others don't. One reason is, believe it or not, that they need the routine an office job provides. Make up your own routines. Dress up for work (put on your *good* sweats), commute to the office at rush hour (while the kids get ready to rush off to school), stop for your morning coffee and paper at the corner, gossip and tell jokes with your co-workers (online), ask your secretary to hold all your calls (turn on the answering machine), put your feet up on your desk and get to work. See, not that much has changed—except that your new routine should take a fraction of the time your old routine did.

Sometimes you have to start early because of time zone differences. Maybe you have to make a call to the Far East (not Hackensack, New Jersey—farther east) and you have to call at three in the morning. Get up, make the call, and then go back to bed.

Everyone has a unique style of getting started. Some start with the most interesting task first, some the easiest, and others tackle the toughest. It doesn't matter how you start your day at home. Just start. Set a goal for the day hooked to a reward. "I will make ten cold calls today before I can watch *The Young and the Restless.*"

Reward hard work with little breaks. For every hour worked, take ten minutes where you can indulge yourself by watching a little TV, doing some gardening, napping, taking some sun time, walking, playing with the kids, smoking a cigar, or, in my case, playing the drums.

A friend of mine who is an extremely talented copywriter went from working at an ad agency to doing freelance work out of her home. I heard from others that she wasn't doing much work anymore. Concerned, I decided to stop by to say hello. I knocked on the door. No answer. I rang the bell. Again, no reply. As I turned to walk away, I heard her yell, "Just a minute!" Several minutes later she came to the door.

"Sorry it took so long. I was taking a nap," she offered, inviting me into her office. No big deal, a catnap in the afternoon is perfectly healthy, I thought. Then I happened to notice her to-do list for the day. It read:

1. Sleep in.
2. Read the paper.
3. Walk the dog.
4. Watch Regis and Kathie Lee.
5. Call Mom.
6. Take a nap.

The irony was, the only things checked off were "Sleep in" and "Take a nap"! She hadn't even walked her dog! Fortunately, she quickly realized she missed working in an office and went back to the agency.

Home Is Where the Office Is

What no wife of a writer can understand is that a writer is working when he is staring out the window.

—Burton Rascoe

Problem: Clients and colleagues may not take the home-based business seriously.

Solution: Put forward a professional front. Quality business cards and stationery, a dedicated fax line, a separate phone line for business calls with a professional outgoing message and voice mail all add to the impression that you're a business—not just some part-timer working at home.

Problem: Too many distractions keep you from meeting deadlines or doing your best work. Distractions include spending too much time online and watching TV.

Solution: Don't use a corner of the kitchen for an office. If you're going to work at home, you need a separate room with a door. Hang a sign on the door that says, "Work in progress, do not disturb."

Problem: You feel isolated and lonely.

Solution: Get out and network with other home-based business owners, attend seminars, meet a friend for lunch.

Problem: You need expensive equipment to start, and can't afford it.

Solution: Take advantage of places like Kinko's, lease instead of buy, barter with other businesses for use of their equipment, buy a little at a time.

Quiz: Will Working at Home Work for You?

1. Are you a self-starter?
2. Do you enjoy being at home?
3. Are you comfortable working alone for long periods?
4. Do you enjoy wearing many different hats and working on many tasks?
5. Are you able to handle finances? Can you budget an erratic income?
6. Can you handle taking calculated risks?
7. Do you hate working long hours?
8. Are you afraid to make mistakes?
9. Do you like to try new ideas?
10. Are you more interested in results than routines?
11. Can you see the big picture?
12. Can you do several things at once?

Answers to numbers 7 and 8 should be "no"; all other answers should be "yes."

Do What You Love

The key to success in the home-based business (or any business, for that matter) is doing what you love. Turn a hobby into a business venture. Opportunities exist in the following career paths:

Photographer or videographer, travel guide, interior designer, writer or writing coach, yoga instructor, music teacher, consultant, graphic artist, party planner, recording studio engineer, editor, jewelry designer, fine artist, Web designer, etc. The list is rapidly becoming endless. The key is to turn your talents and interests into a business, something you wouldn't mind working (or playing) at for fifty, sixty, and sometimes seventy hours a week.

One of my favorite success stories about turning a passion into a business is the story of Clancy "Captain Zodiac" Greff, a landscaper in Kauai who used to spend his weekends exploring the rugged Napali coast in a rubber raft. Pretty soon he was taking friends, then he discovered that people would pay him to take them on this adventure. Today he has a fleet of rafts that explores the waters surrounding Kauai and several other Hawaiian islands as well. What a life!

Work Schedule

My schedule is based on my energy levels, so, although I work eight to ten hours a day, they are odd hours:

9:00 A.M.–noon	Serious writing.
noon–2:00 P.M.	Lunch break.
	Swim, surf, read, work out, make personal calls, run errands, eat.
2:00 P.M.–5:00 P.M.	Lighter work.
5:00 P.M.–9:00 P.M.	Dinner break.
	Early movie, eat, goof off, watch TV, check E-mail.
9:00 P.M.–2:00 A.M.	Serious writing.

Biggest Problem

The biggest problem for the self-employed may be their inability to manage money. Get help.

Top Tip

Want to get something done? Pretend you're going on a vacation when you finish. Better yet, actually go on vacation.

Civilian Life

I've never had a real job. I know they exist because I see all the tall buildings.

—*Jerry Seinfeld*

You can't just create, you have to market what you make. That, loosely translated, means you are in business for yourself, whether you work within a corporate structure or hawk your wares on the street. To be successful, you have to take the business of art more seriously.

Some of us, however, would rather have our toenails ripped off than work for someone else. We want to *own* the business. I am no exception.

My desire to be an entrepreneur started when I was eleven years old. In the summer of 1976, I started my first business venture. I went around my neighborhood sanding and repainting mailboxes for five dollars a crack. It was a perfect little summer business. The hours were flexible, it involved a small amount of creativity and paid well, I was able to see the fruits of my labor every time I rode my skateboard around the neighborhood, and (other than my mom) nobody told me what to do. Since that time, I have founded five companies, everything from surf shops to The Success Shop.

▼ ▼ ▼

FAST FACTS

If you drive twenty minutes each way to work (on average), and you work five days a week, you will spend 160 hours a year on the road. Working at home saves time and money!

▲ ▲ ▲

Think Big, But Start Small

The world will never be happy until all men have the souls of artists—I mean, when they take pleasure in their jobs.

—*Auguste Rodin*

Nearly everyone has a great idea for a business, so what stops them from taking the plunge? They think you need hundreds of thousands of dollars in start-up money. Anita Roddick had very little money when she started The Body Shop. To get the word out, she used her social activism to gain exposure and build her business. Rhino Records was started with three dollars (that's not a misprint). The founders turned a three-dollar pile of used records into a $70-million business selling collections of novelty tunes and past hits.

A couple of college friends (who happen to have offices down the street from me) pooled their money (three thousand dollars), and launched a contact manager software program called GoldMine, which today is a $30-million business. The list goes on and on. This country is full of people who started on a shoestring and built up their businesses or their career. Ed Burns used his friends from *Entertainment Tonight,* where he worked, and a small loan from his father to make the film *The Brothers McMullen.* He parlayed that small success into directing several other movies and even a starring role in *Saving Private Ryan.* Spike Lee used credit cards to finance his first film.

When you start small, your mistakes are smaller, too. A lot of my friends got new cars as soon as they got their driver's licenses. I was stuck with the family station wagon. No matter how you dress it up, a station wagon is *not* cool. I backed that thing into poles, sideswiped parked cars, and basically earned my stripes in what we called "The Green Mana-lishi." The car did have a V-8 engine and a four-barrel carburetor. On an early-morning surf trip to Mexico, a Mustang wanted to race us down the deserted freeway. At sixteen years old, I wasn't going to back down. At 115 mph, I pulled away from the Mustang. At 120 mph, we blew a tire. The car spun out of control, the steel belt from the blown tire ripped open the gas tank, and the car caught on fire. My friend and I escaped unscathed. The car, however, burned to a blackened hulk. I figured my parents would kill me. Instead, they said, "See, this is why we gave you a beater for your first car."

If you take it slow, you're not likely to burn your business down. And if you keep your "must haves" down to "needs" and "can affords," you're more likely to survive any bad initial investments. You WILL make mistakes. Don't waste a lot of time worrying about it. Spend that time learning from your mistakes, and you're way ahead of the game.

There are other advantages to starting small. Your business can be more flexible and offer a higher-touch kind of service in this high-tech world. Starting small also means that you need less capital. With a lower overhead, you keep more of what you make. Chances are that when you start small you will have to wear all the hats and learn to do it all. This will serve you well as you grow bigger and start to delegate. An artist I know actually learned to enjoy bookkeeping. She does it on the computer, using a program that is much like a checkbook for entry (Quicken), but automatically makes charts and graphs, profit-and-loss statements, and more. She likes it even better when the numbers aren't all red.

Paul Hawken, author of *Growing a Business* (a must-read), suggests using your own money as the seed money and growing the business at a slower pace by reinvesting profits back into the business rather than having venture capital (I call it vulture capital) or bank loans to begin. Most of the successful businesses I know borrowed from family and friends, and *not* from banks. These self-financed ventures seem to fare better. Facts bear this out, too. Twenty-three percent of all small businesses began with less than five hundred dollars.

The Lean Years

What convinces is conviction.

—*Lyndon Baines Johnson*

When I began my writing career, I sold my business, my car, my home, and even my dog. I lived the life of a monk and a madman. A monk because I deprived myself of many earthly pleasures while pursuing my business. A madman because I would not give up, no matter how hard it got. I did everything myself, because I couldn't afford to pay anyone.

It was a tremendous learning experience. The lack of money made me mad enough to do the legwork necessary to make it. I paid my dues, and it paid off.

I clearly remember going to the gas station and paying with the change in my ashtray. Do you know how embarrassing it is to say, "give me $1.82 on pump four, please"? I have to be honest, I looked at it as an adventure. I was okay with being broke. I knew I would make it again. I knew these tough times would pass. My wife, however, wasn't as comfortable as I was with our Third World socioeconomic status. She didn't find it as inspiring as I did, especially when we went to the swap meet to sell our old clothes and other remnants from the good life. So I used my creativity to make life fun. We did things that were cheap or free. I wrote a book about it called *Dating in San Diego,* which included free and fun things to do in and around town. Eventually, we were able to buy new cars and a new house (we haven't bought a new dog yet). We made it through the tough times.

The lesson I learned is that a lack of money makes you hungry and a lack of resources makes you more creative. I literally pounded the pavement, handing out flyers, calling on bookstores, speaking for free. One of the best things I did was get free consulting from a retired executive in my field through the Service Corps of Retired Executives. My SCORE counselor saved me thousands of dollars with his sage advice. All those things paid off.

The point is, you have to believe in yourself. Hang in there and things *will* turn around. Stay positive and work hard. Have a goal and hang on to it, knowing that you will come out the other side stronger and better for the struggle. You're making an investment in yourself and your future.

Looking Good

In the process of life planning or career development, our destiny is bound up in the quality of our being rather than the list of things we know how to do. The doing grows out of the being.

—Hilda Lee Dail

Starting small doesn't mean you have to look like you are small. With a computer, you can make impressive-looking business cards and brochures, develop a web site and have an elaborate phone system (with a toll-free number.) Just don't go overboard when you begin. Brand-new office furniture, the latest in computer technology, and fancy office space can eat up all your resources. Give yourself time to develop a client base. Minimize overhead and you minimize risk.

Image is everything. Spend your money on professional-looking marketing materials and invoices, but buy used furniture, rent or lease equipment, use freelancers rather than hiring people, go to Kinko's for copies rather than purchase a copier before you can afford it. One lesson I learned is turning your inventory. When I priced out the printing of my first book, I was seduced by the unit cost of printing three times what I really needed. Needless to say, I got screwed. There are still copies sitting in my garage. Give me a call—I'll give you a great deal.

Success kills many businesses. They try to grow too fast, can't keep up with demand, and basically implode. It's all about cash flow. For example, you develop a prototype and take it to a trade show. You get orders, you fill them, everything is going well. Then a large customer wants to buy a zillion of your widgets. You still haven't collected from the orders you filled from the show, and you have no money left to produce the widgets to fill their order. You stall, you beg, you borrow but can't deliver. Now your reputation is ruined and the big customer goes elsewhere, never to return.

Look at Amazon.com. They don't stock all the books they sell; they order as they receive orders. They don't sink money into inventory, and they don't extend credit. Cash in hand is better than collections in the bush. For years the company was run out of a tiny office, yet their Web presence makes them look huge.

Rhino Records ran their business out of a dungeon, so to speak, but resisted a move until their growth warranted it. The owners didn't buy a copy machine until they reached $2 million in business. "No banks believed in us enough for us to get into a lot of debt," says co-founder Richard Foos.

▼ ▼ ▼

FAST FACTS

There are 8.3 million independent contractors, and that number is rising quickly, according to the Bureau of Labor Statistics.

▲ ▲ ▲

What Is My Business?

Certain professions simply come with higher salaries attached to them, and some people are in them and some people aren't. That doesn't mean you have to make a six-figure income to be a success.
                                                              —*Steve Kelley*

There are several schools of thought on what makes for a good business. The first is to go where the action is. What's hot, in demand, and that you have an aptitude for? The second is to take advantage of your existing talents, skills, background, connections, equipment. Find a need and fill it. Turn your hobby into a business. A lot can be said for doing what you love to do, something that you feel passionate about.

I agree with all those schools of thought, up to a point. For instance, going into something that is hot but that you hate will leave you miserable after a while. Turning your hobby into a business is great, unless your hobby is something like buying and selling eight-track tapes. Is there enough of a demand? Still, the more you combine your skills and abilities with what you love to do, the better off you will be.

In my "other" life (before becoming a writer), I was very involved with the action sports industry (I owned a chain of retail stores). It's ironic that we (surfers, skateboarders, and wakeboarders) are sometimes seen as being one fry short of a Happy Meal. Because we love water and the beach, we must be lazy and stupid. That is, like, so untrue, dude. Some of the most creative and resourceful people I ever came in contact with are in that industry. I saw people take a good idea and not only build a business but create whole new sports.

Scott Olson attached his hockey shoes to a pair of roller skates with in-line wheels and created a $700-million industry when he founded Rollerblade in 1983. (He now has an invention called the Rowbike, and it looks like a winner, too.) In 1977, Jake Burton built the Snurfer, a plastic surfboard you could ride in the snow. He refined it and created the snowboard, founding his pioneering company, Burton Snowboards. Snowboarding is now an Olympic event. We used to tow each other behind our boats on our surfboards for fun. Soon there was a guy riding around Mission Bay on a much more sophisticated board (with foot straps) doing amazing tricks. He had invented the Skurfer—and wakeboarding was born. It is a huge industry, with its own pro tour.

Times are changing—and they favor the entrepreneurial artist. One of the biggest obstacles a self-published author faces is getting his or her book distributed. Now the Web is rapidly becoming the biggest distribution outlet ever imagined, and anybody can get their product in. I remember reading that Todd Rundgren released his latest CD through the Internet. It eliminates all the middlemen, making it feasible to distribute your ideas and your work all over the world.

▼ ▼ ▼

ACTION ITEM

Make a list of all the things you can do that someone would pay you for.

Now make a list of all the things that you can do, not including those on the first list. How would you market the things on your second list?

FAST FACTS

According to the Bureau of Labor Statistics, there are 18.3 million home-based businesses.

▲ ▲ ▲

Business Plans

I've gotten to where I am today because I had a plan. There are plenty of guys more muscular than I'll ever be. There are actors who are far more talented than I am. I just knew what I wanted and I made a concerted effort to follow my plan and work very hard to reach my goals.

—Sylvester Stallone

Every book I have ever read on being in business for yourself includes a chapter on business plans. Do you need one? Yes and no. How do you like that answer?

The Small Business Association says that lack of a business plan is the number-one cause of start-up failure. It is required if you want to get any kind of loan from a bank. And, even though you may never look at it again, the process of writing one helps you flesh out your ideas and define your market.

The point here is, you will most likely run your business by the seat of your pants, so keep it fairly flexible and use your intuition rather than a bunch of numbers. I know this goes against conventional wisdom, but I say write a mission statement backed up by a brief (two-page max) bird's-eye-view type of plan, more a global view than a street map of your business.

I think the macro-view two-pager is short enough that you will actually look at it now and again after you write it. I also believe that spending two to three months writing a business plan when you could be out doing something to bring in business is silly. If that bucks the business books, so be it. My business plan is pictures of my business goals with captions and a one-page summary along with a vision statement. It works for me.

Pitfalls

A good business has interesting problems, a bad business has boring ones. Good management is the art of making problems so interesting and their solution so constructive that everyone wants to get to work and deal with them.

—Paul Hawken

The following is my short course on do's and don'ts for starting up a business:

Don't waste your time (and money) making everything perfect before you begin. You're as ready as you'll ever be. Your idea of what you are and what you need will change with experience, so don't lock yourself in too tight at the start. Make it up as you go.

Do come up with a good name. Brainstorm it with as many people as you can. Try to keep it short—one or two syllables. Try to make it connect with common experience in as many ways as possible (this makes it easy to remember). Think Apple.

Don't get too cute. A graphic artist I know named her company "b graphic." As in "be graphic." Nobody got it.

Don't be a grouch. Whatever product you provide, you're also selling customer service. That means being likable, personable, accountable, and reliable. You have to be pretty exclusively wonderful to overcome poor customer service. If you're naturally a grinch, hire a front man (sales rep) or work in someone else's cubby.

Don't be afraid to put your stuff out there. Yes, people will copy you and steal your ideas. That is a good thing, as long as you remember your contract and copyright law.

Do be aware of what works and what doesn't. You'll have some ideas or explore some marketing areas that just don't work financially, no matter how brilliant they seem at first. Drop the things that don't bring in the revenue. Cut your losses.

Do be your own niche. Use your product or service—believe in it. Nothing sells like sincerity.

Don't quit your day job. Don't underestimate the advantages of medical, dental, and retirement benefits as well as steady income and access to equipment. If your day job is in the business you want to go into, consider it an apprenticeship. Learn the ins and outs while you test-drive it, and you'll make a nice, smooth entry into your own business.

Do be aware of scams and shams. "You could be like me. Big boat, lot of girls. Vewwy expensive cars. Me make lot of money." I'll never forget the first time I saw this infomercial with a man I'll call "Dr. Wu," and his pitch. I thought, who would buy into this? A lot of people. Don't do it. There are no shortcuts (at least honest ones) to making it in business.

Don't leap before you think. Partnerships are like marriages. Some last till death do them part; in others, the partners end up wanting to kill each other. The creative person should consider carefully before committing to a partnership. If the partners bring individual talents and skills that don't conflict (Spielberg, Katzenberg, Geffen), it can work. I work better by hiring freelancers.

▼ ▼ ▼

FAST FACTS

A study by Wells Fargo has found that 71 percent of all startup business begin in the home.

▲ ▲ ▲

Making It Go in Different Directions at Once

Variety is the very spice of life that gives it all its flavor.
—*William Cowper*

Jimmy Buffett is best known as a successful singer/songwriter with several gold and platinum records and sold-out concert tours, but he is also a best-selling author, owns two Margaritaville restaurants, a recording studio, his own record label, a profitable mail-order business, and a newsletter, as well as interests in several minor-league baseball teams. He hasn't had a hit record since 1977 and yet is one of the highest-earning entertainers each year, according to *Forbes* magazine.

What he has created is *multiple profit centers*. This equals multiple stream of revenue.

Entrepreneur Richard Branson (Virgin Records, Virgin Airlines, etc.) started a small mail-order record business in his basement after quitting school to start his own magazine, and is now worth billions, with over one hundred small enterprises.

Rather than focusing on a single source of income, the lesson is to develop several. This covers you during seasonal slumps, tough times, and boredom (you can switch off from business to business or client to client). It also helps you spread the risk around.

The key is to build your businesses so that they support one another. You sell the same thing to different markets, or different things to the same market. Stephen Covey, author of *The Seven Habits of Highly Effective People,* a perennial best-seller, also sells tapes based on his books, does seminars, licenses others to do his seminars, and markets a Seven Habits Planner and related products and services. Publicity from one promotes another. Once a customer buys from him, they're more likely to buy more of his products.

Build one venture at a time, get it up and running, and then move on. I modeled this myself with books, tapes, workshops, an annual conference, clubs, a newsletter, a mail-order business, and a publishing company. When each new business supports the other, it works very well. When I get sick of being on the road doing seminars, I can switch gears and stay home and write.

One way to avoid getting too fragmented with this approach is to farm out responsibility for different ventures. Have an intern process the mail orders. Hire a specialist to take care of conference details. You get the idea.

▼ ▼ ▼

FAST FACTS

More than 40 percent of America's 30 million teens describe working at home as extremely important, says a survey by Drexel University.

▲ ▲ ▲

Garage Business

People don't realize that the "big break" is a cumulative thing. The "big break" comes from small fractures.

—*John Kapelos*

What do Apple Computers, Hewlett Packard, the Ford Motor Company, and Disney have in common? They were all started in a garage.

Working out of the home is nothing new. Thomas Edison worked out of his home, as did the Wright Brothers. How many bands began in a garage? Richard Branson ran his business from a houseboat for years.

In the old days, merchants lived above their stores and artists in their studios. So why all the hype about telecommuting and home-based businesses? I have one word for you—*traffic!* That and *family values.*

This is the age of technology, and it is easier than ever to work from home with faxes, modems, Zip disks, and videoconferencing. One of my favorite commercials is for MCI; it shows a woman in her pajamas and funny slippers, with a cup of coffee, participating in a conference from her home. She tells us of her day, ending with, "I just hope they don't get video conferencing."

ASK A PRO: BETH HAGMAN

Beth Hagman works out of a home office in a multilayered business that includes editing two monthly magazines, art-directing a small local newspaper, designing and editing books (including most of mine), consulting, and writing the occasional article.

How did you get started in your own business?

I got laid off from a good job supervising the graphics department of a good-sized printing company. My boss told me he thought I was too good to be working for somebody else, that I should start my own company. At the time, that was the last thing I wanted to do. But I landed a client and then I was stuck. I researched and bought a computer, learned to use it, and put out a magazine in the space of about a month. Serendipity.

What's your typical day like?

My husband brings me cappuccino and the paper before he leaves for work at 7:00 A.M. I'm up, showered, and at my desk by 8:00 A.M. If I have a meeting planned later in the day, I might bag the shower until just before, and get started a little earlier instead. I start off finishing up any projects that are due that day, then do my E-mail chores. As editor for a regional magazine, I get quite a bit of mail, story queries, and press-release stuff. Then I edit any stories that have come in, or work on my own stories. Around 9:00 A.M., I stop and make my phone calls while the dog sleeps at my feet. Then it's back to editing or doing layouts until lunch at 11:30 A.M.—that's usually when the phone calls start. Afternoons are filled with scanning, layouts, errands, meetings, bookkeeping, and responses to queries or a trip to the zoo or museum. When my husband gets home, I quit for the day . . . except I usually go back to my desk for at least a little while after dinner.

What's your home office like?

It's gone through several incarnations, starting small, in the spare bedroom, and eventually taking over the family room. It's big, airy, and attractive, equipped with two computers (my husband mostly uses the second one, which is a backup in case mine goes down), scanner, laser printer and color printer, two phone lines (one for fax and one with an automatic voice-mail service), and a cable modem.

It sounds ideal. Are there any drawbacks?

I have a hard time turning down work, because you never know whether you'll have any work at all next month. In ten years of a progressively more successful business, I've still never gotten over that insecurity. Which means there are times when I really work my tail off, just to keep up.

Does it get lonely, working at home?

Because the nature of my work is often very personal, I often develop lasting friendships with my clients. I've become involved in neighborhood projects and community groups, too—a spare-time thing that has brought me several new clients and a lot of sat-isfaction. Between my clients, my community work, my family, three cats, and a dog, I have a very full life. I just wish I had time to take a vacation.

Help! I Need Somebody

No man is an island.

—John Donne

Having to do everything yourself limits your growth and your career. Control freaks struggle. If you plan to write, direct, produce, act in, edit, and publicize everything, you miss out and burn out. Even the most creative person can only be in so many places at once. More important, you can only be an expert in so many different things. Spread yourself too thin, and things start falling through the cracks.

Put out an SOS. It's nice to be a part of the tribe. Let the elders help, push you, teach you. Be willing to learn. Band together for support and protection.

There are several ways to do this. Most of them come under the heading of networking. Reach out to your friends and family, to co-workers and clients and bosses, to suppliers and bankers, to your competitors and everybody else you can think of. Develop a group of people who are in your corner, who know what you're doing and what you need, and who are willing (at least by extension) to help you. Give them a reason for helping you. Your mom will help to get you out of the house finally. Your boss/client will help because you'll make them look good. Your friends will help because they are your friends. Make it worthwhile for people to help you, and you're well on the road to success.

There are a lot of networking ideas in this chapter, and they *do* work. But a freelancer I often work with insisted that I include this caveat: Simply hitching your wagon to someone who is a great networker can gain you many networking benefits for minimum effort. She has a couple of clients (I'm one of them) who have extensive networks. She makes sure we are happy with her work and her prices, and so far she's been kept busy with referrals from us and from past clients (who are also happy, because she does very good work and always goes the extra mile for them). I worry that she has too many of her eggs in my basket. She worries that she has too much work to keep everybody happy.

Networking is working for her—even though it's *my* network.

Cheering Section

*The key to persevering in your art is to build a strong enough struc-
ture so that you're happy without success.*

—Carol Lloyd

The difference between successful creatives and unsuccessful creatives comes down to this: a healthy support system. It is wonderful, intoxicating, and addicting to find people who believe in you and want to see you do well. It is the antidote for your inner critic. Sometimes you can't see how special your work and your talents are, and you need people to support and assist you. You need the feedback.

Nobel Prize–winning author Toni Morrison joined a writing group early in her career. "I went because they were really good company and they had great food." Join a support group to help fight isolation.

Look for a like-minded group of people in the same boat you're in—working at home, in a big corporation, in a small company. Each has its challenges, and talking to others facing the same problems can be stimulating. Use their experience for your own benefit.

Unable to find a support group for maniac goal-setters (like me), I formed one. Goal Stars met for breakfast twice a month for four years and provided support, encouragement, ideas, and brainstorming. I brought in experts in different areas to speak, and at the end of each meeting we broke into pairs, or "goal partners." We'd set out what we planned to do before the next meeting, and exchange goals with a partner, who would follow up with a call between meetings to make sure we were staying on track. Networking was never the goal, but it was a by-product of people caring about and trying to support one another.

You don't always have to go so far afield to find support, however. Todd Oldham's mother taught him how to sew, which led to his amazingly successful career as a clothing designer. He is still tight with his family, and they support him as much as he supports them. His mom is the president of the company, his grandmother is head of quality control, and his sister works in customer relations.

Swimwear designer Malia Mills began her career as an assistant dress designer before deciding to strike out on her own after *Sports Illustrated* featured one of her suits. The photos generated so many orders that she had to beg her family to help. "Mom and Dad contributed money, my sister designed the logo, my lawyer brother handled the legal details, and another brother helped me develop a business plan." Her success secret? "Don't be afraid to pick up the phone, ask for advice, and use it."

Matthew McConaughey gets honest feedback from his brother Rooster, who tells it like it is. "If he don't do somethin' stupid, he might be a big movie star." When Matthew was considering a career in law, Rooster also offered his two cents' worth. "I told him if he became a lawyer, I wouldn't have nothin' to do with him."

In 1972, Stephen King wrote his first novel, *Carrie,* but after several rejections from publishers, he threw it away. His wife rescued the manuscript from the trash can and encouraged him to submit it for publication again. That book, and the subsequent film, sold 3.5 million copies and launched his career.

When someone believes in you, he or she can push you beyond what you think is possible. Mel Gibson's sister signed him up for Australia's National Institute of Dramatic Arts without his knowledge. While a student there, he made his film debut in 1976's *Summer City,* before landing the title role in *Mad Max.*

Nobody believed in Ozzy Osborne. Sharon, his manager and wife, got him cleaned up, told him he could do it, and got him through the tough times, like when his guitarist and co-writer died in a plane crash and Ozzy wanted to quit. She helped him hold it together.

Feedback and support can be as close as your computer. I live for feedback from readers. I love it that Amazon.com allows readers to make comments. I read those religiously. The best part of being an author, to me, is fan letters. All the work that goes into writing a book is worth it when I get a letter from a reader saying that the book has helped them in some small way. Yes!

Artists and creatives help each other. There is an energy produced by creatives that you can tap into without taking anything away from anyone. Try to be around as many positive, creative people as possible, no matter what their field. You'll feel energized. Hanging with others in your own field can be helpful, too. You may get their overflow business, learn new techniques, find others to take some of *your* overflow or share responsibilities on a big job.

There is plenty of room at the top. Nicolas Cage and Jim Carrey share their own award, which looks like a tiny Chihuahua dog. They pass it back and forth, depending on who has a hit. (This began *before* the Taco Bell commercials hit.)

Don't Let 'Em Get You Down

Praise is like sunlight to the human spirit; we cannot flower and grow without it.

—Jess Lair

Okay, not everyone will support you. Some won't understand you. Criticism is not always mean-spirited. Parents, for example, may try to persuade you to take a conventional career path because they are worried about you. They think the corporate world is safer than a career in the creative arts. (They haven't got the memo.)

When Jacquelyn Mitchard's husband died of cancer at the age of forty-five, he left Jacquelyn with the kids and mounting debt. She worked part-time in the public relations department of a university, but dreamed of supporting herself full-time as a writer. Her father recommended a full-time job with a ball-bearing company, while an author friend encouraged her to write. She decided to pursue writing. Her father didn't understand. "Think of the kids," he said. "I am," she replied. "Does a good mother teach her children to be timid, to trade down their dreams?" Her first novel, *The Deep End of the Ocean,* made both the hardcover and paperback best-seller lists and was made into a feature film.

I never got much support from my parents. I once showed them a manuscript, but I glued some of the pages together to see if they actually read it. Either they didn't read my book, or they didn't mind that pages were stuck together. They never mentioned it.

If you're not getting support at home, look for support elsewhere. But find it. Form a whole network of helping hands. Just be careful not to confuse support with hangers-on. Many celebrities have entourages that rival the president's. Admittedly, some entourages are positive (Sean "Puffy" Combs surrounds himself with his musical protégés and often brings along his mother, Janice). But MC Hammer went broke supporting his "friends" and those who "supported" him.

Is Your Net Working?

Knowledgeable people know facts. Successful people and prosperous people know people.

—John Demartini

There is a strong correlation between networking and farming. You are probably wondering, "Now, what would a Southern California surfer know 'bout farmin'?" Not much. But when it comes to networking, I can plant, pick, and produce with the best of them. So listen up.

Start with a good soil. You must start out on the right footing and make a strong first impression.

All plants need some sunlight to grow. You have to get out and meet and mingle if you expect to get ahead. Getting out and standing around by yourself watching people isn't enough. Introduce yourself. Talk to people. And don't forget to listen.

Not all seeds will take, so plant more than you need. Some will bloom beautifully, others will wither and die. Meet as many people as you can, and tell everyone what you're doing, what you need.

Diversify your crops. This means networking outside of your company, industry, or art form. Sometimes these connections can prove extremely valuable, and broadening your scope creatively is always valuable.

Rotate your crops. Contact every member of your network at least once a year. Keep your mailing list up-to-date.

Not all plants will take right away. You have to be patient when networking, even if it seems like a waste of time. One day when you least expect it, you will reap the fruits of your labor.

Most plants need lots of care, fertilizing, and watering. Don't wait for people to do something for you. Do something for them first. And always follow through on your promises.

Plants like to be touched. Don't skimp on "skin time." Talk to people face-to-face, take them out to lunch (it's cheaper and easier to manage than dinner), invite them to come and see your latest project. Don't rely entirely on E-mail and phones—they're too impersonal for a real connection.

Don't try to harvest too soon. Don't push. If you have nurtured your network properly—paid attention to other people, helped them when you could, and passed along their needs to others, while making it clear what you need and what your goals are—people will be glad to help you, and they'll find ways to do it that you never thought of. Give synergy a chance.

Don't let your harvest rot on the vine. When you do get help, or a referral or an introduction, take advantage of it right then. Don't waste somebody else's effort.

Plants need both sun and shade. Some people want credit, while others prefer to remain behind the scenes. Be sensitive to the needs of others. But remember, too, that every plant needs sun sometimes, and those who say they don't want or need credit will still be pleased if you acknowledge their help in a personal way.

Focus on cash crops. This doesn't mean you should only be friends with those who can help you, dumping the others, because you never know who might help you. It means periodically weeding out the deadweight—those who have died or moved out of the country, for instance. It means spending more of your time with the most effective part of your network.

My Network

If you're to succeed, you must understand that your rewards in life will be in direct proportion to the contribution you make.

—David McNally

I have been a believer in networking since I was a child. I was the kid in school who was "connected," who knew everyone and got along with the ASB (student government types), surfers, jocks, rockers, and stoners. I often brought these people together for mutual projects—like beach parties!

I have put networking to good use throughout my career, but in 1993 I hit the Rolodex jackpot with an idea I had for a book about famous and successful San Diegans. I wanted to meet the elite people who called San Diego home, the power brokers, star athletes, celebrities, media personalities. I was curious about how they reached their lofty positions.

How could I meet these people? What could I offer them? I could write a book profiling successful San Diegans—which is exactly what I did. I started by contacting the media (they rarely get profiled by competing media), and they liked the idea of being profiled in a book. After I interviewed them, many offered to introduce me to other celebrities or athletes. It was amazing! By offering a benefit while asking a favor, I was able to befriend several key media personalities, meet some of my heroes, and learn the secrets of the success of stars like Whoopi Goldberg.

How did the book sell? Who cares? The contacts I made and the goodwill I gained from writing that book are priceless. I use the present tense because it is still paying off. My Rolodex reads like a *Who's Who* of San Diego. (The book sold 4,500 copies locally and was a critical success.)

People—even "important" people—are more accessible than you think. The worst thing they can do is say no—and the potential benefit is huge.

I wouldn't be writing this book if it weren't for networking. A few years ago I joined a group of writers who were also speakers. We pooled our resources, joined our local convention and visitors' bureau, and shared leads. Through that group I met Harriet Schechter. Harriet was offered a contract to write *Time Management for the Creative Person* (the second book in this series). Facing a conflict of interest, she recommended me for the job. I wrote the book, it did extremely well, and here I am again.

Without Harriet—without networking—it never would have happened.

Networking Is a Two-Way Street

Politeness and consideration for others is like investing pennies and getting dollars back.

—*Thomas Sowell*

Do unto others before they do for you. That's my motto when it comes to networking. I believe you have to give to get. It's like a checking account. As you help and support others, you start to build up an account with them. You now have a balance that you can write checks against. If you try to write checks against a negative balance, they bounce.

It is *not* about using people. It *is* about relationships and a long-term approach. People who are only takers wear out their welcome very quickly. Eventually they burn so many bridges that there's no way to get back in with people. The word does get out.

So how do you ask for help without looking like a taker? Start by looking at your goals. How will accomplishing these goals help others? Who benefits besides you? You'll feel better about asking for help when you know it will benefit others as well.

My good friend Alan Hack is always asking me, "How can I support you?" He has helped me several times—and whenever he needs me or needs something from me, I'll be there. His checking account is now a money market account drawing interest and compounding.

He's a good listener. Thoughtful. He sent me a beautiful book after I sent him a potential client. The client didn't work out for him, but he still sent the book. If you think you can't afford to do something like this, let me disabuse you. You can't afford not to.

Networking allows you to barter services and get things done on a shoestring. What do you have to offer that others would pay for? Alan has asked for nothing except that I teach him to surf. Not a bad deal.

What do you need? Can you trade lessons for studio time? I know a jazz guitarist who produced his own album entirely on trade. Can you trade artwork for clerical help? Have someone proofread your writing while you proof theirs? Think about it.

Be a do-gooder. Volunteers get back more than they give. You may meet VIPs in a situation where you can bond and interact. Charity work is also newsworthy, and you might get well-earned and much-needed free publicity. Find a cause you believe in and that ties in with what you do. It's good for your career and even better for your soul.

Help others, and offer support when they are in need. That's the sign of a true networker—and a caring person. It's easy to support someone when things are going well for them. You show your truest colors when they are down and you still stand by them. When they bounce back, they will remember and reward your loyalty.

Trade your services for hands-on experience, portfolio pieces, and connections. Offer to do the church or community association newsletter if you need experience in graphic design. (Warning: Once you become the newsletter editor, it will never end. You may have to move away or die to get out of it. Still, it's a great trade.)

One of the best things I did was form an informal speakers' bureau. When I am asked to conduct a workshop and I am already booked or get a request for a topic that's not in my repertoire, I refer the request to another trainer—it's a win/win/win situation. I win because I get a finder's fee from the trainer and I get a reputation as a reliable source for speakers, so I get more requests. The other trainer wins because they get business they wouldn't have had otherwise. The client wins because they get the speaker they need without much extra effort on their part. It works.

Stay in touch with people on a regular basis. Once a year, E-mail, call, send a birthday card, fax a joke or an interesting or pertinent article. Notice their successes and congratulate them.

Send postcards from the road. Since I'm on the road doing workshops so often, I take my mailing list and send personal notes to keep in touch with people from exotic places like Boise and Duluth (and Fiji, Tahiti, and the Caribbean). It turns out that many people put these postcards up on their fridges and bulletin boards. One even posted his on his web site (it had a naked native on it)! The point is, a postcard doesn't take much effort, but it makes a big impact. You don't want to be calling someone you haven't talked to in a year and asking them for a favor. Stay connected.

Show appreciation for those who have helped you. Thank-yous are the number-one networking tool. Be diligent about showing your appreciation. Thank-you cards are the *minimum* you should be doing for those in your network who have helped you.

Send birthday cards. I'm big on birthdays. Everyone sends holiday cards, but I have had people tell me that they were blown away that I remembered their birthday when their spouse or parent had forgotten. It makes a big impact, it's fun to take a break and go browse the Hallmark store (lots of creative ideas there)—and I like doing it.

Be there. If you think I don't notice who comes to my events, you're wrong. Oh, I remember. I believe that when it comes to supporting people, you should make the effort to attend their openings, shows, signings, weddings. It means a lot to me when people come, and I notice when they don't.

Tools of the Trade

You cannot mandate productivity; you must provide the tools to let people become their best.

—*Steve Jobs*

To start networking, all you need are business cards, a Rolodex, and a calendar. As you get more involved, your networking bag of tricks will expand to include the following:

Follow-up. This requires some kind of system to remember appointments, commitments, birthdays, and any other opportunity to look as if you have it together. It could be a simple calendar/planner or tickler file, or a software program like ACT, GoldMine, or Sharkware.

A mailing list (by the way, let others know when *you* move). This is essential, and well worth the time it takes to keep it current. Mine is set up like a phone book, with white pages (personal) and Yellow Pages (professional) divided into categories and then A–Z. In the front are emergency numbers.

A prototype, portfolio, or brochure. This gives you credibility and allows for show-and-tell.

Stationery, including letterhead and invoices. You can save on envelopes by just using white business-size ones and stamping them. You can get a stamp with your logo, name, and address at most office-supply stores. Postcards are my most often used item, so I stockpile them, along with thank-you notes and birthday cards. Don't forget to keep postage stamps on hand, too.

Pens. Don't be caught without one. (Paper is good, too.) Write down what you told that person you would do, and then do it. A colleague of mine buys steno pads in bulk—they fit nicely in her purse.

Samples to give away. I carry my books with me at all times. I started giving them to bookstore managers, who, in turn, showed increased interest in promoting my book.

An "A List." I made a list of my "team." This includes the top ten people I count on for my career. I will bend over backwards to help them, and it seems to be reciprocal.

Power tools. Computer, web site/E-mail, cell phone, answering machine/voice mail, toll-free number.

A phone/cell phone/answering service. On David Geffen's phone are twenty speed-dial numbers, next to which are names like Katzenberg, Spielberg, Calvin Klein, Paul Allen (Microsoft's co-founder), and Barry Diller. These are the people he talks to nearly every day. Who is on your speed dial (besides the pizza delivery companies)?

Use an answering service/voice-mail service so you're always reachable. I was getting pretty irritated with my editorial consultant because her line was always busy. Then she got a messaging service through the phone company. Now, if the line is busy, I'm patched straight through to the message center. She hears a beep that lets her know she's got a message, so she calls me right back. Don't take a chance on missing that important call.

E-mail. If you have a computer, get yourself on the Internet with an E-mail address. You'll be amazed at what an effective communication tool it is. You can send and receive messages any time you have free—day or night—so you won't put off making contacts because you only remember to do it at 3:00 A.M. People tend to get to the point better when they're typing it out, and you have a written record of what they said. Just don't rely on E-mail for all your human interactions. Face-to-face still works best.

First Impressions

A movie is like a parachute—if it doesn't open, you're f——ed.
                                                          —Robert Evans

Networking and dating have more in common than many people care to recognize. You can probably recall all the details from your first dates, both the good and the bad.

I'll never forget the time when a first date decided to meet me at my house rather than wait for me to pick her up. (I wasn't even running late.) She arrived at my house nearly an hour early. (This was a bad sign, I know, and in hindsight I should have just run away from the woman.) My roommate had left the door open on his way out. I was in the shower and didn't hear the doorbell ring (if she ever did ring it). She decided to just walk right in! I thought I heard someone going through the drawers downstairs. My house was on the market at the time, so I figured it was the realtor showing people around.

I made possibly the worst decision of my life at this point. I ran naked and wet into the closet of my home office (which was filled with office supplies), hoping the realtor would look around and go away.

I heard footsteps coming into the room. I heard someone rifling through my drawers. Then I saw the closet door begin to open. I tried to hold it shut with all my might, but my hands were wet and they slipped off the handle. The door burst open.

"What the hell!!" I screamed. A high-pitched "Aaaaaaarrrrghhhh!!" came from the other side.

I guess she was impressed, because she still wanted to go through with the date. I, on the other hand, could not get past the fact that she had seen inside my drawers.

It's hard to recover from a bad first impression. Blow people away with a positive first impression. You can resort to your old ways later. For now, be on your best behavior.

Do your homework. Even if it's obvious that you checked them out, people are usually flattered that you took the time to find out their hometown, their hobbies, and maybe even their golf handicap. (Of course, having compromising pictures taken can make them a bit edgy.)

When I was to meet with a filmmaker, I wanted to find common ground to help break the ice. I discovered through a quick background search at the library that he was also a surfer. We had that in common, so conversation came easily and we became fast friends.

Prepare what you are going to say before you are introduced. Have a verbal brochure of sorts that succinctly tells others what you do, what makes you special. Add a touch of humor. Make it memorable. Practice it so that you can make it sound natural, and yet have it honed. Put your name last. For instance, "I'm an editor and a graphic artist specializing in publications—I work on books, magazines, and the occasional newsletter. My name is Beth Hagman. What's yours?"

Look professional (at least be clean). Yes, you are a nonconformist. We get that. But at least make an effort to look like part of the tribe you are meeting with. (Every tribe has its own garb—lawyers, doctors, and even creative people. For a while, a ponytail was standard issue for an artist.) A tattoo signifies youth and lack of judgment. Recognize prevailing preconceptions even if they're misconceptions. When you need to be serious, it really helps to *look* serious.

Be on time or early to meetings. Stand and deliver. Don't sit down and start doing paperwork so that either you miss opportunities to meet people or when you meet it is awkward. Put the magazine down and sit up straight (get your feet off the table while you're at it).

Eat before you get to an event so you don't look like a pig. If it gets all over the place, it doesn't belong in your face. At least in public. This way you don't spend your schmoozing time in the buffet line or with your hands and mouth full.

Get to networking opportunities early to find the best seat, get comfortable with the surroundings, and, if registration is necessary, get that out of the way. Then make sure you meet the presenters and hosts.

Look around for someone who's standing alone and approach him or her first. Someone alone is usually more receptive, and you can use the practice being the approacher.

Stay sober? Early in Matthew McConaughey's career, he was in a hotel bar with his girlfriend, talking about how much he wanted to become an actor. The bartender informed him that there was a Hollywood casting agent seated at the other end of the bar. McConaughey went over and introduced himself. The two hit it off and began to order drink after drink, prompting Matthew's date to leave and the bar to eventually eject them. The casting director was Don Phillips, mentor to a whole generation of actors, including Sean Penn. Ironically, the meeting led to a part in the movie *Dazed and Confused* for McConaughey.

George Jean Nathan said, "I only drink to make other people interesting." Just don't embarrass yourself.

Good handshake and eye contact. Anything that resembles a wet noodle or a dead fish is not acceptable. Neither is a secret handshake, Boy Scout salute, or bone breaker.

Learn names and use them. (Didn't catch it? Ask them to repeat it.) A person's name is music to their ears. The more you use it, the easier it will be to remember. Remembering a person's name shows you are paying attention.

Learn the art of small talk. Ask questions. Start with family, job, activities, interests. Find some common ground. Get personal. Try to stay up on current events so you know what people are talking about. Larry King, who obviously has the gift of gab, says, "Whether you are talking to one person or a million, the rules are the same. It's all about making a connection. Show empathy, enthusiasm, and a willingness to listen, and you can't help becoming a master of talk."

Keep it clean. You can have collagen injections in your lips, a hundred-dollar haircut, and an Armani suit, but if the minute you open your mouth you start spewing four-letter words and bad-mouthing everyone and their brother (you never know whose brother you're ripping, by the way), you look like trash. I always pretend I'm talking to a nun (be careful—this can bring back haunting memories for some). If what I would say would offend a nun, I won't say it. We live in a PC world (that's *politically correct,* not *personal computer*), and I have found out the hard way how easily people can be offended. So don't curse. And stay as apolitical as possible until you know your audience.

Adapt to the atmosphere. You can talk to anyone about anything for about five minutes. Then it's time to move around and mingle. Just when they are about to find out I'm a fraud, I'm off to the next person. Use your divergent thinking style to learn about a lot of different topics. And if you come up against a conversation you're not up to date on—listen.

Think before you speak. Seriously! How many times have you put your foot in your mouth by blurting something out? Practice pausing before you open your mouth. John Cage, a senior partner in Ally McBeal's law firm (on the TV show by that name), has a whole repertoire of techniques to give himself time to think when something unexpected happens in the courtroom. He pours a glass of water—slowly—and sips it—slowly. He stands up, carefully buttons his jacket, advances—slowly—to the witness box. He never, ever, says something he hasn't thought out or that he doesn't mean. He never even says something he does mean but that is inappropriate. The result? People *listen* when he talks.

Be sincere, warm, and honest in your praise of, and interest in, other people. Smile.

Let other people talk. Don't brag, and don't monopolize the conversation. People really don't care about your success anyway. Let them be the star of the conversation.

Carry your card—and keep it handy. You don't want to open your purse and expose your personal items (a pack of condoms or hemorrhoid suppositories, for instance). Be Bond-like—"My card." "I'll call you." Shaken, not stirred.

Ask for their card. Show an interest in following up on your conversation. Make a note on the back of their card to remind you what you said you would do, or some identifier to remember them by. (I like to include what they like to drink.) Just the act of making a note will leave the impression that you really do want to reconnect with them.

Make a strong exit. Know when to move on. Pick your spot.

Send a thank-you note or an "it was a pleasure meeting you last night" card. Send it right away, before they forget who you are. That little note will earn you a solid spot in their memory bank.

Schmooze or Lose

In business, contacts are the name of the game. Why, in the art world, are they considered dirty?

—Brett Singer

Set networking goals. Make a plan. Otherwise, you end up wasting a lot of time and energy. It can be expensive, too. Knowing where you want to go helps streamline your efforts. Get serious about it. Who needs what you have to offer? How can you reach them?

Whom do you know? Start close to home. Find an ally to carry the torch for you. Guy Kawasaki got his job at Apple when a college pal hand-carried his résumé to the human resources department. Apple was getting ten thousand unsolicited résumés a day at the time, so Guy's chances of landing a job otherwise were about as good as Microsoft going bankrupt.

Start local, then go global. Contact old friends and associates, class-mates, clients.

While attending Yale, Frances McDormand (*Fargo*) and Holly Hunter became friends (both went on to win Oscars), and Hunter gave McDormand a tip that resulted in her film debut. McDormand also met her future husband, filmmaker Joel Coen, on that shoot.

Tell everyone what you are up to and what you need. Don't assume your family and friends know your situation. Usually they are too wrapped up in their own little worlds to pay much attention to yours. Bring them into your orbit.

CNN's Meredith Bagby wrote a book during her junior year in college and paid $2,000 for two hundred copies. Her father sent the book to a columnist at the *Miami Herald*. The next thing she knew, Ross Perot held the book up while testifying before congress on NAFTA. The giant suck-ing sound Bagby heard was Ross Perot inviting her to appear on *Larry King Live.* That led to a network job on CNN. Thanks, Dad.

Get to know your contacts—bankers, agents, editors, producers, directors, reporters, influential people, talk show hosts, and city coun-cilpersons—*before* you need something. Become a resource for them. Ask to be used. Find out what they need and fill that need (I'm talking business, not sex here). You'll get to be known as an expert by supplying information, articles, artwork, a good sound bite, or connections. When there's a need for similar information, articles, artwork, sound bites, or connections, you'll be remembered.

Get to know local shop owners, leaders, and other creatives. Be friendly, be interested—not interesting, *interested*—and people will gravitate to you.

Work from the bottom up. Get to know up-and-comers and support staff.

Get a rep. A good one.

Acknowledge people when they are exceptionally warm or help-ful. I pass out "good finder cards" to tellers, clerks, flight attendants, and others who mostly do great work but don't get recognized for it. The cards simply read, "You are special! And don't ever forget it." The reac-tion I receive is priceless. I have had people call, E-mail, and write to thank me for noticing.

Be nice to everyone. You never know. Today's schmuck could be tomorrow's Spielberg.

Follow up and follow through. I have even given people assignments, like little scavenger hunts, to prove that they are reliable and worth spending my time to help out. It sounds cold, but I can't tell you how many times people come to me for advice, assistance, or just acceptance. I am not about to recommend them to agents, other authors, or anyone for that matter, until I find out if they are reliable. It's my reputation that's on the line.

Be a card collector. Collect business cards as if they were Nolan Ryan rookie cards. They may be worth more than the Hall of Fame pitcher's trading cards someday. Put *x*'s on the cards if they have helped you out, *o*'s if you have assisted them. Put nicknames, pronunciations, the gatekeeper's name, kids, hobbies, etc., on the back. These are their stats. Want to hit a home run? Use them.

Be a joiner. (But don't overdo it.) Organizations, associations, and professional groups can be a source of inspiration, contacts, and information. They can also be a giant time-waster and means for procrastination. Not to mention expensive. Choose wisely. There is a national organization for professional speakers. When I first started to get paid to talk (and not just a free lunch), I joined for eight hundred dollars a year. What a waste! Two years later I took that same eight hundred dollars and invested it in marketing materials, a much more effective use of the money.

Give to get. You will say I am crazy for doing this, but I truly walk the walk. When I teach a class on graphic design, I will inevitably have people ask me to critique their work. It isn't part of the course description and I don't charge for it. But I will take their newsletters, brochures, and ads home and rework them—free of charge. Why? Because when I do this I have won a customer for life. I enjoy doing it, and I learn from it, too.

Speak or teach your way to the top. The Learning Annex is an organization that conducts seminars on both coasts. I have taught seminars for them for the past eight years, off and on. The exposure I get from their extensive promotion of my classes is tremendous. I have had old high school classmates call me (as well as new clients) as a result of Learning Annex publicity. It also gets my name out, which makes it easier to approach strangers.

Master written or verbal skills. When I first inquired about doing seminars for a national seminar company several years ago, they asked me to fly out and audition for them. After I did my thing, I asked what they were looking for in their trainers. They told me that although it's nice to have trainers who know a subject inside and out, it's more important that they are good communicators. Why? They feel they can teach prospective trainers the technical stuff, but they can't teach them how to be good speakers.

Bone up on your writing and speaking skills, but remember, the number-one communication skill is listening. Asking questions and listening. People are always amazed at the details I remember about their lives. Did I do fewer drugs than they did, and thus have more brain cells left? Maybe. There are a couple of years in my teens that are pretty fuzzy, though. Mostly, I remember people because I pay attention, and I'm genuinely interested in others.

Get out!!! How many garage bands were discovered when a neighbor came over to complain that the music was too loud? Not many. Get out. Gig. Give talks. Be seen and be heard. You never know who may be sitting in the audience waiting to discover you.

Always give people more than they expect. Before Harrison Ford became Indiana Jones, he was a carpenter. While building a new portico for Francis Ford Coppola's office, Ford made an impression on the director. Before he knew it, Ford was cast in Coppola's *The Conversation,* which led to his role as Han Solo in *Star Wars*. If you have to work a day job, be the best possible cabbie, waitress, or usher you can be.

Advanced Schmoozing Tips and Techniques

Losing my virginity was a career move.

—*Madonna*

As a college kid, I was driven to learn the secrets of success. (I eventually learned there are no secrets, just work your ass off.) Back then, I was naïve, and I was a geek. I wore a tie to class and carried a briefcase. I was inspired to design and print up a little flyer inviting the local multimillionaires to lunch. I drove to the center of the richest area of town and started putting my flyers on the most expensive cars I came across—Rollses, Bentleys, Jags, and so on. I got a couple of calls praising my initiative—and one lunch invitation. It turns out that the former head of one of the largest book publishers in the country had retired to my hometown. He asked me over for lunch, and I picked his brain all afternoon. I am still applying some of the things I learned from that meeting.

That's advanced schmoozing.

One of my good friends, "Boris" Bromley, isn't afraid to go up and talk to anyone (which served us well when we were single). He knows and is friends with most of the key athletes in the area. When the Super Bowl was in town, Boris was riding around in limos with players from both teams. A couple of times when players were being interviewed on TV, I could see Boris standing in the background.

What's his secret to getting to know celebrities? He looks for ways he can help them. He is honest and trustworthy.

What do you have to offer a celebrity in your field? Establish a relationship. It really is lonely at the top. You can meet celebrities through their agents, accountants, attorneys, family, friends. I met Jimmy Buffett through a mutual friend who played for the Padres and is currently the third base coach for the team. It turns out Jimmy is a big baseball fan (he owns two minor-league teams) and likes to surf. That was my entree.

Be memorable. Some of my promotional materials sport a picture of me wearing a suit, standing in the surf carrying an inflatable rubber shark. Some show me with an arrow through my head. Don't be afraid to look a bit silly.

Use technology. Chat rooms, web site, E-mail . . . Put the word out on the Internet. Give out your E-mail address.

Use personal touches. Handwritten notes, fresh-baked cookies. A personal gift is worth far more than an expensive one.

Golf your way to the top. Or play basketball, fish, hike, ski, shag softballs, play racquetball. Finding something you can do with the people on your network list that gives you a natural point of contact (even if you suck).

You are always on. Television executive Geraldine Laybourne, a former schoolteacher who has held top positions with MTV Networks, Disney, ABC, and Nickelodeon, was attending an NBA basketball game and wound up sitting next to Michael Ovitz and family. (Ovitz was probably the most powerful person in the entertainment industry at the time.) Once Ovitz's nine-year-old found out Laybourne was the head of Nickelodeon, he was more interested in her than in the game. When Ovitz was named the president of Disney a few months later, he remembered Laybourne and asked her to become president of the newly created Disney/ABC Cable Networks.

Find a backer. Every person out there who believes in you is a dollar in your pocket. Toni Morrison has benefited immensely from her friendship with Oprah Winfrey. When Oprah announced that Morrison's 1977 novel *Song of Solomon* was the latest selection for Oprah's Book Club, the book sold over 500,000 copies. Who is your Oprah?

Making the Connection

Be careful the environment you choose for it will shape you; be careful the friends you choose for you will become like them.

—W. Clement Stone

Your own personal network reaches much farther than you think.

Make a bunch of circles, each standing alone, each large enough to contain several names. Across the top of each circle, write one of the following categories: friends, family, classmates, shop owners, co-workers, clients, associates, neighbors, charities, suppliers, professionals, acquaintances, volunteers, church (you'll need a very big piece of paper, and you'll need to write very small).

Write the name of every person you can think of that fits each category. When you run out of ideas, switch the pen to your other hand and keep going. Using both hands lets both halves of your brain work for you.

Now let your circles sprout other circles. Draw an arrow between them. The "Friends" circle begets the "Friends of Friends" circle. "Family" begets "Extended Family" and includes all the relatives of your relatives. Fill in as many names as you can, off the top of your head. If you kept begetting circles, you'd find a connection, however tenuous, between yourself and practically everyone in the country, if not in the world.

Do As I Do

Working with the media is like a game. You win some, you lose some, but once you know the rules, you can win more than you lose. And, as with any game, the more you play, the better you get.

—Lee Silber

Someone once said about me, "Two-thirds of the planet is covered by water. The rest is covering events by Lee Silber." I was touched. Here are a few of the successes I have had in promoting my businesses (surf shop, speaking, and publishing) and my books, using the tips I gave you early in this chapter.

- College radio stations and newspapers are media that are often overlooked, but I've had good luck with them.
- I became a spokesman for the surf industry and was profiled in *Action Sports Retailer,* the trade magazine for that "industry." We were not the biggest chain (two stores), but we got the most ink!

- My favorite promotion was a campaign built around the premise that not all surfers are dumb. We gave customers gifts for grades. If they brought in their current report cards, we gave gifts in relation to their GPA. We got letters from school principals. The parents loved it, too. So did the local papers and news shows.
- I gave free surf lessons one summer. Not only was it a kick to teach kids how to surf, but I took the news media surfing as well. I got endless PR from that one.
- It was always important to me to keep the beaches clean. I started doing beach cleanups with local kids. A great promotion—and the environment won, too.
- I first began speaking in 1987, when I was asked to give a talk to kids on water safety. I was terrified. (Have you ever tried to talk to eighth-graders about anything?) It turned out great, and I got turned on to speaking in public.
- One of the best things I did was to offer a discount to repeat customers by forming a membership club. It included a T-shirt and a newsletter. That little idea has been taken up successfully by huge corporations and boutique stores alike.
- I was always Johnny-on-the-spot. With only a moment's notice, I was a guest on a talk show arguing for free parking at the beach. The guest they booked didn't show, so they called and I rushed down to the station. It actually went extremely well, and added to my reputation not only as an expert on beach issues but as a handy fill-in. Be available.
- When I started getting involved in goal-setting, I wrote a book. As part of that project, I invented my own planner and to-do pads as a giveaway. They helped get the word out about my book and showed that I had some creative ideas. I quickly became "the Goal Man."
- Bookstores are not the only places to sell books. I have tried to tap underdeveloped markets and practice the "big fish in a small pond" theory whenever possible. Markets that I've come up with include corporate libraries, warehouse stores, art-supply stores, cruise ships, college bookstores, health and alternate-lifestyle stores (I do live in California). Often, managers of these venues are receptive to carrying a small number of self-published books. Some of them have even set up lectures and book signings, with great results.
- Whenever I was in a bookstore, I pitched other self-published authors, too. (Always turn fellow authors' books face out. It's the law!) I have benefited by having others sell my books at their talks. Co-op promotions can double your visibility. Don't be afraid to ask

if you can bring your work along when someone you know is doing a signing, a lecture, a concert, or a showing. If they say no, take it with good grace, and you might get invited along next time.

- When I became interested in public speaking, I needed a hook to make me appeal to clubs and seminar-holders. I wrote a book on dating and published it myself. With a book, you exist. It doesn't matter so much what you write about. Just write something.

- Because my book was on dating, I was swamped with media requests around Valentine's Day. The media is big on timely topics. Find a tie-in and play it up.

- I got ink for my wedding because it was on Maui. A Jewish wedding on Maui? Remember, never be boring.

- Having a web site has increased my visibility more than any single promotional idea.

- I began speaking for SkillPath Seminars in part because they pay my way to speak all over the country, and while I am in a city, I do book signings and interviews. In a way, they underwrite my book tour. Meanwhile, I work very hard for them, doing all-day seminars with no support staff. It's a win/win.

- Free in-store seminars bring people in. While they're there, offer a special price, a freebie, an autograph. Have order forms available for the procrastinators. I've done free thirty-minute talks on a variety of subjects, all linked into one of my books, in big and small bookstores. I usually also help publicize the talks, putting up flyers, talking it up to my friends, calling in favors, and getting mentions on local television and radio stations. It helps to have a great hook for your talk. I drew huge crowds to a series of "How to Get Published" free seminars at Barnes & Noble.

- I have gotten a ton of press in obscure, small magazines and newsletters that my publicist thought were too small. But these publications hit my target market. I think it *is* worth the effort.

- I've given freebies and a preview the night before a seminar— sometimes even free drinks and a mini-seminar—for the staff of the hotel. It creates a buzz, and they recommend my seminar to hotel guests.

- Make sure whatever you are talking about on Oprah is on the shelves or available through an 800 number. Getting people to go to the store is only half the battle. You have to make sure there is something there (of yours) available to buy.

- I love Amazon.com. Don't overlook this avenue for promoting yourself.

- I have put out a newsletter since 1991. It is the single best way to build a grassroots following.
- I had my own column (the magazine folded, not my fault) for *San Diego Celebrity Magazine*. It was a kick—and it paid.
- A friend and I created a motivational seminar and ended up with standing-room-only crowds and lots of exposure.
- While I was in Canada, I called the local paper and told them about my books. They sent a photographer and a reporter to my seminar. Then they made me stand in chest-high snow for an hour for the photo op. They were probably just having fun with the kid from California, but so what? It was worth it!
- I wrote a nice letter to my publicist's boss. He said NOBODY had ever done that. I believe I am in like Flynn from now on. It was a very nice letter.
- After Orville Redenbacher passed away, I was asked to come on a couple of news shows to talk about my relationship with him. Sure, I'd be happy to help you out and do it, I said. A few weeks later I had an important event that I wanted to promote. When I called to pitch it on an interview, they said, "We can't have you on again, you were just on." "But I was only doing you a favor!" Charlie Rose usually has guests on only once. Same with *Booknotes* on C-SPAN. Don't waste it.
- I give a good message. When I call producers, I am ready with my mini-pitch for their voice mail. My machine is equally upbeat.
- I have served as a radio talk-show host and plan to have a new show on the air by the time you are reading this. I have found this builds credibility and gives you all kinds of perks.
- I am always asked what a right-brainer is. It's my hook. What's your schtick?

▼ ▼ ▼

FAST FACTS

Ninety-four percent of executives polled by Accutemps think having a mentor is important for professionals just beginning their careers. Seventy-five percent of those same executives say they have had mentors help them on their way up.

▲ ▲ ▲

Mentors: Been There, Done That

If I have seen farther, it is by standing on the shoulders of giants.
—*Sir Isaac Newton*

During the summer before his senior year in high school, Steven Spielberg took the Universal Studios bus tour. During a bathroom break, he got off the bus and never got back on. He decided to take his own behind-the-scenes tour. He wandered around the lot and watched film crews until dusk. That's when Chuck Silvers, head of the studio's film library, asked him what he was doing on the lot unsupervised. "I want to be a director," Spielberg replied. "But I wasn't learning anything on the tour, so I started looking around myself."

Laughing, Silvers told him to come back the next day and he would get him a week's pass. The next week, Steven found someone else to sponsor him. On the third week he took a chance and walked past the guard, waving and calling him by name. The guard was used to seeing him by that time and waved back. Spielberg found an empty trailer and put his name on the door, "Steven Spielberg, Director."

How does this tie in with mentors? After high school, Spielberg made a twenty-six-minute film called "Amblin." He showed it to Chuck Silvers, who took it to the head of Universal's TV production. Impressed, the executive offered the aspiring director a long-term contract. By the age of twenty-one, Spielberg had launched his career.

Mentors have been there, done that. Their experience can take years off your learning curve. They can teach. Point out the pitfalls. Attach you to their own network. They encourage and support you when things are tough.

Singer, songwriter, and producer R. Kelly has a familiar rags-to-riches story. He grew up in poverty and hardship, raised by his single mother in the housing projects on the south side of Chicago. When Kelly was sixteen years old, he met his mentor, Lena McLin. McLin helped Kelly polish his raw musical talent, and pushed him to pursue a career in music. She encouraged him to sing in the choir, take piano lessons, and sing on the sidewalks of Chicago, where he earned several hundred dollars a day singing on the street. This led to a bona fide R&B outfit called MGM. The street group won a $100,000 prize on a talent show, and in 1990 Jive Records signed Kelly to a deal. Describing the influence of his mentor in *People* magazine, Kelly said, "She made me feel like I could do anything."

A mentor will not only point you in the right direction; they can help you see the light at the end of the tunnel or open up vistas of possibility you never imagined.

The spot where I surf most often (and have since 1978) is called Big Rock, just south of Windansea Beach, about which Tom Wolfe wrote *The Pump House Gang*. This is a very heavy wave, one that heaves over a shallow ledge in about a foot of water in front of a big rock. People have broken their boards, their heads, and their backs there. One surfer even had his kneecaps ripped right off. Ever since I can remember, there has been a core crew of guys that just dominates this wave. When I first started surfing there, I was scared out of my mind—I was twelve, and I wasn't sure I could handle it.

I was afraid to take off and just sat beyond the break on my board while the other guys rode the waves. One of the crew guys, Rex, called me over. He said, "Sit here and wait with me." He began telling me a little about the wave and how to ride it. When the next set came, my stomach was doing flips. Trying to look as though I belonged, I started to paddle for the wave, not really wanting to catch it—it was all for show. Just as I was about to pull back, Rex screamed, "Go! You got it!" I went, I made it, I got tubed out of my mind, and I haven't looked back since.

He believed in me. Or he was playing a cruel trick, I'm not sure. I never would have gone on a wave like that without him, and I'd have missed out on years of pure adrenaline fun. Now I encourage others from time to time. (This is how I can tell I'm getting old.)

Keep Your Mouth Shut and Your Ears Open

We learn best when we are learning about ourselves, when we're discovering truths that speak of inner and outer realities, when we're finding out what makes us unique—and like others— within the community.

—*Marsha Sinetar*

They say that when the student is ready, the mentor will appear. I say, go get a mentor. In fact, get more than one. Seek one out.

A good example is John Frizzell, one of the hottest young composers in Hollywood. The major reason for his quick rise to the top is his use of mentors. As a nineteen-year-old, he saw the great jazz guitarist Joe Pass perform at the Blue Note. After the show, he badgered the jazz great for a lesson. Though Pass didn't give lessons, he agreed to a once-in-a-lifetime opportunity for the persistent Frizzell. A year later, Frizzell interned with vibraphonist Mike Mainieri, followed by several others, including noted composer James Newton Howard, each time learning valuable lessons. When Frizzell struck out on his own, he was armed with a lifetime's supply of knowledge.

You might say Frizzell learned his way to the top. He developed confidence over years of being taught by the best.

Look for a mentor who has something in common with you. Jonathan Silverman auditioned for the role of Eugene Morris in Neil Simon's Broadway play *Brighton Beach Memoirs,* winning the part and the heart of Simon. Simon and Silverman developed a mentor/protégé relationship because they had so much in common. Both were avid baseball fans and came from close-knit Jewish families that had suffered through divorce.

When you do find a mentor, you have to do your part. A mentor will help, guide, encourage. You must do two things:

Do the work. A mentor's reward is seeing you succeed. Don't make yours feel that his or her time and energy have been wasted on you.

Shut up and listen. Take notes. Accept your mentor's criticism and suggestions and try to use them, even if you don't always agree (and you won't always agree. A mentor is not God, but just someone who's already gotten where you want to go).

Important Questions

In the book *The Artist's Way,* author Julia Cameron suggests asking yourself the following:

- Whom do I know who has an agent? Ask them how they got one.
- Whom do I know who has done a successful rewrite? Ask them how to do one.
- Whom do I know who has survived a savage review? Ask them what they did to heal themselves.

While these questions are obviously geared to would-be writers, you get the idea. If the answer to any of your questions is "nobody," join a professional association for the field you're interested in. It's the best way to find contacts with the skills you need, and many professional associations have mentorship programs already set up to help newcomers.

Creative People and Their Mentors

Throughout history, creative people have relied on and benefited from having a mentor. Here are some past and present creatives and their mentors:

Student	Mentor
Aristotle	Plato
Monet	Manet
Leonardo da Vinci	Verrochio
Sheryl Crow	Don Henly
Edward Burns	Robert Redford
Trisha Yearwood	Garth Brooks

Everybody Is a Mentor

*My teachers called me a daydreamer. They would write comments on
my report card like, "He seems to live in a fantasy world and prefers
that to paying serious attention to serious subject matters that will
prepare him for life."*

—*Jimmy Buffett*

I have an associate who rejects the idea of mentorship. "I am my own
hero," she says loudly (and often). However, she admits that she learns
something from every client she works with. And from co-workers. And
from books, manuals, magazines . . . She's also very willing to share
what she's learned (whether you ask or not).

The bottom line is this: As long as you keep your ears, eyes—and
mind—open, as long as you're willing and able to learn from mistakes—
yours and others'—you're using the mentorship concept to your advantage. There really is no downside.

▼ ▼ ▼

ACTION ITEM

List three people who have what you want to have, who are doing
what you want to do. Write a brief description of each. Then ask
yourself, when faced with a tough challenge, what would _____
do? Make them an imaginary advisory board. Or put the great
thinkers on your wall and ask them, "If you faced this same challenge, what would you have done?"

▲ ▲ ▲

Role Models

*The people I admire and aspire to be like, model the role I most want
to play. I read their life stories and try to do what they did—with my
own unique spin on things, of course.*

—*Lee Silber*

Whom do you most admire? What do they have that you don't? How did
they get it? What steps did they take? Can you contact them? (You'd be
surprised at how accessible many people are, and how receptive they can
be.) What would you ask them if you could?

If you can't reach them, you can still pattern yourself after them. I
have done this my entire career. I have always been a big biography
junkie. I love to read how people got where they are. (I could watch
A&E's *Biography* day and night.) At different times in my career, I

have emulated and applied techniques from Phil Collins, Jimmy Buffett, Stephen Covey, and Tony Robbins. I'm also inspired by the *Chicken Soup for the Soul* authors' struggle to get published and their subsequent success.

Learning from others' success helps you formulate a path and plan to follow. Success does leave clues. Read biographies as if they were the Bible. Highlight passages that inspire you. If they can do it, so can you. These are ordinary people who have done extraordinary things.

A young Goldie Hawn, dreaming of becoming a professional dancer, was a great admirer of Maria Tallchief, a prominent ballerina in the 1950s. Honoring her role model at an award ceremony, Hawn stated, "Maria Tallchief gave me the chance to say, 'That's what I want to be.' She gave me a sense of mastery. I didn't become exactly that. But the truth is, there's something of her in everything I do."

One warning: Don't lose your uniqueness and don't compare yourself to your heroes. Don't get down on yourself because you didn't make it the same month and year they did. Your success is your own, with your own script, timing, and ending. You may discover that you don't want what your mentor achieved after all. That might even be the most valuable lesson you learn from them.

Pick Teams

Create your own team of advisors, your own board of directors, that you can turn to for advice, guidance, and support.

The first thing you need to do is admit you need help.

The second thing you need to do is ask for help.

Hired Help

Absolute individualism is an absurdity.

—Henri Frédéric Amiel

I am not cut out for collaboration or group projects. I much prefer to hire freelancers on a contract or project basis. I work with an editor on my books, consulting her on organization, handing chapters over for tightening up. She helps me stay focused, gives me insights (and a different perspective), reminds me not to overwrite, keeps my page count down when I can't, and keeps me pumped up when I'm wondering why I ever got into this business in the first place. She's as interested and involved in my book as I am—but it's *my* book. I like it that way.

When I give seminars, I have a hired assistant in every city. They do all the detail work while I focus on what I do best—speak and schmooze. The assistants register attendees, handle book sales, check me out of my hotel room, run errands during the day, deal with the hotel staff, and more.

Still, I do a lot of the scut work myself. It's easy to OD on help, to get lazy, to lose touch with your projects because you've handed off too many bits. Don't become codependent. Don't hire a publicist for seven thousand dollars a month when you could have done it yourself. When you do hire help, look over their shoulders. Pay attention to what they do. Learn from them.

Or teach them. Hire college students or get interns to do your dirty work, and teach them everything you know. Then they'll do things just the way you like them. Then they'll graduate and leave you (sigh). Just remember, every time you lose a great intern, you've added a new component to your network.

The latest rage for people stuck in a rut is to hire a personal coach. (Not a personal trainer, but a personal coach—to help them with their bottom line, not their bottoms.) These trainers can help you focus your goals, shift careers, and unleash your creativity. They bring you a new perspective, a wider choice of options, different types of expertise. A coach will ask the hard questions, and try to bring clarity and account-ability to help you reach your goals. They are your personal cheerleaders, mentors, counselors (who help you look ahead, not back), and people who truly want to see you do well. It's nice to have someone 100 percent in your corner, but then you paid them to do it, so . . .

When anybody starts saying "I know what's best for you," weigh that against your gut. Take their advice into consideration, but your inner voice (intuition) should have the last word.

Jerry Maguire: Agents and Managers

Agent: "I was swimming in shark-infested waters and I got away."
Herman J. Mankiewicz (screenwriter): "I think that's what they call professional courtesy."

I hate to get involved with negotiations and the fee part of the business. I get too emotional, or I cave too easily. Having an agent fight for what's right, and rightfully yours, is the only way to go. They can be the bitch so you don't have to be. They take care of the detail work, sell you or your art, negotiate, collect the money. A good agent also has a huge network of business contacts, and favors to collect in your behalf. That's what you're paying for, and it's worth every dime.

I dislike handling money deals so much that I hired an agent for my speaking engagements. I pay Susan 25 percent of the fee, but she gets me

50 percent more than I got on my own, so I still come out ahead. And I don't have any of the hassle of doing it myself.

In some fields, and some cities, you need an agent to go to the bathroom. Everything is done by appointment, and only agents can get an appointment. Even in areas that aren't sewn up so tight, it's hard to get people to accept unsolicited material. Most publishers don't even look at a manuscript unless it comes from a reputable agent. You can send your tape to a hundred labels, but you've got no guarantee that anybody will even open the box.

Agents open doors, make you look professional. Choose an agent with a solid reputation, a track record of success, someone who is enthusiastic about you and what you do—if possible, someone with some clout.

There are books that list agents with different specialties (check the library). Find several near you who cover your field (literary, art, speakers, music, etc.) and ask them to look at your work. Be persistent. Find out which seminars, retreats, or workshops will have agents attending, and be there, too. If you really are talented, someone will take you on.

Expect agents to say they aren't looking for new clients. Don't take no for an answer. Bring them business. Have someone put in a good word for you. Produce something they can see. Invite them to a performance. Give them a copy of your most recent book, article, or review.

When you do get an agent, don't leave them unless or until you have another one. Pay attention to the contract. Turn any leads that come to you over to your agent. Do not try to make any deals without them. But don't expect your agent to do it all. Be active and visible. Create a buzz—"Oh yeah, I've heard about him." Look for opportunities to showcase your talents. Be on time to meetings, follow through, meet your deadlines.

Never make the mistake of thinking your agent is working solely on your career (unless your agent is your mom, in which case you might want to keep looking). It pays to remind him or her of your presence and your needs. Be the squeaky wheel. Keep your agent up-to-date on what you're doing and what you want to be doing. Ask what you can do to help yourself. Be accessible. Return your agent's calls quickly.

Come up with ideas and pitch them to your agent. Books, movies, plays, shows. *The Gambler* was a vehicle for Kenny Rogers concocted and pitched by his manager, Ken Kragen. If you can get your agent excited about a project or about you, he or she will be a better representative on your behalf.

It is nice to build a relationship with your agent. He or she will work harder for you if you are likable and easy to work with. Don't forget to give your agent thanks and credit. Yes, agents get paid. A thank-you is still important. (Thanks, Susan and Toni!)

If you don't have (or can't find) an agent, you're going to need a lawyer. I know, I know, but this may be a case where a lawyer is not just a bottom feeder. Attorneys work for an hourly fee rather than a percentage, and can look out for your best interests in a deal. They can help you with copyrights and trademarks and handle any lawsuits or legal matters. They can also put you in touch with an agent, a label, or a manager. They can be a catalyst for putting deals and people together.

Another option is a manager. (Managers do everything but sing and wipe your nose.) They take care of all the day-to-day details, handle the lawyers, financial advisers, travel agents, and publicists, and coordinate your team, making sure everyone does their job. I'm laughing as I write this. Oh sure, my entourage. Ha! It consists of a dog, a cat, and a lot of birds. Still, when you hit the big time, it can get difficult to handle the business side of things and still be a great performer/creator.

Quiz: Self-Assessment

Yes or No:
1. I return calls within twenty-four hours.
2. I religiously send thank-you notes to those who have assisted me.
3. I remember people's birthdays, and call or send them a card.
4. I have a system to keep track of things I promise to follow up on.
5. I always give people more than they expect.
6. I do what I say I will do, when I say I will do it.
7. I send handwritten personal notes and stay in touch with my network.
8. I have a mailing list, and use a contact manager to keep it updated.
9. I am an avid business-card collector.
10. I believe that networking is a two-way street, and I try to help others whenever I can.
11. I have mentors and role models whom I can turn to for sound advice.
12. I give credit to those who have helped me whenever I can.

In a Nutshell
- Try to help others with a win-win solution to any problem.
- Always look your best.
- Carry networking materials with you everywhere (cards, brochures).
- Give people more than they expect.

- Be reliable, stay in touch, look for ways to help.
- When you collect a card, write notes on the back about the person.
- Follow up.
- Spend your time with the 20 percent of people who bring you 80 percent of your business and personal satisfaction.

▼▼ 10 ▼▼

Expose Yourself

> *The Compass Rose Book Shop is looking for artists to expose them-*
> *selves on the wall of the shop.*
> —*Announcement in the* Cape Cod Chronicle

In order to have the freedom to create, you must build a successful business. To build a successful business, you must build some sort of buzz
with your PR and promotion. I'm not saying you have to take off your
clothes to promote yourself or your work, but the naked truth is that you
may have to go to extreme measures to get people to pay attention to you.

This is a weak area for many talented and creative people, yet what
separates the haves (creative people with deals, exposure on Oprah,
money, fame) and the have-nots (starving artists struggling to get by) is
simply attitude. Embrace the fact that you have to publicize yourself.
There are specific things you can do, many of which are free, to get the
word out, but you must take action. Even word-of-mouth promotion
requires some action on your part.

Most creatives are overly protective of their ideas. Sure, you should
take precautions to keep your ideas from being stolen, but if people are
going to come forward to help you, you must at least give them an
inkling of what you've got brewing. They may have the missing ingredi-
ent to make it a success. Although my literary lawyer will disagree, I find
that very few people possess the ability, resources, desire, or malice to
steal your ideas. On the flip side, there are a great many people who
know something, or someone, who can help further your idea and career.

Quiz
Do you work for yourself? Are you responsible for promoting your
creations?

(The answer is YES, no matter if you work for a corporation, have your own label or publisher, or are married to the gallery owner.)

Legendary literary agent Jan Miller (Stephen Covey, Tony Robbins, Susan Powter) says she looks for authors who are media-savvy, with an uncanny ability to promote themselves and their books, before she signs them.

Just Do It

Drop your pants here and you'll receive immediate attention.
—Sign in a dry cleaner's window

Why is it so hard to promote yourself? You might be able to do it for others, but when it comes to marketing your own talents, you freeze up. One of my favorite writers (and former Navy SEAL), Richard Marcinko, says, "Thou hast not to like it—thou hast just to do it."

Do you resent the fact that you have to do publicity? Could it be because you're not confident enough? It helps to have a clear, focused vision. Many people are afraid even to say what they want, let alone shout it out. It gets easier with practice, though, so practice saying who you are and what you want. Make a mock-up of *USA Today* with your photo prominently displayed on page one. Visualize yourself on *Oprah*. I do mock interviews all the time. Oprah, if you are reading this, I'm ready, baby.

If you believe in yourself and what you do, say so. Don't expect people to figure it out for themselves. To be brutally honest, people just aren't that smart. Tailor your self-promotion to your own personality and product, and it will be stronger and more memorable. Use your creative genius.

The best example of tailoring self-promotion to the product that I can think of involves rocker Ozzy Osborne. Sharon, his manager (and now his wife), set up a meeting with the executives of Epic Records to get them excited about Ozzy's comeback album with the label. She had him bring in live doves and was going to have each Epic exec release a dove to symbolize a new beginning. Sharon wanted to show them that Ozzy had turned over a new leaf—a nicer, gentler Ozzy Osborne.

As Ozzy was passing out the doves, he (for some inexplicable reason) decided to bite one of their heads off. People were puking. Ozzy stood there with blood running down his chin and a dumbfounded look, as if to say "What? Was that wrong?"

Anyway, the record was still made and the publicity surrounding the incident was priceless. After that, Epic put some serious effort into promoting the record.

Clever Concepts

I can fix anything your husband can—and I'll do it now!
                                                    —Ad for a handyman service

An advertising rule of thumb is that you should spend 3 to 5 percent of your gross income on promotion. Even if your business is successful, continual promotion will keep it successful, keep new customers coming in, and keep old customers aware of what you offer. Whether you work for yourself, in somebody else's office, or in a big corporation, the same idea holds true—you must invest in promoting yourself to be successful in the long term. As a creative person, you can invest more time and less money for the biggest payoffs of all.

The first step is to think outside the box, vow to be an original, and keep an open mind. The following are creative ways other people have promoted themselves:

Play on Words. From a job-seeker looking for work as an art director: "I'd like to be an art director at your agency, but I can only work half days—8:00 A.M. to 8:00 P.M. I can work weekends, too." From an illustrator looking for new clients: "You can hire me for free . . . lance." Here's one that maybe went too far: "Hire me because I am bi . . . lingual." Hmmmmm.

Use Humor. Christopher Conerly's promotion pieces read, "Hire an art director that really shines" with a picture of his bald head shining. Inside reads, "They said that to get anywhere in the advertising business, I'd have to use my head. So I did." Or how about this one for a hypnosis center? "If you doubt the effectiveness of hypnosis, consider that David Copperfield is dating Claudia Schiffer."

Do the Hustle. Harvey MacKay's *Swimming with the Sharks Without Being Eaten* sold over 2 million copies. To do it, he met with the sales staff at Ingram, the largest wholesale book distributor in the United States. He spoke at his publisher's annual sales meeting. He gave back part of his advance to help promote his twenty-six-city book tour. Pounding the pavement pays off.

Gimmicks. I once sent a sales pitch message inside a Magic 8-Ball. No matter how much you shook it, the answer always came up "Hire Lee!" I also made a snow globe and put my picture in it. It was supposed to be a reminder to a speakers' bureau that I prefer warm-weather climates for speaking engagements, but that idea backfired. They sent me to Alaska in January!

Family Feud. My family was lucky enough to be on the game show *Family Feud*—twice. (Nothing like embarrassing yourself in front of millions of viewers.) One of the questions posed was, "What could you purchase that would win you more friends?" I pounded the buzzer and blurted out "A rock band!" Ray Combs, the host at the time, stopped the show because he was laughing so hard. When he finally calmed down, he asked, "Are you sure you want to say that? Did you understand the question?" I assured him that I did. So he said, laughing, "Show me a rock band!" Bzzzzzzzz. It was horrific.

Well, it may not have been a popular idea, but it could work. A band called Sonic Joyride is giving away an opportunity to win them. They will play a gig in your front yard. Radio stations are helping to promote the contest. (Hint: great PR.) The band also tours the country in a custom bus complete with a sixteen-track recording studio and a two-hundred-watt sound system. They perform in stadium parking lots, for lunch breaks at factories, at tourist spots, anywhere. I love it! I have been redeemed.

(In case you were wondering, the correct answers to that fateful question were: a pool, a boat, a vacation home, a Jacuzzi, and a truck.) The real moral of the story is, get out and do something (and if *Family Feud* comes knocking, just say no!).

Target Practice. Kathy Ennesser, the manager of a Barnes & Noble in San Diego, tells a story about an unknown romance writer who wanted to do a signing. These signings usually don't draw a big turnout, so they brainstormed, trying to come up with a way to draw people to the event. Kathy asked the budding author what hobbies she had, and discovered she was also a psychic. They decided to offer a free five-minute psychic reading for people who bought the book. There was a line out the door. This promotion had all the elements for success—a sense of fun, a hook, and it was unusual and targeted to the audience.

How Am I Driving? A skatewear designer I know painted his car like a *Mod Squad* rerun. It looked like a bad acid trip, but it stood out. He drove it to all the hot spots in town and parked it in front of his shop next to the freeway. He used miniature toy cars painted like his "Magic Bus" with his phone number on them as giveaways. It worked, too! I had to borrow his car one day to run an errand, and the looks I got were precious.

Off the Wall. My first book, *The Guide to Dating in San Diego,* was sold in "adult" bookstores. These days, some bands are creating their own labels and selling them at such unusual places as skate shops, concerts, the beach, and in parks and clothing stores. Don't let yourself get locked into a single market.

Avoid Clichés. If I hear "We have the lowest prices, excellent service, and the best selection" one more time, I will gag! A women's clothing store, rather than saying "We are having a 15-percent-off sale," sent a bag with this printed on it: "Everything that you can fit in this bag is 15 percent off." Bravo! If you think there is nothing new under the sun, think again. I love the show on TNT called *Dinner and a Movie*. It's a new twist on the same old thing, reruns and leftovers. Find a new way to say the same old thing or tweak a cliché to give it a new meaning.

Cookie Crumbs. Debbie Fields, the founder of Mrs. Fields cookies, was twenty, just married, and made a mean cookie. She opened a store to sell her product. By noon of the first day, nobody had come in, so she filled a tray, went out on the sidewalk, and gave samples away. It's called the "puppy dog" approach. Once someone tries your product, they'll like it and want to keep it (or want more).

Make It an Event. Charlie Chaplin's father staged a contest for the best imitation of the real Chaplin. Contestants dressed like Chaplin and did a skit. Without identifying himself, the real Chaplin got up and did the routine. He came in third.

Turn That Frown Upside Down. One designer who was doing the ads for a pizza chain forgot to take out an ad in the Yellow Pages. Oops. That's a big deal. Missing the deadline means your ad won't be in there for an entire year. (I have pizza places on my speed dial, so I understand how this could be a big problem.) Desperate, she created an ad that read, "If you will bring in the Yellow Pages ad of any other pizza place, we'll give you half off your pizza." People began tearing out all the other pizza ads from their phone books to use as coupons. Within weeks, most phone books in town were bereft of pizza ads, and the designer had minimized her mistake.

As Albert Einstein said, "The world we have made as a result of the level of thinking we have done thus far creates problems we cannot solve at the same level of thinking at which we created them."

Emotional Appeal. A florist sent letters to customers about the beauty of relationships and the power of flowers. Around Valentine's Day, she sent a second letter warning that the relationship was in jeopardy. A few days later she sent a letter marked "Court Order." Inside it contained a small booklet called "A Couples' Guide to Divorce" and a note saying, "We hate to see your marriage end this way," with a P.S. noting that it wasn't too late to send flowers. Sales were never better.

Whatever It Takes. Aspiring screenwriter Mark DiBello flew from New York to Los Angeles a few days before the Oscars to find an agent and meet and mingle with the power people. Of course, he didn't get within five blocks of any Hollywood types at the Oscars, but he wore the name of his screenplay, *The Archangel,* in blue felt letters on a white T-shirt. It made the papers (and I am writing about it here).

How badly do you want to succeed? Are you as hungry as DiBello? I love it when someone is so passionate about something that they will fly three thousand miles to promote it. Get fired up!

Pizza! Pizza! An ad agency sends pizzas at lunchtime to potential clients. The outside of the box is a design tool, with the words "For a larger slice of your market, call us," along with the agency's name, phone number, and address. Inside, a single piece is missing. Making it more cost-effective, the agency traded with their printer for free boxes.

Be Outrageous. Nicholas Graham of Joe Boxer Corp. (the underwear people) hung from a crane a hundred feet above Times Square and threw bagels with silk boxers as parachutes at the crowd to gain attention for his company's web site. Author and self-publishing guru Dan Poynter occasionally parachutes into his seminars.

Laugh and the World Laughs with You. Nerds rule! Geek Squad, a computer repair and consulting company founded by Robert Stephens, has "special agents" (employees) wearing black suits and skinny ties, white socks, and black shoes, wielding Geek Squad badges. They arrive in old ice cream trucks and vintage cars with the Geek Squad logo. Humor doesn't cost anything, Stephens says. But he makes a point of returning calls in under ten minutes. Back up a clever gimmick with good service, and you're on your way.

Animals and Babies. You have about three seconds to grab someone's attention with your marketing materials. You can have an extra seven seconds if you use a child or an animal. I know a guy who took his faithful four-legged companion "Rocky" surfing. To promote himself, he had a photographer take pictures of the now world-famous "surf dog" boogie-boarding, windsurfing, and surfing. He made the photos into postcards and used them to promote himself and his business. The postcards themselves became popular, and the press coverage "Rocky" got for his owner was endless (and priceless).

Walk Tall and Carry a Big Schtick. Or a chain saw. A sculptor was unable to generate any interest in his work, so he started doing wood-carving with a chain saw. He was featured on the news and profiled in several papers.

Wake Up and Smell the Coffee. A publisher of several athlete-oriented magazines was putting together a big shindig for advertisers and prospective advertisers at the Ironman Triathlon in Kona, Hawaii. The invitations went out printed on bags of Kona coffee.

Become a Brand

One of the greatest self-promoters of all-time was Muhammad Ali. How did Ali get to be "The Greatest"? Sure, he was an amazing athlete. But it was more than that. He became famous, a brand unto himself. Here's how:

His phraseology was memorable. "Float like a butterfly, sting like a bee" and "rope-a-dope" are vivid reflections of his style, not to mention his boast, "I am the greatest."

He was a rebel. Ali went against the flow. He stood out, took a stand, and did not compromise his values in a sport that had a bad reputation. He appealed to people who had never trusted or cared about boxing before.

He was outrageous. He was bold. He didn't give stock answers to questions.

He was confident. One day, Ali was flying to a fight. The flight attendant saw that he hadn't buckled his seat belt. She told him he would have to buckle up. Ali replied confidently, "Superman don't need a seat belt." The flight attendant smartly returned, "Yeah, well, Superman doesn't need a plane, either." You can't overestimate his confidence. He was able to promote himself shamelessly. It isn't easy to say "I am the best."

Do you have confidence? A logo? A tag line? A color scheme? Why not?

Self-Promotion 101 (The Basics)

I didn't think anyone besides myself really knew how to promote me in the first place, so I decided to make a connection with the people who enjoy my music.

—*Jimmy Buffett*

To focus your self-promotion ideas, answer the following questions:

Who is my audience?
Dilbert: "What are you writing?"
Dogbert: "A new self-help book for compulsive shoppers."
Dilbert: "What do you know about compulsive shoppers?"
Dogbert: "I know they buy a lot of books."

How much should I spend? Ten to 15 percent of your time, and 3 to 5 percent of your gross revenue (or more; more time, less money). Create things people will keep, like a newsletter, bookmarks, booklets, T-shirts, calendars, anything useful that they will hang on to for months to come, and won't cost an arm and a leg.

Where do I start? If I were looking to hire me and I was new to town, where would I look first? How would I find me?

Should I have a mailing list? Create what Ken Blanchard termed "raving fans." Start a fan club. Begin with your friends and families, business contacts, media contacts. Exchange lists with others. Look at how the Deadheads support the Grateful Dead. They have become "evangelized," as Guy Kawasaki would say.

Be seen and heard. Is my field different in terms of promotional possibilities? A friend of mine got a record deal. How? He committed to being a musician, got a good manager, worked on the gatekeepers, performed everywhere he could, got some visibility, became an opening act for established artists. Hone your act and be ready to perform live—it's a good program for any creative field.

What sets me apart? Spend some time thinking about this. You have to understand clearly where you fit in the marketplace before you can answer. Armed with that information, you can give yourself a unique selling position. Sum it up in one sentence. Memorize it and be ready to tell everyone and anyone who will listen.

This statement is called a "unique selling position"; for example, from *Star Trek,* "to boldly go where no one has gone before." Your own statement should both reflect and guide your marketing plan and positioning. A small video store realizes it can't compete with Blockbuster, so it stocks hard-to-find movie classics.

Why should anyone use my services/buy my product? Don't be diffident or shy. Arm yourself with benefits. (Hints: people buy to make money, save money, save time, be popular, have something beautiful, be in style, gain praise, get laid.)

Do I need a publisher? A label? An agent? What do Mark Twain, George Bernard Shaw, and Edgar Allan Poe have in common (besides being dead)? Each started out as a self-published author. (So did Ben Franklin, M. Scott Peck, and *What Color Is Your Parachute?* author Richard Bolles.) Writing and publishing a book, a newsletter, an article, or a song is a great way to make money and gain exposure.

What can I do differently? Take an idea that has worked for someone else and add a twist that personalizes it for your own needs.

Why should they like/want me? Get involved with people, interact, make personal contact. You can make lifetime customers out of casual contacts by being interested in their ideas, their projects. A successful book editor I know has a knack for making an author's project her own. Her authors feel that she understands and cares as much about their books as they do—and they're right. Consequently, people who have worked with her recommend her highly and come back to her themselves, over and over.

How can I get them to buy more? Expand on your original success. Teach your clients new uses for your products and services. It's much easier to build customers into better customers or make them repeat customers than to keep finding new ones.

What should I focus on? Divergent thinkers and multitalented creatives have to learn to focus. When you focus on what you do best and who wants, needs, and will pay for it, everything gets easier.

You may be able to do everything, but nobody can do everything *best*. Maybe you should market your flexibility. Your creative scope. Find a way to fit your talents into a small bag. One way to do this is to devise a strategy connected to your mission (objective). Make it active, intense, filled with practical ways to get things done. Keep it visual, flexible, colorful, brief. Sample:

> *Mission:* Keep Carmel Valley clean.
> *Objectives:* Clean up beach, roads, shopping areas.
> *Strategies:* Get help! Set good example, talk at schools, put together fund-raisers, get publicity, start a group, find a corporate sponsor, talk to councilmen, make and sell T-shirts.

If you feel stifled by this admittedly left-brain approach, branch out. Just try to be sure your branches attach directly to the main goal (in this case, speaking, writing, radio, Web, club, newsletter, etc.).

How can I be in three places at once? Open a store or gallery. Frank Zappa made a catalog called Barking Pumpkin, which grosses a million dollars a year, for more exposure. It has the added benefit of residual income. Royalties rule!

Will trade shows help me? Be a showman! Demonstrate. Be interactive. Collect business cards everywhere and follow up with a note, a phone call, or E-mail.

How will people remember me? When you have a hook or an angle, it is easier for people to remember you. Johnny Cash dresses all in black. Drew Carey's crew cut and glasses are his trademark. Alfred Hitchcock and Jay Leno have the most famous profiles in show business. A middling mountain biker named Missy Giove got a lot of press because she always wore a dead piranha around her neck. Best-selling author Leo Buscaglia became known as "Dr. Hug" for ending his seminars by hugging all members of the audience. Tony Robbins got his start with the firewalk. Zig Ziglar carried around a handheld pump.

Steve Martin started his stand-up career like many comics in the early 1970s, dressed like a flower child with a beard, long hair, and squash-blossom necklaces. After two years with little success, he shaved his beard and donned a white three-piece suit and a new persona—the dim-witted, arrogant guy we all know—and quickly became famous. Separate yourself from the crowd—it pays to be different!

How can I keep the ball rolling? Build on the attention you already get. People will think something's good if somebody else thinks so. Act as if people should know you. Become known as an expert in your field. Hit them from different directions. Be innovative. Concentrate your efforts into a short period of time for maximum impact. Do TV interviews, host Web chat rooms, get endorsements, teach a class, speak in front of any group you can find, contribute your services to charity, write articles and send them to every publication you can think of, put on performances—do it all. Take an ad out. DO NOT rest on your laurels. Leave your mark.

How do I sell? Be your own customer. What would excite *your* interest? Mail things to potential clients—free trial, free information, free sample, free gift. Create a club or a contest. Give them content. Guitar Center sent out a brochure titled "How to Buy a Guitar" that provided several useful and timely tips. Stress benefits. Back up benefits with facts and features. Be believable. Overcome possible objections—remove the risk with a guarantee. (One speaker offered money back if he didn't get a standing ovation.) Ask for the order and make it easy to respond.

Should I rethink my name/logo/package? Repackaging helped Harriet Schechter sell her book. It was billed as an organizing guide for busy couples. Years went by with no takers. She changed the title to *More Time for Sex* and it sold to a publisher almost immediately.

If you're image-impaired, do some brainstorming. Start with words that roll off the tongue, will stick in people's minds, and that convey a clear idea of what you do. One- and two-syllable company names work best.

How can I overcome negative stereotypes? Diversity can work to your advantage. Race (unique perspective), sex (woman to woman), age (how to reach a younger market), parent (help company understand kids), geography (know the media and market), nationality/language (*No quieres Taco Bell?*). Take any negative you perceive that you have, and spin it into a positive.

ASK A PRO: BRANDMASTER ORVILLE REDENBACHER

Before the Popcorn King passed away, I was lucky enough to get to know him personally and interview him several times. (Orville lived near me and even asked if I wanted to work on his autobiography.) As he liked to say, there may not be a grocer named George Whipple or a baker named Betty Crocker, but Orville Redenbacher is the genuine article. He even listed his home phone and would answer the phone to curious callers who wanted to see if he really existed. He was the master marketer and spokesperson extraordinaire. Here are some of his thoughts on branding:

Your face is recognized by millions and your name is a household word. How did it begin?

I needed a name for my popcorn company, so I went to a Chicago ad agency. They talked with me, they interviewed people, they hired copywriters, they did research, and they came back with the name they thought best—Orville Redenbacher. What do you know about that! The same name my mother gave me over eighty years ago. Yet I paid $13,000 to the ad agency for that name!

Not only is your name memorable, but so is your look. The horn-rimmed glasses, bow tie, and white hair parted down the middle. What image are you trying to project?

Integrity. Someone you can trust. A brand you can trust. That's why my picture is on every box. I stand behind every bag of my popcorn.

Do you mind being recognized and stopped wherever you go?

It would bother me if they didn't! In a recent survey, it was discovered that over 75 percent of the country recognized my face or my name. Besides, popcorn is fun. You never see anyone in a bad mood eating popcorn.

The Tools of Self-Promotion

Web people don't care about your dumb design.

—*John Schmitz*

If I have a pet peeve when it comes to design, it is this: I don't care how much equipment you have, how well you know your software, how many colors of ink your design is. If it stinks—it stinks. I meet many people who understand their equipment but don't understand design. To make things even more complicated, what makes good design changes depending on the product.

A Web page has specific needs relating to the time it takes for a computer to draw it, clarity on the average computer screen, and downloadability (among other things). A printed piece—brochure or direct mail—is limited by budget and printing requirements, and the fact that it must grab attention fast or be tossed. A video should be short, crisply shot, with good sound and a direct message. A business card should express personality, yet be completely readable and provide the necessary information. Get my drift? The first question to ask is, "How/when/where will this be used?" All right, that's three questions. So sue me.

Other things to think about when putting together your promotional piece:

Borrow from the best. Steal ideas from other designs you like.

It's only junk mail when you receive it. When you create it, it's *direct* mail.

Give them a reason to retain your piece. Incentive items can be a coupon, an 800 number to call for information, a special offer. Or the piece itself can be an incentive item, such as a calendar.

Triple-check for typos and grammatical errors. Here is a classic blunder from a maid service: "Tired of cleaning yourself? Let me do it." How do you catch this kind of booboo? Read it aloud, then let someone else read it. (Believe me, people *love* to find mistakes in your work and then laugh at you. Let them do it *before* you go to print.) Find a left-brainer friend to proof your piece, or hire a professional.

Make it appetizing. When you can't finish your food at a restaurant, they put it in a doggie bag. Yuk. It does not look appetizing the next day. That's how people look at your proposals. Jazz up the cover to make it more appealing.

Make it different. If you have a stack of proposals and all of them are letter-size, and then some wiseass sends you a smaller proposal, would you put it on the top or bottom of the pile? Right! The top. I'll take those odds over being buried on the bottom.

Don't assume you know your audience. Ask questions, get feedback, get to know them intimately before you send out your promotional piece. You might send fewer pieces, but they'll be more effective.

Go visit your audience. Where will they be when they receive your piece? I went to a bookstore buyer's office and saw how much clutter there was. No wonder we didn't get any response to our flyer! I created a binder to put on the shelf, and three-hole-punched my flyers. I sent them with a reminder to "put this in your binder."

Facts tell, but stories sell. Turn your dry description into a story and people will read it and remember it. Be conversational. Be personal. Be real.

Cut it down and break it up. People tend to scan rather than read. Make your pieces skimmer friendly. Use bullets, sidebars, pull quotes, cartoons, and illustrations. Vary the font, type size, and boldness for emphasis.

Keep it simple. One main point per piece and a focal point (one large image) are far more effective than two or three or ten or twelve. Many advertisers think they need to tell their whole story in an ad. Think again. Most of the time, all you need to do is to entice the reader to call you. Then you can talk to them, interact with them—sell them—in a way no promotional piece can.

Save money at the printer's. Use a dark ink and screen it at different percentages for a variety of tones with a single spot color cost.

If you are doing a four-color piece, print a large quantity of just the color. Then you can have the body of the piece overprinted in black, changing your message as often as you like for the price of a quick print job or a run through your own laser printer. It's called "making a shell," and it's far cheaper than having a four-color piece printed every time you need one. Many companies use shells for their business cards, making it possible to print cards for new employees quickly and cheaply.

Buy your own paper at a wholesale house and supply it to the printer. This won't actually save you much money, but it will guarantee that you get the paper you want.

Tell your printer you'll put their name on your piece if they'll give you a discount.

Men love blue, women love purple. Red is the best attention-grabbing color. It's very difficult to get an effective printed green. Black ink on yellow paper offers the best contrast, but black ink on off-white or cream paper is easiest to read. Gray ink (or black screened back to 70 percent or so) gives a sophisticated feel. Whole books have been written about the science of color. Invest in one, trust your instincts, look for printed examples that you like, or ask someone with experience in printing. To be honest, it's better to trust your instincts *after* you've developed those instincts and backed them up with a bit of knowledge (via the other techniques mentioned).

ASK A PRO: CHUCK GREEN

Chuck Green is a Virginia-based graphic artist and the author of *The Desktop Publisher's Idea Book.*

What are the keys to self-promotion for the creative person?
There are ways of doing things, formulas developed over

time that work for the masses. When people are looking for work, for example, they send a résumé. When a freelancer is promoting their talents, they show a portfolio. When an entrepreneur is starting a business, they design a three-panel, two-fold brochure that fits a number-10 envelope.

Sounds boring to me.

Exactly. Formula thinking is b-o-r-i-n-g. Memorable self-promotion happens outside the box. Before you resort to doing what everyone else is doing, ask yourself three questions: What is the purpose of your promotion? Why is it typically done the way it's done? How can I do it more effectively?

What is the biggest mistake people make when they create marketing materials for themselves?

Don't make the mistake of focusing on yourself. Folks who don't know you start out wondering what you can do for them—not how they can help you out. It isn't selfish—it's natural. Forget all the self-aggrandizing stuff and focus on filling a need. No matter what you're marketing, talk about the benefits, not the features.

Business Cards

One of my favorite TV shows is *Law & Order.* Sometimes when Briscoe or Logan is trying to get a snitch to talk, Lenny will pull out his business card and scribble something on the back. He calls it his "get out of jail free card." Whenever he hands one to a perp or a snitch, they cradle it like a wad of twenties. I always thought it would be great if someone would do that with my business card. So when I owned a chain of surf shops I had some waterproof business cards printed, and I always kept one in my wet suit. Things like that make a business card so much more than just a piece of cardboard.

Don't cheap out with ink-jet cards. Prefab, perforated cards that are thin enough to go through your printer are too thin to make a good impression. You deserve better. Invest in yourself.

Paper can make more of an impression than color. Go for matte or thick, rag or speckled or textured. High-quality paper feels rich, and gives the impression of wealth, power, sophistication.

Use the back side of your card for something interesting. A travel agent puts the 800 numbers for the airlines on the back of his card, making it handy to keep around. I keep it in my wallet because it is useful.

You could put keystroke shortcuts for a software program. A freelance editor puts all those squiggly little symbols and their meanings on the back of her card. You could include links to related web sites or a list of your books, credits, or awards. My latest card has a quiz on the back to see if you are in your "right" mind.

Photos

Use photos in your promotional materials. Why? Because they work. Studies have shown that people will look at pictures, particularly of faces, then children, then animals. Even if you don't photograph well (heck, we all think we're ugly in pictures), you can use pictures of yourself as a baby or child, pictures of yourself with someone ugly (so you look better by comparison) or beautiful (hoping they'll think that's you). Use humor to cover up any lack of movie-star quality—draw a mustache on your face, or stick an arrow through your head. I have personally used all these techniques. I have a brochure showing me in the water with a blow-up shark, a newsletter with pictures of me with celebrities, a book cover showing me with an arrow through my head, and my web site shows my baby picture (it's funny, I am starting to look more and more like my infant self, balding and drooling).

I even went underwater in a suit and tie. My wife was supposed to be off to the side with an air tank while the photographer took my picture. I would take a breath, swim to the spot set up for the shot, then swim back to my tank for more air. I nearly drowned when my wife wandered off with my tank, as I was thirty feet underwater off the coast of Maui. The point here is that these unusual photos captured my personality and helped me to stand out.

If you are a speaker, teacher, or lecturer, or if you write articles or columns for publication, include a photo with your bio. Be sure to put your contact info on the back, along with a photo credit.

If you come up with a great or unusual or funny photo, send it to the media. Write a caption and put it on the back, along with your contact information. This kind of thing is often used as filler, and the free publicity can't hurt.

The Web

When freelance computer graphics designer Jennifer Ringley set up a camera attached to her computer in her college dorm room and began "exposing" herself on the Web with real-time images of herself "doing stuff" in the "privacy" of her own bedroom, JenniCam was born. Soon it developed a cult following that made it one of the Internet's Top Ten sites, viewed by millions.

You don't have to get naked to have a successful web site. You do need to have a reason for being there. Yes, the Web is the place to be. Yes, you'll reach more people on the Internet than you can possibly reach any other way. That doesn't necessarily mean the Web is for you.

Think about it. What can you offer? Content is king. People want to stay informed and learn new stuff. Tell them something they don't know. Keep it fresh. You can add success stories (your own or others'), interviews, excerpts or samples of your work, free advice, special offers, contests, links to other cool sites, quotes, illustrations, tips. Stand-up comic Gallagher's site has goofy pictures (downloadable), jokes, a funny map showing where he'll be playing, with all the details, a chat room, a game, and more.

Whatever you put on your web site, it should be fast, easy to navigate, and interactive. Ideally, it will match your marketing materials. Even if you have someone else put up your site for you, you've got to pay attention and work at updating and upgrading all the time. You need to be ready with a quick response to any requests for information or special offers. The more successful your site is, the more work it will be for you, so make sure you're getting something out of this—referrals, sales, or contacts.

Faxes

People treat faxes with a sense of urgency that you don't get from mail. Just make sure they can read your fax when they get it. Don't use screens or photos—stick to line art and fax-worthy typefaces (Clearface was invented to be faxable). And make sure you use wide margins. Many fax machines will only print out seven to seven-and-a-half-inches wide, so your margins on letter-size paper should be a full three-quarters of an inch on both sides.

That doesn't mean it has to be dry and businesslike. My favorite fax cover sheet says, in huge letters at the top, "Just the Fax, Ma'am."

If you use the fax a lot, get a separate telephone line and number for it. Then you can have a twenty-four-hour fax line, which should always be listed next to your telephone number. This is a benefit to yourself as well as your customers; your phone won't be tied up, you won't have to manually switch over, and you won't get that screech in your ear.

Fax your newsletter and save postage. (Better yet, E-mail it and save on your phone bill.) Use polling to make sure your fax gets where you sent it. Put your own number on the cover sheet with a request that the recipient call immediately if they have any problems with the fax. Finding out right away that a foundation didn't get page three of your grant request is far better than simply not getting the grant and wondering why.

If you want to weed out your faxees, give them a way off your list ("If you want to be removed from this list, check this box and fax back").

Sales Letters

Make the first sentence pop, and put a key wrap-up in the P.S. Refer to any previous conversation with the person, building on any connection you've already made. Then get to the point. If you're trying to sell something, don't be afraid to say so. Be specific, be direct. Use large margins with lots of white space. This makes it readable, forces you to write less (less is more), and also makes the end result faxable.

> Dear Mr. Slick,
>
> I enjoyed discussing my ideas for Elvis print ties with you last Thursday at your office. I've done more research on prices, and I believe I can prepare three designs for silkscreening by March 1 at a cost of $300 each. My research also suggests that the market will support a retail price of $29.95 per tie, making it a potential bonanza for your company.
>
> As you know, Elvis's sixtieth birthday will be celebrated next year, and I believe these ties will make a real splash in the memorabilia market.
>
> I'd be happy to discuss this project further with you at your earliest convenience.
>
> Thank you very much,
> Joe Schmoe
> P.S. Time is of the essence if we're to have these ties ready for the nostalgia buffs commemorating Elvis's birthday.

You don't have to reinvent the wheel. If you have one successful letter, you've got a hundred. Use mail-merge software to customize them to individual recipients.

Brochures

A brochure is like a salesperson for you when you can't be there. It doesn't need a commission and it never complains about travel. Use it as an extended advertisement. Use it to respond to requests for information from prospective clients. Keep it lively, with photographs or illustrations, odd sizes or folds, and minimal, skimmable copy. Keep it professional, with details of your work, credentials, and clients.

Keep your brochures handy, and make sure everyone you know has several so they can pass them out whenever they detect even the faintest glimmer of interest.

There are ways to personalize a brochure. Send a cover letter with it. Mark key points with a highlighter, or make notes in the margins geared toward a particular client.

I know a cartoonist who has his portfolio on a Zip disk, with a clever cover. He uses low-resolution images to make sure people don't simply use the art without paying him. An artist who does book covers did a four-color flyer shaped like a book cover, showing examples of her best work, cleverly making her contact information into a title. The jury's still out on which method is most cost-effective, but each artist used a form of brochure that best reflected the type of work they did.

Some creatives may even spring for a video brochure, although this is expensive and most applicable in the performing or film arts. Animators frequently send out samples of their work in two-minute clips. Copyright laws must be carefully observed here, to avoid getting your ideas or your work stolen.

Tag Lines

When someone says, "So, what do you do?" you should be ready with a clever and concise response. Write it out. Say it over and over until you develop a smooth delivery. "Hi, I'm a freelance artist currently specializing in web site designs. My company is called Rover, named after my dog. Believe it or not, *my* name is Spanky."

Quiz: Memorable Tag Lines

Name the company that goes with the tag line:

1. Quality Is Job One.	a. Yellow Pages
2. We Love to Fly, and It Shows.	b. Avis Rent-a-Car
3. Let Your Fingers Do the Walking.	c. Ford
4. Reach Out and Touch Someone.	d. AT&T
5. Good to the Last Drop.	e. Delta
6. The Quicker-Picker-Upper.	f. CBS
7. We Try Harder.	g. Bounty
8. Welcome Home.	h. Maxwell House

Try to create a simple tag line for yourself.

Answers: 1.(c); 2.(e); 3.(a); 4.(d); 5.(h); 6.(g); 7.(b); 8.(f)

Postcards

Postcards are a cheap and easy way to get your message out. The largest size the post office recognizes as a postcard is four and one-quarter inches by six inches. That's big enough for the cover of your latest book with contact information on the back, an invitation, a coupon, or a friendly reminder. If you're willing to spring for a first-class stamp, you can go even larger, putting your newsletter on it, or your book cover with an entire bio on the back, or your latest publicity still in a size big enough to put up on the wall.

In general, a letter or postcard with a handwritten address will be tossed less frequently and less speedily than one with a printed label.

Direct Mail

When you send a promotional piece through the mail, you have the reader's attention for about three seconds. 1-2-3, gone. Extend that time by using a cool envelope with a teaser on the outside. I saw one that said, "Find out how French men last longer . . ." I opened up the one that said "Everything you need to organize your desk and your office is inside this envelope."

The other horrifying statistic about direct mail is that a 2-percent response is *excellent*. Don't blow your budget on one mailing. Break it into smaller components, two to three times a year. Try to aim your pieces at the people who will be most interested in you or your product. You can buy mailing lists from companies that break them down into detailed markets—"Women under thirty in the greater Chicago area who read *Cosmopolitan* and buy from the Victoria's Secret catalog at least twice a year."

Surveys

I keep saying you have to know your audience. How are you supposed to do that? You can hire an agency to run surveys and focus groups. Or you can do it yourself. One guy sent a box of crayons and construction paper to former clients, asking for feedback. People could draw their answers. He got some excellent insights, and his former clients got a reminder of how clever and creative he was.

If you do a survey, make it easy to fill out and easy to send in. Provide a stamped, self-addressed envelope. Try sending your surveys via E-mail or fax. The people at 3M ask people to write in uses they have found for Post-it Notes. You can't make this stuff up.

Classified Ads

I've sold a ton of books through the classified ads. I've even read a book about finding love through the classified ads (without dialing a 900 number). So don't just assume you can't sell your product or service in the back pages of the newspaper.

Newsletters

I've mentioned newsletters several times already—faxing them, putting them on postcards, putting one on your web site. So you already know it's a self-promotion tool with many applications. But spending the time and energy to put together a newsletter has benefits in itself. It gives you a reason to contact and interview leaders in your field. It gives you a way to connect with your clients and fans, building lasting, personal relationships. It lets you reward and acknowledge those who have helped you. It can add to your image as knowledgeable in your field by providing useful information. It updates your clients and fans to changing business information—hours, products, prices, etc. It increases your exposure in a format that might be shared, or referred to by the media.

You can use a newsletter to sell stuff, but most newsletters don't sell, they serve and inform. If you do sell products through your newsletter, make sure it's a soft sell. Offer, don't push.

The trend these days is to keep newsletters short, one letter-size page, two-sided, or at most a tabloid-size page folded in quarters. Keep type clear and relatively large and easy to read. Use photos of yourself, your employees, your products. Make a connection.

Clever Promo Pieces

A promotional piece can take almost any form, as long as it's functional, memorable and (preferably) not offensive. A female graphic artist sent cheap wallets to prospective clients with art inside like photos and credit cards in the plastic sleeves. The recipient had to search through it for clues about who sent it.

Here are some promo ideas that you can tailor to most creative fields:

- Create your own award. Give it away or maybe even display it in your office.
- Create a mini-booklet that teaches people how to use your services better. I made one the size and shape of a CD box.
- Create things-to-do pads. I send out a whole-brain planner pad.

- Create a tent. I sent an invitation to a Warwick's book signing in the form of a tent on card stock. I knew that if I sent a regular invitation it would be lost in some pile. It said, "This invitation was designed to be a visual reminder. Put it where you'll see it. Hey, I'm not a nag, I'm a motivator."
- Do a survey or send a quiz. I made a right-brain/left-brain quiz. I have one that lets you color in the brain based on your score, so you have a visual reminder of your dominant brain.
- Have your logo imprinted on T-shirts, key rings, pens, mugs, hats— or anything useful you can think of.
- Door hangers can be used to carry all sorts of information.
- Post-it Notes can be imprinted with your contact information and passed out.
- Rolodex cards can be imprinted with your name, logo, and contact information. I received one from a local congressman, who managed to imply that I was a very special person and he wanted his number at my fingertips so I could call day or night with my important observations. Ha! Image is everything.
- Buttons can be made up very cheaply. It gets more expensive when you have to bribe people to wear them.
- Signs, temporary or permanent, can be very effective. You do have to be careful about city, county, and state ordinances regarding where and to what you can affix your sign.
- Make a dump (a display for your products).
- Create a recipe book. People love recipes, and they keep recipe books around even if they don't use them.
- Create stickers. I made one for my friend's motorcycle repair shop, with his phone number on them, and we stuck them on the bikes he worked on. He got a ton of repeat business.
- Calendars are always handy, up on the wall with your name and number prominently displayed for all to see. Unfortunately, the competition in this category is fierce. Be willing to spend some money, show some skin, or find a goofy hook.
- Make personalized playing cards or baseball cards. I made a baseball card résumé once.
- Create a booklet style portfolio.
- Create a faux book dust jacket.
- Make a binder or folder with your logo prominently displayed.
- Create thank-you cards custom-designed with your art.
- Magnets are very popular these days (except around computers).

- Make your own distinctive "Hello, My Name Is . . ." badge for those hellish times when you can't get out of wearing a name tag.

Self-Promotion on a Shoestring

Necessity is the mother of invention, it is true—but its father is creativity, and knowledge is the midwife.

—*Jonathan Schattke*

I have found that having no money makes me more aggressive and creative when it comes to self-promotion. In fact, some of my best and most successful self-promotion pieces were done on a very limited budget.

Never let a lack of funds be an excuse to stop you from doing creative self-promotion. In this brains-versus-bucks approach, brains win, as long as you have a clear understanding of yourself and what kind of work you do. Money is *not* the answer. Use what the other guys don't have—creativity, time, well-thought-out strategies. Be thought-provoking, original, humorous, personal.

Be a "rogue warrior" when it comes to promotion. Be resourceful, living off the land (use any scraps left over from the printer, create rubber stamps, ink-jet computer printouts). Be fast on your feet, ready to take advantage of sudden opportunities. Do the grunt work yourself to save money (I'll stuff my own envelopes, glue things on by hand, whatever it takes). If you can't get your foot in the front door, try a window, the chimney, the back door.

What can you do right now to promote your talents? Think before you spend. Is there a better way? A cheaper way? Here are some free, almost free, and affordable ideas to help you get the word out. (Some even pay you back!)

- FREE. Tell everyone what you do. Befriend the person who serves you your latte—she could be the daughter of a studio executive.
- ALMOST FREE. Barter your services with printers, other creatives, accountants, and sales reps. Pool your resources. Team up with complementary services and put together a package. Co-op(erate) and save.
- AFFORDABLE. Buy remnant space in magazines. Last-minute leftovers are cheaper, but you need to have your ad materials ready to go.
- FREE. Blow people away. Wow them with your ideas, carry your prototypes around with you, modestly show pictures of your work when everyone else is showing baby pictures.

- FREE. Have a unique personal greeting. While watching *The Dating Game,* it struck me that the guy who got the girl was always the one with the best opening line—unique, clever, and confident, yet sincere.
- FREE. Who said there is no free lunch? Rotary and other service clubs will feed you in return for a short talk on your area of expertise. Seminars are a great way to generate leads. Speak at trade shows, conferences, bookstores, extension classes. Be a panelist. Trade for cool stuff like a trip to Maui for the Wailea Maui Writers' Conference (Barbara Santos, I'm available!!!!).
- FREE. Turn your passion into a cause. Evangelize it. Make people feel a part of your team. They will spread the word.
- AFFORDABLE. Posters or flyers are your weapon. Remember the Staples commercial where the secretary wanted her boss to buy a new copier that Staples had on sale? She put little flyers inside the elevator, in his coffee cup, plastering pictures of the copier all over the office. Put flyers where they will be seen, in high-traffic or high-attention places. I have put them in bathroom stalls and over urinals, where I know they'll get undivided attention.
- FREE. Get celebrity endorsements. Just ask. If they say no, ask somebody else.
- ALMOST FREE. Seek feedback with contests and questionnaires. Surveys also communicate the fact that you're there, and you're interested in what they have to say.
- FREE. Make words work for you. A school in Virginia couldn't get kids signed up for a course called "Home Economics for Boys," so they put themselves in the shoes of the students and changed the name of the class to "Bachelor Living." Ta-da. It worked.
- AFFORDABLE. Be willing to use the recording studio during off hours, have your stuff printed during the first week of the month (not the last), hire a hall during January or August. When you're buying during the slow time, you can negotiate for a better price.
- FREE. Do pro bono work, and make sure your name is on promotional pieces and press releases for the charity. Let them announce you at their meetings and events. Perform at a charity event. Donate a piece for an auction, or books to the library. Offer free seminars or consultations. Get your name associated with positive things. The caveat here is to use this as an introduction to your services. Don't spend all your time working for free, or you'll starve to death.
- FREE. Follow up. When somebody calls, make sure you get back to them right away, even if it's to say you can't help them. If you say

you'll do something, get it done. More than anything else, this kind of service will make you stand out.

- AFFORDABLE. Sponsor a cause or a team, and make sure your name is displayed on uniforms and promotional materials. A local realtor runs a two-page ad—one page with his real-estate offerings, one page spotlighting a community group or feature that makes the area a good place to live. The second page has a simple line at the bottom, "Presented by Ken Pecus." He becomes known as a community supporter, readers get an added incentive to buy in the area and he gets more clients. Win/win/win.

- FREE. Tell two friends . . . Word of mouth is the ultimate way to expand your business and grow your career. Spread the word, and get others to spread the word. If you do a great job for a client, there is nothing wrong with asking for a referral. It sure beats having to cold-call. Offer a kickback to prime the pump. Give clients materials to help them promote you—a stack of cards, flyers, samples. Put on your invoice, "Tell a friend."

- AFFORDABLE. Willy Wonka was no idiot. By putting a winning gold ticket in five candy bars, he gave the kids an extra incentive to buy chocolate, lots of it. Do a contest or giveaway.

- FREE. Referrals are a two-way street. Network with other creatives, and be free with your overflow work. Be a good neighbor. Share leads.

- FREE. Give testimonials for others to get your name out. Just be sure you know what (and whom) you're talking about.

- AFFORDABLE. Sell T-shirts and other items sporting your art/name. When I was in Tahiti, I saw one of my shirts. I danced around, shouted, pointed, and said, "I did that!" The person thought I was a freak, but that's beside the point.

- FREE. Offer demonstrations. A carpenter talked concierges at local hotels into putting his woodworking shop on their maps, offering tours and demonstrations. He did small carvings on the spot—a *huge* hit, and loads of PR.

- ALMOST FREE. Offer coupons. An illustrator offered coupons for free caricatures of you and your staff. He put his name and number on each one—a constant reminder that this guy is not only cool, he's *good*.

- FREE. To bring in traffic, office supply stores often post work offers for temps. A coffee shop offers free space to a local theater group to rehearse. People come to watch the live practice, interest in the play is generated, and lots of coffee is consumed. A hair salon plays a video made by a local band and gets a reputation as having up-to-the-minute style. Find somebody who can benefit from your product or service, and work with them.

- FREE. Enter bulletin boards and chat rooms on the Internet, and talk up your product.
- FREE. Offer free online consulting.
- ALMOST FREE. Get celebrities to use your stuff. Maybe Cher will be hawking your stuff on TV someday.
- FREE. Be real, warm and fuzzy. A landscaper I know tells a moving personal story in his brochures. As a young boy, he put his pet turtle in a pond, thinking it would make the turtle happy. It died from the stagnant water. Crushed, he needed to find out why his turtle had died. So he got interested in pumps and water and ponds. Today he runs a successful pond business.
- FREE. Hang your work in a coffeehouse, dentist's office, a bank.
- AFFORDABLE. Let people see your work. Have it up in your home. Have an open house at your studio. Throw a party. An artist used an empty storefront to display his work. A surfboard shaper rented floor space from a surf shop and allowed people to watch him work. I used to love watching the DJ for KPOI through the window in Lahaina. The DJ in the TV series *Northern Exposure* worked with a window on the street, where he could see, be seen, and interact with people passing by. You might feel like you're in a zoo, but you might just get some creative buzz from being out front.
- FREE. Make your answering machine message a sales tool. A yoga instructor might use motivational messages, a speaker might give out upcoming class dates, an author can give new book info. (I say, "I'm working on my new book, *Career Management for the Creative Person,* right now, so I might not get back to you until September.")

Quickie Quiz
Which of these are "shoestring" marketing methods?

Post articles
Invoice as a promotional tool
Attire
Speed
Service
Follow-up

Follow-through
Publicity
Seminars
Canaries
Testimonials
Barter
Word of mouth

Publicity (Snagging Your Fifteen Minutes of Fame)

We now sadly live in a country in which publicity has triumphed over culture.

—*Yale Udoff*

I knew from other "mid-list" (i.e., not on the *New York Times* best-seller list but still successful) authors that the fantasy and the reality of being published are two entirely different things. If you expect your publisher to support you with unlimited publicity, you are either extremely naïve or delusional. (I was neither.) I understood that my publisher wasn't going to take out a full-page ad for my book in *USA Today* (I did make it into the *San Diego Union Tribune*), that I would not be sent on a whirlwind twenty-five-city book tour (I made my own), that bookstores wouldn't be making endcaps around my new book (just getting the books in stores was a challenge), and that my chances of appearing on *Oprah* were slim to none—so I got busy. I had a publicist assigned to me by my publisher, but I made it my own business to find clever and cost-effective ways to build buzz about my book.

Some acts have picked up corporate sponsors to underwrite portions of their concert tours. These sponsors range from restaurants (LeAnn Rimes has Red Lobster) to beer (Jimmy Buffett has Corona) to cars (Eric Clapton has Lexus) and even shoes (Rancid has Vans). Some bands, like R.E.M. and Pearl Jam, prefer to take the high ground on this type of corporate sponsorship, but those of us without gold records and millions in the bank can benefit from some type of sponsorship. One way to do this is to become a spokesperson for a product or service that you use or believe in.

A few of my author friends have been able to do book tours and gain media exposure for their books by promoting everything from software to cameras to Post-it Notes. The sponsor paid them handsomely for their time and landed them interviews on major media where they pitched their books and, in a soft-sell way, the related products. I have personally benefited from this approach by conducting workshops for a large seminar company. They help me reach hundreds of people a week, all across the country (and Hawaii!) by providing travel expenses, filling the seats in my seminars, and allowing me to promote my books and services (and they pay me a salary, too). With publishers reluctant to send authors on book tours, I had to find a way to get out and spread the word. While I am in a city doing a seminar, I also schedule a book signing or two and make myself available for interviews. Everyone wins.

Since I come from a self-publishing and entrepreneurial background, I knew what to do. I once heard someone say, "Expecting a publisher to turn your book into a best-seller is like giving birth to a baby and expecting the doctor to parent the child." Yet an author's career depends on publicity. This includes knowing how to make word of mouth work for you and being able to use the media to get the word out. Survival depends on press releases, coverage that furthers your career, interviews, book tours, networking.

Understanding at least the basics of PR helps you break through the clutter. It doesn't hurt to consult professionals, even if you intend to take charge of your own promotion. One idea from a good PR firm can be more beneficial than any amount of money you would have spent on advertising. They can bring out strengths and clarity you never would have been able to do yourself.

I know, the last thing you want to do after you have completed a twelve-month project is talk about it. You're sick of it, and ready to move on. Maybe the gallery or your assigned publicist is supposed to handle the PR. Don't rely on them. I look at it like this: whatever they do is icing on the cake of what I do myself.

Avoid a haphazard approach, and make a plan. Most magazines have long lead times, so find out about editorial deadlines and make sure your press release reaches the appropriate person well before that date.

Mark Victor Hanson and Jack Canfield, the authors of the *Chicken Soup for the Soul* books, sold millions of copies with this simple philosophy: Do one interview a day. It's so simple and so powerful.

I know some creative types who feel they are above having to publicize their work. Then they wonder why other, less talented artists get the showing, land on the best-seller list, or have a hit record. It's simply not enough to be a writer anymore. You have to hawk your work. It's showbiz, baby.

How to Get It On

My goal is to say or do at least one outrageous thing every week.
—Maggie Kuhn

A struggling actor died and, at the funeral, the funeral director said to his agent, "Judging by how many people came to pay their respects, he must have been a greatly admired man." The agent turned and smiled, "Yeah, if he had known he'd have a crowd like this, he would have died years ago."

Find a way to explain the uniqueness or newsworthiness of your product or service in the simplest, most direct manner possible. That's the art of the pitch.

I spent a day with the producer of a local newscast and followed her around to gain insights into what works and what doesn't. She scans headlines of several papers (media coverage leads to more media coverage), checks the AP wire for stories, sifts through E-mail but reads only ones with catchy or clever subject lines—and then the mail arrives in a big bin. A *very* big bin.

Over the years, this producer has learned to open the mail standing next to the trash. Most pieces are tossed in unopened (ouch!). Why? She won't look at mail with a computer label, or envelopes on which her name was misspelled, or where someone was too lazy to call and get her name and just put "editor" (that's not even the right title, it's "producer"). She isn't willing to take the time to open anything that the sender didn't take the time to do right. She will, however, open hand-addressed mail.

Even if she opens a piece of mail, it'll get tossed if the sender doesn't get to the point right away. Of what makes the cut, some things get forwarded to other shows' producers. For interesting or newsworthy items, she takes notes on the release and throws the rest of the packet away. She'll keep one or two pages, but the bulk of the package is overkill.

What I learned is this: Get to the point *fast,* in the first sentence. Keep press releases to one page. Include phone numbers and contact info on every piece. E-mail is better than paper, but the subject header must be a grabber. FedEx gets opened first, but doesn't necessarily rate a longer look.

▼ ▼ ▼

FAST FACTS

Top executives were asked what was the best way employees could earn a promotion and/or a raise. (From the book *Why Good Girls Don't Get Ahead But Gutsy Girls Do,* by Kate White.)

1. Eighty-two percent said ask for more work and responsibility.
2. Eleven percent said publicize their achievements.
3. Two percent said work longer hours.

▲ ▲ ▲

Electronic Media

I used to see my mug in the dailies and groan. Now I see it and think, hey, you look like an aging Chinese character actress—and they still hire you!

—Kevin Spacey

I once heard there are over one thousand talk shows in America. If they each average three guests per day, that's twenty thousand guests per week.

What am I driving at? It's a great time to get out and blow your horn. The media needs you! There's a high demand for guests, and not just the Jerry Springer kind.

Take out an ad in *Radio-TV Interview Report* or other books that producers read for leads on prospective guests.

Know the show. Nothing is a bigger turn-off than making the wrong pitch to the wrong station in the wrong market. Once you know the market and format, tailor your message to match the media. If you want to be on *Oprah,* focus on heartwarming, personal, and helpful ideas geared to women. If you want to be on *Charlie Rose,* go cutting-edge, political, hard-hitting.

Record your experiences with photos or video. Before and after, step by step, show what you do. Film it. Can TV tag along to record your experience? Get a tape from the producer of any show you do get on— bring them a blank tape to copy their original on.

Find a hook. How can you explain the uniqueness of your talents in the simplest, most direct manner? Come up with a hook. Pitch the package. Suggest show ideas. Put on a panel discussion.

Write a book. Ever notice how much publicity authors get? If you're not ready for that, try writing a column or Q&A for your local newspaper or magazine.

Enter contests. Make a list of contests in your area of expertise. Enter the same piece in several contests and it won't take up all your time. If you win, you get media attention and a credit for your portfolio.

Avoid the turkeys. Remember on the TV series *WKRP* when the radio station dropped live turkeys from a helicopter as a promo—only to discover that turkeys can't fly? A little research can save a lot of embarrassment.

Create a contest. A coloring contest, a battle of the bands, a cook-off, a fashion show, an art show, a 10K race—these take a lot of time and help, but they generate a lot of goodwill and much PR. Or you can go simpler, and give out an annual award: best-dressed, best web site, worst pun. Have fun with it.

Create a sensation. Abbott and Costello's press agent took out a policy with Lloyd's of London that would pay $100,000 to the survivor of anyone who died laughing during one of their performances. Hyatt Hotels had a party to which they invited people named Hyatt. Three hundred showed up! They got tons of ink for this one.

Be considerate. Call the producer, not the host. Find out how they like to be contacted. Patty Nager, a producer with *Good Morning America,* prefers faxes. Yvette Vega of *The Charlie Rose Show* likes letters. Be prepared to handle a couple of tough questions. If you can't cut it on the phone, they figure you'll choke under the pressure of a live interview.

Persist or perish. It's hard to be sure when no means N-O! Your timing may just be wrong. Don't blow a chance at a future appearance by being a jerk.

Tie in with current events. Use Chase's book of annual events to find interesting or peculiar horses to hitch your wagon to. National Procrastination Day is my favorite, but I never get around to sending out the queries.

Think small. Cable-access shows are always looking for programming. Blitz the local media. That's a great angle, local celebrity/artist/talent.

Join the club. Professional associations are listed in a book called *The Encyclopedia of Associations,* which you can find in the library. They almost all have newsletters, meetings with speakers, and annual events.

Be available. If you're known as a handy, last-minute, stand-in guest, you're likely to get on, especially in regional shows. If it's radio, you're only a phone call away.

Give your stuff away. Get your book in the hands of industry leaders or influential people who may pass it on to media friends.

Be a do-it-yourselfer. Host your own show. Start your own magazine.

Go for a record. Check out Guinness and go for it.

Pay attention. Call local stations as an expert offering your opinion when a newsworthy event in your area comes up. A friend of mine who wrote a book on being prepared for disasters (she sold it to insurance companies, which gave it out with their policies) was on television for a week when a big fire consumed an entire neighborhood.

Teach them. Invite a media personality to take your class, attend a show. (I taught newspaper editor John Gregory how to surf, and he wrote several articles about it.)

Create as many tie-ins as you can. We had Orville Redenbacher appear at an event, and sent bags of popcorn with our press releases. A BIG hit.

Hold a press conference in an unusual place. In a gallery, at an amusement park, a historical place, or a cemetery, on a ship, at the beach, in a fire station. It helps to make it a place where tired, blasé reporters might want to go (although a bar is not a good idea if you want a coherent story), and it needs to tie in somehow with what you're announcing.

Be Printable

In this world of ours, it's all on how you can sell it. Then it doesn't matter if you end up telling them the same thing that everyone else has told them, because you've sold the sizzle.

—*Michael Gelman*

Bill Zanker, founder of The Learning Annex, told me this story about being outrageous: To show he was an advocate of profit sharing, he tried to throw ten thousand dollars' worth of one-dollar bills off the Empire State Building. He was detained when a crowd showed up (gee, I wonder how they found out?!). He was ushered off in a patrol car for his own security, before he threw out a single dollar, but the story made the front page.

Most editors these days are overworked, underpaid, and on multiple deadlines. They don't have time to chat on the phone, go to lunch with you, or hear your life story. Don't call around deadline time (find out when that is—it varies from publication to publication). Find out the name and number of the appropriate editor (most publications have several). If you get an assistant editor, treat him or her with respect and you're more likely to get bumped up to the big dog. Be prepared to pitch your story quickly and follow up with printed materials and appropriate art. Send E-mail whenever possible. Make sure your written materials are clear, concise, and factually and grammatically correct. In a word, be professional. *Then* you can be clever, cute, and interesting. But be professional first. If an editor feels they're going to have to rework your stuff or hassle with someone who doesn't understand deadlines, you're dead in the water.

Don't ignore specialty or fringe publications that are targeted to your audience. These are actually your best bets for getting published or covered. Once you get anything published about you, get reprints of your articles and use them in future publicity releases. It's the old "I can't get a job because I don't have any experience and I don't have any experience because I can't get a job" routine. Once you've been published, it's much easier to generate interest in getting published again.

Send a photo with your clip. Publications are more and more visually oriented (check out a newspaper from 1900 or so—all tiny print, no pictures, small headlines). Anytime you can provide art—of you, your logo, your product, your dog—you improve your chances of getting a mention.

If you have something positive to say—a change in policy or address, a new client, a new product, a big increase in profits, a partnership or connection with a well-known person or group, an event announcement, results of a study, or new information of widespread interest—send press releases out to every publication within 250 miles.

Press releases should be short, no more than two pages (double spaced), written in the inverted-pyramid style with the most important information first. Pay attention to your headline and your first paragraph. Include contact information at the top of each page, and end the release with your mission statement, a clear one-liner about who you are and what you're doing. Use quotes whenever possible, even if you're just quoting yourself. Customize it for specific publications with a quick change here or there, but don't bother with a cover letter. It'll only be tossed.

If you send out press releases often, it might be worthwhile to put together a complete press kit. This is a folder with a place for your business card and separate sheets for your bio, a history of your company, quotes from people about you or your product, article reprints, photos (prints or slides), a list of credits or information on all your products, and complete contact information as well as the current press release.

Keep an eye out for listing opportunities. Many magazines do annual listings of various kinds, and it's often free or very inexpensive to be listed in the appropriate category. People do read these, and they are fairly easy to get.

Be (Inter)Viewable

After I got nominated for an Oscar, I expended a lot of useless energy going "I'm not ditzy." But on talk shows, I'm so excited to be there I talk four times as fast as I normally do. So I think I contribute to it, too.
—Jennifer Tilly

Most interviewers are not prepared, so you'd better be. Figure out in advance what your main points are going to be. Shoot for clear, catchy, colorful answers. Turn them into sound bites. Come up with anecdotes or stories. Figure out the worst thing they could ask you, and get a response ready. It helps to practice.

Be energetic, excited, animated, even ridiculous, but never, ever be boring.

Radio interviews are often done over the phone, so you can keep a glass of water handy to avoid "cotton mouth" and notes in front of you to prevent "brain farts" (you know, where your brain goes dead in mid-word). If it's a call-in program, you can have some friends call in with prearranged questions. If not, send the interviewer a cheat sheet of information on you and possible questions to ask.

Just make sure you're in a quiet place with no distracting background noise. Be confident, and let it show in your voice. Relax and have fun. Don't argue, even if the host or caller is belligerent. They can't make you *look* bad—it's radio!

When you're talking up a product, book, or service, make sure it's available. Response to radio and television interviews is usually short-term, and if you generate an interest that can't be satisfied, you've lost an opportunity, and you've ticked off a lot of people. Not good.

On-camera interviews are a lot harder, since most of us are self-conscious to begin with. Practice until you have what you want to say down to where you don't have to think about it, because you won't be thinking very clearly when those lights first hit your face. If you've never been on TV or film before, consider getting a media coach or having someone tape a mock interview. The less you sweat on camera, the better.

Don't be late. Make sure you know how to get to the studio and when you need to be there for makeup and preshow run-throughs. Dress like a pro. Solid dark colors work best. Stay away from white shirts and busy ties. Look as wild and interesting as you want, but look clean.

Try to get the producer to put any relevant information (such as a phone number) on the screen. I always carry books with me to the interview, making sure to get them on screen. Then I give some away to the host and staff. Any samples of your work or other visuals, clips, or props will add spice to the interview. Bring them along.

Many interviewers will end an interview by asking, "Is there anything you would like to add?" Be prepared with a strong closing.

▼ ▼ ▼

FAST FACTS

In a survey of more than one thousand adults by *Prevention* magazine and *NBC Today Weekend Edition,* 36 percent of men and 38 percent of women say they have been told by someone that they talk too much. (Only 22 percent of men and 35 percent of women admit to being the teller.)

▲ ▲ ▲

Getting a Leg Up in the Corporate World

The only way you can fail these days is not to try new stuff.

—*Tom Peters*

Power does not flow to invisible people. Be visible. It's not enough to do the job well. You have to prove your value and make sure others are aware of it. If you are working hard, producing results, you may as well get the credit. Always remember that you work for yourself—you are the product.

If you were a product in a grocery store (I know this is a little weird, but bear with me), would you be located on the top shelf (requiring effort to reach), on the bottom shelf (at kick-me level), in the middle of a row filled with similar products (hard to distinguish), on the picnic supplies row (one nobody goes down except by accident)—or would you be an endcap, with a whole display built around you? Think about that (not for too long, please), and use these tips to make sure you are positioning yourself properly.

Be a Team Player. "You promote yourself every time you take on a new responsibility," says author William Gore. Volunteer for extra work, and be available when needed. Play additional roles on different teams and projects. Is it just me, or does it seem that companies expect you to be able to do it all? Play right into their hands and make it work for you. In this project-driven world, be able to adapt and morph to fit the current needs of the company.

There are times when this technique doesn't work. Don't spread yourself so thin that you're not doing a good job. And make sure every team you attach yourself to wants you there. Otherwise you can become the goat, the person to blame, the odd man out. Not good for your career, your confidence, or your sanity.

Be proud. I think it was Fred Astaire who said, "Even trash can be picked up artistically." Turn the mundane, menial job into an art form. Take pride in your work and others will notice.

Become your own publicist. Don't be afraid to tell others when you accomplish something worthwhile, finish a project, bring in a new client, improve a concept. Don't brag. Just let yourself be excited about your own gifts—and share that excitement with others.

De-sterilize your space. One creative person put a punching bag in her office. Whenever someone was frustrated, they came into her office, whaled away, then walked out, sometimes without saying a word. (Sometimes they said lots of words—bad, bad words.) While this might make you popular with the rank and file, it's not likely to endear you to the management, who expect you to get your work done (hard to do with constant interruptions). A better idea would be to create a cubicle that is conducive to creative work. Paint the walls, put up interesting art and memorabilia, use your space to show off your talent.

Speak out. Position yourself as the spokesperson for your company. Join committees and even chair a committee or serve in some capacity.

Create your own mystique. Choose a paper color or ink color that is exclusively yours. Send memos on your purple paper. (Hint, choose something distinctive.) Give out a signature candy. (Looking for Mr. Goodbar? Good & Plenty? Hot Tamale?) Create your own personal logo, or add your personal touch to the company logo (IBMary Smith). Reinvent your role in the company and give yourself a new title to match—High Priestess of Purchasing.

Dress to impress. Be outrageous or classy—anything but understated. Funky suspenders, trippy hats, vests, rings. Create a signature look, but keep it somewhat within corporate guidelines.

Get a reputation. Not like Elaine on *Seinfeld* when she became the "office ho." Be the person to go to for information (not gossip), be the person with integrity and a willingness to pitch in. Make sure your reputation is flawless.

Don't complain. Look for the positives in any situation. If it's that bad, find a way around it or get the hell out. Marcia Kilgore, who owns Manhattan's ultra-hip spa Bliss, said, "I just keep thinking, how can we do this better?" That is a great attitude to have in the corporate world, too. Stop complaining and ask, "How can we do this better?"—and then do something about it.

Hang out with the leaders. Be seen with key players. If you're nowhere close to the big dogs, just make sure you hang out with other people who are doing a good job. Don't be damned by association with slackers.

Smile. Bring fun into the workplace. Plan parties. Organize brainstorming sessions. Be positive.

Learn a new skill and train others. Teach your boss a handy-dandy new software program, and you will make a positive impression.

Organize a nonprofit group that goes out into the community and paints over graffiti, cleans the beach, speaks at schools, or gives awards to up-and-coming artists. Invite students to watch what you do. Use it to promote your company.

Ask for feedback. If others around you are getting assigned the choice projects, receiving promotions, or getting pats on the back, find out what they are doing that you aren't. Improve your weak areas or make your strengths stronger.

Offer to build the company a web site. Use your creativity to show off what you can do. Put up your picture as the webmaster. Being in charge of this new medium and the one who maintains it translates to added power and prestige (plus some skills that will come in handy in the future).

Get connected. Get to know the players, work with people in other departments. Volunteer to be a part of teams and projects outside your normal scope. Help people get what they want so that down the road you can collect.

Extra effort means extra credit. "Always do more than you are paid for, and soon you will be paid for more than you do," says entrepreneur John McCormack. My mentor always told me to give people more than they expect. Do you know how much that advice has cost me? Seriously, it has become a way of life. Don't just finish things on time, how about a day early and under budget? (I can hear my editor laughing right now!) Take "That's not in my job description" out of your vocabulary, and replace it with "I'll do my best," and then proceed to blow them away!

Be a superstar, not a prima donna. People respect talent, but they resent those who act as if that talent allows them to be a jerk. Don't let this be you. Offer to help others (Lord knows, they need it, right?), pretend to be modest (fake it!), and be a team player (even though it *is* all about you).

Speak the language. Want to make yourself more promotable? Learn another language. Spanish would be good. How about a more obscure language? Portuguese? Chinese? Japanese? (Any of the "eses" would be great.) You may even get a free trip out of it. You might be called upon to represent your company in one of the countries where you know the language. Choose wisely, grasshopper.

Make a good first impression. When you are first hired, remember, they are watching you. This is your chance to set yourself up for easy days ahead. If you start out with a bang, you can milk that early success for months to come.

Parting Thought

I was reading the July 1998 edition of *Success* magazine (when I should have been writing this chapter), which included a fascinating profile of Jeff Bezos, the billionaire founder of the hugely successful online bookseller Amazon.com. The author of the profile was Lesley Hazelton. At the end of the profile appears the following credit: "Lesley Hazelton's new book, *Driving to Detroit: An Automotive Odyssey,* will be published in October by Simon & Schuster." Are you seeing what I am? Not only did this writer get advance press for her upcoming book, but she also got to build a relationship with one of the most important booksellers today. Brilliant! She gets it! Do you?

▼▼ 11 ▼▼

The Seven (Bad) Habits of Highly Ineffective Creative People

I think if a woman were behaving like these men, not only would she not get hired, but she would be considered a junkie scumbag.
—Drew Barrymore on Christian Slater and Robert Downey Jr.

Sometimes you are your own worst enemy. Nobody can sabotage your career as well as you can. Why do creative people often become career kamikazes who crash and burn? The right-brainer (that's you) is more susceptible to some of the pitfalls and problems that befall many people in business for themselves. It's important to be aware of the dangers that lurk ahead in your career and be properly prepared to slay them one by one as they rear their ugly heads.

The Seven Deadly Sins

1. **Sloth.** Procrastination, a problem that leaves you a day late and a dollar short, and eventually puts you out of work. Failure to do what you say you will, *when* you say you will do it, will cost you clients, friends, and spouses.
2. **Gluttony.** When you want it all, when you can't say no to any job, you end up torching the candle at both ends, burning out—and charring both your reputation and your chance for new business.
3. **Avarice.** When it comes to money, there never seems to be enough—and there are far too many ways to lose what you have.
4. **Pride.** A big head, egomania, complacency, selfishness, "artistic" temperament, bad decisions, and bad behavior are very human side effects of success that can knock you from the top to the bottom quicker than you can say "Gary Coleman."
5. **Lust.** Sex, drugs, and rock 'n' roll. Creative people are particularly susceptible to addictions of many kinds. I'm addicted to

work, and I don't think that's so bad, but my wife disagrees. It stops being just a matter of perspective when your health, happiness, and livelihood become threatened, however.

6. **Lack of Discipline.** When you are all over the "bored" and lack focus and discipline, it is very hard to build a body of work or a meaningful career.

7. **Deceit.** Be honest with yourself as well as others. Don't settle for second best. Don't be afraid to dream—that's your strength. Share your dreams with others—that's your gift.

1. SLOTH: TOO LITTLE, TOO LATE

Procrastination is like a credit card; it's a lot of fun until you get the bill.
—Christopher Parker

You will notice I didn't put off procrastination. I put it first. That doesn't mean that I haven't suffered from the affliction known as "hardening of the oughteries." There are several reasons why the right-brainer is susceptible to this disease. These include fear of success, fear of failure, and fear that it won't be perfect. There are many more reasons, but the bottom line in most of them is fear.

There are ways to deal with fear. You don't always have to face it. You can sneak around it, hand it off to someone else, fool it. For instance:

Cram it. "A perfect method for adding drama to life is to wait until the deadline looms large," says author Alyce Cornyn-Selby. Do you like the rush of waiting until the last minute? Do you work better under pressure? Creatives are indolent by nature. Left to their own devices (and vices), many people's music would die with them. Sometimes you need a push, or the pressure of an impending deadline, to get you off the couch and into action.

Wait for inspiration. It's a romantic notion that you wait around for an epiphany, that "aha!" revelation, and then work like mad to finish. That makes for interesting headlines, but the successful artist works day after day through blocks, bad habits, urges, and distractions to create their art. There is no perfect time to begin. Begin now.

Cut it up. When you're faced with a big project, start by cutting it into workable pieces. That does two things: it gives you a better overall picture of what needs to be done and how everything works together, and it makes it less overwhelming to start. You negotiate the staircase to the top in small steps, not one huge leap.

Take a trip. You know how just before a vacation you can get twice as much done in half the time? You are on a mission. Set up a vacation for just after a deadline. Use the extra energy that a pre-holiday provides.

Kick ass, then kick back. My wife disagrees with me on this one, saying she has to do all the packing, shopping, planning, and pre-vacation preparation because I'm so busy meeting that deadline. Maybe that's why I find it such a motivator.

Stop making excuses. All I hear from other would-be writers is "I want to write . . . but I don't have an agent, my kids are home from school, my job is too time-consuming." With that attitude, it's never going to happen. Try saying affirmations every day. Work on thinking positive, shoot down those negative thoughts before they take wing. "I will write ten pages today." "I will call/write three agents today." "I will hire a high school student to watch the kids four hours a day." Thinking that you can becomes thinking that you will becomes knowing you will becomes doing it.

Mind over matter. Get into a creative mind-set any way you can. Mahler stroked fur, Brahms shined his shoes, Beethoven poured ice over his head, and Van Gogh beat himself with a stick. Find a method that works for you and use it.

List the pros and cons. Pros get things done, take proper steps to beat procrastination, and finish on time. Cons lie and cheat (and do time). Write down all the negative consequences of procrastinating on a particular project on the left side of a sheet of paper. On the right side, list all the benefits of starting and completing it. (Include a personal reward.) If the pros outweigh the cons, you've got all the more reason to start. If the cons win, maybe it's not worth doing. This is an intellectual exercise, and procrastination is primarily an emotional problem, but you need all the ammunition you can get.

Just do it. In a creative career, you can't tell a client or boss you aren't feeling like being creative today. Very few people have the luxury of waiting for their muse to show up. Find ways to do the work. Develop a bank of "starters." Then use them.

Set limits. Say to yourself, "I'm only going to work on this for five minutes." You can put up with anything for five minutes. John always hated roller-coaster rides—he's not ashamed to admit they scared him to death. Somehow a friend talked him into going on Montezuma's Revenge at Knott's Berry Farm—one of the absolute worst—by saying "It's only thirty-two seconds long. You can take *anything* for thirty-two seconds!" The longest thirty-two seconds of his life that was, and some of the best. Now he loves roller coasters! Just five minutes—yet that's all you need to get started. Before you know it, an hour has passed and you're in the zone.

Minimize it. A page a day keeps procrastination away. Set a minimum amount of work you will do per day. Make it minor. This works much like the "only five minutes" idea. Anybody can do a page! Usually, it's hard to stop there. Just don't give yourself the guilts if you have a hard time doing that page. Write big. Draw a picture. Have fun with it.

Throw a kick-off party for each new project. Give yourself a reward for just beginning. You usually reserve the reward till the end, which for someone with an impulsive personality is too long to wait. Give yourself credit for just starting.

Perfectionism is like a muscle cramp. Just get it out. Don't worry about how perfect it is, or your creativity cramps up. It does not have to be perfect the first time out. Part of the fun is in the polishing.

Ignore it. My biggest problem is too much data. Doing insane amounts of research does give me confidence to begin, but it can scare me. (The more you know, the more you realize how much you really *don't* know!) There is so much information out there, you will never get it all. (I try!) It can overwhelm you. I start swimming in it, but then the undercurrent starts to pull me down. The answer is to tap internal wisdom. You know more than you think you know. "No," says my editor. "The answer is focus. Go back to your goals. Figure out what you want to do here and dump the other stuff, no matter how interesting." Sometimes I hate my editor.

Don't major in the minors. Let some things go. You will never get all your errands done, your social obligations covered, your car or dog or house clean. That stuff is just a renewable source of procrastination. Minimize it. Hire a maid, send a mass E-mail, pay your bills online, let the errands pile up. Spend your time where it counts.

Make a movie. You know they don't shoot movies in sequence, right? (Oops, did I let the cat out of the bag?) *You* don't have to begin at the beginning, either. Find an easy place to start. You don't have to do things in a linear fashion (yeccch). In fact, it's often better not to do things that way. This book was not written in order. In fact, the first chapter was written last. I began with the dedication and acknowledgments. Then I could say, "Hey, two pages down and three hundred to go."

Get help. Find a goal buddy. Brainstorm with others for ideas. Have someone hold you accountable. Delegate a portion of the project.

Force yourself. This one is harsh. Using an egg timer, and sitting at your work space, put a blank page in front of you and set the timer for ten to fifteen minutes. Then stare at the paper until the timer bings. No matter what, don't begin. Ten minutes is a long time to do nothing, so your mind will take off, and you will usually end up with so many ideas you are itching to begin.

The longer you procrastinate, the harder it is to start. Oh, the guilt. You beat yourself up—you start thinking shoulda, woulda, coulda. Then tension, anger, and jealousy raise their ugly heads. Which, of course, wastes more time and makes you feel worse about yourself. You spiral down into procrastination hell. You are no longer in control. I've been there. The only way out is to *do something*. Anything. Make a sketch. Write the acknowledgments page. Run through your scales. Race around the block (doing something physically energetic puts your brain into high-energy mode somehow).

Success breeds success. Action comes before motivation, not the other way around.

Don't Beat Around the Bush

Those who can, do. Those who can't, bitch.

—*Kenny Rogers*

There is nothing wrong with letting things simmer until they reach a boiling point. You don't have to *look* like you're working to *be* working. Creatives need time to allow the subconscious to well up into the conscious with new ideas pieced together from past experience. It's called inspiration. Although you're going to have to work without it sometimes, the real excitement in your work will come here. So don't plan your days too tightly. Don't lock yourself in. Get plenty of sleep. Go for a drive or a walk sometimes, heading nowhere. This is not the same as procrastination, and the distinction should be very clear.

The big difference between the two is energy. Procrastination drains your energy, making it harder and harder to do anything at all. The creative process, even when you're not working directly on a project, is energizing. It brings you to life.

Part of your job as a creative businessperson is to nurture that creativity. Despite all the stories of hit songs written on cocktail napkins—the Gettysburg Address written on the back of an envelope—these are exceptions. Abraham Lincoln was smart enough to take advantage of inspiration when it hit—whenever it hit. Inspiration isn't always convenient or appropriate (you may be working on widgets and have a fantastic idea for dingbats). But you can develop patterns that make it possible for your genius to work for you.

Creative people *are* creatures of habit. Surprise! I know many artists who have a rather regimented routine. You probably think you prefer total freedom and chaos, but you need some structure to create. You need to have a work space and materials (instrument, computer, drawing pad and pencils, and so on) and a certain amount of uninterrupted time to create effectively. A routine provides the framework to get things started (and completed) on time.

Get all your ducks in a row and then shoot them. Get mundane tasks out of the way first. Clear your mind. Don't try to complete *all* of your piddly little projects before you start, however—that's one of the worst forms of procrastination. Everything is more interesting than what you are working on when you are stuck. But completing a few of them sometimes gets you motivated to begin on your more serious stuff. It's been proven that ideas come to you when you are doing such mundane things as making copies, washing the car, cleaning the house.

Set a regular time to start. It worked for Pavlov. Just as you can teach yourself to be hungry at six o'clock instead of at seven, or sleepy at midnight instead of at ten, you can train yourself to be at your desk, facing your work, at a particular time every day. It takes only twenty-one days to make a firm habit.

The hard part is training others to leave you alone to work during your "working hours." I have certain times when I don't answer the phone or the door. Of course, I do a lot of my writing late at night, so it's not so hard to ignore the outside world and focus. Maybe you should get lost— find a retreat somewhere without all the distractions.

Just sitting down at your desk or your instrument at a regular time every day is the best antidote to procrastination. Once you're there, you have to do something (it's hard to sleep in your chair—I know. You fall out, land on your head, wake up, and there you are at your desk again). Once you begin, there is a magical thing called momentum that builds and builds until you are up and running at full speed.

It's like going to the gym. Once you drag yourself there, get dressed, and start your workout, the motivation starts to kick in. You say to yourself, "Oh, what the hell, I'm here, I may as well do something." Before you know it, forty-five minutes have gone by and you're sweating away, in the zone.

There is magic in the morning. No guilt throughout the day if you get the job done early, and then you can move on to the fun stuff. Give yourself permission to take time off if you get your work done. Three good hours of work is better than six hours of crappy time. It isn't about the amount of time spent working, it's about the quality of that time.

Emily Brontë said, "A person who has not done one half of his day's work by ten o'clock runs the chance of leaving the other half undone." What if you aren't up at ten A.M.? Hey, many of us aren't morning people. So just apply this technique to the first few hours of daylight you see (even if they are in the afternoon). It's about getting to your art before your left brain is fully awake and functional.

Successful artists have rigorous rituals. Pour themselves a strong one, light a smoke, put on some coffee (yeah, I know, not healthy—so do some yoga, go for a run, call your mom, whatever works). The point is to relax and prepare mentally for the coming session.

Becoming successful as a creative doesn't mean living a dog's life. Actually, it's more like a squirrel's life. It requires discipline to practice, think, create. If you really want to make a career of your creativity, you have to make some sacrifices in order to produce something.

Meanwhile, enjoy the journey. You're much less likely to procrastinate if your work is fun. Be creative! If you're good, you can find a way to make even the yucky parts fun (or get rid of them somehow).

If you can make the journey more enjoyable, the whole process is better. Whenever my brother and I wanted to go surfing in Fiji, we had to take a long boat ride out to the cloud break (outer reef). Imagining the perfect waves made the trip out exciting. On the way back, I enjoyed the scenery, talked with the boat driver, and relived my best rides.

Procrastination doesn't only paralyze your day-to-day work. It can stunt your career. You have to make your own breaks, take matters into your own hands. Make an independent film, self-publish your novel, stage your own show, form your own record label, sell your art at the flea market or on the Internet, *move forward*. Get some momentum going. Put your money where your mouth is. Don't let not having a "deal" stop you.

Thoughts on Procrastination

The hardest part of any project is beginning it. Don't procrastinate, just attack it.

—*Evelyn Lauder*

Action is the antidote to despair. You don't get to choose how you're going to die or when. You can only decide how you're going to live. Now.

—*Joan Baez*

Anyone bellying up to a bar with a few shots of tequila swimming around the bloodstream can tell a story. The challenge is to wake up the next day and carve through the hangover minefield and a million other excuses and be able to cohesively get it down on paper.

—*Jimmy Buffett*

2. GLUTTONY: CRASH AND BURNOUT

I'm learning to relax, doctor—but I want to relax better and faster! I want to be on the cutting edge of relaxation.

—*Unknown workaholic*

You are a star on the top-rated show on television (*ER*) and you are earning close to $70,000 per episode. You have the proverbial fame and fortune. You are on top of the world. So what's your next move? If I told you to quit, you'd say I was nuts. But that's exactly what actress Sherry Stringfield (who played Dr. Lewis) did in 1996. She explained, "It's a whole lifestyle thing. Do I want to continue to go down this road? I had a taste of what fame meant, and I just realized it's not for me."

Wow. If you read between the lines, it sounds like the show consumed her and she wanted her life back. These days, many people are choosing life. In fact, they are OD'ing on life. The same passion they put into building their careers, they are throwing into their personal lives. The problem comes when you add performance pressure to your personal life. "I gave everything up for this, so it has to be perfect."

Life isn't perfect.

The real trick to beating stress is learning to enjoy life with all its pimples and dandruff. Don't take yourself too seriously. Smile at people; laugh every day. Revel in your success, learn from your failures. That's my philosophy in a nutshell.

But, true to my subconscious belief that more words are always better, I'll elaborate.

Stress Test

Work is my norm. I have mad energy, insane energy, a kind of stamina in terms of work that's a little crazy.

—*Sidney Lumet*

Not all stress is bad. The stress of an impending deadline (like the one for this book) can energize you . . . or not. Take a quick stress test. Do you:

Like risk?
Relish change?
Work better under pressure?
Feel energized after an all-nighter in which you finished a big project?
Like to have a million things going at once?
Live life as a drama, and if there isn't one you'll create one?

If you answered yes to all of these, see your doctor—you're a candidate for heart attack or stroke. Some stress is good. *All* stress is bad.

Road Warriors

You need to recognize what gets to you, and set your own limits.

What burns me out is the road. It sounds so romantic to go from city to city, meet new people, get away from home. But the reality stinks. The airports, layovers, lost luggage, time-zone changes, hotel food, packing and unpacking, performing, it all burns you out—quickly. It is also lonely. I try not to do more than three weeks in a row. (Do you know how much E-mail can accumulate in three weeks?)

I know a guy who travels with his own pillow, a picture of his wife, and a few other touches from home. One of the strangest stories from the road is a guy who tried to lighten his load as he went. After a few days he mailed his dirty underwear and other items home. Unfortunately, he forgot to tell his wife of this ingenious plan. She opened up the mail one day only to find a smelly package filled with dirty laundry. She's still having nightmares about it.

I travel all over the country to conduct workshops and seminars. When I first started, I began collecting frequent-flyer cards, as well as a credit card that gives me miles back. I put them in a sleeve made for business cards, and carry them with me when I travel, making sure to earn my points. My goal was to fill up both sides (twenty frequent-flyer and hotel membership cards.) I did it. But what did I really win? I love doing the seminars, but I am getting tired of the road. One day in line at the airport, a woman commented, "Wow, you must be lucky to be able to travel so much," nodding at my impressive sheet of cards. "I bet you have a lot of free tickets, huh?" she asked. I thought about it. I do have several free tickets, but the fact of the matter is, after being on the road so much, I never want to use them.

One of the good things about being on the road is that your problems at home seem far away. You are focused on the work. The bad thing is that your problems are there waiting for you when you get home.

Here are some tips from a road warrior to others who spend a lot of time on planes, trains, and automobiles:

Don't lose touch with the real world. I send postcards from the road to my friends and family to let them know I am thinking about them.

Pack the night before you have to leave, so that you're not stressed in the morning.

Have a separate travel toilet kit. I even have clothes that I wear only when traveling, so that packing is fast and easy and I don't forget anything.

Carry extra batteries for your laptop so they don't think you are a terrorist when they ask you to start it up at the security check and the darn thing doesn't respond.

I always end my room charges with the number five. That way I can quickly skim through my bill and make sure it's kosher.

Pencil in some time out. See the sights, catch a movie, go for a run. A nonstop, whirlwind road trip leaves you stressed out and irritable.

Lighten your load. I packed up for a road trip, then grabbed my bags and walked around the block. When I got back, I ditched the deadweight. (Every ounce counts.) Less stress on your back.

Don't sweat the small stuff. On the road, things *will* go wrong. Try to keep calm and look for solutions instead of stressing out. Being the squeaky wheel and kicking and screaming doesn't get me to my destination or room any faster; it just irritates those who are trying to help.

Go with what you know. I rent the same kind of car every time so I don't have to relearn all the controls.

Anything that can be lost will be lost. Put all your valuables in your carry-on bag. (These include presentation materials, passport, traveler's checks, medication, etc.)

Join the club. Those executive clubs are a nice respite when you are on a long layover. You can nap, work, or relax in a quiet environment.

Decompress after a long trip and plan a catch-up day. Don't tell the office when you really return.

Try to come back to a clean office. That means cleaning up before you go.

Don't book the last flight of the day. If you miss it, you're out of luck. If you catch it, you're home very, very late, nobody wants to come pick you up, and you're wasted for the whole day after.

Keep your passport current so you don't miss out on the cool overseas trips.

Take vitamins and other supplements, and wash your hands often. Germs, lack of sleep, and time zone and weather changes leave you vulnerable to all kinds of nasty little bugs.

▼ ▼ ▼

FAST FACTS

Nineteen million Americans have pagers.

Inc Magazine did a poll that revealed that 19 percent of workers check their E-mail during vacations.

In a recent study, adults averaged roughly forty hours of "free time" per week; 15 percent of that time was used to watch TV, 7 percent to socialize, and 4 percent to talk on the phone.

▲ ▲ ▲

Overstimulation

I don't think I will ever mellow out. It's not in my blood.
—*Van Morrison*

Our society keeps speeding up as technology makes it possible to go faster and faster. Because of this, laborsaving and timesaving devices have actually added to the stress of the average worker—not to mention the creative worker. It is theoretically possible to know more and do more, faster than ever before—but it's not necessarily the best thing. Know your limits. Don't overload your circuits and burn out.

Share the work. Even taking a vacation can cause stress. Handling all the details of planning a trip when you are in the middle of a key project and you can't quite afford it anyway can be stressful. That's when a spouse (or travel agent) comes in very handy.

Control interruptions. When you're on the phone all day, you can't get much creative work done. Limit your phone time and save a little sanity.

Communicate when you need to. E-mail helps you manage the phone problem, because you can send and read your E-mail anytime that's convenient for you. Still, many people fall into the trap of believing they should E-mail everybody all the time. It can become your only social outlet. Worse, it can become an excuse for procrastinating.

Take your time. E-mail makes it easy to send art and copy (almost) instantaneously, which means clients will feel free to make last-second (it used to be last-minute) changes. Even the best system doesn't always get the message through for hours. And even the littlest change can take a long time to incorporate. Insist on appropriate lead time. It'll actually get you some respect.

Own your tools, don't let them own you. Computer technology is developing so fast there's always new software to learn, upgrades to install, techniques to master. When you start becoming a slave to your computer—when you spend more time maintaining it and working on it than you spend on your home life—you're in trouble. When your computer bombs, you'll understand just how deep that trouble is.

Get real. Stress can come from unrealistic expectations. Trying to be perfect and do perfect work is a major one. Trying to make everybody happy is another. Admit you aren't perfect and let some things go.

Trim your to-do list. Is it really necessary to do this? What is the worst thing that would happen if you don't do it? Can you live with that? Cut it. Cut back on what you feel you have to read. Learn to skim through for the meat and leave the potatoes behind.

Keep your promises. The guilt causes more strain than whatever it was you were avoiding. Maybe you'll even learn not to promise things you don't want to do. "Just say no" doesn't only apply to drugs.

Save for a rainy day. Having a little nest egg set aside in case of an emergency can relieve a lot of stress. If you're constantly concerned that you are one bad month away from being a bag lady, knowing you have a stash puts your mind at ease. (You can have the best bag of all the bag ladies. Do it in style. Just kidding.)

Love your work. Work that you are excited to get out of bed for in the morning is less stressful than work you dread.

Live in the moment. You can't live in the moment if you are always worried about what you have to do next, or guilty about what you should be doing or should have done. You'll never feel serene or satisfied.

Shit happens. Leave room in your schedule for it. There will be storms that you can't forecast. Leave yourself some elbow room. I know a woman who has one morning meeting a week with a particularly large and demanding client. She doesn't schedule anything else for the day because, as she puts it, "that office is a black hole for time." Although the meeting is scheduled to last an hour, it's four to six hours before she gets back to her desk. Even with less demanding clients, she recommends scheduling no more than two meetings a day (one morning, one afternoon). That way, you have time to prepare for and digest after each meeting.

Don't isolate yourself. There will be times when things in your private life spill over into your work. When your life is falling apart, you have to try to keep it together at work. To do that, try not to spend too much time in isolation. Spend time with positive people you can interact with and talk to about your problems. Ask for a leave of absence to regroup. Ask for a lighter load.

Breathe deeply. To calm my mind, a more enlightened and centered friend told me to close my eyes, breathe deeply, and picture the word "relax" in my head while repeating it over and over. I was skeptical, but it worked.

Take a vacation in your mind. Hang a picture or poster of a peaceful place over your workspace. By looking at it, you can transport yourself there. (May I suggest Bora Bora?) How about going to a funny movie?

Let it go. There are days when everything turns to mud. It starts when you can't find your keys and spill coffee all over yourself, and ends when you get a flat tire on the way home. Don't let one of those days turn into one of those months. Tomorrow *is* another day.

Surf's up. For my money, surfing is the best stress reliever in the world. When I am bobbing around in the Pacific, sharing waves with friends and sliding across a glassy wave of nature's creation, I am at total peace. Nothing, and I mean *nothing,* bothers me then.

Save the world? Who has the time? Save yourself. Deal with the world, the art market, the recording industry, Hollywood, Silicon Valley, the way it is, not the way you wish it were. The best way to make it better is by *being* better.

Relax. These are uncertain times. There is a lot of anxiety about the future and the pace of change. What if I told you you'll be okay—would you relax? Okay. You will be fine. If you can come up with ideas and embrace your creativity, you have nothing to worry about. I know you feel powerless. You have the power!

Handling Stress

Research on people who have been able to manage stress effectively in their lives shows they have three things in common:

1. They consider life a challenge, and not just one damn thing after another.
2. They have a mission or purpose in life and are committed to it.
3. They don't feel like victims, but believe that, despite temporary setbacks, they have control over their lives.

The Rat Race

The problem with the rat race is that even if you win, you're still a rat.
—*Lily Tomlin*

Did you happen to catch the hype when a doctor at Bowling Green State University discovered that rats laugh? If you tickle their tummies, they make the rat equivalent of a chuckle. They noticed these high-pitched noises while the rats were playing games in the lab. It's been proven that extended time on a treadmill stresses the rat out. Makes you think.

Balance and Align Your Life

There is no obligation on us to be richer, or busier, or more efficient, or more productive, or more progressive, or any way worldlier or wealthier, if it does not make us happier.
—*G. K. Chesterton*

Statistics show that you are working harder and longer than ever before (and, in many cases, for less money). One reason is that you want/need to capitalize on opportunities as they present themselves. This can lead to conflicting projects and overload.

You need to have a life in your life. It feeds your creativity, lowers your stress, keeps you grounded. Unlike her character "Elaine" on *Seinfeld,* Julia Louis-Dreyfus balances being a TV star with being a hands-on mother by setting limits. She refuses to travel to locations to do movies. People in the business have told her that would spell tragedy for her career. She replies, "People in show business don't realize that there's a life outside their universe. They don't know what they're missing."

Obsessiveness is a trait common to creatives, but there are good workaholics and bad workaholics. Studies have found that achievement-oriented workaholics, who work a lot because they enjoy their jobs, seem to thrive. The bad type of workaholic uses his or her job to escape personal problems. Stephen King maintains a grueling writing schedule, taking only three days off per year. For relaxation, he plays poker with his friends, including author Amy Tan and cartoonist Matt Groening (creator of *The Simpsons*).

My definition of a good workaholic is that if you ask them, "Is there anywhere else you would rather be, or something you would rather be doing?" they'll say no. Leave them alone. But trying to avoid issues in your life by overworking is only a stopgap measure. Eventually, you have to live your life and deal with your problems.

Art can't be created in a vacuum. "It can't come out of your horn if you don't live it," said a jazz great.

Those who report the greatest satisfaction on and off the job are people who embrace technology to make their lives simpler. They use pagers, cell phones, and laptops to bring work home or take it to the beach, the park, or anywhere their kids are. One of my favorite commercials features a working mom with three little girls. It's summer, and the kids want to go to the beach. The mother explains that she can't go to the beach because she has an important meeting with a client. Then one of the little girls asks, "Mommy, when can I be a client?" Guilt registers, and they go to the beach, where the woman conducts her meeting on her cell phone.

Bernadine Healy, M.D., said in a speech that she is privileged to share the final moments of people's lives and that, while facing death, these people don't think about their degrees, their wealth, or their businesses. At the end, what really matters is who you loved and who loved you. I have conducted goal-setting workshops for years and, when I ask people to list the three most important things in their lives, nearly everyone includes family.

What are friends for? They encourage you and console you, and are there to talk to and support you. In our jam-packed lives, sometimes friendship gets squeezed out. Yet people with friends are generally happier and healthier, with fewer illnesses, less depression and anxiety, and longer life spans. Call that old college pal. Drop a note to a childhood buddy. Meet for coffee with current friends. Make the time.

Not all friends are good influences, though. Make a list of everybody you spend time with, and put a plus or minus next to their name to indicate whether they give positive or negative energy. (Ever been around people who drain your energy?) Start spending time with the positive people.

What does it mean to live life to its fullest? That depends on the person. But I will say this: for the creative person, it means spending time alone, engaging in playful activities, using your creativity, and doing nothing. Nothing? Just napping under a tree, going for a long, leisurely drive, listening to music, walking on the beach, watching the sun rise, playing with your pet, watching a movie. For me, it's things like browsing around a bookstore, surfing, hanging out with friends, lounging by the pool, riding my bike. Spend more time "being" and less time "doing" for a happier and healthier life.

I guess in a way I have a surfer's mentality. (No, I'm not mental, I just have a laid-back approach to life.) One of the ambassadors of the sport was Rell Sunn, who succumbed to breast cancer at the age of forty-seven. She was first diagnosed with the disease at thirty-two. On more than one occasion she was told she had six months to live. She lived every day as if it were her last. Why wait to start living until you only have six months left to live? Do it now!

When I interviewed actor Robert Hays (*Airplane,* the *Starman* TV series) he told me that his daughter was born nine months from the day of his wedding (to singer Cherie Currie, formerly of the band The Runaways). He admitted that, with their hectic schedules, they hadn't had sex in weeks before the wedding. You need to carve out some time for romance in your life. Maybe you actually have to make an appointment in your planner. Make regular "date" nights during the week. I know it isn't as spontaneous as many right-brainers would like, but otherwise even romance can get pushed aside and your relationships suffer.

Need more stress reducers? Try these:

Clean house. Getting your home or office in order is one way to relieve stress. Get organized. If you can't do it yourself—and many of us just can't—hire somebody.

Take a long lunch. Remember when a lunch hour really was an hour? You need that time to regroup. Leave the office, and don't take your phone.

Cultivate interesting people. Preferably ones in different fields, from diverse cultures. Spend time talking about the world, about life, about ideas instead of just discussing what happened today.

Take advantage of flextime and telecommuting. Match your workload to your energy cycles whenever possible.

Time is more valuable than money. Are you trading your life for fame and fortune? Is it worth it? Are you happy? Grammy-winning singer-songwriter Marc Cohn took five years off after his initial success. "I had to choose between whether fans would remember me or my kids would remember me. It wasn't a hard choice to make."

Get a life. Don't neglect your emotional and spiritual side. Take time out for bad behavior. Let yourself go and feel things, experience new sensations. Get naked, act crazy. It's good for the soul—and very good for the creative spirit. (Just try not to get arrested, okay?)

One story in *Reader's Digest* illustrates the stress people are under at work. One boss admitted he might have been pushing his people too hard. Everyone was feeling the pressure of deadlines. One day the boss passed by the desk of one of his top workers, whose wife was expecting their first child. He casually asked, "When's the due date?" The star employee stopped dead in his tracks and, with a look of panic, asked, "Which project?"

In the book *Work This Way,* author Bruce Tulgan points out that there are both workaholics and *life*aholics. Lifeaholics work like hell, then say the hell with it and drop out of the rat race and regroup. It's an all-or-nothing approach. When they are in regrouping mode, they work primarily to pay the bills, move back home, reconnect with key people, travel, pick up a hobby or two, go back to school—they basically binge on life. But, just as workaholics get sick of work, they get sick of life and start to itch to get back in the game.

Action Item

When projects come your way, ask:

How does this fit in my life?
What does it add to my life?
What will I have to give up (personal projects, time with family, hobbies, a cause)?
Will I have to deal with a bunch of nimrods?

How long will it take?

Is it worth the money?

More on Stress and Burnout

One reason there is so much job dissatisfaction in the marketplace is that in return for security, you do the same thing every day and the excitement goes out of the whole process.

—Andrew S. Grove

Burnout—we've all heard of it, and most of us have experienced it. You go brain-dead. You get depressed. You make stupid mistakes. Your personal life can burn you out as easily as your business can—and for you, it's all the same thing. It's worth spending a little more time on how to avoid it:

Put at least one fun thing on your to-do list. While you're at it, trim that list down.

Try to remember why you are working so hard. If you aren't sure, it's a certain indication that you need to either cut back or find work you love.

Celebrate your successes. Treat yourself with some much-needed rest.

Don't spazz on the small stuff. Don't hit the panic button for minor problems. Printers from hell, bosses who do a hatchet job on your work, collaborators who steal your ideas. If you can't do anything about it, leave it, learn from it, and move on. Try not to put yourself in that spot again, but don't obsess.

Get off the freeway. Take a pit stop, look under the hood, choose a new direction, and get a map to help you get there. Even if you love what you do, burnout is a signal that it may be time to slow down, or even try a new road in your life.

Pick your moments to fly off the handle. When I was in Hawaii doing a seminar, and the hotel shuttle was late to pick me up at the airport, I had a conniption. Then I remembered, I'm in Hawaii! So I went to the bar and had a Mai Tai (or two) and relaxed. Why let a little thing ruin your day?

Fun lubricates the creative flow. To get the juices going, try adding some play to your daily routine. Take a recess and get into some mayhem.

Back off. When you start biting heads off, shut your mouth, go away, and give yourself time to come to terms with whatever's bugging you.

Let it out. When you get to the point where you feel like screaming, go into a closet and let it out. Scream, shriek, holler. So it feels stupid at first. Get into it. When it starts being fun, you can stop, go back and be human.

Smile a lot, and laugh every day. Some companies don't think that humor has a place in the work world. I believe it is essential and solves a lot of problems. Look at Southwest Airlines. They are having fun, and the airline is laughing all the way to the bank.

Browsing a bookstore has a very calming effect on me. Try it sometime.

Stress comes from the unknown. Try to stay in the loop at work, in your industry, and with your clients.

Be positive. Dwelling on the negative is stressful and hard on the body. "I'm positive this is going to turn out god-awful . . . er . . . great." See how easy that is?

▼ ▼ ▼

FAST FACTS

The average Fortune 100 worker receives eighty-three messages a day.

The Louis Harris poll says eighteen days are missed because of stress every year.

▲ ▲ ▲

Living the Simple Life

Some stress is good. Your body is built to handle stress, just not massive doses of it. When you have no responsibilities, no risks, nothing to do, no competition, no challenges, you get bored, your metabolism actually slows down, you get sluggish both physically and mentally. Sometimes stress adds just the right amount of challenge and motivation you need to have a happy and productive life. Balance is the key.

Stress Busters

- Lighten the load and get some help.
- Get a pet—or get rid of a pet.
- Listen to music. Not just relaxing music. Any kind of music. Classical is best for concentration. I find that a solid rock beat energizes me.
- Help others.
- Spend some time at Walden Pond (figuratively speaking).
- Get things down on paper.
- Minimize meetings and paperwork.
- Delegate more tasks.
- Find a state of calm, a tranquil center amid all that chaos swirling around. Yoga, meditation, self-hypnosis.

- Get plenty of sleep.
- Get regular exercise.
- Eat several small, nutritious meals a day. Skip the potato chips.

Power Outage

I write between 6:00 A.M. and 10:00 A.M., when I can access aspects of my brain that become unavailable as the day's trials and tribulations knock me into submission.

—*Peter Berg*

If you aren't getting enough sleep, you can thank Thomas Edison. Before he invented the lightbulb, people slept nine hours a night. Today we're lucky if we get six. And for some reason the creative person has a difficult time getting to sleep and getting enough of it.

Cutting back on sleep in order to get more done is a sure ticket to burnout. It is also counterproductive. Skipping sleep plays havoc on your body and your brain. People who are sleep-deprived pay the price in a lack of creativity and the inability to concentrate.

One way to deal with this is power napping. Christa Miller, who plays Mimi on *The Drew Carey Show,* naps in her trailer before a 7:00 P.M. taping of the show. At 5:00 P.M. she hangs a Do Not Disturb sign out and sleeps for a half hour, emerging refreshed and energized. Power naps work best if they're only ten to twenty minutes long—thirty minutes max. Otherwise, you end up feeling sluggish (not what you were going for).

If you're tired during the day, start eating smaller meals. A big meal will send a lot of blood into your digestive system, diverting it from the brain and muscles, making you feel exhausted. Eating several small, nutritious meals or snacks will eliminate the problem, your digestion will improve, and you'll be less likely to gain weight. Talk about win/win/win!

Fear makes you tense up your muscles, which leads to fatigue. You may also not be breathing properly when tense, so you're not getting enough oxygen.

There is a connection between depression and a lack of sleep. You are grumpy, unmotivated, and exhausted. The best way out of this cycle is to exercise. Exercise will tire your muscles, supply your brain with happy-making endorphins, and lead to healthy sleep. The more tired you are, the more exercise will help.

Energy and purpose are related. The stronger your sense of where you are going and why you want to go there, the more energy is at your disposal. A positive outlook allows people to use their positive energy to solve problems and achieve goals. When they encounter challenges, they believe they will overcome them and don't waste their time and energy worrying about it, which leaves them more time and energy to do something about it.

3. AVARICE: DEBT AND TAXES

We act as though comfort and luxury were the chief requirements in life, when all we need to make us really happy is something to be enthusiastic about.

—Charles Kingsley

I have had lucrative offers to take a "real job" in a "real office" with "real hours." I didn't even think twice. No amount of money would make me want to trade in my freedom or my love for what I do. (As I write this, I'm sitting in my shorts, tank top, and flip-flops under a palm tree in my backyard—and it's a weekday!)

Let me be honest here; I am not independently wealthy, but I do have a wife who works (benefits, steady income, and discounts on clothes—she works for Nordstrom) and I have a "day job" conducting workshops and doing keynote speeches. Yet, although I may not be a millionaire, I feel like I am the richest guy west of the Mississippi.

How much money would it take to make you feel as though you had enough? Five hundred thousand dollars? A million? What would you do if you had that kind of dough? Would you still work? Would all your problems be gone?

Actually, having money will not solve all your problems. It will make you feel good for a half a second. You'll have a lot more friends until it runs out. You'll get some new problems—investing, hiring financial help, worrying about losing what you've got. Money won't bring you peace of mind, freedom, or the sense of security you probably think it will. You'll find out you can never have enough. As you earn more, you spend more, and after a while you can't understand how you lived on less.

People with money to burn will always find themselves surrounded by people with matches: deadbeats, cheats, and creeps who want to take your hard-earned money; jealous rivals and critics who want to bring you down; people eager to work for you, do for you, supply you with whatever you desire.

You've undoubtedly heard the saying "Do what you love and the money will follow." They don't say when. For the creative person who sometimes has to work on spec, negative cash flow can be disastrous.

People don't pay you on time, but you're expected to pay your bills on time or face hefty penalties, repossession, loss of credit.

Actress Julianna Margulies was dealing with the dead when her big break came. Actually, she had a job packing up estates of the recently deceased in New York when she got the call to come to Hollywood and make a movie. She dropped what she was doing (not literally) and took the train home to Brooklyn, grabbed an overnight bag, and went to the airport, where a first-class ticket awaited her.

"I was in heaven. I'd been living hand-to-mouth, and then, when I got off the plane, they handed me three hundred dollars in per diem money. I was so overwhelmed with joy, I ran to the first pharmacy I saw and bought myself the conditioner that I always wanted to have," said the soon-to-be-rich-and-famous actress.

Even successful creatives often have to deal with periods of low income (everything's great until the play closes, and then it's months before you get another gig). The only way to deal with it is to go with the left brain and start a savings program during the good times to tide you over in the slow times.

Most right-brainers don't want to deal with filthy lucre. They don't want to worry about money—they just want to have it when they need it. I repeat: the only way to have it when you need it is to learn how to manage your money. If you don't balance your checkbook as you go, you never know how much you really have, and it doesn't seem real. Same thing with "funny money," i.e., credit cards. Paying cash for things gives you a raw appreciation for the value of a dollar. And it keeps you from going into debt.

It's easy to go overboard when you hit a good patch. Easy to play Big Spender and spread the joy around. But if you indulge that tendency, you're apt to find yourself playing Big Sponger somewhere down the road—a role that will not endear you to your friends, family, or associates.

It helps to have the kind of personality that can handle ups and downs—emotional as well as financial, because they often go together. It especially helps to have a spouse who can handle the uncertainty of life with a creative. My wife likes a steady income, and she deals with that by earning her own regular paycheck. We've come to terms with that, though it's a bit hard on the old ego. But I couldn't handle a regular job! There are negatives: With no steady income, I've got no credit to speak of. It was hard to buy a home. I had to provide tax returns for the past four years, and couldn't get the best mortgage rate.

Creative ups and downs will also affect your income. Ballplayers often have their best years when they are in their last year of a contract, when they are playing for less but trying to earn more in a big fat new deal. When they get the new contract, they often nose-dive, whether from complacency or burnout, for a year before they get back into the swing. Pressure to perform doesn't affect only your sex life, you know.

Sometimes you just have to wait for the timing to be right. Mario Puzo's first book got great reviews but didn't sell well. After a suggestion from his editor to write about the Mafia, he began to write *The Godfather,* but that same editor turned the finished manuscript down and he couldn't get an advance for it. At that time he was writing book reviews at two hundred dollars a pop. He was still basically broke. He borrowed money from his brother Tony and promised him 10 percent of the book if he could get it published. He ran into someone at Putnam and gave him a copy of the manuscript, then he took his wife and kids to Germany. While he was there, he found out that with American Express you could borrow five hundred dollars against your card in each European city you visited. By the time he got home he was deep in debt, with no job and no deal. He called his agent and told him he needed money. The agent replied, "Don't worry—we just turned down $400,000 for the paperback rights for your book." He ended up with $480,000, not including the movie rights.

▼ ▼ ▼

ACTION ITEM

Write one sentence about what money means to you. What's your financial philosophy?

▲ ▲ ▲

Just a Thought

Personally, I don't believe the world owes me a living—although for the amount I get, an apology would be nice.

You Deserve It

If you don't feel you deserve the money you make, you will find a way to sabotage your own success. If you don't feel as though you're making as much as you deserve, you're just like all the rest of us. Ask for a raise. Increase your rates.

Setting a value on your work is perhaps the most difficult part of a creative career. It pays to know your market, and to know where you stand in that market. What is the going rate in your area for what you do? Sometimes you can increase your income dramatically by moving to a better market. Many creative jobs pay twice as much in Los Angeles as they do in San Diego, though the two cities are only a hundred miles apart. There are complex economic reasons for this, but the bottom line is they have to pay you better to make it worth living in L.A.

Are you low-end, middle, or high-end, price-wise? Is that where you want to be? Think about positioning yourself, the kind of customers/ audience you want, the type of work you want, the amount of money you'll be satisfied with. Aim your marketing at a specific target and you're more likely to hit. You may have to work up from low end to high end, but it's actually easier to start out asking for more than to ask for a raise after you've been working for less. If you've got confidence, and good work to show, employers will believe you're worth more if you tell them so.

▼ ▼ ▼

FAST FACTS

Four out of five Americans in their prime working years believe that they will not have enough money for retirement, and more than 40 percent of women worry that they will be living in poverty when they retire, according to a survey conducted by SunAmerica. More than 50 percent of respondents said they had little money left over after paying bills to save for when they retire.

▲ ▲ ▲

One More Thought

The pursuit of money is a large part of people's lives. Once you get it, you have a huge hole to fill. You don't feel as good about yourself as you thought you would. What you're lacking now is a goal. Yeah, I know, you just reached your goal. Set another one, maybe one that doesn't involve money.

Parade of Dollars

Every February, *Parade* magazine runs the feature "What People Earn," in which they take a random sampling of the earnings of people in a variety of professions. I began saving these articles a few years ago. Let's just look at the fields that involve the creative person and examine their annual salaries.

Restaurateur	$85,000
Celine Dion	$34 million
Comic-book author	$250,000
Jerry Seinfeld	$66 million
Audiovisual technician	$34,000
Robin Williams	$23 million

Arts administrator	$23,000
Andrew Grove, Intel Chairman	$50 million
Floral Designer	$18,500
Leonardo DiCaprio	$2.5 million+
Marketing/PR director	$39,250
Tim Allen	$47 million
Artists' representative	$45,000
Mary Kay Ash	$500,000+
Executive chef	$53,000
Actor	$18,000
Musician	$24,000
Glassblower	$30,000
Newspaper reporter	$14,750
Art director	$40,000
Massage therapist	$23,500

ASK A PRO: GABRIEL WISDOM

Gabriel Wisdom is a San Diego financial guru, radio and TV talk-show host, and all-around creative person. He owned a surfboard repair business, lived in a treehouse on Kauai, sold radio time, had his own nationally syndicated radio show, was a rock promoter, studied to be a lawyer, completed a doctorate in psychology, served as a marriage counselor, sold real estate, went broke, and finally became a stockbroker and very independently wealthy. Now he has his own nationally syndicated radio talk show on the Business News Network.

Quite the zigzag approach to your career. I love it!

The zigzagging began in the 1960s (remember Captain Zig-Zag?). My "true calling" has always been personal growth, only the vehicles have kept changing. For example, there has been surfing, where I learned about timing and cycles. Radio, where I learned about media and marketing. Psychology, where I learned about human behavior. Harvard Business School, where I learned about financial engineering and business management. You get the picture.

How does the creative person and his money get parted?

When I was a rock-and-roll DJ, I had the good fortune to know many great recording artists. I knew these people because I was busy helping them gain more success. Unfortunately, some of them were too preoccupied with their art and neglected their bodies. These people died before they got old. Others neglected their money and didn't hang on to it, partly because they didn't covet money, or give it enough importance. Some lost it by taking unnecessary risks, others through get-rich-quick or harebrained schemes, but most just pissed it away.

You have to be involved with your financial life. If you don't want to be bothered with all the details, then it's a good idea to hire professionals who, for a fee, and without conflicts of interest, help you achieve your stated financial goals.

What advice would you give artists to help them manage their money?

Well, since these people are pretty good at forming habits (and usually not the good kind), I would try to get them to develop a savings habit. If they could save 30 to 50 percent of what they earned, it would lead to financial independence.

Is it unusual to find creative people in your field?

The great misnomer is that good financial people are linear. Many of the great financiers are creative people who, through a savings habit, have the money and cash flow to hire good detail people.

How can the right-brained person get started down the road to financial independence and financial freedom?

Kahlil Gibran wrote in his classic *The Prophet,* "When you yearn for things that you cannot name, and you grieve knowing not the cause, be certain that you are growing as all things that grow, and rising towards your higher self."

Yo, Gabriel, English please!

Keep daydreaming and imagining your best scenario for the future, because that's the one you'll eventually inhabit, in one form or another.

So what you are talking about is some form of goal-setting, right?

Right. But the creative person has to be able to visualize that goal. There is nothing inspiring in linear goal-setting. Instead, you should involve your art in creating your goal—draw it, paint it, try to feel its effects. Your goals should come from inspiration and involve all of your senses. Describe the lifestyle you want and what the benefits would be from reaching it. Also, enjoy the ride.

Funny Money

I've just gotten my first ATM card and am figuring out how money works. I'm dealing with such huge numbers that my perspective is way off. It's scary.

—*Claire Danes*

Fact: Forty percent of U.S. adults play the lottery at least once a month.

Tip: You will not win the lottery. (My chances of being wrong about that are 16 million to one, about the same chance that Ed McMahon will hand you a Publisher's Clearinghouse check.)

Hey, it's not easy to make and hang on to wealth. If it were, we would all be millionaires. You've got the talent and most of the information you need to earn all the money you want. But it'll take some work. Don't resent that, don't hang back from it. The work is the best part!

How is your financial health? Is it in critical condition (bankruptcy)? Intensive care (moving back in with Mom)? Burn unit (loaned money, ripped off)? Cancer (bad debt)? Just a common cold (too many payments)? Clean bill of health (savings are growing)?

If you want to be wealthy (healthy), study self-made wealthy people and the principles they followed and actions they took. "Prosperity begins with an idea. Become convinced that it's available; persuade yourself to obtain it, and accept it as it arrives," say Mark Victor Hanson and Jack Canfield, two guys who know how to make money on their ideas (they came up with the idea for the *Chicken Soup for the Soul* books).

Be a charity case. The more you look for ways to help others, the more you will earn, both financially and spiritually. You will be less preoccupied with success and more likely to achieve it.

Don't play the blame game. Stop blaming others for your predicament: It's the market, the economy, the company, my clients. You have a choice. To save or not to save. To charge or not to charge. Take charge of your money.

Bounce back. Even if you go into debt, you can bounce back better, stronger than you were before. When Kenny Rogers began his solo career, he was over $65,000 in debt. That was in 1976. First Edition had broken up after ten years of hit records, concerts, TV appearances, and even their own TV show. He had all the trappings of success. "I figured it would last forever. In fact, I was counting on it. So when it didn't last, I was devastated. I was also broke." His manager insists that Rogers hasn't earned less than $10 million a year since. The past is the past. Forgive yourself, but don't forget, and don't mess up again.

Be a budgeter. Make a budget, scrimp and save, pay off your credit cards, quit smoking, and save 10 percent of everything you earn. That's all there is to it. If you think it's boring, you fail to realize how much creativity it takes to make macaroni and cheese appetizing six nights a week.

Invest in yourself. Promotional materials, equipment, and training that are focused on bringing you closer to your goal are worth many sacrifices. I did my own PR and used the money I saved to finance my own book tour. A new suit is an investment in my speaking career. Sometimes you have to spend money to make money. Sometimes you don't.

Creative accounting. I'm not talking about cooking the books. I'm talking about finding ways to save, little bits you cannot spend. Look for little things to cut back on. For example, Chinese takeout at $15 per week costs $780 per year. Caller ID at $8 per month and call-waiting at $2.50 run you $126 annually. A $2 latte every morning adds up to $718 by Christmas.

Using charts and graphs may make income/outgo make sense to you. Do it yourself or let your computer do it for you. Numbers aren't necessarily work. They can be play. I like to play at making a budget that doesn't end up in the red. It's a good game, I never tire of it. I'll win someday, too, I will.

Lower your overhead. You hear about all these enormous salaries, but when you take away everyone's cut (manager, agent, lawyer, business manager), it's not quite so grand. When a band goes out on tour, even more money goes out to food, the backup, the roadies, equipment, lodging, lights, wardrobe, and TAXES! Then, if you put half into savings, you're sitting on a very small pile, but people expect you to spend big because all they know is the mega-number you started out with. It's hard not to live up to the expectations of those around you and toss about money you can't afford to toss. It's even harder to resist your own expectations of what it would be like when you got this far. Only it isn't like that, is it? That's why so many already wealthy people blow it all on get-rich-quick schemes. Enjoy what you do have, and leave it at that.

Are there ways to cut back on, or cut out, some things that maybe are hidden cash drainers? Do you need a personal hairdresser? Could you get by with only thirty pairs of shoes? Lean and mean, that's how I run my business.

If it sounds too good to be true, run away. It's that Vegas mentality that leads people to risk it all with the smallest chance of ever hitting it big. Be sensible. It's what they'll least expect. It'll make you a true original.

Take the "free" out of "freelance." Limit how much you're willing to do for free. Ultimately, people won't value your work unless you place a value on it. I believe you should be paid what you're worth and always overdeliver. It's funny, when I raised my fees to try to slow down my speaking business (I was getting way too busy to suit my chosen lifestyle), my bookings actually increased. I have learned that you can't make it on volume. There just aren't enough hours in the day.

I know a graphic artist who, to get rid of difficult clients, doubled her fees. The real problem was that she was too busy with the little pain-in-the-ass clients to go after bigger and better fish. She got rid of her most difficult clients, and makes more money with less work and far less stress. The people who stayed on despite higher rates don't seem to mind—they're still getting great product and service for the price. She looked at the 20 percent of her business that gave her 80 percent of her income and satisfaction, and restructured.

Want to get rich? According to the book *The Millionaire Next Door,* the best way to make a million is to become self-employed. They learned that about two-thirds of the millionaires who still worked were entrepreneurs. "Self-employed people are four times more likely to be millionaires than people who work for others."

Recycle old ideas. Without selling pills, potions, or pie-in-the-sky products, look for ways to earn residual income (and I am not talking about multilevel marketing!). Can you resell your work? Turn chapters into articles, illustrations into clip art, original art into prints, or photographs into stock photo disks. A local photographer I know sells his photos to stock photo agencies, which pay him handsomely and get him exposure in areas he never would have received otherwise. Could some of your art be merchandised or licensed? *Peanuts* characters are on everything from clothing to cosmetics. Subsidiary licenses by Charles Schulz's Creative Associates, Inc., make him millions of dollars a year, mostly for work he has already done.

Diamonds are a carpooler's best friend. Carpooling saves the ecology, saves time (you can ride in the diamond lane), saves money (you spend less on gas, tolls, and parking), and lets you make new friends, connections, and fun. According to one study, only 35 percent of people polled like to drive alone. You can actually save up to one thousand dollars a year that you can use for things that bring you joy.

Be a do-it-yourselfer. Do your own PR, stretch your own canvases, clean your own office, wash your own car, type your own letters . . .

Chump change. Write down in a notebook all the little incidentals you spend your chump change on. Don't be judgmental, just note when, where, how much, and why you spend on things you don't even enjoy, like ATM fees.

The sky IS falling. Play the "what if?" game . . . What if a dealer came to my studio and tripped on an easel and broke his back? What if I got sick? Was in a car wreck? Plane crash? Robbed? What if there was a flood and it destroyed my equipment? Art? Don't forget mudslides, earthquakes, hurricanes, tornadoes, fire, riots. Or, more likely than all those scenarios, what if I have a nervous breakdown? Ever play the game of Life (you know, the one with the little cars that you load up with kids to make more money)? In that game (and in the real world), you are far better off with the big four: health, auto, life, and home insurance. Join associations for group discounts if you are a freelancer. Videotape your belongings so you have a record. Back up your computer files regularly, and store them away from your office.

Money magnet. If you are worried about never having enough money, you never will. It's funny how that works. Fear prevents you from doing the things required to get it. (Some risk is involved when it comes to acquiring money.) Take a chance. Be a money magnet. It doesn't always have to make financial sense. Jimmy Buffett bought a bar in the Caribbean. Billy Joel (now there's a sad story, about how he was burned by his money manager) decided to build boats, knowing it won't make him wealthy. Enjoy *some* of that money you are earning. Money is meant to be spent, right? This won't be too hard for you, I can tell.

Crap[s]. Don't gamble with your money. This includes getting greedy when it comes to returns on investments. Don't gamble, ever, with more than you're willing (and able) to lose.

Loan sharks. Don't lend money to others. Help a friend in need and they'll never forget you. Especially when they're in need again.

Don't shop when you are depressed. Or hungry. Window-shop when you're broke, but don't go inside. I have a friend who shops catalogs. She checks out the clothes and the hair and all that female stuff. She chooses what she likes, circles it with a pen, or dog-ears the page and puts the catalog away for a while. When she goes through it again, sometimes she still likes what she highlighted before, sometimes not. If she really likes it, she saves the catalog for a little longer. By the third time she goes through it, she's had all the pleasure of shopping and choosing, with none of the expense of buying, and she's ready to move on to another catalog.

Barter your services. Haircut for taxes. Logo for housework. Lodging for baby-sitting. An illustrator I know traded her services for those of a personal trainer, and the two ended up doing a children's book together.

Trade a raise for more time off. Money isn't everything. Did I say that already? Well, it isn't.

Plastic or paper? Credit cards can get you in trouble, because you don't realize how much you're spending. It's just a signature, right? It's not dollars out of your pocket. Wrong! Put a picture of your mother on your card—that should curb your spending. "But, Ma, I really need . . ." Stick to a single credit card so it really is just for emergencies. Keep a lower limit. Get a mileage card so that you can earn travel miles. Pay it off every month—those finance charges can really add up. Get a low-interest card for those times when you can't pay it off right away.

Do not live hand-to-mouth, from paycheck to paycheck, from client to client. Save up for changes in the market, lulls, slumps, necessary equipment, and other investments. Saving gives you a sense of security. It means you don't have to do things that suck just to pay the rent. It means more freedom, less stress, room to make better long-range decisions. With savings, you can take a position in a start-up company for low pay at first. You can invest in things like alternative energy sources. You can travel, take a break, start your own business. You won't fight with your spouse over money so much.

Automatic debit is a great way to make saving painless. It's not money out of your pocket, because it never got into your pocket in the first place. "I think it is worth keeping in mind that the businessmen who run banks are so worried about holding on to things that they put little chains on all their little pens," says Miss Piggy.

Live for today and plan for tomorrow. My motto.

There is a difference between cheap and frugal. When you leave a 5-percent tip, that's cheap. Frugal is when you use a two-for-one coupon. (And tip on the total, not the discounted amount.) Thomas Edison was frugal. He encouraged guests at his summer home to tour the grounds and inspect the various inventions he had on display. To enter his garden, each visitor had to pass through a turnstile, which was not easy to push. "Why do you have this thing here?" a guest asked. "It's a pain." Edison smiled and said, "Every single soul who pushes his way through that turnstile pumps seven gallons of water into a tank on my roof."

Live below your means. Esther Dyson has been described as the most powerful woman in Silicon Valley. Her conference (PC Forum) is attended by hundreds of cyber-stars annually, and her newsletter (*Release 1.0*) can make or break new high-tech ventures. While other cyber-moguls collect planes and boats, Dyson lives very modestly. If you met her on the street, you would never guess at her success. She prefers to invest her money in enterprises she finds intellectually intriguing and useful. "Money enables me to invest in things I think should exist."

Hang in there. Many of the rich and famous went through their "Spam" days. Michael J. Fox sold portions of his sectional couch to pay the rent, and used a pay phone for his office.

Lifestyles of the Not-So-Rich and Almost Famous

As a child, a library card takes you to exotic, faraway places. When you're grown up, a credit card does it.

—*Sam Ewing*

Sometimes you need to splurge. You need to put on a good show for a potential client, you need to impress your boss, you just need the ego boost of spending some money on yourself. These times often come when you're not exactly loaded. (Not that kind of loaded!) I tried to put my creativity to good use and come up with some clever (and somewhat crazy) ideas to live large when you are largely broke.

- Treat friends to breakfast instead of dinner (or meet for dessert and coffee).
- Rent a sailboat for a day rather than buying one. (Owning a boat is like a hole in the water that you throw money into.)
- Fix the outfit that's been lying on the floor of the closet for a year because it's missing a button.
- Create your own art to hang on the walls.
- Go to the library.
- Matinees are a great way to get out and see a movie without having to sell your firstborn.
- Get involved with a support group instead of a shrink—er, psychologist.
- Make birthday and holiday gifts using your art.
- For vacations, swap homes. Living someplace else, even in your own town, changes your perspective.
- Travel during the off-season, cash in frequent-flyer miles.

- Offer to get bumped off a flight for a free ticket.
- Take the train.
- Create your own drive-in theater. Put the TV in front of the car, pop a bag of popcorn, rent a movie. There you are!

Raise Money

They say it's far worse to have had money and lost it than never to have had it at all. There are ways to raise money—some of them admittedly painful—when your banker turns you down. These might include the following:

- Sell your car or home.
- Sell your ideas (consulting pays far better than what you did to get the expertise to consult with).
- Sell your business.
- Sell your clutter.
- Sell overstock.
- Teach or speak.
- Barter.
- Ask your granny.
- Suggest an early inheritance—it saves on taxes later, too. But it only works if your parents or grandparents actually intended to leave you something. It works better if they have some savings of their own. It works best if they already have a trust set up for you.
- Refinance your house, or take a second mortgage.
- Get a roommate, or move back home.

Get Paid

It's not show me the money, it's give me the money!
—*Harriet Schechter*

Most graphic artists get paid half up front, the rest on delivery. Many performance artists get a small percentage up front as earnest money (unfortunately, huge signing bonuses such as the ones sports stars get are uncommon), and then a regular paycheck for the duration of the gig (or a flat payment when it's over). Publishers usually give one-third when they accept the proposal, one-third when they get the manuscript, and one-third when the book is published, often with royalty payments depending on book sales. When you work for a business, either on contract or as an employee, you will get paid either once or twice a month.

Payment setups vary by industry. Within those general parameters, you can often set things up your way. But get a signed contract, whatever your situation. Small-claims court will take you much more seriously with a contract—and so will your client. A contract should spell out what you're going to do, when you're going to do it, how much you're going to be paid, in what form and when. The clearer the contract is, the less chance you have of misunderstandings that will cost you time and money.

Many creative services have boilerplate contracts you can get from books or find in an office-supply store. You can make your own by writing it up in letter or proposal form and adding words like, "Initial payment indicates acceptance of this proposal in full." ALWAYS get some payment up front—preferably enough to cover your expenses. That way, if they flake out on you, you're out only your time and energy, not your working capital.

For a big job, there's nothing wrong with asking for references and running a credit check. A reputable company will not be insulted by this. It's part of doing business. I did a lot of work for a start-up magazine once, not knowing the publisher had just come out of a bankruptcy in another state. He bankrupted again, and I was out two months' work, plus the time it took to go to court and testify against the guy.

Keep accurate records. You don't want to hound people who have paid, and you don't want to forget to send an invoice and follow up when past due. Most people won't pay without an invoice. You can use a prefab one or make your own—it's pretty simple. List who the client is, who authorized the job, what the job was (in detail), what the agreed price was, any expenses (long-distance phone, fax, travel, materials, etc.), the total and payment-due date. Mine say "Invoice is due and payable upon receipt." That means pay *now,* please. Even with that, *now* means "within thirty days" to most people, "within sixty days" to some, and "when you get a chance" to others. If you want to get paid, follow up. I make those calls on the first of the month and get them out of the way (not my favorite thing to do).

You can offer discounts for cash up front to avoid all the invoice hassle, although many clients will still want an invoice for their records. Discounts are usually reserved for hard goods and not services, however—a painting, not a logo, a handmade dress, not a performance.

Be creative in your approach to deadbeats. Light but serious. Don't let them blow you off, but don't get angry, either. This is business. If they refuse to pay, take 'em to small-claims court (under $5,000). Small-claims court is designed for the nonlawyer; the system is user-friendly and nonthreatening. Use it. You fill out a form, they set a date, you go tell your story in front of a judge, they tell their story, the judge decides—Judge Judy, here we come. The only problem with small-claims court is that it has no enforcement capability, which means you may end up with a judgment but no money. Most people will pay if the court tells them to, however.

If the worst happens, you can write bad debts off your taxes, although this is not as straightforward as you might think. There are very specific rules about what constitutes a bad debt. Check with your tax person or accountant before you stick your neck out.

Taxes

> *Internal Revenue Service: We've Got What It Takes*
> *to Take What You've Got.*
>
> —*Bumper sticker*

In the mail was a plain white envelope. I glanced at the return address, which read, "IRS." My legs got all rubbery, my head got light, and I started to sweat profusely. I squinted and double-checked to see if maybe it was addressed to someone else and mistakenly put in my box. I held it at arm's length and looked again. Damn, that *was* my name on it. I dropped the envelope as if it were burning hot. When I finally got around to opening it, it was worse than I thought—I was being audited. They wanted me to come to IRS headquarters.

Chances are you will never be targeted. Statistics show that only about 1 percent of all returns are ever audited. (Feel better already, don't you?) On the other hand, home-based businesses are more likely to be flagged than most. The laws about independent contractors and home office deductions are very strict, very confusing, and often abused.

Now that I have been through three of these (lucky me), I realized that if you are honest, keep good records, and save your receipts, there is nothing to fear. You *can* beat the IRS! Yet there are creative people (Willie Nelson, for example) who have lost everything (and then some) because of their reluctance or inability to get their taxes in order. So here are some tips on how to avoid an audit and, God forbid, how to survive one if you are ever asked to come before the (now supposedly friendlier) Internal Revenue Service.

File a neat return. One of the quickest ways to have the IRS come down on you is to file a return that can't be read. They will wonder if you are trying to hide something. Consider using a software program to file. The forms are in the program, so you don't have to go scrambling for a 1437-whatzis on April 14, they cost less than a professional tax preparer, and the expense of the program is a built-in write-off. MacInTax and

TurboTax are surprisingly easy, they walk you through the process step by step with plenty of help and lots of suggestions, and they're updated annually so you don't get caught out, thinking that last year's tax law is the same as this year's tax law. And MacInTax won't let you print out the form unless it's complete. The IRS seemed to be suspicious of these programs at first, but now it accepts them readily.

List all reportable income. That may include advances, royalties, fees, commissions, and whatever else may have been reported to the IRS. If you get a Form 1099 from somebody, they've told the IRS they paid you. There's no getting around it.

Home office deductions are a red flag. So are deductions that are way out of line with your income. My advice is to keep good records if you file a Schedule C (for self-employment income). I know a cartoonist who was audited because her office supply expenses were triple the norm. She took her box of receipts in and explained that she had put art supplies under the office supplies heading—there was no place else to put them. It made sense to the auditor, and she got a "no change." Which means the IRS accepts your numbers and won't look into them again for a couple of years. Hooray!

Have someone else prepare your taxes. The devil is in the details, and for most right-brainers, preparing your own taxes is not going to be the best use of your time or energy. It might be worth it to get a professional to deal with all your little scraps of paper shoved in a shoebox. Unfortunately, most professionals are going to want you to deal with those scraps and just give them the totals. Face it, taxes are going to be a pain in the neck no matter how you deal with them. The big advantage of using a professional tax preparer is that they will go with you and justify your numbers if you do get audited.

Write it off. Remember, they only tax you on your profits if you are a freelancer. So do what you can to lower your taxable income—defer invoicing to another calendar year, buy more equipment and supplies, invest in a retirement plan to offset income.

If you are audited, remember, loose lips sink ships. Don't give them more information than they ask for. Most audits are limited, covering a specific area (like travel expenses). Don't open up a whole other can of worms. Do not ask questions. Bring all your receipts. Be able to find things. Be nice. Be on time. Be helpful. Leave the gun at home.

The Art of the Deal

The minute you settle for less than you deserve, you get even less than you settled for.

—Maureen Dowd

Negotiation is an area you're likely to be very good at. At the same time, you're likely to be very uncomfortable with it. Many creatives can use a professional to do their negotiating for them, and in most cases that's a good idea. But if you're a freelancer, or a wage earner, you're going to be on your own when it comes to making the deal. Here are a few guidelines to make it a little easier:

Keep your mouth shut. Let them make the first offer. Remember when Kramer on *Seinfeld* burned himself with scalding hot coffee and sued? The coffeehouse was about to offer him lattes for life *and* a large cash settlement, but when they mentioned lattes for life, Kramer blurted out, "I'll take it!" If you can be patient, they may keep putting things on the table.

Western Union offered to buy one of Thomas Edison's inventions. Edison didn't know how much to ask for, so he stalled and asked for a couple of days to think it over. He asked his wife for her opinion. She said it was worth $20,000. He was stunned. When he was asked again what he wanted for his invention, he couldn't get "$20,000" out of his mouth, it sounded like so much. So he stood there speechless. An impatient Western Union executive blurted out, "How about $100,000?"

Look for a win/win solution. You win and then you win again. Seriously, it's poor form to bully people into submission or be a whiner and guilt people into agreeing. In any negotiation, there's a trade—what you have/they want for what they have/you want, usually services for money. Ideally, everybody gets what they want and walks away happy.

Use your creativity to come up with unique solutions to seemingly impossible situations. They want to pay you less, so give them options.

Don't take it personally. This is business. Both sides have a viewpoint that deserves respect. They want to get as much as possible for as little as possible. It's called capitalism (greed). You want to earn as much as possible while getting the strokes you need to keep that creative ego alive. A smart businessperson will give you lots of strokes and less money—a great title and a small salary. Is that what you want? Try to be dispassionate and realistic (left-brained).

Don't deal with the devil. If it doesn't feel right, if it causes you to compromise your values, don't do it. You may see dollar signs and be tempted to take a deal that will ultimately cost you in other ways. Look at the whole price before you make a decision.

Be willing to walk away. When you are willing to do that, you have all the power. If you're too needy, they'll take advantage of you—or they'll decide you're not good enough. If you come on like a loser, you'll get treated like one.

Ask for the sun and the moon. Have a bottom line. What is fair, what is the fair market value, what other options could make up for money? Know your lower limit—and don't go near it.

Knowledge is power. Step one is to find out as much as you can about the person or organization you are dealing with. That way, you can anticipate their moves, get an idea what their bottom-line (or top-line) amount is, how they made past decisions, what their goals are, and how you can help them. Go in with a game plan. What are others in comparable positions getting paid?

Don't lock yourself in. With creatives, more than with most people, things change, fast and often. Be wary of long-term deals, no matter how attractive they might seem.

Take your time. No matter how good an offer sounds at first, give yourself a day or two to think about it. Don't say yes on impulse and regret it later.

Use the car-salesman routine. "Let me talk to my boss (my agent, my whatever), and I'll get back to you." Then say that the boss, agent, whatever didn't go for it. You fought for it (ha!), but they didn't bite. They would, however, go for . . .

Use your intuition. Read the person, and change tactics if necessary. It's not so much *what* they say, it's how they say it. Watch for body language and other hidden clues. Read the subtitles when you are negotiating with someone. Most people ignore their gut reactions. "Shut up, can't you see I'm in an important meeting right now!?" they will say to their subconscious, while their instincts are shouting, "But . . . but . . ." Later your gut will say, "I told you so, but you never pay any attention to me." Listen to this built-in baloney detector. It is there to protect and serve. Let it.

An oral agreement is worthless. In any dispute, it's only your word against theirs. After negotiations are complete, put these items into a letter of agreement.

The early bird gets to see who the worms are. Try to get to a meeting early enough to see people when they have their guard down, in a relaxed state.

Timing is everything. Pitch it at the right time. When someone is desperate for what you have, you have the upper hand. Pitch things when you are hot. If you were just featured in a national magazine, that's the time to try to land a book deal.

Do NOT lose your cool. Many deals fall through because a creative person was emotional and/or irrational. When you are on top, you can get away with a lot. You've heard stories about the perks that big-name stars negotiate (no green M&Ms, a private jet, a massage therapist). But even when you are on top, if you are seen as difficult, nobody will want to work with you. I can think of several actors and actresses whose careers came to a standstill because of their unreasonable demands and difficult behavior. Don't get carried away. Nobody is irreplaceable.

Be confident. Babe Ruth was asked to take a salary cut during the Depression. He insisted on getting $80,000, the same salary he earned the year before. Yankee officials pointed out that even President Hoover didn't make that much money. "I know," Ruth said, "but I had a better year."

Bad Deals

When a person with experience meets a person with money, the person with experience will get the money and the person with the money will get some experience.

—*Leonard Lauder*

Agents, publishers, dealers, record labels, chain stores, studios, and galleries all have more experience than you when it comes to doing deals. They bring that experience to the table, and turn the tables on you. They will play games at your expense. Being aware of that fact is the first step to getting into the ball game. They see you as a piece of meat. It's not personal. It's business.

Get a good agent with negotiating experience. Let him or her know your bottom line. When Tommy Lasorda was asked about what terms Mexican-born pitcher Fernando Valenzuela might settle for in his upcoming contract negotiations with the Dodgers, Lasorda replied, "He wants Texas back."

Beware of dealers who don't use contracts or formal agreements. Get it in writing, *especially* if you are dealing with friends. State your terms clearly and up front. As Samuel Goldwyn once said, "A verbal contract isn't worth the paper it's printed on."

Contracts always favor the party who created them. Once you sign one, it is very hard to reverse it. So you want to balance what they want and what you can live with. Fight for key things. Protect your rights. Play "what if" scenarios; cut through the legalese and put it into perspective. Money isn't everything. What about percentages, royalties, clauses, buy-back rights, when you are paid, how much promotion will they do, how easy is it to get out of, are there arbitration clauses in case of a lawsuit, and so on? Will you get credit for the work you are doing? How will you be paid? If you get a percentage, is it of the retail or wholesale price? Will you get a bonus if you finish on time and under budget?

Don't sign anything you don't understand. Get a lawyer to read the fine print and inject a dose of paranoia for you.

I am not a lawyer. Let me say that again. I am not a lawyer, nor do I play one on television. That's my disclaimer. Now, you will have your ideas ripped off. Sorry, but it's true. If you are as talented and creative as I think you are, someone, somewhere, will steal one of your ideas. So what? You should be flattered. My philosophy (remember the disclaimer a minute ago) is that I can always come up with newer and better ideas anyway. You can have the old ones; I'll win out in the end by coming up with the new and improved version.

Get all the trademarks and copyrights and patents you want, but they are useless if you can't afford to sue. Be better, faster, and more cutting-edge; that's your protection. If you are too guarded with your ideas, they will never see the light of day. Have people sign a nondisclosure contract if it makes you feel better.

I read an interesting article about inventor Ed Cohen, who has created over a hundred products. He said, "Flood the market with a new product, ride it until it's knocked off, then move on to a new one." He never got patents for his creations—too involved and time-consuming, he says.

4. PRIDE: BIG HEAD, BIG PROBLEMS
The only disability in life is a bad attitude.

—Scott Hamilton

Albert Einstein never understood why anybody treated him as anything more than a physics professor. His modesty is nicely illustrated by this story: A girl stopped in to see him every day on her way home from school. One day the girl's mother met Einstein and asked, "What do you two talk about every day?" Einstein laughed, "She brings me cookies and I help her with her arithmetic homework."

Early in Cheryl Gould's career as a radio correspondent and researcher in the Paris bureau of NBC News, she was asked to book her bureau chief's appointments. At first she was offended. Then she realized what a great opportunity it would be to get on her bosses' good side. She did a bang-up job, thanks to her fluent French. Her reporting assignments quickly doubled, and today she's a vice-president at NBC News.

Don't decide you're too good now to do the things that made you a success in the first place. How many opportunities could you be missing out on? Burt Reynolds took a minor role in *Strip Tease* and a supporting role in *Boogie Nights,* and did a great job and revitalized his career. Bruce Willis makes cameo appearances all the time. (Can you say *Pulp*

Fiction?) You don't always have to be the star. You just have to make the most of the opportunities you have.

Chris Rock put it well: "You know how it can be in this business. Fickle. Here today, gone today."

Be nice to people on the way up, because you'll see them again on the way down. After a rocket to the top, Rock fell like a stone. Couldn't even get an agent. Regrouped and came back, doing whatever it took. He did commercials, including the voice of Li'l Penny for Nike. He hosted the MTV Music Video Awards. He took small roles wherever he could get them, eventually earning two Emmy Awards and gaining a lot of momentum. *Lethal Weapon 4* put him right back on top again.

Drew Carey owns the one-bedroom house in the modest Cleveland neighborhood where he was raised. "I've noticed a lot of comics who were really funny when they were young and struggling. Then they acquire their big houses and their movie deals and they're not so funny anymore. No matter how big or small my career gets, I just don't want to give up my roots."

Meredith Brooks, who hit it big with her gold record "Bitch," claims success hasn't changed her. "I talk to my friends every day. And I still take out the garbage and make my own bed." Conversely, Jim Carrey left his wife during the filming of *Ace Ventura: Pet Detective* because, in part, he couldn't deal with domestic life anymore. He mentions taking out the trash as the turning point.

Dawson's Creek's James Van Der Beek had a *Hard Day's Night*-type experience when he made a personal appearance in Seattle and had to be rescued from the mob of eager teenage girls who wanted to rip his clothes off. After appearing in the flop *Angus,* he experienced a long dry spell. That memory has helped to keep him grounded. "I was unemployed and depressed. I didn't even have an agent."

Mary J. Blige grew up in a public housing project in Yonkers, New York. At seventeen she went to a shopping mall karaoke booth and recorded a cover tune. Her stepfather got the tape to a manager, who got it to Uptown Records and, before she turned twenty, Blige had a contract and a career. Her debut album went to number one and sold nearly 3 million copies. Unfortunately, rumors of bad behavior were becoming part of her résumé. She was rude, unreliable, and unstable. She cleaned up her act and cleaned house, getting rid of some of the negative people around her who were bringing her down. "There were people telling me I was fat and ugly and that I couldn't sing. There was such a cloud of negativity around me, so many people who didn't want me to see that I was worth something."

There are hundreds of stories of people who made it big and blew it. You don't have to be one of them. You can choose not to make it big. Or you can be prepared to handle it when you do.

Take on a variety of projects. It's all too easy to be pigeonholed, and you'll lose out on opportunities to spread your wings. Don't let yourself be known for only one thing.

Don't brag. You will alienate people, and your circle of friends will dwindle. You need people to keep you grounded. It's all too easy to surround yourself with sycophants when you're very successful. They will not help you stay successful. Stick with your friends, those who are willing to tell you your head's up your butt. Listen to them. They're in your corner.

Bad attitudes are contagious, and companies try to get rid of them quickly. It's not okay to be boorish, selfish, and cruel, and behave like an idiot. Too many people think that means you have power. Power is having choices. Don't choose to be an ass.

Control the temptation to be bizarre. Many people feel that you have to get farther and farther out there just to be different in today's anything-goes society. To pull your pants down and moon the paparazzi. You can be weird and quirky. But do it to please yourself, not to impress somebody else, because you're likely to be impressing the wrong people, or the right people the wrong way. Remember that dealers, agents, and record executives live in the real world and they may not get it.

Act like a pro. "The artistic temperament is a disease which afflicts amateurs," said G. K. Chesterton.

To keep a true perspective on their importance, everyone should have a dog that worships them and a cat that will ignore them.

Ego

One thing I hope I'll never be is drunk with my own power. And anybody who says I am will never work in this town again.

—*Jim Carrey*

Runaway ego can ruin your chances for clarity and lead to poor decisions. You feel you are invincible. Drunk with your own power. The Greeks called it *hubris,* the feeling that you're as good as the gods. In Greek myths, the gods usually got ticked off by that attitude and proved you wrong. Thunder, lightning, suffering, and failure tended to follow.

Fame

Fame is delightful, but as collateral it doesn't rank high.

—*Elbert Hubbard*

My dad understood the basic law of show business—you're never as good as they say you are. Once you understand that, you'll survive anything.

—George Clooney

I'm very leery of thinking that I'm somebody. Because nobody really is. Everybody is able to do something well, but in this country there is a premium put on stardom.

—Stephen King

5. LUST: SEX, DRUGS, AND ROCK 'N' ROLL

I think nearly all of us have some kind of defect.

—Tennessee Williams

Addictions kill talent. There are so many examples of celebrities who lost everything due to drugs that I had a hard time narrowing down just which stories I would use. Then I had a worse revelation: for every Robert Downey Jr., there are tens of thousands of gifted and talented people who never had a chance to fall, because their drug abuse kept them from realizing their potential.

Addictions often make us impotent as artists. (Although, as you read on, you'll see that some were able to fight through their impotence and find other ways to sabotage their careers.) You have to rise above these temptations.

You don't have to be a heroin addict to get yourself in serious trouble. Self-indulgence of the wrong kind at the wrong time can do you in, all while you're feeling smug that you've avoided the big pitfalls. Staying up all night clubbing before a big presentation or when you are on deadline can do it. Spending more than you have. Playing around on your spouse. Goofing off when a client is expecting results. Being snotty to people who can help advance your career. Speeding down the freeway (*mea culpa*). There are all kinds of self-destructive behavior. It catches up with you.

Sex

I'm such a slut. But who else is there? You're on the road for two years . . . You don't want to start to shag groupies.

—Sarah McLachlan, on dating her keyboard player
and marrying her drummer

When you hear Hugh Grant's name, what's the first thing you think of? How about Pee Wee Herman? President Clinton? These are people with successful careers who let sex take them down a peg or three.

Nat King Cole's widow admitted that he was less than faithful. She realized it was par for the course. Not all partners are that understanding. Loni Anderson and Burt Reynolds, Mia Farrow and Woody Allen come to mind. Nasty breakups, huge settlements, loss of contact with your kids, depression, bad publicity, loss of respect, loss of clients, friends, and support can all follow indiscretions of the sexual kind. Not to mention illness, suffering, and death.

It took Rob Lowe years to get past an incident with an underaged girl, a hotel, and a video. Ted Nugent doesn't do drugs, doesn't drink, but talks about his addiction to sex. "Mona" sleeps with everyone on the set of a shoot and wonders why she gets no respect. Just say "Ho!"

Temptations are everywhere when you are a rock star, actor, or celebrity in your field. And it's lonely when you're away from home for long stretches. Dating co-workers is one answer, but it has dangers, too. Look what happened to Fleetwood Mac.

Don't talk about your sex life with co-workers. Don't open that door. Blatantly flaunting your sexuality is a no-no. Interoffice romance is another not-so-good idea, especially with the potential problems posed by sexual harassment laws. Will that stop you? Of course not. My advice is, be discreet. Getting caught doing it in the supply room would not go over well in most companies. Lock the door. In the movies, why doesn't anybody lock the door?

Use common sense. If you don't have any, get some. Showing up wearing the same thing you did the night before is tacky. Keep a spare toothbrush and a change of clothes in the trunk of your car.

The NFL had a mandatory seminar for rookies who just came into major money, fame, and freedom. During the seminar weekend, they had two especially attractive women helping the players with their needs. Several of the players took their best shot at trying to line up dates with these women. At the end of the seminar, it was announced that the two women had HIV. The players were floored. Hopefully, it taught them the intended lesson. Be careful out there. Wear your raincoat.

Drugs (The High Life)

I think the only reason I ever used drugs was to overcome self-doubt. I didn't use drugs actually to create, but simply to buffer those feelings of inadequacy.

—*Don Henley*

Creatives are very susceptible to substance abuse. (Try to say that fast ten times.) History bears this out. Yet many people's worst drug problems come out when they are at the height of their careers. Why would you want to drown out the best time of your life?

Dealing with success can be harder than getting there. Lenny Bruce started doing heroin when his club career was taking off. Calvin Klein became addicted to Valium and vodka after he got married, bought a new home in the Hamptons, and launched the highly successful Eternity perfume.

Abusers are taking steps backward, not forward. Drugs aren't all they are "cracked" up to be, anyway. So you get wired, then what do you do? Work? Usually you are too hyped up to sit still enough to create, so you end up cleaning the house, or partying loudly enough to bring the police calling. Drugs and alcohol do not make you more productive, interesting, or creative. They make you loaded. They make you stupid. They make you very, very vulnerable.

Besides the obvious problems, addictions are expensive. One DUI is said to cost a person eleven thousand dollars before all is said and done. Yikes! If you get drunk and have an accident, it could cost you your life. It could cost someone else's life. It could cost you a relationship. It could cost you your job.

A cocaine habit can cost you five hundred dollars or more a day, not to mention what it takes to supply the "friends" you party with.

The people who are all too eager to supply you with drugs are not your friends. They are entrepreneurs themselves, and you're helping to make them successful at the cost of your own career. Those who want to drink with you all night long are enjoying your life more than you are. Get rid of them.

When you're high, you do and say things you regret later. (I don't even remember getting that tattoo of Scooby Doo on my butt.) Maybe you are a good person, but when you drink . . . You sleep around, get violent, or say ugly things. Any way you look at it, this is not going to enhance your life or your career.

Dennis Hopper was voted Most Likely to Succeed by his high-school classmates in 1954. He got off to a good start with a role in *Rebel Without a Cause* (remember the switchblade fight in the Hollywood Hills?). He also wrote, directed, and starred in *Easy Rider*. Then alcohol and drugs robbed him of his prime years. When he sobered up, he worked like mad to build a body of work, including the horrible film *Super Mario Brothers*, to overcome his reputation as a loser, a flake, and a boozer. His young son asked him why he made that film. "So you can have nice shoes," said Dennis. The boy looked his dad in the eye and said, "Dad, I don't need shoes *that* badly."

Drugs and alcohol can be a crutch. You're afraid you won't be good this time, you won't hit the mark, you'll be found out as a fraud. So you drink to make the fear go away. And you do more as the fear grows, the habit grows, and the conviction that you can't do it without your drug of choice grows. Eventually, you lose your ability to be good, to hit the mark, to prove you're not a fraud.

Another phenomenon is the James Dean factor. He made fast living and self-destructive behavior cool: "Live fast and die young." Many creative people live too much in the moment and have no future vision. Also, many highly successful people have unlimited access to everything from pot to prostitutes (and the money to afford it). It's hard to hang back when "everybody's doing it." Some have fought through it and are clean and sober; others weren't so lucky.

Tommy Boy is one of my favorite comedies. I am a big Chris Farley fan. He was thirty-three when he died of a combination of too many drugs and too much weight. Chris Farley was the poster child for self-destructive behavior. He was insecure, emulating his idol John Belushi, who also died of a drug overdose. Try to find positive role models.

If addiction and failure happen to so many gifted and successful people, how can you possibly avoid it? The answer is to find satisfying, rewarding, and challenging work and create a solid personal life so you don't want to escape reality by getting stoned, eating sweets, and watching *Love Boat* reruns. Get addicted to life!

Look, I am no saint. I could party with the best of them. (I still boogie from time to time.) It's a hobby, not a habit. I decided not to make it a way of life. (I can't bounce back from hangovers the way I used to.) When I look back to my younger days, I realize I lost a lot of time.

A couple of books ago, I started smoking cigars. It got to the point where I couldn't write without a cigar. It's a surprisingly expensive habit, and they stink. It started out as my reward for finishing a chapter. Then it became my reward for finishing a couple of pages. As soon as this book is done, I swear I'm gonna quit. I just have to find a reward to replace them with.

Did you know that cigarettes make you less creative? The capillaries that bring blood to your brain shrink when you smoke.

Paul Thomas Anderson, who wrote and directed *Boogie Nights,* described his morning work routine: "I write early, like 6:00 A.M., and I can only really write for three hours. That's because I smoke myself into a sickness."

ONE OF US

A homeless guitarist playing in front of Horton Plaza, where my wife works, caught my attention. He was there for weeks, then one day he disappeared. Before he left, I took my microrecorder, bought him lunch at Burger King, and asked him to tell me his story. I also spent some time listening to him play. He was good. Really good.

Let's start with your name.
If it's all the same to you, I'd rather not say. My friends at the shelter call me "Wet Dog."

Dare I ask why?
Because they say I smell like a wet dog. [I should tell you that his answers were rather short at first because he was inhaling a Whopper with cheese.]

Let's back up. You said your friends at the shelter. Is that where you live?
Yeah, when there's room. Otherwise I like to crash down by the Convention Center. Ya know, that way I'm near the water and all. But it's tough, man, 'cause they keep kicking me out.
[At this point, he went off about cops and politicians and a big conspiracy.]

You have some of the best chops I have ever seen. Did you ever play professionally?
I was a hired gun for a while. Ya know, doing studio gigs in L.A. I've played with some of the best. I've got licks on tracks by some big names. BIG names. I've done gigs all over the world. For a while I was touring as a rhythm guitarist for this band and we played to sold-out crowds every goddam night. Shit, I was making money hand over fist. Livin' the good life, if ya know what I mean. I had it all. I was even married for a while and I got a son. Check this out, I even bought a house and turned the garage into a sixteen-track recording studio.

Without being too blunt, how did you end up where you are today?

You mean homeless and shit. Take a guess.

Drugs?

Yup. And I was into everything, big time. I guess I have what you would call an addictive personality. This was during the seventies and eighties and nobody thought twice about it. Man, shit was everywhere. I didn't think it was that big a deal. I actually believed that blow wasn't addictive! Ha! After a while I had to be juiced just to play. At first I'd just do a coupla lines and booze it up a little before a gig. But when I started doin' smack, man, I was all f——ed up.

What happened next?

I was hardcore. The guys I'd be jammin' with partied, too, but I was like over the edge. I pissed so many people off and was so strung out, I couldn't get no work. I was blackballed. You know, persona non grata. But at least I had my family. Then I blew it.

So your wife left you?

No man, I left her! Can you believe that shit? I was so messed up I didn't know which end was up. I did some really stupid shit in my time, but that was my biggest screwup by far. I got my act together for a while and I tried to go back, but she split with my kid. That pushed me over the edge, man. I've been on the streets ever since.

What advice would you give to other young musicians who have amazing talent, like you, but are on the verge of throwing it all away on drugs?

Honestly, if somebody tried to tell me "just say no to drugs" when I was younger, I woulda laughed in their face. I felt like I was invincible. Like I could do nothin' wrong. I got it under control. Right? I was a fool. People think I don't know what's what, because I'm homeless. I got ears. I hear some of the crap on the radio and I think, "Shoot, that coulda been me." I coulda been big. The only reason it ain't me on the radio is cause I started messin' with drugs. It took over my life and I was powerless to stop it. So I'd say go ahead, take a hit, but if you do, you could end up just like me. And being me sucks.

Rock 'n' Roll

There is nothing that more obviously separates the powerful from the powerless than graciousness.

—Sherry Suib Cohen

What has being late cost you? Missed dates. Lost clients. Angry friends. Late for your own wedding? Usually, you're late because you're trying to fit a few more things in before you leave, run five miles, answer E-mail, plant a few plants, wash your hair, call your mom, find your keys. Have you tried setting the clock ahead, listing phony meeting times in your planner, making extra sets of car keys and placing them around the house?

A study by Westclox, a clockmaker, found that one in ten workers admit to being late often, with an average tardiness of 9.3 minutes. (Women and younger workers were more likely to be late.)

Many people are late because they're afraid to be early. Plan ahead for things to go wrong. Leave extra time for bad traffic, finding lost items, changing your outfit because a button pops off. Go ahead and be early. It won't kill you. It might even be a good thing.

A friend of mine was exasperated because she showed up on time for a meeting and nobody was ready. She had even called the day before and confirmed the time. As she started to sizzle, a co-worker pointed out that they knew when she said she was coming, but they didn't know when she was going to show up. "The boss told me you said you'd be here at nine, but nine for you could be ten, ten-thirty, or eleven." It was true. She had to shut up and waste an hour waiting for the rest of the group to arrive. A reputation for being on time can save you a lot of embarrassment and aggravation.

A woman was running late and frantically trying to get ready as her husband looked on in amusement. As she was about to pull on her panty hose, she noticed a run. She grabbed another pair from the drawer, also ripped. She was exasperated. She grabbed her briefcase and dashed off to work, making it just in the nick of time. Once there, she opened the briefcase, and on top was a neatly folded pair of panty hose with a note from her husband. "The stockings you are wearing have a large run behind your right knee. Try these—and have a nice day."

Think of your life as a performance. Let it be a comedy or even the news sometimes—you don't need all that drama in life. Flakiness is not cute in business. Be reliable.

Things take longer than you expect them to. Give yourself some cushion. Not delivering the goods on time will not only cost you now; it'll ruin your chances for getting work later.

Respect other people's time. Constantly rescheduling is bad manners. There are people who depend on you, and when you screw up, they suffer. These people have mortgages, car payments, budgets, and people to answer to. You won't last long if you let them down. When you blow them off, you are taking bricks out of the wall that you call your career. Take enough bricks away and the whole thing will collapse.

People pay a price for blind ambition and self-centered behavior. Love yourself and love others. When you don't have time for kids, spouse, friends, it's time to regroup and reconsider your priorities. That's why they say it's lonely at the top. You don't need to end up with a hollow victory and a miserable existence.

Don't be afraid or unwilling to help others, to be kind, to be generous. There is plenty of room at the top. Even if you don't believe in karma, believe this: Your good deeds will come back to help you, just as your bad ones will haunt you.

6. LACK OF DISCIPLINE: LOSS OF FOCUS

My MO growing up had always been that I was distracted, always the kid with the short attention span. Creativity allowed me to express myself positively. This is why I gravitated to the fashion business.

—Tommy Hilfiger

Tommy Hilfiger's lack of focus nearly cost him his business. He had to file for chapter-eleven bankruptcy protection from creditors. "I had allowed myself to become distracted, and I paid the price. I was bankrupt at the age of twenty-five," he admitted. "Fashion was exciting. It was perfect for me. It offered change all the time, along with music, color, different people, different cities, all set against this wild revolutionary period in American culture."

Unfortunately, Hilfiger was so busy trying to get his new designs made that he ignored the nuts and bolts of his business. It taught him a valuable lesson. "Ideas can carry you far, but you have to keep your eye on the bottom line—all the time."

Lack of focus can make you feel like a loser. Everyone is disappointed because you have so much potential but you are all over the place. "If you would just apply yourself," they say. Or the even better one: "If you could only stick with something."

I'm bored! Okay? I fought people who said I wasn't smart. "Why can't you understand economics like your friend here?" If only I had a witty comeback. I wasn't interested in economics. I was out of my element. (I managed a C in the class because of my paper on a kelp-harvesting company. *That* interested me.)

You're not a bad person if you like to juggle several things at once. It isn't an excuse for bad behavior and never following through. It's just an explanation. The problem is, when you're going in six directions at once, you get lost, run out of gas, and end up nowhere.

Lack of focus can be the root cause of marital infidelity, frequent job changes, substance abuse, auto accidents. Your life is a roller-coaster ride. Although it is exciting, it has the potential to jump the tracks at any time. Spontaneity and variety are wonderful, but without a specific goal, they don't usually lead to creative work. Harness that energy with some discipline, order, and direction.

The clearer you are about your vision, purpose, and goals, the more that unexplained universal force brings things to you, and the more able you are to recognize them as opportunities.

Thomas Edison once commented that the reason he was able to achieve great things was his ability to focus: "The trouble is, most people do a great many things, and I do about one. If they took the time in question and applied it in one direction, to one object, they would succeed."

▼ ▼ ▼

ACTION ITEM

Do you often rush through tasks without any preplanning? Do you end up wasting time and money? Does your carelessness lead to errors? Does a short attention span affect the quality of your work? Does your behavior drive other people crazy? Do you leave total chaos in your wake—unfinished tasks and clutter everywhere?

Do you think these are just natural attributes of the creative person? Do you take pride in your flakiness?

Think again.

▲ ▲ ▲

Quiz

When I was in school, I always had a dilemma: did I want to be a scientist; did I want to be a computer programmer; did I want to be an economist? You have to pick; you can't do everything. I like so many things, but I think that I chose the right job for me.

—*Bill Gates*

You are just too talented—in too many diverse areas. Lack of focus will ruin you, for more reasons than you probably realize. Take this test:

	True	False
I find it hard to market myself and my art because I am into so many different things.	___	___
I have a hard time choosing a career path because I am interested and talented in several areas.	___	___
I can't figure out what to do with my life because I have a hard time making a decision, and when I do, I'm afraid I made the wrong one.	___	___
I take big risks. Sometimes I reap the rewards, but mostly I pay the price.	___	___
I am easily distracted.	___	___
My mind tends to wander in the middle of a project.	___	___
I am impulsive. My failure to stop and think without considering the consequences has caused me problems in the past.	___	___
I often rush to finish a task so I can get to the next thing, not doing my best work and making careless (and costly) mistakes in the process.	___	___
I have so much energy I sometimes find it hard to go to sleep.	___	___
I am easily bored.	___	___
I like to approach projects in a haphazard fashion.	___	___
It often looks to others as if I don't care or won't try. But the truth is that it takes twice the effort to maintain my motivation.	___	___
I find it impossible to relax, so I take on hobbies or habits to fill the void.	___	___
I tend to drift off when people are talking to me.	___	___

As with many of the quizzes in this book, there are no right or wrong answers, no score to add up. Just things to think about.

Choose Between Better and Best

I admire people who always knew what they wanted to be when they grew up. Take *ER* star Eriq LaSalle, for instance. When he first saw a dance troupe come through town at age ten, he was captivated. At age sixteen, he was willing to risk vicious teasing from his peers by taking ballet lessons—not the thing to do in his neighborhood. People laughed at him and questioned his masculinity. He knew what he wanted, and he would not be deterred.

Not everybody knows exactly what's the best thing to do at any given time. Concentrate on what brings you the highest reward both financially and emotionally. You will have to make some tough choices, many times between better and best. Pick best.

Don't give till it hurts. Joan Baez is probably as well known for her work with antinuclear and animal-rights causes as she is for her music. She lost focus, eventually realizing that she needed to concentrate on her music career. "At the moment, I have really retreated like a turtle. I don't want any more responsibilities apart from making the most beautiful music I can."

Get in the zone. Jim Carrey talks about being in the moment when shooting a scene, rewriting a joke, or working at the drawings and sculptures he's done since childhood. "I was concentrating, I was lost in it, it was like being in the womb, like meditation or something—you don't care about anything." This is the same Jim Carrey who was a whiz in school and would finish his work and then have to wait. With his amazing energy, he got bored. One thing led to another, and he'd end up in trouble for goofing off. One day a teacher said, "If you think you're so funny, why don't you come up here and try it?" He did—and he's been a comedian ever since.

Choose your rituals. One highly creative person I know changes her shoes at lunch. I had to ask, "Why don't you just use Dr. Scholl's Odor Eaters?" "No, it's my way to take a moment, look at myself, focus in, then move on." Too deep for me, but it works for her.

Don't spread yourself too thin. Some people have been able to manage two careers at once. Harry Connick Jr., for one, has been successful at film and music. But he warns about spreading yourself too thin. "I think it's best to establish one career first. Don't try to build them both at the same time. If you try to do them both at the same time, you do both an injustice."

Take out an umbrella policy. Combine a variety of interests and a tendency to hop around into a broader field or category. "Entertainment," for instance, can offer room to move about without getting too far afield. How about finding different ways to do the same job? Play in two bands, a rock band and a jazz band, for variety. Channel some of the need to jump around into your hobbies. If you were on the freeway, you might get sick of the fast lane, so you merge to another lane, but you are still going in the same direction, at approximately the same speed. If you get off at every off-ramp, as interesting as it may be, you will only fill up on fast food and waste a lot of time and energy trying to get back up to speed.

Keep your eye on the ball. In football, a receiver often drops the ball because he tries to run with it before he has it in his possession. Coaches will tell you to "look the ball into your hands." The same goes in your career.

Binge and purge. I binge when I am on a deadline. (No sleep, lots of caffeine.) I kick ass, then I kick back. I make sure to allow myself plenty of recovery time between big jobs.

Practice your juggling. Establish limits on how many balls you will try to keep in the air at once. When the balls marked *relationships, health,* and *quality* start hitting the ground, cut back.

It's feast or famine. Creative work is rarely regular. Sometimes a month's worth of work will all hit in the same week. Sometimes you'll have empty weeks and get your windows washed and go see some movies. It's hard to turn any work down today because it might not be there tomorrow. But if you get too busy, you have to really discipline yourself, focus, and drive yourself to meet all the deadlines. I have this problem. It takes me weeks to prepare for a seminar, and sometimes all these lucrative opportunities come at the same time. It's tempting to take them all, but I don't want to live that way. I try to be realistic about how much I can handle, and I trade the rest to other speakers in exchange for a referral fee. (I keep the best opportunities, of course.) If I yield to the temptation to take on just one too many jobs, I won't do my best work, and it will hurt my reputation. Try to pace yourself. Life isn't a sprint, it's a marathon.

Variety pack. True, one project at a time isn't enough for most divergent thinkers. You need to be able to shift gears to stay interested. That's why I switch between speaking, writing, promotion, and PR and design. All tie in with each other, so my efforts overlap, while still letting me dabble in lots of different projects. When I have too little going on, I actually get depressed.

Remember the ten-times rule. It's ten times harder to get a new client than to keep an old one. Don't spend all your time trying to get new ones. Cultivate the ones you have. Make them happy. That's the best way to get new ones, anyhow.

Know your limitations. How many actors want to be musicians? I'll tell you, nearly all of them. Some will make it (David Hasselhoff, John Tesh), some won't.

Don't try to do everything. If something is interesting but unrelated or you are unqualified to do it, don't be afraid to say, "That's something I'm not good at," and give it a pass. Even if you could do it, but it would sidetrack you from your goals, say no. Just because you *can* do something doesn't mean you *should.*

You need balance. You can have some order and routine without stifling your creativity and need for variety. Freedom and order. Solitude and quiet. One hour of uninterrupted time is worth days working beside a constantly ringing phone. You need calm and stillness to create—not just outside you, but inside you, too. Don't let yourself get too busy, too harried and distracted. Life will pull you away from your art if you let it. Choose a career and a situation that will let you get into the zone.

Thoughts on Discipline

Writing a novel is like building a wall brick by brick; only amateurs believe in inspiration.

—*Frank Yerby*

Do we not find freedom along the guiding lines of discipline?

—*Yehudi Menuhin*

Concentration is the secret of strength.

—*Ralph Waldo Emerson*

The principles of war could, for brevity, be condensed into a single word—concentration.

—*Sir Basil Liddell Hart*

Discipline

When I first started getting into music, I developed a strong sense of discipline. I practiced incessantly. When I went away to music school at Interlochen Arts Academy, I sort of got the informal award for the person who practiced the most. This was a big-time music academy with people from all over the world. I was used to being one of the best guitarists, but when I got there I was nothing special. I saw a lot of people with God-given talent pissing it away. I decided to utilize what I had.

—*Peter Sprague*

The only way to rise to the top is to defeat your weaknesses. For many, that means doing the work and staying with it despite being distracted. Learn to love your work—even the prickly bits—and you won't be so distractable, and self-discipline will feel more like self-indulgence, which is my favorite way to go.

Make it a habit. Even if you're not making money from your art, get in the habit of working on it (before or after your real job) every day. If you're making a living at it, don't take it for granted. Work it, practice it, keep learning. Don't let it get old.

Don't forget the details. Do the errands, save the receipts, dot the *i*'s that must be dotted. It pays off—mostly in headaches you won't have later.

Set daily goals for how long you will work on art or practice your music, or how many pages you will write. Don't get up until it's done.

Make it easy to get started. Leave your supplies out. Keep everything set up.

Find the time during the day when you have the most energy, and don't waste it. Use it to focus on your art. Most people have biological low times and high times. Between one and three in the afternoon and four and six in the morning are the most common low times. Don't try to do your best work then. Take a nap. Do your filing.

Get interested. When you are interested in something, you can focus for hours at a time. Don't worry so much about the money or the deadline. Enjoy the process. Have fun. Play around. Experiment.

Hit the ground running. Are you like me, full of excitement and anticipation at the start of a project? Go from brainstorming and ride it till it runs out of steam. Keep the momentum until you're bored. Get as much done as you can, and then hand it off to somebody who's good at finish work.

What turns you on? Recognition, feedback, helping others, deadlines? Set up your work so you maximize the motivation these provide.

Learn your lines. Spencer Tracy said, "The best advice I can give to a young actor is this: Learn your lines." Be prepared. Practice.

Clear your plate. Eliminate distractions. I like to take my work out to my backyard. It's a little tropical paradise. But when it was halfway done, I couldn't concentrate on my work out there. I kept seeing things that had to be done. So I powered through the landscaping one weekend, and now my yard is the peaceful retreat I hoped it would be.

Set goals. When you are clear about your vision of what you want, it is so much easier to focus, to keep heading toward those goals instead of wandering around in the ozone. Setting goals forces you to be honest about yourself, your needs, your dreams. It's hard to do. It is the first, last, and best discipline for the creative person. If you take nothing else away from this book, take this: set goals for yourself. Put your dreams into words and those words down on paper. Then say them aloud, not just to yourself, but to everybody. Repeat them daily. Then start working toward them.

7. DECEIT: LET'S BE HONEST, HERE

Perhaps the worst failing common to creative people—and the one that leads to many of the others—is dishonesty. Not slipping-a-little-something-into-your-purse-at-the-department-store dishonesty. Not walking-out-of-your-workplace-with-a-few-extra-pens-and-a-ream-of-paper dishonesty, or cheating on your taxes or robbing-the-liquor-store dishonesty. It's worse than that. It's not being honest with yourself.

Face yourself. Recognize who you are. Understand who you want to be and why. That's the first, most vital step toward setting goals, and setting goals is the first, most vital step toward success.

Be honest about what you want—even if it sounds silly or stupid or impossible, even if it's not what anybody else in the world would want. Say it out loud. Let them laugh at you if they're going to. That can't hurt you—and being afraid to admit your dream can. You have to be willing to say out loud what you want before you're ever going to get it.

Be honest about wanting, needing, dreaming about your success. Stick your neck out. Don't waste time being cool, pretending that you don't want or need anything. That's the surest way to failure—and failure is not cool by any standard.

Admit your mistakes. It's the only way you'll learn from them. There's nothing wrong with making a mistake—everybody fails sometimes. Yes, you're unique, you're special, but you're still human. That's not a bad thing. It is a bad thing to gloss over your mistakes, to pretend they don't exist, to dodge responsibility.

Accept your weaknesses. Nobody's good at everything—even Leonardo da Vinci had his poor subjects (public relations, for instance). Be willing to admit your failings and then honestly decide whether it's worth spending the time to overcome them or the money to work around them.

You can't make good choices without all the facts, and you can't get all the facts unless you're willing to look at the whole picture. You can't see your options unless you can look past your ego. An ego is a good thing—a healthy ego gives you confidence in your vision. But a healthy ego isn't afraid to look on the dark side and deal with it.

Nobody sees themselves absolutely clearly all the time. That's where friends, family, and support groups come in. Someone I thought was a close friend once told me, "If you were my friend, you'd support me, you'd tell me I was right no matter what." I was flabbergasted. To me, a friend is someone who will tell you when you're wrong, and love you anyway. Cultivate real friends, ask for honesty from them, and reward them for offering it. Your feelings might be hurt now and then, but in the long run you'll benefit.

I'm going to be your friend now and tell you a few hard truths about creative careers.

It's hard work. There are no shortcuts, no quick fixes. Most of the overnight successes you hear about spent years in the trenches, learning their craft, waiting for their moment. Most financial successes spend seventy hours or more every week, week in and week out, year in and year out, to achieve their goals.

It takes dedication to succeed. Often not just yours, but the dedication of your family. It takes loving what you do so much you can't *not* do it. It takes working toward your goal, even when that means you have to do yucky stuff.

You need that left brain. Get friendly with it. Use it. Take advantage of all those qualities you have that maybe aren't so interesting. You may find out you have an affinity for numbers (many creatives are remarkably good at math, if they let themselves be). You may surprise yourself in other ways. Explore.

Your success may not show up in dollars, or fame, or any measure our society respects. Success is when you're happy doing what you're doing. It's personal fulfillment. It's being responsible for yourself. Past that, it can be whatever you make of it.

It takes great strength of character to succeed. It takes even more strength to handle material success. Don't neglect your personal growth, don't let personal issues slide. They will come back and bite you in the butt. Take care of yourself and those you love.

▾▾ 12 ▾▾

PMS: A Positive Mental State

*Some see the glass as half empty, some see the glass as half full.
I see the glass as too big.*

—*George Carlin*

Do you ever feel as though your life is like being in a boat without a rudder and at the mercy of the winds? Being unemployed or underemployed doesn't help.

You must keep your head above water. Stay away from the rocky shoreline and keep the boat afloat with positive thinking, even if you have tried all the traditional advice and still can't find work or clients. You're losing your confidence and unsure if this is the right path for you. Don't feel sorry for yourself, even if you feel as if your ship is sinking fast. Keep bailing and hang on. If you feel like grabbing a life vest and want to take a grab at getting a "real" job—DON'T.

This is the moment of truth. This choice, whether to hang in there and stick it out or hang your head and sell out, is crucial. Get your sorry rear in gear and paddle your boat if you have to. Let it fuel you. Go ahead, get mad. Life isn't fair, I know. And you aren't the only one out there in the turbulent sea. Others before you have come through the storms of life, battered but intact. They captained their ships with the belief that they would survive and make it to paradise. You can do it, too.

What sinks ships? The "if they find me out" syndrome. Feeling like a fraud is one way to capsize a creative career. You must believe you deserve good things, and enjoy them when they come. "The greater the artist, the greater the doubt; perfect confidence is granted to the less talented as a consolation prize," said Robert Hughes. It doesn't have to be that way.

Cut yourself some slack. Two-time Pulitzer Prize–winning author J. Anthony Lukas was regarded as one of the best nonfiction writers of our time. His book *Common Ground* was a critical and financial success. At age sixty-four he had everything to live for. He was just wrapping up a new book, *Big Trouble,* when he committed suicide in June of 1997. One of the contributing factors was that he didn't feel his new book was up to the standards he had set for himself in his earlier work.

Maybe you're on course but moving a little slower than you'd like. Maybe you should change course and head for a different destination. It isn't easy, but you must change to grow. You can do it. You *must* do it.

"If you expect the worst and get the worst, don't you suffer twice?" asks C. W. Metcalf. Cut out the catastrophizing and what-if-ing and get on with the work at hand. Everything will be fine. It almost always is. Stop freaking out, make a plan, and start putting your plans into action. Pay attention to where you are now and where you want to go. That's what's important.

Kill the Inner Critic

Tell me, George, if you had to do it over, would you fall in love with yourself again?

—Oscar Levant, to George Gershwin

Wherever you are in your quest for creating the career (and life) you want, you must stay positive to stay afloat. "Left to its own devices, my mind spends much of its time having conversations with people who aren't there," said writer Anne Lamott. Fall in love with yourself. "What you believe to be yourself, you are," Claude Bristol pointed out.

Trust yourself. You will remember your lines, you will perform well, you will do a good job. You must believe that.

It's not called *self*-esteem for nothing. You, and you alone, are in charge of your thoughts. This is one area where you are the boss. (Let's face it, nobody gets enough strokes from supervisors or clients.) Positive people have positive thoughts, and prosperous people have prosperous thoughts. It's really that simple.

Full esteem ahead. It does take time to undo the negative thoughts you have had all your life. But the past is the past, and all you can concern yourself with is the present. From this time forward, make an effort to see yourself as successful. Speak kindly to yourself.

Get out of your own way. "My life has been one long obstacle course, with me as the biggest obstacle," admits Jack Paar. Lisa Kudrow (from *Friends*) said that she was very encouraging when others were unsure of themselves and pushed her friends to go for it. But when it came to her own career, she was less than positive. "I thought everyone talked to themselves with a tremendous amount of harshness and called themselves 'losers' and 'stupid.' I had to learn to allow myself to make a mistake without becoming defensive and unforgiving."

Don't be a junkie. Being a natural-born risk-taker (and adrenaline junkie), you may be the one putting yourself in peril. The life-on-the-edge, fly-by-the-seat-of-your-pants approach works only until you OD on anxiety and pressure. Give yourself some time to "dry out" and kick back between big projects.

Right brain, wrong problem. The right-brainer loves to grapple with problems, and sometimes sees things that need to be better when good enough is good enough. You don't have to save the world. You're the only one who wants or expects you to be perfect. Know your limits. You aren't Superman or Wonder Woman. Kryptonite kills.

Self-employ your self-esteem. If you decide to go the route of the self-employed, there will be constant challenges (and when I say challenges, I mean just trying to hang on to what you have), and you will have to deal with occupational hazards like setbacks, rejections, and mistakes (all before lunchtime). This is the trade-off to being in business with yourself. The secret is in how you deal with these challenges—and learning to love dealing with them.

Your time will come. Everybody has their share of tough times. The ones you see who are getting ahead have put the past behind them and are creating a better future. Instead of wallowing in self-pity, they take the Mr. T approach and say, "I pity the fool" who tries to stop me from getting what I want. You look around and see others (far less talented) with juicier jobs, fatter paychecks, better connections, bigger deals, and choice gigs and you say, "How did that happen?" Hang in there, your time will come.

No matter where you are, there will always be people with more than you, and others with less. That's not important. Real success is inside you. Appreciate where you are.

What Does This Say?
IAMNOWHERE

If you said, "I am now here," congratulations. If you said, "I am nowhere"—well, then, aren't we just the negative one?

Self-esteem Is an Inside Job
The new frontier of the nineties is an inner one.

—Peggy Noonan

Expect the best. If all you can focus on are negative outcomes, your possibilities shrink and eventually you *will* need to seek professional help. Your internal thoughts, good or bad, manifest themselves in your external world. People who believe they deserve success and happiness usually attract it. Take, for instance, George, the balding, often jobless, and frustrated character in *Seinfeld.* One day he decides to do the opposite of "common sense." He decides to take a chance on himself, something he's never done before. He goes up to an attractive woman and says, "Hi! My name is George, I don't have a job, and I live with my parents." The response? "Helloooo. My name is Cathy."

If you believe you're worthy of good things, you'll take a chance. If you're not willing to take a chance, you're not going anywhere. Period.

When you undervalue yourself and your work, so do others. So when you lowball your prices, you cheat yourself. The more people pay, the more they appreciate your work. You deserve to be paid well for your work. You deserve nice things. You must believe that, because if you don't, you will never have money—and when you do, you'll blow it. Repeat after me, "My work is worthwhile. I deserve good things to happen to me. I deserve to be paid well for my work." Feel better?

Envy is another career-killer. Comparing yourself against others is unhealthy and, ultimately, meaningless. I teach a course in creativity, and I always begin by asking the audience this question: "How many of you believe you are creative?" A smattering of hands will go up. After some prying, I find out that those who don't believe they are creative are setting themselves against an unrealistic standard of what being creative is. They aren't Leonardo da Vinci, so they're not creative at all. I go through a series of exercises and, by the end of the day, prove to everyone in the room that they are more creative than they give themselves credit for. The paper-airplane races and coloring with crayons help, but it is really just lowering the bar a bit that helps them see the light.

The best thing (and sometimes the worst thing) about being human is your uniqueness. Learn from others' mistakes, but don't make the mistake of thinking they are better or worse than you are. They are different. You are different. Exploit that fact, and rejoice in it.

Another career-killer is the false belief that there is too much competition, not enough money to go around, and no room at the top. Baloney! Use that imagination of yours. Find a niche. Fill a need. Create a space for your work. That's how you will succeed. It's a big world out there, with plenty of room for everyone. You just need to mark out some territory for yourself.

Get to know yourself better. Enlist help. Look back at your past accomplishments. Spend some time reviewing your success. Research yourself. Many of us work so hard to have buns of steel and washboard abs that we don't work on our inner muscles. Say what you will about Jean-Claude Van Damme (The Muscles from Brussels), but, by his own admission, the musclebound actor was flabby on the inside and went about pumping up his self-esteem to match his pecs. (I like action flicks, so shoot me.)

Find people who believe in you. There have been times throughout my career when the encouragement of others carried me through. In my head, I had these stereo speakers playing heavy metal all the time, a broken record of doubts, fears, and insecurities. Others would spin the dial to a soothing symphony of self-esteem with comments like "You're going to be a big star" and "You have so much talent it makes me sick." People around me could see things about myself that I could not. This was the one time when Stravinsky was able to drown out Metallica. Tune in and turn on.

Dump those who only add to the heavy metal in your head (not those who offer constructive criticism or advice, however). If they say, "Isn't that a very competitive field?" or "Wal-Mart has a very good manager's program and I heard they have openings," cut them loose. If they say, "If you're having a hard time getting started, maybe you should try an internship program, or go back to school," listen, take it for what it's worth, and make your own decisions.

I realize it is hard to find outsiders who understand your plight as a creative person. That's why it is a great idea to find a support group of others who, like you, could use some support. In the end, however, you will need to be your own support group, and founder and president of your own fan club.

▼ ▼ ▼

ACTION ITEM

If you had a "black box" or data recorder in your head like the ones on airplanes, the dialogue might frighten you. Clip off negative thoughts and replace them with reassuring and respectful ones. Every time you tell yourself you can't do it, repeat after me, "I can do it. I will do it!"

▲ ▲ ▲

Self-esteem Quiz

1. When I receive a compliment I will
   a. smile and thank the person for noticing.
   b. downplay, deflect, and dismiss the compliment.

2. If I were offered the chance to trade places with anyone else, I
   a. wouldn't trade places with anyone for any reason.
   b. would gladly trade places with another person.

3. At this point in my career, I am
   a. proud of what I have accomplished so far, but know I can and will do more.
   b. wish I had done more, made more money, and achieved more recognition.

4. My future looks
   a. bright and filled with unlimited possibilities.
   b. dim and uncertain, filled with fear and apprehension.

5. I am usually
   a. happy, able to enjoy my life at any given moment.
   b. unhappy and unable to enjoy even myself when things are going well.

6. When I reflect on my life, I
   a. am able to focus on the positives and have very little regret.
   b. tend to dwell on my shortcomings and always have a twinge of guilt.

7. If someone were to ask my friends, they would say
   a. I'm basically upbeat and fun to be around.
   b. they often wonder why they even hang around with me.

8. When it comes to my physical appearance,
   a. I take good care of myself.
   b. I have let myself go.

9. When it comes to getting paid for my work,
   a. I have no problem asking for and getting what I am worth.
   b. I have trouble asking for and receiving fair compensation for my work.

10. I generally tend to hang out with
   a. people who are my equals, and some that I look up to.
   b. people who are struggling and tend to look up to me.

11. Which statement is more accurate?
   a. People don't expect enough of me.
   b. People expect too much from me.

12. When it comes to decisions, I
   a. stick to my guns.
   b. am wishy-washy and easily swayed.

13. In social settings or meetings, I
   a. have no trouble voicing my ideas and opinions.
   b. usually keep my opinions and ideas to myself.

14. If I lost everything and had to start over,
    a. I could bounce back.
    b. Oh God, what a horrible idea!
15. When it comes to my attire, I
    a. am a nonconformist and have my own style.
    b. prefer to fit in and dress unobtrusively.
16. Which statement is more true about me?
    a. I am above average.
    b. I am about average.
17. To get through the day, I
    a. prefer to be alert and avoid controlled substances.
    b. prefer to get high and numb my senses.
18. When faced with a difficulty,
    a. I will rise to the challenge and meet it head-on.
    b. look for an easy way out.
19. When it comes to my work,
    a. I strive to do more than people expect.
    b. I will do just enough to get by.
20. Are you a creative person?
    a. Yes.
    b. No.

Before I tell you how you scored, let me reassure you that you are good enough, smart enough, and that people like you. Okay, here goes. If you had fewer than ten "a" answers, you could use a bit of a boost to your self-esteem. If you had five or fewer "a" answers, you may need professional help. Nothing I say will convince you that you're worth a damn.

Put Your Money Where Your Mouth Is

In a survey conducted for the American College of Prosthodontists, a quarter of the respondents said their teeth, or smile, is the physical attribute that most affects their self-confidence.

Look in the mirror right now. Do your lips naturally curve up or down? It actually takes fewer muscles to smile, yet somehow smiling can affect your whole outlook on life. Try it.

False Evidence Appearing Real (Fear)

Fears are learned—and if they are learned, then they can be unlearned.

—Karl Menninger

I hardly noticed the discomfort from sitting on cold metal with my knees pulled into my chest, the cold air rushing in, making my hands numb. What I *did* notice, however, was that the small plane I was in was banking sharply to the west. This meant that in just a few minutes I would hurl myself out of the plane. My mind wrestled with thoughts like "Why am I jumping out of a perfectly good aircraft?" and "Does my insurance cover things like this?" My stomach was in knots.

I have gone diving with sharks, bungee-jumped from a balloon, and jumped off Dead Man's Point, but this! This was fear I had never felt before. As we neared the designated jump site, the jumpmaster grabbed me by the straps, looked me in the eye, and screamed above the sound of the prop, "Are you ready, Silber?" He sneered as he said it, maybe sensing my fear. "Hell, yes!" I exclaimed, faking a bravado I did *not* feel. "Let's do it!" He then held me over the edge of the open hatch and pointed to a spot on the ground known as "the box," so small I had to squint to see it at this height, and said, "You land there. Good luck. Now climb out onto the wheel." "What?!" I screamed. He repeated his command to climb out onto the wheel of the plane to get into position for the jump.

This was not in the brochure! What the hell, I thought. If I slip and fall, I'm no worse off than if I jumped right out of the plane. So I inched my way out onto a small step on the arm that held the wheel of the small plane. The jumpmaster yelled, "Don't look down." I looked down. He yelled, "Are you gonna jump or sightsee?" I have a picture of me (taken from the camera on the wing) making a rude gesture at the instructor as I leaped. I looked fear in the eye and spit in it.

I have never felt so charged, before or since. This was life-or-death-type stuff. (One of the other jumpers, who froze up when she left the plane, got seriously hurt when she drifted off course and crash-landed in Mexico.) Now, when I feel any kind of fear, I ask, could it kill me? Chances are it can't. The more you face your fear, the stronger you become.

Bobby Bowden, the college football coach, in describing one of his best players, said, "This player doesn't know the meaning of the word *fear*." Bowden continued, "I've seen his grades, and he doesn't know the meaning of *a lot* of words."

I have seen fear all but destroy many talented people's dreams. The worst part is that when their worst fears come true, it's because they made them happen. I've seen writers not turn in their manuscripts on time, musicians show up hours late for recording sessions (which costs a small fortune), actors get wasted before going on stage to perform when they know a VIP is in the audience. They made their fear a reality.

Why? Good question. It could be a fear of responsibility, of taking their craft to the next level and having a whole new set of expectations to live up to. A fear of losing their independence. A fear of failing. The number-one fear, if you ask me, is fear of not having enough money, of being homeless. That is always a fear for the creative person (especially the freelancer).

What is worse, working at a job you despise for the dollars, or doing what you love for the love of it? Follow your passion. Your sense of security comes from within, knowing you are working on purpose and using your gifts. It is riskier to not follow your dream. The cost is extremely high.

One fear I never considered was revealed in the book *The Career Guide for the Creative and Unconventional Person,* by Carol Eikleberry. She points out that if you fear for your physical safety, it is difficult to be creative. If you live in an unsafe area or are in an abusive relationship, this kind of fear is real and should be dealt with immediately.

Another fear is undue worrying about what others think. Will they like my work? Will anyone pay me for this? Will I lose my friends and family if I become too successful? The answers are usually yes, yes, and no. Others, usually out of concern for you (or jealousy), will say things like "most businesses fail in the first two years," or "you're too short," or "play it safe." *Safe* is a one-way ticket to nowhere. You must stand strong, thank them for their "concern," and move on.

In baseball, there are players who thrive and come alive in pressure situations. They are fearless. They come through in the clutch. They say, "Hit the ball to me." Watching Padres outfielder Greg Vaughn face down pitchers is a treat. For some reason (maybe because he has hit fifty homers), pitchers seem to be gunning for him by aiming ninety-five-mile-an-hour fastballs at his head. He dives for cover, as any rational person would. But after he dusts himself off, he gets mad. I can't tell you how many times after he was knocked down that Greg Vaughn came back and hit a home run.

A lot of ballplayers give the cliché answer before a game that they will do their best and not worry about the rest. That's actually pretty good advice. Sounds incredibly simple, but it is so powerful not to worry about the outcome and focus on the process. So what if others "don't get it"? You did your best.

See?

Life comes with risks. Either you take them on or you sit at home and watch the rest of us on TV or read about us in the newspaper.

▼ ▼ ▼

ACTION ITEM: FEEL THE FEAR

Feeling fear isn't all that bad. In fact, it's normal. You must work through it and, as the title of the book says, *Feel the Fear and Do It Anyway.*

- Don't downsize your dreams. Just start small and build minor successes into monumental ones.
- Make a list of all the things you are afraid of doing, and put a start date next to each one, because action has a way of canceling out fear.
- Complete this sentence: "A fear I have always had about myself is _____." Get your fears out in the open and then deal with them.

▲ ▲ ▲

Happen-Chance

Our doubts are traitors, and make us lose the good we oft might win, by fearing to attempt.

—*William Shakespeare*

Nothing happens until you take a chance. There is no success without risk. You simply can't play it safe and expect to come out on top. As an entrepreneur, you must be willing to take risks. I am not saying you should take reckless risks, but be daring and do what others are afraid to do, and you will succeed where others have failed. Pat Metheny is one of the greatest guitarists of our time. He won nine Grammy Awards and has a string of successful records that go back to the 1970s. One of the things that make him great is his ability to venture into new and uncharted territory with his playing. He does not take the safe path with his music; he is unpredictable and experimental and, so far, that has served him well.

Jeff Bezos, the founder of Amazon.com, gave up the success and security of a cushy job on Wall Street to pursue a dream. He packed up and drove across country in an old Chevy Blazer (with his wife and dog) to Bellevue, Washington, to start "Earth's Biggest Bookstore." Pretty gutsy, eh? Even more so when you consider that E-commerce was an entirely new and untested field. He looks at it differently. "I call it a regret-minimization framework," he told *Success* magazine. "I projected myself into my eighties and asked what regrets I had about my life. And I realized that, at eighty, I probably wouldn't even remember all the things that seemed so important right then, like forgoing the end-of-year Wall Street bonus. But I would have definitely remembered that I'd ignored the emergence of the Internet just as it was happening, and tell myself I'd been a fool."

I always ask myself, what is the worst thing that could happen? Could I deal with it? Yes! Okay, then, onward and upward. If I can't deal with it, how can I scale this back a bit?

The bottom line is that the saying "the bigger the risk, the bigger the reward" is true. When it comes to careers, big success comes to the bold, those who went for it when they had the chance. It may not seem sensible to those around you, but it is what you must do if you want to live a life without regret.

At the Crossroads of Life

Think back to two transition points in your life. Write a key word for each. Now ask yourself, What was I feeling at the time? Was I fearful? Looking back now, did it turn out okay? Better than okay? Was it a blessing in disguise?

Quiz: Are You Afraid of Success?

To live a creative life, we must lose our fear of being wrong.
—Joseph Chilton Pearce

Answer the following questions:

	True	False
I have a hard time finishing what I start.	____	____
When working on something I am almost certain will be a success, I get anxious and lose my concentration.	____	____
I lack discipline and desire when it comes to key work and will goof off, missing deadlines.	____	____
I tend to be overly critical of my work and will set impossible standards that I am unable to meet, so I don't do it at all.	____	____
I have sabotaged my success at one time or another by being late or unprepared, or by failing to perform to the best of my abilities.	____	____
When new clients or projects fall through, I feel an incredible amount of relief (as well as grief).	____	____
I get lazy and lethargic when I am working on a sure thing.	____	____
I have been known to "act up" and alienate key people who could have helped me reach my goal.	____	____

	True	*False*
When I have been successful, I feel more uncomfortable than if I had failed.	___	___
I feel more pressure from being successful, so I have done less than my best at one time or another in the past.	___	___

Some Thoughts on Fear

Everyone has talent. What is rare is the courage to follow the talent to the dark place where it leads.

—Erica Jong

It's not what we fear that happens to us.

—Oscar Wilde

Ingenuity, plus courage, plus work, equal miracles.

—Bob Richards

Confidence is preparation. Everything else is beyond your control.

—Richard Kline

Being a celebrity made me so uncomfortable that I would have preferred standing behind the amplifiers.

—Linda Ronstadt

Fear stops action. Action stops fear.

—Margaret Bourke-White

No Excuses

I don't try to dance better than anyone else, only better than myself.

—Mikhail Baryshnikov

Whenever you feel as though you've got it tough, read and reread the following stories for inspiration. You have no excuse for not reaching for your dreams, especially when you consider what others faced on the way to achieving their goals.

As a child, Jean Michalski accidentally touched a high-voltage power line and had to have both arms amputated as the result of his injuries. This did not stop him from becoming an accomplished painter. Jean painstakingly paints by holding a brush in his mouth, and uses his toes to squeeze the paint onto the palette.

Maria Ilena was turned down by all the major computer companies when she tried to get the rights to market personal computers in Latin America at a reasonable price. She was told that Latin Americans were too poor to afford computers. Maria finally convinced a company that she could sell $100,000 worth of their products in a year. Using the Yellow Pages as her sole source of contacts, she reached her sales goal in only three weeks.

Karen Duffy awoke one morning with an excruciating headache that was later diagnosed as a rare and dangerous disease that attacks the central nervous system. At the time the lesion was discovered, Duffy was set to star in two films and had a Disney sitcom in the works. (She had already made her mark in films like *Dumb & Dumber* and *Reality Bites,* was an MTV DJ, a model, a columnist for *Cosmopolitan,* and a writer for television.) Instead of complaining and asking "Why me?" she forged ahead through the chemotherapy, continuing to work and doing it with dignity, courage, and a sparkling sense of humor.

Eileen Goudge went from a single mother on welfare (who would water down frozen orange juice to make it last another day or two) to a best-selling novelist. Along the way, she left a bad marriage and moved to New York to make it as a writer. She was a college dropout who remembered receiving high marks in high school English. Working on a borrowed typewriter, she managed to get twenty dollars for an article on how driving tactics can save gas. The money went to groceries, but the encouragement went a long way to reinforcing her belief that she could make it as a writer. And she did.

Ronnie Milsap is a multiple Grammy Award–winning singer/song-writer. His song "Any Day Now" became a Billboard Song of the Year, and he has been festooned with awards ranging from Entertainer of the Year to Male Vocalist of the Year. Milsap is an extremely talented musician. He was also born blind and into poverty, abandoned by his mother and placed in the custody of strangers by the age of six.

Aimee Mullins wants to change the common idea of what beautiful is. She believes that "Confidence is the sexiest thing a woman can have." As a double amputee, Aimee aims to make it as a model, TV talk-show host, and motivational speaker. The twenty-two-year-old is already in demand as a model. She says, "As a model I can confront society's emphasis on physical perfection and say, 'Hey, look at me. You think I'm hot, but guess what? I have artificial legs!' There is no ideal body. Mine is very imperfect, and I can't change that—but I can still be attractive." This is a woman who is beautiful both inside and out.

So, what was your excuse again? That's what I thought. Whatever it was, it is totally bogus. You can do *whatever* you want to do if you want it badly enough.

Failing Your Way to the Top

There is no such thing as failure—only people who quit.

—*Phyllis Diller*

There were no outs in the top of the ninth inning and the bases were loaded. I had great stuff and nobody had been able to hit me all day. I had pitched as close to a perfect game as I could. Now, in the closing minutes of the game, I was having a meltdown. I was tired, and all I had left was my off-speed pitches, which I couldn't get over the plate. I was frustrated, and I took my frustrations out on the ump. The more I protested, the less the calls were going my way. Before I knew it, I had walked the bases loaded. Seeing I was out of gas and going out of my mind, the manager came out to pull me. I lost my cool. I trashed the dugout, trashed the manager, and yelled at the ump. (This really was as embarrassing as it sounds.)

Finally, the ump threw me out of the game and made me leave the dugout. I can remember this like it was yesterday, because it was the first time my father or my grandfather had ever seen me pitch. Even though we went on to lose the game, I came out ahead—because I learned a valuable lesson that day. Failure is a great teacher, if you are willing to learn.

My editor, Beth Hagman, has told me over and over, "Failing to *learn* from your mistakes—that's failure."

You've heard the saying "you win some, you lose some." Nowhere is this more true than in sports, where a batter in baseball can fail seven out of ten times trying to get a hit and be called a success. Or, as Padre Eddie Williams once said, "In baseball, nine times out of ten, you're going to struggle half the time." The year Mark McGuire and Sammy Sosa set the new standard for home runs in a season, they were the leaders in strike-outs as well. You have to fail to succeed.

I was fishing with my dad in the Hudson River (if you know the Hudson, you know we had just as much chance of hooking a dead body as a live fish) when he saw my frustration at not catching anything. He told me, "If you caught a fish every time you put your line in the water, they would call it catching, not fishing."

So you will fail. Sorry, but it is true. But that doesn't make you a failure. Author Harold Kusher said it best: "When things do not turn out (as we expected), we feel like failures. We will never be happy until we stop measuring our real-life achievements against that dream. We will never be comfortable with who we are until we realize that who we are is special enough."

In Silicon Valley, there are a lot of "failures" that still move innovation along. As software companies push the envelope, they push others to try harder as well. Eventually, they are able to go further than they would have thought possible, finding new frontiers to push against. Thomas Edison failed twenty thousand times before finding the material suitable for lightbulb filament. When asked about his failures, he said, "I didn't fail. I found twenty thousand ways *not* to make a lightbulb."

When you push yourself beyond your comfort zone, occasionally you will stumble and fall. The more you try to do, the more you will fail. But because you try to do more, you ultimately accomplish more. Beverly Sills said, "You may be disappointed if you fail, but you are doomed if you don't try."

You have already failed if you're trying to hold on to past success. You can't stay still. You are either moving ahead or falling behind. "As far as I'm concerned, people who think they fear failure have got it wrong. They really fear success. If you truly feared failure, you'd be very successful. People who truly fear anything stay as far away from it as possible," says Barbara Sher.

When bad things happen to good people (like you), it is a natural reaction to ask, "Why me?" Go ahead and do that. But ask the question with a purpose. Why *did* this happen to you? What can you learn from it so it won't happen again? How can you be better, stronger, faster? Find some meaning in it. You know how people always say "all things happen for a reason." Figure out what the reason is, and see the silver lining.

Don't take failure personally. *You* didn't fail, you failed at *something*. You are not a failure. Don't blow these things out of proportion. Learn from it, laugh at it, and then leave it behind you. Look for opportunities, see solutions, be as positive as you possibly can, and you will rise from the rubble.

If it helps, maybe you could describe a difficult time as a temporary setback rather than as a permanent failure. The word *temporary* is the key. You will bounce back. Heed these words by Michael Eisner: "Recovering from failure is often easier than building from success."

Finally, rather than dwelling on the disaster, do something that can bring some order to your life and help you get your bearings. After a failure, you may feel out of control. Do something small that you can count as a victory. When I say small, I am talking *tiny*. Like cleaning or organizing or dealing with details that will take your mind off your problems and help you get your balance back.

Those Who Can't, Criticize Those Who Can

No statue has ever been put up to a critic.

—*Jean Sibelius*

Critics are everywhere. Rejection comes at you from so many angles you aren't sure if you should duck, jump, or run. Sometimes it's a sniper attack. Other times it's a full frontal assault by a whole platoon of these numbnuts.

Look, you'll never be able to please them all. So please yourself. Do good work and move on. Firing back is a mistake. Get a bulletproof vest and a helmet, because it is dangerous out there. And you *do* need to put yourself in the line of fire if you want to get anywhere in the creative arts or have your innovations and ideas turned into something tangible.

When I read through my evaluations after a workshop, I sometimes wonder where the 1 percent of the people who wrote the negative and nasty stuff come from. Were they in the same room as the other 99 percent who were entertained and educated and generally enthralled?

Sometimes critics want to take shots at you for reasons that have nothing to do with you personally, or with the quality of your work. Just knowing that helps ease the blow to the ego. It's really not a big deal—unless you let it get to you.

When George Lucas told studio executives that he wanted to have two robots star in his movie, they said he was nuts. He had the last laugh when *Star Wars* was made. Theodore Geisel's first book was rejected by twenty-three publishers, but his Dr. Seuss books went on to sell 6 million copies. Fred Smith was told by a professor in graduate school that his business proposal for a package delivery company would never get off the ground. It almost didn't. He was turned down a hundred times before he got the money to start Federal Express. Jimmy Buffett was turned down by every record label in Nashville before he finally got a deal with a brand-new label created by Andy Williams.

It is important to take "constructive criticism" and use it to improve. It is counterproductive to take plain old criticism to heart. What's the secret to dealing with unjust rejection? You could get angry, and I mean that in a good way. Let it fuel your inner desire to do better, try harder, and prove them wrong.

You could just let it go. If you are an actor, you already know you're too tall or too short (or both, according to some crazy casting directors). What you are hearing is "I am not good enough." If you let that get to you, then you will have a very tough time maintaining any kind of self-worth. Actress Kathy Bates (*Misery*) was told from the very beginning that she wasn't pretty enough to be an actress, that she needed to lose weight and maybe she should think about doing something else. "When I did my first press junket for *Misery,* the very first question I got was, 'You know, you don't look like Michelle Pfeiffer.'" She admits that she has made peace with it and just continues to do great work in movies like *Titanic* and *Primary Colors.*

Rejection comes in many forms. It could be a canceled contract, a poor review on a performance, losing a key client, or getting fired, to name a few. The point here is that it is almost never personal. It's part of the professional life of a creative person.

Realize that sometimes criticism has nothing to do with you at all. Actress Minnie Driver (*Good Will Hunting*) says she doesn't depend on others to make her happy, and she doesn't take rejection personally. "A director once dumped me from a project without explanation," she says. "Two years later he admitted that at the time he had just split up with his wife, and he thought I looked identical to her."

The bottom line is this: Don't wait for others to validate your work. Give yourself approval and praise for doing good work, even if nobody else notices. Awards and accolades may or may not ever come your way—but you're not doing this for awards, are you? If others approve, that's just icing on the cake. Oh, I admit it is nice to have others tell you your work is worthy. And it certainly increases how much you can charge for your labor. Seek some feedback and, when it is positive, save those comments, write them down, and use them. Create a "praise page" in your planner. Use it as a sales tool—to sell yourself on yourself, or to show to prospective bosses or clients.

▼ ▼ ▼

ACTION ITEM

When others are trying to set limits on you, or to discourage you and drag you down, write them a nasty letter. I mean *really* nasty. Read it over out loud. Then flush it down the toilet—great symbolism, but a bit hard on the plumbing—and let it go.

FAST FACTS

In a recent Harris poll, it was discovered that 50 percent of Generation X-ers lose sleep worrying about money, compared with 32 percent of all adults who had trouble relaxing because of financial worry.

▲ ▲ ▲

Keep the Faith

I never wrote anything that was published until I was forty.

—*James Michener*

Just engaging in foreplay is not enough. I want you going all the way, all the time. People will respect you for it, more so than if all you did was fool around. Besides, it's far more satisfying. What I am talking about, of course, is persistence when it comes to your career. It's like a marriage. There will be ups and downs, but you are in it for the long haul. Because when you are madly and passionately in love with your career, you want it to work out, so you work at it and work through the tough times.

In 1969 the New York Mets were the surprise team of the National League. I was a Mets fan back then, and I remember that all my Yankee friends were skeptical that the hapless Mets would ever make it to the World Series. Tug McGraw, a Met reliever, coined the phrase "You gotta believe," and it stuck. Flash forward to 1998 and the San Diego Padres, another team that is a frequent cellar-dweller. Not many picked the "Swinging Friars" to amount to much. But as the season wore on and it looked as if they might make it all the way, fans started chanting, "Keep the faith." Sure enough, the Padres had a magical season. When it comes to your career, "you gotta believe" you are going to make it, and when the going gets tough, remember to "keep the faith." Hang in there and the tide will turn. You *will* end up on top.

There is a saying that "genius is perseverance in disguise." No matter how bright or how talented you are, there will be obstacles between you and your career goals. It's a jungle out there, but the successful people keep whacking away, clearing a path, sweating it out, dealing with the snakes, the heat, and the pitfalls, until eventually they reach a clearing. Beaten and bruised, maybe, but stronger for the struggle and appreciative of their new surroundings (hot meals at Spago and a warm bed at the Ritz).

To make it means refusing to take no for an answer, fighting for what's rightfully yours. Once you get that first deal, you are halfway there. But you have to keep at it. If that sounds like too much work, then maybe you don't want it badly enough.

It took author David Baldacci eleven years and ten thousand discarded pages before his first book was published. *Absolute Power* became a best-seller, and Baldacci became a millionaire. And all it took was eleven years of just plugging away, writing from 10:00 P.M. to 3:00 A.M. every day while practicing law full-time.

L. Frank Baum couldn't keep a regular job, and his friends and family called him a loser to his face all the way through middle age. It wasn't until he wrote a story called *The Wizard of Oz* (in forty minutes) that he achieved success. Baum went on to produce thirteen more Oz books.

Probably the most upbeat and unsinkable person I know is Wally Amos. A high-school dropout making it as a talent agent with William Morris, he left that rather cushy job to turn his aunt Della's chocolate cookie recipe into a multimillion-dollar business that featured his likeness on every box. He was rich and he was famous (Famous Amos). That's the good part. In more recent years, he lost his business, lost the right to use his own name, almost lost his home, and is being sued. But you would never know it by talking to him. He is starting over and is confident he can do it again, despite the setbacks. I have no doubt he will bounce back.

Don't Take My Word for It

Some thoughts on perseverance:

*The lesson is an important one—writing is not magic,
but perseverance.*

—*Richard North Patterson*

*Beyond talent lie all the usual words: discipline, love, luck—but, most
of all, endurance.*

—*James Baldwin*

Be tenacious—don't let anyone tell you it can't be done.

—*Ricki Lake*

*I'm not a natural singer, it's just sheer, slogging hard work for me. It
takes me six weeks of solid practicing before I am actually ready to
even let a soul hear me.*

—*Julie Andrews*

*I've often made my own luck. You make your own luck by knocking at
every door, approaching every possible opportunity with optimism and
enthusiasm, and, most of all, moving on after each and every setback.*

—*Richard Branson*

*I always hoped that some kid who liked me when he was young was
going to turn into a filmmaker and hire me.*

—*Robert Forster*

We are made to persist. That's how we find out who we are.
—*Tobias Wolff*

If you can't excel with talent, triumph with effort.
—*Dave Weinbaum*

A Hug a Day Keeps the Blues Away
The average person needs at least four hugs a day.

I'm Not Okay, You're Not Okay, and That's Okay
*It took me fifteen years to discover I had no talent for writing,
but I couldn't give up because by that time I was too famous.*
—*Robert Benchley*

The world needs your ideas and your talent. You can, and will, have all the success you desire. Do you really believe that about yourself? Chances are you don't. But it is true. Every word of it.

If you can stay upbeat and hold on to the belief that you are going to make it, you can deal with the setbacks and stay focused on the big picture. Renoir said, "The artist, under the pain of oblivion, must have confidence in himself."

A creative career is challenging and fraught with pitfalls for positive thinkers. It is impossible for those who have a negative self-image. The creative arts and creative careers breed insecurity and uncertainty. You must stay positive to protect yourself, no matter where you want to end up—in front of the crowd or behind the scenes.

You can think your way to success. Super-successful creative people I know think positive and prosperous thoughts and are rewarded for that kind of mind-set. They believe success is right around the corner. They can visualize it happening and see themselves as successful. It works. They believe so much in a positive outcome that they see opportunities, they do the work. Dolly Parton said, "I have more confidence than I do talent, but I think confidence is the main achiever of success." If you act as if you are successful (without the attitude, please), you might just fool yourself into *being* successful. It's even easier to fool other people. They pick up on your confidence and they believe in you—which makes it easier for you to believe in yourself. Sort of a catch-22, but a good one.

When you feel good about what you are doing and you believe things will work out for you, your whole life looks better. There is less stress, and worry is replaced with good work. People notice you are having fun, and they want to be a part of that, so they help you. You also get respect for knowing where you are going and sticking your neck out. A belief that you will make it sustains you through the strained times.

Believing in yourself and your work eliminates many of the distractions and drawbacks that worry, anger, jealousy, and frustration can create. That doesn't mean you don't have to do anything and good things will happen. Positive thinking empowers you to do what is necessary to bring about positive things in your life. As Rafe said, "Positive thinking is working for something and expecting it to happen—wishful thinking is hoping for something and waiting for it to happen." There is a difference.

Farai Chideya is an author, a television correspondent (ABC, CNN, MTV), and a reporter for *Newsweek*. All this and she isn't even thirty yet! The hardest part was the first step, she says. "Applying for the much-coveted *Newsweek* internship when I was a Harvard student. There were so many other people who I assumed had more experience. I learned not to underestimate myself."

You want to hear something crazy? I used to introduce myself as an author before I really became one. I believed so much that it would happen that it just came out of my mouth. It wasn't easy, but I made it happen—otherwise I would have been a liar.

Sarah Bernhardt made this statement in 1906, but it still holds true today: "One should have absolute self-confidence, even in the early stages of a career . . . Be willing to learn from others, but at the same time appreciate the actual value of the knowledge you already possess."

Two-time Oscar winner and pioneering animation director Chuck Jones, who created such characters as Bugs Bunny, almost dropped out of art school when he saw how talented his fellow classmates were. But, like his creation Wile E. Coyote, he stuck with it.

Great things will happen to those around you, and you will want to strangle them and take their money. That's a natural reaction. Of course you want these wonderful things to happen to you, right now. And being so close to others who are having their dreams come true can be a little disheartening. It will eat away at your self-confidence, if you let it. Instead, let it fuel your fire and desire to do more for yourself. Sure, you'll still want to spoil their opening, steal their expensive new car, and burn their mansion to the ground, but working on your own career is a much more positive and productive tack to take. So get a grip, your time will come (or, if you act on your impulses, you'll be doing time).

There are some things you can control (your thoughts and your actions), and some you cannot (crazy clients or market conditions, policies and procedures, rules and regulations). You have to deal with what is, not with the way you wish things to be. You can spend your time and energy trying to change the system (usually futile and not much fun), or you can work within the situation and the system to make things happen. Don't expend all your energy trying to change something you can't. And, please, don't blame others if things aren't going your way right now.

Now Is the Time to Get Started

Reading about what you should do, and answering the hard questions we've asked here, is a first step, but it's only a first step. The next step is to take action. From here on out, it's up to you.

Don't set limits on yourself because you are lacking in some area that you believe is crucial to your career. Remember that songwriter Paul McCartney can't read music, screenwriter Stephen Cannell can't spell, actress Marlee Matlin can't hear, and author Stephen Hawking can't speak or write without assistance. In the advertising business, I was around art directors who could not draw to save their lives. (They know what good drawing is, however, and that's their job.)

Finish what you start. Seeing something through to completion, whether it is a hit or not, fills you with a sense of pride that nothing else will. If, when faced with adversity, you get discouraged and ditch your plans, that is a drain on your confidence.

Hang out with positive people. Spending all your time with struggling artists isn't healthy. Look for supportive people who believe in you and want to help. Then let them. Hitch yourself up to those who have already made it and let them take you along for the ride, then unhitch when you feel ready to go it alone. When a seven-year-old boy stricken with leukemia started chemotherapy and lost his hair, his classmates (and teacher) shaved their heads and called themselves the "Bald Eagles Club" to show support for one of their own. We need more people like that in our lives.

Feed your self-esteem a steady diet of positive affirmations instead of that junk food you've been choking on all these years. I realize that, to the highly skeptical creative type, affirmations sound hokey, but they really do work. Being a negaholic is not productive or particularly helpful. Affirmations can help you change the channel on your inner dialogue from head-banger to easy listening. When your inner dialogue is filled with "I can do this," "I know I have talent," "No matter what, I'll manage," "I deserve to be able to find work that I love and be well paid for it," rather than "Who the hell do you think you are, trying that?" "It will never work" and "You'll poke your eye out," you have a better chance to make it. One of the best books on affirmations is Dr. Eric Maisel's *Affirmations for Artists*.

Visualize yourself making it. Go back and read the chapter on goal-setting to get a clear picture of what you want, then focus your mental energy on that image.

Reward yourself. It has helped me to pay attention to what went right, and to celebrate some of my small victories. Try giving yourself an award for doing something right, even if nobody else noticed. Celebrate your success with a victory party or a prize.

Free-associate without passing judgment on some of the highlights of your past. Write, draw, paint, cut out pictures from magazines to make a visual documentary of your past accomplishments. Try to include as many things as possible. (There are some key messages buried in those past successes you may want to take note of.) When you are done and feel as though you got them all, sit back and smile as you look on in pride at all that you have done in your life. Make a collage to remind you of your past success, or narrow it down to a "top ten" and post them up where you will see them.

Guilty as Charged

A 1991 study found that the average person spends two hours a day feeling guilty. The answer is to make peace with the past, accept your shortcomings, do the right thing from now on and live each day as if it were your last.

Don't Worry, Be Happy

*I don't measure my worth by how much people pay me
or what I look like.*

—*Ally Sheedy*

Life is never exactly the way you want it to be. Life isn't perfect. That doesn't mean you can't be happy. You can wish things were different, but that won't do you much good. If you make avant-garde art and wish that mainstream America "got it" because it's so good, that may be wishful thinking. If, on the other hand, you just concentrate on making great art and don't worry about the way others perceive it, you will be much happier and healthier. You can bitch about the current state of the arts, but some things are beyond your control and you need to let them go. Or—and this is a big piece of advice for peace of mind—do something small to correct the bigger problem. For instance, as I travel the country I am appalled by how much trash there is on the side of the road. This is a problem too big to tackle on a national scale. So I am taking action on a local level and working with politicians and organizations to keep my own hometown clean. On an even smaller scale, whenever I see trash, I pick it up, on land or in my boat. I feel as if I am making a difference—and on a small scale, I guess I am. So now I can enjoy visiting other parts of the country without all the worry. Do what you can with what you have.

This Is the Time of Your Life

It is good to have an end to journey toward—but it is the journey that matters, in the end.

—Ursula K. Le Guin

If you were stripped of your condo, car, credit cards, and career, would you still feel worthy? These things we spend our lives working for, are they worth it? For the creative person, the answer is likely to be no. It takes a long time to create a career in the arts. Don't waste your early years wishing you made more money, had a better car, got good gigs. Celebrate small victories and live in the here and now. A little girl said to her smaller brother, "Yesterday is the past, tomorrow's the future, but today is a gift. That's why they call it the present." No truer words have ever been spoken.

Today is a gift. Unwrap it with all the zeal you would a present on your tenth birthday. Find the joy in today. Don't put off living until you get a record deal, make a million dollars, or have a best-seller. It could (a) be a long time coming, and (b) when you get these things, they won't be enough. It's human nature not to be satisfied with what we have.

We have such a short time here on earth, and we squander so much of it on trivial things. If only we could celebrate the small things. A single father raising his teenage daughter leaves her Post-it Note messages every morning before he goes to work. He does it because it is important to him to show how much he cares for and appreciates his daughter and all she means to him. Leaving these sticky little love notes takes very little time but brings so much joy, whether she reads them or not, he feels it was time well spent. One day, when he was in her room, he noticed that, carefully stuck to the back of his daughter's door, was every single Post-it he had ever written. At that moment, nothing else mattered. Not that his publisher omitted his picture from the back of his new book. Not that the radio interview he was scheduled to do was preempted by a breaking news story, not that his agent dumped him and he was unable to find a publisher for his next book.

You get the picture. What matters most is what is happening now. There is no *there* when it comes to success. There is only a series of tragic and magic moments strung together on a thin line called life.

I experienced a roller-coaster ride while writing this book. There was the euphoria of signing the contract and cashing the advance check. Then the anxiety that set in with the realization that in six months I would have to turn in a completed manuscript. It was made more difficult because of the success of my previous book. Could I top what I had already written? Would it sell as well? Would it be embraced in the same way by readers? I took solace in the fact that I had done it before and I could do it again, but it was still a very trying time. I buried myself in research. After months of hard work, I came to the realization that the more I learned about this subject, the less I felt I knew. So I continued to study until I amassed a mountain of material that was quite frankly overwhelming. I felt pinned down and paralyzed by all that I wanted to say.

To make it more manageable, I began to break the book down into bite-sized pieces. I shuffled and reshuffled the outline before I began to get a handle on how to proceed. Then I forced myself to put pen to paper and begin writing. I focused on why I wanted to write this book in the first place—to help my fellow creatives come up with a career that would center on their talent and their passion. To share practical tips and techniques that they could use, to offer advice they could take to heart. Yet every chapter was a struggle. There was so much I wanted to say. Before I knew it, I was a hundred pages beyond my page count. I reread what I had written. I couldn't believe it. It was exactly the kind of book I would want to read myself. A book filled with practical tips and positive thoughts.

I am so proud of the way this book turned out. To me, that is what success is, helping others to help themselves. This book has changed my life, and I hope it can do the same for you.

You would think this is where I would conclude by writing "The End." But I want to practice what I preach by pointing something else out. When this book comes out, there will be a big push of publicity and a feeling of importance as I conduct interviews and talk the book up (hopefully on *Oprah*!), but then the publicity machine will move on and I will be left with my life—a life that was fulfilling before, during, and after this book.

I spent eight months (I was a teensy bit late turning it in) with this book. While working away, I was able to write at my favorite coffeehouse, on my boat, in my backyard next to the waterfall, and even in Fiji, Maui, and Key West. The process was a pleasure. Now that the book is complete, I have something positive to point to and say, "I did that!" I will also continue to promote, publish, and plow ahead with other projects. That's okay, because I have found my true calling. I love what I do (even when it is very, very hard and I am very, very frustrated). I am living the life that I hope everyone who reads this book will experience. A life filled with passion and purpose, and in which if today isn't a great day, yesterday was and tomorrow will be.

If I can do it, so can you.

Contact Information

We would love to hear from you. Please tell us your success stories (and you will have many, I promise), and how this book helped you reach your career goals. If you have any tips or techniques that may help your fellow creative person, please pass those along as well. We will do our best to publish your letters in our newsletter or post them to our web site. (Hey, here's your chance to expose yourself and garner some free publicity.)

Write to us at:

CreativeLee Speaking™
P.O. Box 4100-186
Del Mar, CA 92014
E-mail: leesilber@earthlink.net
Visit our web site at: http://www.creativelee.com

For a FREE *CreativeLee Speaking* newsletter, please send a self-addressed stamped envelope.

Bibliography

My name is Lee Silber, and I am a bookaholic. It is becoming an increasingly hard (and expensive) habit to kick. I am now about to become an enabler, too. I highly recommend you look into the following books for further insights and ideas on career management. I have read each of the books listed, and have found them helpful in the preparation (or is that procrastination?) of this book.

Albrecht, Donna. *Promoting Your Business with Free or Almost Free Publicity.* Englewood Cliffs, N.J.: Prentice Hall, 1997.

Anderson, Nancy. *Work with Passion.* San Rafael, Calif.: New World Library, 1995. Sound advice from a seasoned career specialist.

Barkley, Nella. *How to Help Your Child Land the Right Job Without Being a Pain in the Neck.* New York: Workman, 1993.

Boldt, Laurence. *How to Find the Work You Love.* New York: Penguin, 1996.

Brown, Les. *Live Your Dreams.* New York: Avon, 1992. Les is one of the best speakers you will ever see. His books get you pumped up, too.

Buchanan, Carol. *Best Small Budget Self-Promotions.* Cincinnati, Ohio: North Light Books, 1996.

Buffett, Jimmy. *A Pirate Looks at Fifty.* New York: Random House, 1998. If you haven't figured it out by now, I am a card-carrying Parrothead.

Buzzell, Linda. *How to Make It in Hollywood.* New York: HarperCollins, 1996. Just as the title says, if you dream of making it on the big (or small) screen, you must read this book.

Cameron, Julia, and Mark Bryan. *The Artist's Way.* New York: Putnam, 1992. This is simply the best book available to foster a more creative lifestyle. Do your morning pages.

Capacchione, Lucia, and Peggy Van Pelt. *Putting Your Talent to Work.* Deerfield Beach, Fla.: Health Communications, 1996. I read this book while I was on *vacation* in Fiji. Now that's saying something!

Carlson, Richard. *Don't Worry, Make Money.* New York: Hyperion, 1997.

Dail, Hilda Lee. *How to Create Your Own Career* (Audio). Boston: Shambhala Publications, 1990.

DeLuca, Mathew, and Nanette DeLuca. *Wow! Résumés for Creative Careers.* New York: McGraw-Hill, 1997.

Drummond, Erica. *Quotes for Kids.* Rancho Santa Fe, Calif.: Polished Presentations, 1997. Erica Drummond is wise beyond her years (she was fourteen when she wrote this book). It is filled with her keen and clever insights on life.

Drummond, Mary-Ellen. *Fearless and Flawless Public Speaking.* San Diego, Calif.: Pfeiffer & Company, 1993. This is the best book out there if you get sweaty palms when you hear your name called to get up and speak. (Mary-Ellen Drummond is Erica's mother.)

Edwards, Sarah, and Paul Edwards. *Finding Your Perfect Work.* New York: G.P. Putnam's Sons, 1996.

Eikleberry, Carol. *The Career Guide for Creative and Unconventional People.* Berkeley, Calif.: Ten Speed Press, 1995. I give this book "two thumbs way up." Carol understands the unconventional person, and offers outstanding insights and ideas that really ring true for right-brainers.

Field, Shelly. *100 Best Careers for Writers and Artists.* New York: Macmillan, 1998. The single most comprehensive source on job opportunities for the creative person.

Grappo, Gary Joseph. *The Top 10 Career Strategies for the Year 2000 & Beyond.* New York: Berkley Books, 1997.

Green, Chuck. *The Desktop Publisher's Idea Book.* New York: Random House, 1993. Am I a geek because among my heroes is a graphic-arts guru? Chuck Green is the man with the magic touch when it comes to desktop publishing and design.

Herrmann, Ned. *The Creative Brain.* Lake Lure, N.C.: The Ned Hermann Group, 1995. The best book I have ever read regarding our "right" minds.

Hiam, Alex, and Susan Angle. *Adventure Careers.* Franklin Lakes, N.J.: Career Press, 1995. If the words "safe and secure career" or "nine-to-five" scare the living daylights out of you, then read this book.

Hooks, Ed. *The Audition Book.* New York: Watson-Guptill, 1996.

Kawasaki, Guy. *How to Drive Your Competition Crazy.* New York: Hyperion, 1995. I bet when Guy writes out his shopping list, it's entertaining. What talent!

Kragen, Ken. *Life Is a Contact Sport*. New York: William Morrow, 1994. A magnificent book by a man who managed the careers of Kenny Rogers, Lionel Ritchie, and Trisha Yearwood.

Kremer, John. *1001 Ways to Market Your Books*. Fairfield, Iowa: Open Horizons, 1993.

Lamott, Anne. *Bird by Bird*. New York: Anchor Books, 1994. I have read this book at least a dozen times, and each time I learn something new.

Levine, Michael. *Take It From Me*. New York: Perigee, 1996.

Levinson, Jay, and Seth Godin. *The Guerrilla Marketing Handbook*. Boston: Houghton Mifflin, 1994.

Lloyd, Carol. *Creating a Life Worth Living*. New York: HarperPerennial, 1997. This book is so good that I found it a little intimidating when I first read it. "How can I top this?" I asked myself. I didn't. Instead, I covered new ground and left this gem for you to read after you are done with my book.

Lois, George, and Bill Pitts. *What's the Big Idea?* New York: Bantam Doubleday Dell, 1991. Weird. But in a good way.

Maisel, Eric. *A Life in the Arts*. New York: G.P. Putnam's Sons, 1994.

Marcinko, Richard. *Leadership Secrets of the Rogue Warrior*. New York: Pocket Books, 1996. This is the most kick-ass, take-no-prisoners book of its kind. Attack!

Mayer, Bill. *The Magic in Asking the Right Questions*. Solana Beach, Calif.: Bill Mayer International, 1997.

Michels, Caroll. *How to Survive and Prosper as an Artist*. New York: Henry Holt, 1997. Resources. Resources. Resources. Nearly a hundred pages of addresses and phone numbers for everything from artists' agencies to virtual art galleries.

Peters, Tom. *The Circle of Innovation*. New York: Random House, 1997. A breath of fresh air for those of us who find most business books boring. Tom Peters is NOT boring!

Richards, Dick. *Artful Work*. New York: Berkley Books, 1995.

Richardson, Bradley. *Jobsmarts for Twentysomethings*. New York: Vintage Books, 1995.

Popcorn, Faith, and Lys Marigold. *Clicking*. New York: HarperCollins, 1996. Reading this book makes you feel like a voyeur, peeking into the future for a glimpse of what's to come and how to become an active participant in it.

Rozakis, Laurie. *The Complete Idiot's Guide to Making Money in Freelancing*. New York: Alpha Books, 1998.

SARK. *The Bodacious Book of Succulence*. New York: Simon and Schuster, 1998. Read anything and everything you can get your hands on by SARK. She's a genius!

Salmansohn, Karen. *How to Succeed in Business Without a Penis*. New York: Three Rivers Press, 1996. This is a great book, whether you have a penis or not.

Silber, Lee. *Time Management for the Creative Person*. New York: Three Rivers Press, 1998. If you're a right-brainer struggling with time-management in a linear, left-brained world (filled with anal retentives), then this book can help you get a grip.

———. *Aim First!* Del Mar, Calif.: Tales from The Tropics Publishing, 1994. I still get gobs of orders for this book from Amazon.com—simply because it is the best book out there on goals and goal-setting.

Tracy, Diane. *Take This Job and Love It*. New York: McGraw-Hill, 1994.

Tulgan, Bruce. *Work This Way*. New York: Hyperion, 1998. Every time I see this title, I hear Steven Tyler singing "Work This Way." Good book.

Tye, Joe. *Personal Best*. New York: John Wiley & Sons, 1997.

Weinstein, Matt. *Managing to Have Fun*. New York: Fireside, 1996. How to make your workplace more conducive to creativity.

Winter, Barbara. *Making a Living Without a Job*. New York: Bantam Books, 1993. This is one of the better books about being your own boss.

Wycoff, Joyce. *Mindmapping*. New York: Berkley Books, 1991.

Zdenek, Marilee. *The Right-Brain Experience*. Santa Barbara, Calif., Two Roads Publishers, 1983.

Index

Abbott, Bud, 245
addiction, 12–13, 253–54, 294–99
affirmations, 68, 255, 331
agents, 212–14, 290
Ali, Muhammad, 222
Allen, Paul, 194
Allen, Rick, 50
Amazon.com, 178, 188, 205
Amiel, Henri Frédéric, 211
Amos, Wally, 65, 328
Anderson, Paul Thomas, 297–98
Andrews, Julie, 328
Andrews, Markita, 112
answering services, 194–95
appearance, 113, 116, 122, 133,
    196, 248, 250
apprenticeships, 139–40
Aristotle, 39, 209
Astaire, Fred, 249
attire. See dress
attorneys, 214
auditions, 109, 110, 113–14
Aykroyd, Dan, 130

Baez, Joan, 259, 304
Bagby, Meredith, 199
balance, 2, 265–68, 306
Baldacci, David, 18, 327
Baldwin, James, 328
Barrie, J. M., 129
Barry, Dave, 169

Barrymore, Drew, 253
bartering, 192, 237, 282
Baryshnikov, Mikhail, 321
Bates, Kathy, 325–26
Baum, L. Frank, 328
Beene, Geoffrey, 92
Beethoven, Ludwig van, 255
Beltzer, John, 38
Belushi, John, 130, 297
Benchley, Robert, 329
Bender, Frank, 86
Bennett, Tony, 94
Bennett, William, 95
Bennis, Warren, 86
Benson, George, 136
Berg, Peter, 271
Berle, Milton, 160
Bernhardt, Sarah, 330
Bezos, Jeff, 251, 319–20
Bishop, Stephen, 74–75
blame, 149, 278
Blanchard, Ken, 152, 222
Blaurock, Donna, 107, 137–39
Blevin, Doug, 82
Blige, Mary J., 292
Bolles, Richard, 223
Bourke-White, Margaret, 321
Bowden, Bobby, 317
Bradbury, Ray, 84
Brahms, Johannes, 255
Brandt, Dorothea, 62

Branson, Richard, 130, 182, 183, 328
Brashares, Ann, 93
Bridges, William, 140
Bristol, Claude, 311
brochures, 112, 177, 194, 232–33
Brodie, Richard, 67
Bromley, Boris, 201–2
Brontë, Emily, 258
Brooks, Meredith, 292
Brower, Charles, 119
Brown, H. Jackson, Jr., 127
Brown, Les, 94
Bruce, Lenny, 296
Buchwald, Art, 19
Buffett, Jimmy, 13, 66, 74, 76–77, 153, 182, 202, 210, 211, 222, 241, 259, 281, 325
burnout, 253, 260–72
Burns, Ed, 175, 209
Burns, George, 49
Burrows, V. W., 22
Burton, Jake, 179
Buscaglia, Leo, 93, 224
business cards, 112, 121, 177
    networking, 194, 198, 200
    as promotional tool, 229–30
business etiquette, 124, 125, 163
business mathematics, 135–36
business meals, 122–23
business plans, 180
business writing, 134–35, 200–201
Butler, Samuel, 75
Buzzell, Linda, 60–61, 99

Cage, Nicholas, 188
Cameron, Julia, 209
Campbell, Joseph, 27
Campbell, Lori, 93
Canfield, Jack, 242, 278
Cannell, Stephen, 331
Capra, Frank, 82

career planning, 72–99
    fact-finding, 84–85, 88–89
    interim work, 97–98
    money issues, 78, 87, 96–97
    unusual/odd jobs, 83–86
Carey, Drew, 95, 224, 292
Carlin, George, 27, 30, 310
Carnegie, Dale, 145, 157
Carrey, Jim, 67, 96, 188, 292, 293, 304
Carter, June, 74
Cash, Johnny, 74, 224
Chaplin, Charlie, 220
Cher, 87, 240
Chesterton, G. K., 265, 293
Chiat/Day, 83
Chideya, Farai, 330
Clapton, Eric, 241
classified advertisements, 120, 235
cleanliness, 116, 122, 196, 248
clients, 118, 148, 162, 167, 223–24, 239
Clooney, George, 94, 95, 294
clothing. See dress
Coen, Joel, 199
Cohen, Ed, 291
Cohen, Sherry Suib, 300
Cohn, Marc, 268
Colette, 13, 33
Collins, Phil, 23, 211
Combs, Ray, 219
Combs, Sean (Puffy), 189
communication skills, 134, 151, 157–58, 163–66, 193, 200–201
Conerly, Christopher, 218
Connick, Harry, Jr., 304
contracts, 181, 285, 290
control, 24–25, 27, 42–44, 73, 98, 152–58
Coppola, Francis Ford, 201
copyrights, 181, 214, 233, 291
Cornyn-Selby, Alyce, 254
corporate sponsors, 241

Costello, Lou, 245
cover letters, 106–7, 118
Covey, Stephen, 45, 182, 211, 217
Cowper, William, 182
Crawford, Joan, 150
credo, 60
Cricco, Cristin, 112
criticism, 158, 325–26
Cromwell, Oliver, 82
Crow, Sheryl, 10, 209
Cunniff, June, 139
Currie, Cherie, 267
Curtis, Jamie Lee, 122
Cusack, John, 169
customers, 118, 148, 223–24
customer service, 181

Dail, Hilda Lee, 177
Danes, Claire, 278
Davis, Al, 145
Davis, Bette, 150
deadlines, 61, 66–67, 117
Dean, James, 297
delegation of work, 152–58, 256
Dell, Michael, 130, 153
Demartini, John, 189
De Niro, Robert, 113
Denver, John, 74
DiBello, Mark, 220–21
Diller, Barry, 194
Diller, Phyllis, 323
direction, personal
    determining, 24–48
    lack of, 51
    See also goal setting
direct mail, 227, 234
discipline, 14–15, 254, 301–7
Disney, Walt, 117, 133, 159
Donne, John, 186
Dowd, Maureen, 287
Downey, Robert, Jr., 253, 294
Drescher, Fran, 54
dress, 122, 248, 250
Dress for Success New York, 101

Driver, Minnie, 326
Drucker, Peter, 142
Duchovny, David, 134
Duffy, Karen, 322
Dyer, Wayne, 58
Dyson, Esther, 283

Ebert, Roger, 50
Edison, Thomas, 50, 110, 183,
    271, 282, 288, 302, 324
education, 77, 79, 91, 130–33
ego, 293, 308
Eikleberry, Carol, 27, 318
Einstein, Albert, 10, 77, 97, 98,
    130, 220, 291
Eisner, Michael, 324
Ellington, Duke, 66
E-mail, 104, 121, 195, 202, 263
Emerson, Ralph Waldo, 163, 306
endorsements, 238, 240
Ennesser, Kathy, 219
entrepreneurs, 2, 77, 175–76, 179,
    182
Evans, Robert, 195
Ewing, Sam, 283
excuse making, 65–66, 69–71,
    321–23
exercise, 133, 271
experience, 133, 136–40

failure, 323–24
fame, 78, 293–94
family, 157, 187–89, 267, 308
Farber, Barry, 110
Farley, Chris, 297
faxes, 104, 231–32
fear, 9, 70, 142, 254, 271, 316–21,
    324
Fields, Debbie, 220
financial issues, 26, 47, 56–58,
    135–36
    agents and, 212–14, 290
    career planning and, 78, 87,
        96–97

financial issues (*continued*)
  contracts and, 285, 290–91
  fee collection, 284–86
  money-saving tips, 228,
     237–41, 283–84
  reserve funds, 97, 264, 273, 282
  in self-employment, 167, 174,
     176–77, 253, 272–91, 313
  taxes, 286–87
focus, 2, 14–15, 46, 67–68, 80,
    224, 301–7
follow-through, 14, 123, 200,
    238–39
Foos, Richard, 178
Ford, Eileen, 124
Ford, Harrison, 96, 201
Ford, Henry, 156
Ford, Henry, II, 94
Forster, Robert, 328
Fox, Michael J., 134, 283
Franklin, Ben, 22, 23, 223
Franks, Michael, 58
freelancing. *See* self-employment
Freeman, Shelley, 86
friends, 116, 267, 308
Frizzell, John, 208
Fromm, Erich, 95
Frost, Robert, 154
fun, 1, 12, 54, 158, 269

Gallagher, 231
Gates, Bill, 23, 67, 113, 130, 302
Geffen, David, 140, 182, 194
Geisel, Theodore, 325
Gelb, Michael, 163
Gelman, Michael, 246
Gershwin, George, 311
Gibran, Kahlil, 277
Gibson, Mel, 188
Gillette, King, 129
Giove, Missy, 224
Givens, Chuck, 69
Glass, Philip, 11
goal setting, 2, 37, 45–46, 49–71,
    117, 277–78, 307, 332

Goddard, John, 53, 55
"Godfather" calls, 120, 121
Goethe, Johann von, 57, 88
Goldberg, Whoopi, 93, 191
Goldwyn, Samuel, 290
Gore, William, 249
Gorin, Fern, 46–48
Gossett, Lou, Jr., 100
Goudge, Eileen, 322
Gould, Cheryl, 291
Grabowski, Marilyn, 96, 130
Graham, Nicholas, 221
Grant, Amy, 74
Green, Chuck, 228–29
Greene, Stephen, 169
Greenwald, Julie, 93
Greff, Clancy, 173–74
Gregory, John, 245
Groening, Matt, 266
Grove, Andrew S., 269, 276
Gwynn, Tony, 151

Hack, Alan, 192
Hagman, Beth, 183–85
Hall, Doug, 109
Hamilton, Jane, 129
Hamilton, Scott, 291
Hammer, MC, 189
Hanft, Adam, 19
Hannaker, Harold, 82
Hanson, Mark Victor, 242, 278
happiness, 332–33
Harrington, Jane, 170
Hasselhoff, David, 305
Hastings, Robert, 161
Hawken, Paul, 176, 180
Hawking, Stephen, 331
Hawn, Goldie, 95, 211
Hays, Robert, 267
Hazelton, Lesley, 251–52
Healy, Bernadine, 266
Henley, Don, 209, 295
Hewlett-Packard, 83
Hilfiger, Tommy, 301
hiring, of help, 156, 211–12

Hitchcock, Alfred, 224
home-based businesses, 170–74,
    183–85
honesty, 124, 151, 254, 308–9
Hooks, Ed, 114
Hopper, Dennis, 296–97
Hore-Belisha, Leslie, 164
Howard, James Newton, 208
Hubbard, Elbert, 293
hubris, 12–13, 293
Hughes, Robert, 310
Hui Hai, 39
humor, 218, 270
Hunter, Holly, 199

Ilena, Maria, 322
Industrial Light and Magic, 88,
    139
insecurity, 12, 310–12
Internet, 88, 179, 202, 240. See
    also Web sites
internships, 139–40, 212
interpersonal skills, 142–66
interviews, 110–13, 247–48
intuition, 11, 31–33, 116, 147, 289
inventory, 178

Jefferson, Thomas, 95
Jennings, Waylon, 123
Jewel, 21
job descriptions, 150
Jobs, Steve, 1, 110, 130, 194
job/work searches, 100–126
Joel, Billy, 72, 281
Johnson, Lyndon Baines, 176
Johnson, Nunnally, 124
Johnson, Stewart B., 22
Jones, Chuck, 330
Jong, Erica, 321

Kapelos, John, 183
Katzenberg, Jeffrey, 182, 194
Kawasaki, Guy, 146–47, 199, 223
Keeslar, Matt, 22
Kelley, Steve, 178

Kelly, R., 207
Kennedy, James, 101
Kennedy, John F., 158
Kettering, Charles, 39
Kiam, Victor, 111
Kidman, Nicole, 94
Kilgore, Marcia, 250
King, Larry, 197
King, Martin Luther, 164
King, Stephen, 22, 188, 266, 294
Kingsley, Charles, 272
Klampert, Ruth, 38–39
Klein, Calvin, 194, 296
Kline, Richard, 321
Koch, Ed, 116
Kohe, J. Martin, 24
Kragen, Ken, 213
Kramer, Scott, 25–26
Kristofferson, Kris, 12, 74
Kudrow, Lisa, 131, 311–12
Kuhn, Maggie, 242
Kusher, Harold, 323–24

Lair, Jess, 189
Lake, Ricki, 328
Lamott, Anne, 311
L'Amour, Louis, 130
Lansing, Sherry, 151
LaSalle, Eriq, 303–4
Lasorda, Tommy, 290
Lauder, Evelyn, 259
Lauder, Leonard, 290
Lauren, Ralph, 92–93
Laury, Steve, 169
Laybourne, Geraldine, 202
Leaf, Ryan, 132
Learning Annex, 200
le Carré, John, 90
Leder, Mimi, 93–94
Lee, Spike, 175
left-brain thinking, 45, 146, 309
    vs. right-brain thinking, 1, 2, 9,
        12–15, 19–20
left-handedness, 22–23
Le Guin, Ursula K., 333

Leider, Richard, 46
Leno, Jay, 67, 94, 224
Leonardo da Vinci, 23, 209, 308
letters
    of agreement, 289
    cover, 106–7, 118
    query, 118
    recommendation, 126
    sales, 232
    thank-you, 112, 124–25, 193, 198
Levant, Oscar, 311
Liddell Hart, Basil, 306
Lincoln, Abraham, 164, 257
Lloyd, Carol, 187
Lois, George, 105, 162, 170
Long, Lazarus, 157
Longworth, Alice Roosevelt, 122
Louis-Dreyfus, Julia, 266
Lucas, George, 88, 325
Lukas, J. Anthony, 310–11
Lumet, Sidney, 81, 260

Macdonald, Norm, 126
Machado, Sage, 131
MacKay, Harvey, 218
Macleod, Gordon A., 22
Madden, John, 158
Madonna, 201
Mahler, Gustav, 255
mailing lists, 194, 222–23
Mainieri, Mike, 208
Maisel, Eric, 331
Maltz, Maxwell, 167
managers (bosses), 145–47, 150–59
managers (personal), 214
Mankiewicz, Herman J., 212
Manpower, Inc., 140
Marcinko, Richard, 100, 125, 217
Margulies, Julianna, 273

marketing and promotion, 2, 203–6, 216–52
    basic issues, 222–25
    corporate, 249–51
    cost-effective, 237–41
    media and, 244–48
    publicity and, 241–42
    tools and materials, 226–37
Marriott, Bill, Sr., 156
Martin, Judith, 125
Martin, Steve, 224–25
Matlin, Marlee, 331
McCain, John, 1
McCartney, Paul, 23, 331
McConaughey, Matthew, 188, 197
McCormack, John, 251
McDormand, Frances, 199
McGraw, Tug, 327
McGwire, Mark, 323
McLachlan, Sarah, 294
McLin, Lena, 207
McNally, David, 191
Mead, Mic, 152
Meanwell, George, 31
media, 206, 244–48
meetings, 160–63
Menninger, Karl, 316
mentors, 206–10
Menuhin, Yehudi, 306
Merchant, Natalie, 169
Metcalf, C. W., 311
Metheny, Pat, 319
Michalski, Jean, 321
Michener, James, 59, 91, 327
Microsoft, 83
Miller, Arthur, 151
Miller, Christa, 271
Miller, Jan, 217
Mills, Malia, 187–88
Milsap, Ronnie, 322
mission statements, 58–59, 61, 180, 247
Mitchard, Jacquelyn, 189
Monroe, Marilyn, 23, 124

Montgomery, Joe, 38
Morrison, Toni, 94, 187, 202
Morrison, Van, 263
Mother Teresa, 116
motivation, 17–18, 54–55,
    159–60
Motorola, 83
mottoes, 59
Mullins, Aimee, 322

Nager, Patty, 245
Nathan, George Jean, 197
negotiating skills, 287–90
Nelson, Willie, 286
networking, 15, 120, 186–215,
    239
    basic tools, 194–95
    first impressions, 195–98
    key aspects, 189–91, 198–202
    mentors and, 206–10
    mutual benefits, 192–93
    promotional efforts, 203–6
    support systems, 187–89
Neuharth, Allen, 129
newsletters, 206, 231–32, 234,
    235
Newton, Isaac, 206
Noonan, Peggy, 312
Nordstrom, 140
Nye, Bill, 85–86

O'Brien, Conan, 134
O'Brien, Joe, 34–36
O'Connor, Karen, 61
O'Donnell, Rosie, 27
Ohlmeyer, Don, 126
Oldham, Todd, 130, 187
Olson, Scott, 179
O'Neill, Eugene, 88
Orben, Robert, 94
organization, 12, 170
Osborne, Ozzy, 188, 217
O'Sullivan, Humphrey, 119
Ovitz, Michael, 202

Paar, Jack, 311
Parker, Christopher, 254
partnerships, 181–82
Parton, Dolly, 94, 329
Pass, Joe, 208
passion, 96, 110, 116
past life, 33–34
Patterson, Richard North, 328
Pearce, Joseph Chilton, 320
Pearl Jam, 241
Peck, M. Scott, 15, 223
perfectionism, 256, 263, 312
Perot, Ross, 199
perseverance, 73–75, 117,
    327–29
personal coaches, 212
personal direction, 24–48, 51
personal support, 187–89, 308
Peters, Tom, 146, 249
Philips, Emo, 21
Phillips, Don, 197
photographs, 103, 108, 230, 244,
    246–47
Picasso, Pablo, 17, 86–87
Poe, Edgar Allan, 223
portfolios, 107–9, 111, 112, 194
positive thinking, 68, 112, 114,
    255, 270–72, 310–34
postcards, 109, 135, 193, 234
Poynter, Dan, 221
presentation skills, 163–66
press kits and releases, 243, 247
pride, 249, 253, 291–94
procrastination, 13, 253, 254–59
professional associations, 200,
    209, 245
promotion. See marketing and
    promotion
proposals, 118, 227
prototypes, 194, 237
Proulx, Quentin, 86
psychological problems, 12–13
publicity. See marketing and
    promotion

public speaking, 163–66, 200–201
punctuality, 113, 114, 124, 162,
    166, 196, 300
purpose. *See* direction
Puzo, Mario, 274

query letters, 118

Rafe, 330
Ralph, Sheryl Lee, 92
Ralston, Rick, 93
Ramage, Rick, 68
Rancid, 241
Rascoe, Burton, 172
recommendation letters, 126
Redenbacher, Orville, 206,
    225–26, 245
Reed, John, 161
references, 112, 121, 285
referrals, 117, 126, 239
regret, 52–53, 136–37
rejection, 325–26
reliability, 117, 300–301
R.E.M. (band), 73, 241
Renoir, Pierre-Auguste, 329
reputation, 123, 250
resignations, job, 126
respect, 124, 146, 152
résumés, 79, 101–6, 112, 167
Reynolds, Burt, 291, 295
Rhino Records, 110, 175, 178
Richards, Bob, 22, 321
right-brain thinking, 1–23, 146,
    169–70, 312
Rimes, LeAnn, 241
Ringley, Jennifer, 230–31
risk, 21, 96–97, 119, 319–20
Robbins, Tony, 45, 211, 217, 224
Rock, Chris, 95, 292
Roddick, Anita, 175
Rodin, Auguste, 175
Rogers, Fred, 95
Rogers, Kenny, 44, 213, 257,
    278–79

role models, 210–11
Ronstadt, Linda, 321
Rose, Charlie, 206
Roth, David Lee, 67
Rubbermaid, 83
Rule, Ann, 93
Rundgren, Todd, 179
Ruth, Babe, 290
Ruthman, Todd, 149

sales letters, 232
Salmansohn, Karen, 145, 147, 148
Sanders, George, 51
Santos, Barbara, 238
SARK (artist), 60
Schattke, Jonathan, 237
Schechter, Harriet, 191, 225, 284
Schmitz, John, 226
Schulz, Charles, 60, 280
Schwartz, David, 115, 159
Seinfeld, Jerry, 23, 110, 134, 174,
    275
self-employment, 39–42, 167–85,
    312
  business plans, 180
  do's and don'ts, 181–82
  financial issues, 167, 174,
      176–77, 253, 272–91, 313
  freelancing, 26, 78, 98, 126,
      280
  home-based businesses,
      170–74, 183–85
  multiple ventures, 182–83
  starting out, 175–78
  work schedules, 174
self-esteem, 70, 137, 164, 311–16,
    331
self-knowledge, 36–42
selling yourself, 115–17, 119
seminars, 205, 206, 238, 242
Service Core of Retired
    Executives, 177
sexual relationships, 294–95
Shakespeare, William, 319

Shannon, Molly, 141
Shaw, George Bernard, 223
Sheedy, Ally, 332
Shepard, Sam, 60
Sher, Barbara, 324
Shouse, Deborah, 161
Sibelius, Jean, 325
Sills, Beverly, 324
Silverman, Jonathan, 209
Silvers, Chuck, 207
Simon, Neil, 209
sincerity, 112, 117, 164
Sinetar, Marsha, 208
Singer, Brett, 198
Singer, Irving, 55
Skillpath Seminars, 205
skills, 11, 30–31, 127–41
    business math and writing,
        134–36, 200–201
    communication, 134, 151,
        157–58, 193
    interpersonal, 142–66
    negotiation, 287–90
Slater, Christian, 253
sleep, 114, 271
Smith, Fred, 325
Smith, Liz, 129
Snipes, Wesley, 129
Snyder, Richard, 118
Sonic Joyride, 219
Sosa, Sammy, 323
Sowell, Thomas, 192
Spacey, Kevin, 244
speakers' bureaus, 193
Spielberg, Steven, 10, 94, 182,
    194, 207
spirituality, 39
Sprague, Peter, 306
Stabler, Ken, 145
Stallone, Sylvester, 180
stationery, 107, 121, 172, 194
Steinem, Gloria, 101
Stengel, Casey, 153
Stephens, Robert, 221

Stone, W. Clement, 203
Streep, Meryl, 37
stress, 260–72
Stringfield, Sherry, 260
substance abuse, 12–13, 114,
    253–54, 294–99
success, 1–2, 36, 309, 313,
    320–21
    goal setting and, 49–50
    visualization of, 114, 329
Sunn, Rell, 267
surveys, 234, 238
Suzuki, Shunryu, 129
Szymansk, Joyce, 139–40

tag lines, 233
talents, 30–31, 36, 38–39, 51,
    76–77
Tallchief, Maria, 211
Tan, Amy, 266
Tarantino, Quentin, 91
taxes, 286–87
teamwork, 151–52, 153, 249
temping, 79, 98, 140–41
Tesh, John, 305
thank-you notes, 112, 124–25,
    193, 198
Thompson, Dorothy Balsis, 38
3M, 83, 234
Tilly, Jennifer, 247
Toastmasters, 163
Tomlin, Lily, 50, 97, 265
Tracy, Brian, 14–15
Tracy, Spencer, 307
trade shows, 224, 238
training, 132–33, 141
traits, 40–41
travel, business, 261–62
trends, 11, 86–87, 88
Tripp, Linda, 147
Truman, Harry S., 114
Tulgan, Bruce, 268
Twain, Mark, 102, 123, 223
Tyler, Leona, 16

Udoff, Yale, 241

Valenzuela, Fernando, 290
values, 36–37, 52
Van Damme, Jean-Claude, 314
Van Der Beek, James, 292
Van Gogh, Vincent, 21, 255
Vaughn, Greg, 318
Vedder, Eddie, 73–74
Vega, Yvette, 245
videos, 108, 233, 244
visualization, 63–64, 114, 329,
    332
vocation, 73, 99
voice mail, 121, 172, 194–95
volunteering, 139, 151, 192, 249,
    251
vos Savant, Marilyn, 136

Web sites, 177, 194, 205, 226–27,
    230–31, 251
Weinbaum, Dave, 329
White, Kate, 243

Wilde, Oscar, 2, 321
Wilkey, Walt, 86
Williams, Andy, 325
Williams, Eddie, 323
Williams, Tennessee, 63, 294
Willis, Bruce, 291
Wilson, Carnie, 130
Winfrey, Oprah, 44, 50, 202
Winter, Barbara, 117
Wisdom, Gabriel, 276–78
Wolfe, Tom, 207
Wolff, Tobias, 329
work environment, 9, 17–18,
    249–50
Wright Brothers, 183
Wyland, 38

Yerby, Frank, 306

Zanker, Bill, 246
Zappa, Frank, 24, 72, 96
Zdenek, Marilee, 8–9
Ziglar, Zig, 38, 118, 164, 224

About the Author

Lee Silber is a true creative spirit. In addition to being the author of six books, Silber is an accomplished graphic artist, musician, and founder of several companies, including CreativeLee Speaking™. When not traveling the country conducting his popular workshops for the creative person, Lee resides with his wife in Del Mar, California.